After th... Postmodern

After the Postsecular and the Postmodern: New Essays in Continental Philosophy of Religion

Edited by

Anthony Paul Smith and Daniel Whistler

CAMBRIDGE SCHOLARS

PUBLISHING

After the Postsecular and the Postmodern:
New Essays in Continental Philosophy of Religion,
Edited by Anthony Paul Smith and Daniel Whistler

This book first published 2010. The present binding first published 2011.

Cambridge Scholars Publishing

12 Back Chapman Street, Newcastle upon Tyne, NE6 2XX, UK

British Library Cataloguing in Publication Data
A catalogue record for this book is available from the British Library

ISBN (10): 1-4438-2704-5, ISBN (13): 978-1-4438-2704-1

TABLE OF CONTENTS

Part III: Contemporary Speculative Philosophy and Religion

ACKNOWLEDGMENTS

First and foremost, we wish to thank the contributors for their tireless efforts in making this volume happen. Thanks are also due to the team at CSP for their assistance, Kathryn Bevis, Jenny Bunker, James Carter and Joseph Carlisle for their work in organising the events at which some of the ideas in this volume were first aired, Pamela Sue Anderson for initiating these events as well as her continued support and Jenny Bunker and Hayley Smith for all their encouragement.

FOREWORD

PAMELA SUE ANDERSON

"Modernity Reborn, or Enlightenment—again—in Continental Philosophy of Religion"! This could be the alternative title and something I could contribute as a focus for readers of this collection of new essays. Without a doubt, Daniel Whistler and Anthony Paul Smith give us "Continental philosophy of religion" seen with new eyes. The fresh air and cogency of their Introduction are palpable. Neither the editors nor the contributors pull any punches in the traditional manner whereby positions "for" and "against" (God) must be reinforced by strong barricades on each side. And yet the authors in this collection each "tell it like they see it" with clear voices and attentive eyes equipped with incisive and historical skills. This said, it must be noted that being "critical" is neither their main aim nor the dominant virtue here. In particular, instead of treating *modern* philosophy of religion as a theological taboo, both modernity and philosophy of religion as found in the historical traditions of Continental Europe are freed from the spoof which—as argued cogently by the editors in their Introduction—had wrongly persuaded many (and especially theologians) to think them "illegitimate"!

We, as readers, are offered bold and energizing "test-cases" in speculation, in liberation (of thought) and in heresy. The contributions before us are, then, brave historically and philosophically. This also makes the work political: the volume could generate a storm of free thinking which not only challenges one's own constraints in writing in this field, but opens us to what feels extremely novel here (to me at least), that is, both the secular and the speculative. "Experimentation" might be the new buzzword for this fresh approach to European thought and to philosophy of religion; this also supplements (or moves beyond) what is often perceived as the philosophical approach on the Continent which remains caught up with phenomenology and hermeneutic method. Doing Continental philosophy of religion without current or recent constraints of method and content is meant to be excessive. It is also, as I see it, "revolutionary" in the best sense of this term.

To the credit of the editors and the contributors, what we have here is—in their own words—a "fuller picture of what Continental philosophy of religion can be". To give you a taste for what is to come, for one thing, the obligation is to see how "modern philosophy of religion liberated itself and disrupted claims to orthodoxy. Such modern strategies provide a template for contemporary efforts". For another thing, a crucial imperative is "to think beyond the failures of the moderns (while remaining within that tradition) so as to carry out a speculative inquiry into the very nature of the secular".

From my own point of view, it was at a conference in 2007 at the University of Oxford, entitled, "Transcendence Incarnate," that a new breed of young philosophers came to my attention with Daniel Whistler acting (at least in organisational terms!) as "the midwife"—in the very best Socratic and inclusive sense of this concept. Both Anthony Paul Smith and Daniel Whistler are each owed our intellectual debt and huge gratitude for the hard work and inspiration evident everywhere in this courageous volume of constructive ideas in philosophy for the second decade in the present, twenty-first century. Thanks to Dan and to Anthony—at this point, I turn you over to their capable hands in a most original Introduction.

EDITORS' INTRODUCTION

WHAT IS CONTINENTAL PHILOSOPHY OF RELIGION NOW?

ANTHONY PAUL SMITH
AND DANIEL WHISTLER

I. Madame Curie as Philosophical Persona

Marie Curie was not afraid to get her hands dirty. Her lifelong experimentation with radioactive isotopes was made possible by openness to contamination, and even recklessness in the face of it. In her attempt to understand and work with radioactive material, she continually exposed herself to contamination and (in true Spinozist fashion) this resulted in a fundamental—and ultimately fatal—change in the constitution of her body. There are destructive and constructive contaminations, but more often there are both together: Curie's research led to both cancer treatments and the atomic bomb; it enlarged scientific understanding but also contributed to her death. Curie's risks with contamination engendered both joyous affects and passions.[1]

---

[1] Illustrative of this interplay of joy and passion in Curie's life is an anecdote from Le Doeuff: "The book [my teacher] gave me was a biography of Marie Curie, written by her daughter Eve, if I remember rightly. A week later I gave it back. 'So you saw,' he said, 'how cold she was in her attic room and how she put her suitcase on top of the bed covers...' 'What a woman she was! She could dance non-stop for three days! So that afterwards her shoes were only fit for the dustbin!' replied she who is always suspicious when people start talking about her edifying sacrifices." Michèle Le Doeuff, *Hipparchia's Choice* 2nd ed, trans. Trista Selous (New York: Columbia University Press, 2007), 144. It is here, when we take on the persona of a woman, that we must also acknowledge the lack of a specifically *feminist* Continental philosophy of religion in this volume. Feminist philosophy of religion is part of how Continental philosophy of religion is currently practiced, but there are no essays devoted to it here simply because there already exists two

This volume is also concerned with contaminations.[2] Various accounts of them and strategies to deal with them are given throughout, creating a metaphilosophical debate that forms the unconscious connecting thread throughout the essays. Roughly, there are two groups of strategies proffered. First, a number of the contributions chart the sometimes destructive effects of the recent theological contamination of philosophy. The task here is simply that of finding a way to perform a philosophical operation upon theological material, while retaining something properly philosophical. Here philosophy turns outwards, both as a critical operation on theology and as a liberation of aspects of religion from their own theological contamination. Second, some of the contributions experiment in the possibility of an aggressive alternative: a complementary philosophical contamination of theology. Experimentation here risks a disintegration of the philosophical body, in order to disturb theology's ideological and orthodox identity (that is, to contaminate it). What is at stake in both cases is a practice of philosophy which avoids dissolving into theology or becoming a tool of theological thought.

Contamination is therefore the challenge, and the pertinent strategy for philosophy of religion is twofold: liberation or automutation.

II. The Liberation and Automutation of Philosophy

The religious turn in phenomenology (Marion, Henry, Courtine), a Christian brand of deconstruction (Caputo) and feminist appeals to Mariology (Irigaray), all manifest the "theological turn" of recent Continental philosophy. The epithet "theological turn" itself implies that all these movements share the same intent: to contaminate philosophy with theological thinking. If anything defines the last decade of Continental philosophy of religion, it is the *theologisation of philosophy*.

This contamination, like Curie's, has been both productive and destructive. Its major benefit is the increase in status and popularity Continental philosophy of religion has enjoyed. There is now no longer any need to pause and wonder at its mere existence; rather, Continental

---

exemplary volumes that focus specifically on the feminist practice of Continental philosophy of religion. See Pamela Sue Anderson and Beverley Clack eds, *Feminist Philosophy of Religion: Critical Readings* (London: Routledge, 2004) and Pamela Sue Anderson ed, *New Topics in Feminist Philosophy of Religion: Contestations and Transcendence Incarnate* (London: Springer, 2010).

[2] It cannot be overstressed that we use this concept in a strictly scientific sense; it is *not* intended to imply any hope of ideological purity.

philosophers of religion are able to get on with deepening and developing the discipline. This volume could not have existed without such movements.

However, we also need to ask what consequences this blurring has had for thought: has it, in fact, failed to challenge theology and philosophy equally? Has philosophy been made the handmaiden of theology once again? If we answer in the affirmative, it is because this postmodern dissolution of philosophy of religion into theology has, in the last decade, given rise to an associated movement within theology itself. The Radical Orthodoxy group has popularised a mode of theological thinking which undermines philosophy's claim to autonomy. Once again (this time from within theology), philosophical thinking has been *theologised*, overrun by a theological virus whose intention is to obliterate the distinctiveness of philosophy of religion in the name of theology.

Both the postmodern and the postsecular[3] contamination are two sides of the same coin: a one-way injection of theology into philosophy until what is proper to philosophy becomes indiscernible. The deconstruction of the philosophy/theology binary has resulted, not in a true democracy of thought between philosophy and theology, but in the humiliation and debasement of philosophy before the Queen of the sciences, theology.[4]

To designate one of the solutions to this one-sided contamination "the liberation of philosophy of religion" is therefore to call for a critique of such tendencies in the name of philosophy. Liberation is a two-stage operation: it shows up the normativity and partiality of recent contaminations, but it does so in order to free a practice of philosophy of religion from the constraints imposed on it by theological thinking.[5]

---

[3] Although Radical Orthodoxy should not be confused (as we argue in section four) with the postsecular *per se*, but is only a specific theological appropriation of it.

[4] Janicaud's analysis of the theological contamination of phenomenology is exemplary here. See Dominique Janicaud, "The Theological Turn of French Phenomenology" in *Phenomenology and the "Theological Turn": The French Debate*, trans. Bernard G. Prusak (New York: Fordham University Press, 2000), 3-103 and Dominique Janicaud, *Phenomenology "Wide Open": After the French Debate*, trans. Charles N. Cabral (New York: Fordham University Press, 2005).

[5] Again, it needs to be emphasised that "liberation" here does *not* imply the repurification of philosophy. Theology and religion are always necessary material for philosophical thinking (however liberated). What our contributions attempt to liberate philosophy from is not theology *per se*, but the normative constraints the introduction of theology into philosophy of religion has brought about. It is for this reason the concept of liberation is appropriate: it names the freeing up of philosophy's capacities after a convalescence. As Bryant, Harman and Srnicek put

Likewise, auto-mutation aims to first liberate philosophy—sometimes from itself, but also from the theological—in order to create new forms of philosophical thinking. As such, the essays collected in this volume represent no school of thought and propound no orthodoxy; rather, they all undertake the task of experimenting on and with theological and religious material.[6]

The interplay between these two methods, one of liberation and the other of automutation, is best summed up in comments made by Gilles Deleuze in which he makes explicit three themes that we see as essential to any answer to the question, "What is Continental philosophy of religion now?". Deleuze begins a seminar on Spinoza by raising the "problem" of early modern philosophy's obsession with the concept of God:

> It's quite curious to what extent philosophy, up to the end of the 17th century, ultimately speaks to us, all the time, of God. And after all, Spinoza, excommunicated Jew, is not the last to speak to us of God... Why is philosophy so compromised with God? And right up to the revolutionary coup of the 18th century philosophers. Is it a dishonest compromise or something a little purer?[7]

---

it in another context, "The danger is that the dominant anti-realist strain of [the] continental philosophy [of the "theological turn"] has not only reached a point of decreasing returns, but that it now actively limits the capacities of philosophy in our time." (Levi Bryant, Graham Harman and Nick Srnicek, "Towards a Speculative Philosophy" in Bryant, Srnicek and Harman eds, *The Speculative Turn: Continental Realism and Materialism* (Melbourne: re:press, 2011), 3.)

[6] This questioning of the theological tendency of recent Continental philosophy is in certain quarters already well-established. In addition to Janicaud (see note four), Badiou, Le Doeuff, Rancière and Žižek have all risen to popularity (in part) by pointing out the aporia and shortcomings of that postmodern thinking which has been so susceptible to theological contamination. There is also a younger generation of Continental philosophers who have taken up this mantle of suspicion towards the "theological turn": Brassier, Grant, Hägglund and Meillassoux. The approach of this volume is indebted to their work, and many of the essays herein engage concertedly with them (sometimes for the first time). The challenge to think philosophy of religion "otherwise than theologically" has also already been taken up by a number of established philosophers of religion. This volume follows in the footsteps of Pamela Sue Anderson, Clayton Crockett and Philip Goodchild (to name but three) who (in very different ways) have all already begun the process of liberating and/or mutating philosophy of religion.

[7] Gilles Deleuze, "Seminar on Spinoza/Cours Vincennes 25/11/1980", available at <http://www.webdeleuze.com/php/texte.php?cle=17&groupe=Spinoza&langue=2>, accessed 10/02/2010. For another use of this passage, see Philip Goodchild, "Why is philosophy so compromised with God?" in Mary Bryden ed, *Deleuze and Religion* (London: Routledge, 2001), 156-66.

Deleuze rejects two answers to these questions: a pragmatic, extra-philosophical answer (that philosophers needed to conform outwardly to the demands of the Church) and a theological answer (that philosophers of the seventeenth and eighteenth centuries just had more "feeling" for the divine). Both are rejections of the idea of philosophy of religion as a field engendered by external, normative constraints; philosophy, Deleuze insists, refuses to burden itself with constraint. Rather, early modern philosophy speaks of God *as a means of liberation and transformation*. Using an analogy with painting, Deleuze therefore constructs his own response to the question, "Why is early modern philosophy so compromised with God?":

> Could we not make up another hypothesis, namely that painting in this era has so much need of God that the divine, far from being a constraint for the painter, is the site of his maximum emancipation. In other words, with God he can do anything whatsoever, he can do what he couldn't do with humans, with creatures. So much so that God is directly invested by painting, by a kind of flow of painting, and at this level painting will find a kind of freedom for itself that it would never have found otherwise. At the limit, the most pious painter and the one who… is the most impious are not opposed to each other because the way painting invests the divine is a way which is nothing but pictorial, where the painter finds nothing but the conditions of his radical emancipation... [Painters] make use of God in order to achieve a liberation of forms, to push the forms to the point where the forms have nothing to do with an illustration. The forms are unleashed. They embark upon a kind of Sabbath, a very pure dance, the lines and colours lose all necessity to be verisimilar, to be exact, to resemble something. It's the great enfranchisement of lines and colours... So much so that, in a sense, atheism has never been external to religion: atheism is the artistic power at work on religion. With God, everything is permitted. I have the distinct feeling that for philosophy it's been exactly the same thing, and if philosophers have spoken to us so much of God... [it was from] a joy arising from the labour they were involved in. Just as I said that God and Christ offered an extraordinary opportunity for painting to free lines, colours and movements from the constraints of resemblance, so God and the theme of God offered the irreplaceable opportunity for philosophy to free the object of creation in philosophy (that is to say, concepts) from the constraints that had been imposed on them... the simple representation of things. The concept is freed at the level of God because it no longer has the task of representing something... It takes on lines, colours, movements that it would never have had without this detour through God.[8]

---

[8] Ibid.

This is Deleuze's account of the liberation and automutation of philosophy of religion. It is an account which stresses three things: the significance of the early modern period for philosophical thinking about God, the freedom philosophy experiences in acknowledging the atheism at the core of religion and finally the experimental and speculative character (freed from the constraints of representation) of this construction. That is, Deleuze stresses the *modernity*, the *secularity* and the *speculative intent* of philosophy of religion. These three characteristics will structure the present volume.

III. The Contribution of Modernity

The first section of the present volume deals with the *modernity* of philosophy of religion. The six essays contained in this section all attempt to chart the experiments and emancipations immanent to the genesis of philosophy of religion. The questions they answer are: what were the conditions that liberated philosophers to pursue philosophy of religion, and how did it become such a significant part of the philosophical enterprise of modernity? In order to lay the groundwork within which each of the six essays answers these questions, it is worth rehearsing two powerful objections to Deleuze's account of the genesis of philosophy of religion quoted above. These two objections concern (unsurprisingly): the speculative intent and the secularity of modern philosophy of religion.

Speculation and Modern Philosophy of Religion

According to Deleuze, early modern philosophy—in parallel to early modern painting—experienced a colossal liberation when it came to constructing the concept of God. Freed from the constraints of representation, philosophy could be practiced in its most absolute form. No longer need it faithfully depict an already existent reality, for "the theme of God offered the irreplaceable opportunity for philosophy to free the object of creation in philosophy (that is to say, concepts) from the constraints that had been imposed on them." Philosophy of religion was therefore the site of *philosophy as such*—and only "this detour through God" offered philosophy the chance *to come into its own.*[9] With the

---

[9] The fact that the term "philosophy of religion" only emerged in German Idealism—far from being problematic for our purposes—indicates the extent to which, prior to this, "philosophy of religion" was the site of philosophy as such. The following claim of de Man's concerning aesthetics applies equally well to philosophy of religion: "Its being left nameless until the end of the eighteenth

concept of God, philosophers were free to *speculate*, to experiment and to construct without external constraints. Such was the impulse to speculation in modern philosophy of religion—a joyful and exuberant creation of new concepts.

The first objection to Deleuze's account concerns his divergence from more traditional narratives of the emergence of philosophy of religion. That is, philosophy of religion is usually envisaged as a *critical*—rather than a speculative—enterprise. For proponents of this view, philosophy of religion (especially in the early modern period) was (and remains) primarily a political movement, concerned with puncturing and deflating dominant meta-narratives and offering alternatives to religious orthodoxies. This critical philosophy of religion is a tool of the oppressed. Philip Goodchild proposes such a view in his Introduction to *Rethinking Philosophy of Religion*:

> It is important to recognise that... a confluence of theologico-political concerns—the overcoming of dissension, the fostering of true piety, the liberation of religion from political interference, and the exposure of the undermining of ecclesiastical authority by avarice and ambition—contributed to the rational exploration of religion in the seventeenth and eighteenth centuries, and not an abstract love of disembodied reason for the sake of its own purity. The philosophers who engaged with religion in this period must be regarded as a small minority of intellectuals and entrepreneurs... This minority was pitched against the vested interests of church, state and aristocracy on the one hand, and against the religious enthusiasms of puritans and pietists on the other.[10]

For the English Deists, Locke and Leibniz (to name but a few), philosophy of religion could not be abstracted from concrete, political concerns with Church and State. Every enquiry into religion was a specific intervention in the social system of the day. Philosophy of religion, therefore, was not a speculative enterprise free to construct concepts without any external constraints, but a battleground for political interests.

There is patent truth to such an account, and none of the contributors would wish to deny any of the political investment implicitly contained in all philosophy of religion. However, no specific form of critique holds a

---

century is a sign of its overwhelming presence rather than its non-existence." (Paul de Man, *Aesthetic Ideology*, ed. Andrzej Warminski (Minneapolis: University of Minnesota Press, 1996), 92.)

[10] Philip Goodchild, "Continental Philosophy of Religion: An Introduction" in Philip Goodchild ed, *Rethinking Philosophy of Religion: Approaches from Continental Philosophy* (New York: Fordham University Press, 2002), 6-7.

monopoly on the disruption of orthodoxy. As the previous section of this Introduction has argued, such ideological critique is also possible through other means: contaminating orthodoxy by a heterodox virus, or flagging up the restrictions theological thought has on philosophical capability. We see no contradiction between stressing philosophy of religion's critical and its speculative intent. Recent accounts of philosophy of religion have merely stressed one specific mode by which this critique can occur, and so have concentrated almost exclusively on (what we shall call for the sake of brevity) "a genealogy of refusal" which leads from Locke through Hume and Kierkegaard to Nietzsche and finally Derrida.

One of the aims of the "Modernity" section of this volume is to remedy this skewed emphasis by recovering the speculative (but no less critical) element of philosophy of religion that has lain hidden from contemporary concerns. There are two ways in which the contributors approach this aim. First, they do so by setting forth an *alternative genealogy of speculative or affirmatory philosophy of religion leading from Spinoza through Schelling to Bergson and Deleuze*. Michael Kolkman's contribution is paradigmatic here: Henri Bergson is an unjustly neglected figure by Continental philosophy of religion. Not only his explicit foray into the field (*The Two Sources of Morality and Religion*), but also, as Kolkman shows, his corpus as a whole has a significance to which late twentieth century scholarship has been blind.

The second way the contributors to the first section attempt to remedy the neglect of speculation in philosophy of religion is by *rereading figures central to the genealogy of refusal through the lens of speculation*. Exemplary here are James Brown's piece on Toland and Karin Nisenbaum's essay on Rosenzweig. So much emphasis has been placed, Brown argues, on Toland's (and other Deists') political critique of priestcraft and revelation that the constructive element in his project has gone relatively unnoticed. The political attack is, Brown contends, merely a preliminary to the production of a materialist metaphysics. A similar point is made by Nisenbaum with respect to Rosenzweig. While the majority of philosophical readings of *The Star of Redemption* emphasise its existential commitment to freedom, they ignore the metaphysical foundations on which this commitment is grounded: the work is, more than anything else, a speculative system of thought.

Secularity and Modern Philosophy of Religion

According to Deleuze, the philosophical emancipation to speculate we have just been discussing is to be associated with a philosophical atheism.

Atheism is the "power at work" in philosophy of religion. Early modern speculation about God is premised on a release from the constraints of theology. The norms and traditions of theological modes of thinking are cast off in favour of a philosophy that is limited only by its own internal necessity. It is therefore through a distancing from the theological that philosophy of religion can genuinely take place; only by stepping back from the "insider perspective" which informs theological study can the philosopher gain the necessary freedom to exceed the representational. This is the minimal amount of secularity that all philosophy of religion requires in order to take place.

The second objection, therefore, comes from those distrustful of and hostile to this aspect of early modern thought—its secular values. As we will see in the next section, there is no doubting the cogency of some of these critiques or some of the failings of the moderns in this respect; what is at issue, however, is the attitude to modernity such critique engenders.

In one camp stand those philosophers who take their cue from Nietzsche, Adorno, Horkheimer and Lyotard and who criticise the Enlightenment's refusal to acknowledge the "dark side" of modernisation, the cost as well as the benefits of the will to civilisation. Essential reading here is the second chapter of Brassier's *Nihil Unbound* as well as Jonathan Israel's monumental works on the Radical Enlightenment.[11] Not only do Brassier and Israel present a picture of Enlightenment thought which revels in its secularity and speculative intent, they also show its sensitivity to the criticisms which are so often levelled against it.

Another camp hostile to the secular values of modernity is formed of the various strands of postsecular thought, which, in its most prevalent form, bears the name "Radical Orthodoxy" (although, as we shall see, this theological movement has co-opted the label "postsecular" for its own purposes). Radical Orthodoxy—as we argued in section two—is one more example of the "theologisation" philosophy of religion has undergone in recent years. This theological contamination here manifests itself specifically as an interrogation of the "artificial space"[12] of secular existence which modern thought has constructed for itself—a space in

---

[11] Ray Brassier, *Nihil Unbound: Enlightenment and Extinction* (Basingstoke: Palgrave Macmillan, 2007), 32-48; Jonathan I. Israel, *Radical Enlightenment: Philosophy and the Making of Modernity, 1650-1750* (Oxford: Oxford University Press, 2001) and *Enlightenment Contested: Philosophy, Modernity and the Emancipation of Man, 1670-1752* (Oxford: Oxford University Press, 2006).

[12] John Milbank, *Theology and Social Theory: Beyond Secular Reason* 2nd ed (Oxford: Blackwell, 2006), 18.

which "philosophy has its own legitimacy, apart from faith."[13] The backbone of the Radical Orthodox challenge to contemporary thought is a questioning of the legitimacy of this "artificial space". Radical Orthodoxy has constructed an all-embracing genealogy of the history of ideas that attempts to undermine modernity's claims to be a "legitimate" tradition of thought, in favour of the claims of pre-secular traditions such as Thomism and Augustinianism. In consequence, Milbank and others have emphasised the significance of figures within the "counter-modern" tradition, like Hamann and Jacobi, who expose secularity's nihilism.[14]

Radical Orthodoxy, therefore, follows all secularisation theses in contending that modernity relies on pre-modern ideas that have been perverted in the process of being appropriated. They are "Christian by derivation and anti-Christian by consequence", as one early proponent of the secularisation thesis put it[15], and at the same time, in Milbank's more recent words, "Secular discourse… is actually *constituted* in its secularity by 'heresy' in relation to orthodox Christianity."[16] Modernity is "a mistaken deviation from Augustinianism".[17] It emerged not through a great leap forward, but on corrupted Christian presuppositions. Modern thought is thus an illegitimate, corrupt and distorted offshoot of "true" and "proper" Augustinian or Thomist systems of thought. Yet, secondly (and here Radical Orthodoxy goes beyond most secularisation theses), such perversion has disastrous consequences for thought: a pre-modern "ontology of peace" is transformed into a modern agonistic and nihilistic ontology. "Nihilism is the conclusion of 'pure reason'."[18] This is the double bind in which Radical Orthodoxy entraps modernity: it is both derivative of the pre-modern and also its abject, nihilistic other. It is neither innovative nor an improvement! Hence, "the Catholic vision of ontological peace" provides not only the unstained original of which modernity is the perversion, but also "the only alternative to a nihilistic outlook."[19]

---

[13] John Milbank, "Knowledge: The Theological Critique of Philosophy in Hamann and Jacobi" in John Milbank *et al* ed, *Radical Orthodoxy: A New Theology* (London: Routledge, 1999), 21.
[14] See ibid.
[15] Karl Löwith, *Meaning in History: The Theological Implications of the Philosophy of History* (Chicago: University of Chicago Press, 1949), 202.
[16] Milbank, *Theology and Social Theory*, 3.
[17] Michael Hanby, "Desire: Augustine beyond Western Subjectivity" in Milbank *et al* ed, *Radical Orthodoxy*, 110.
[18] Milbank, *Theology and Social Theory*, xvii.
[19] Ibid, 442.

As we will make clear in the next section, there is a valuable truth to the postsecular event that needs to be taken far more seriously than Continental philosophy of religion so far has. However, its misappropriation by theologians—and the visibility this misappropriation has attained—has mostly obscured this truth. Thus, instead of concentrating on the manner in which an "imperial" form of secularity (in part reinforced, it must be admitted, by modern philosophy—sometimes against itself) has prohibited experience of religious particularity, this "theological postsecular" has established a new imperialism, this time tending towards the premodern by means of a persistent polemic against the value of the modern.

It is therefore partially in response to the popularity of such a reading of modernity that the first section of this volume is devoted to "Modernity". The task which the six essays undertake is to mine the resources of a distinctly modern way of philosophising about religion. While this does involve recognising its faults and wrong turns, it also involves a serious examination of the manner in which modern philosophy of religion liberated itself and disrupted claims to orthodoxy. Such modern strategies provide a template for contemporary efforts. To paraphrase Clayton Crockett, engagement with modern thinkers on religion is necessary for the production of "test-cases of modernity and the stakes of any possible modern... thinking."[20] The studies of modern philosophers which form section one of this volume are "test-cases for modern philosophy of religion". Their aim is therefore twofold. First, by highlighting the depth, vitality and complexity of speculation about religion in modern, secular philosophy, the essays form indirect rebuffs to postsecular thought's all-too-quick dismissal of it. Second, and most significantly, by uncovering and subsequently mimicking the intellectual strategies—whether emancipatory or mutative—by which modern thought upset orthodoxy's claims upon it, they also directly combat the "theological postsecular".

The first strategy is pursued by George Pattison and Ashley Vaught. Pattison's careful examination of Heidegger's appropriation of Kierkegaard serves as a preliminary introduction to his wider project of a phenomenology of religious life. Such an enterprise is, of course, central to the volume's commitment to free up latent philosophical operations on religion. Vaught—in a fruitful parallel to Deleuze's comments on the essential atheism in modern philosophy of religion—argues that the driving force of Schelling's 1809 *Inquiries into the Essence of Human Freedom* is a realisation of the "philosophical atheism" at work in

---

[20] Clayton Crockett, *A Theology of the Sublime* (London: Routledge, 2001), 2.

theodicy. This atheism is the result of Schelling's fidelity to *philosophically think* the problems of theology. Again, the concern here is to isolate a properly philosophical operation on religion. A different approach, however, is taken by the first essay of the volume. Rocco Gangle provides a succinct introduction to the practice of automutation. Spinoza's commitment to immanence, Gangle argues, is only fully understood when one acknowledges the strategies by which he subverts and disrupts theological orthodoxy with heterodox, philosophical devices.

All the essays in the "Modernity" section therefore share a concern with uncovering the distinctive history and forgotten resources of Continental philosophy of religion—history and resources which have been covered over by theological critique and postmodern prejudices. This process of uncovering, it is to be hoped, will give us a fuller picture of what Continental philosophy of religion can be and so enable it to enhance its power of acting and being acted upon. For (to continue the parody of Spinoza) no one has yet determined what Continental philosophy of religion can do.

IV. Reinterpreting the Secular

During the 1990's, around the time that postmodernism reached its height in the Anglophone academy, another strange appellation appeared on the intellectual scene sharing the same "post" prefix—the postsecular. The emphasis in philosophy (but also in anthropology and the social sciences) shifted as scholars began to take seriously radical critiques of identity and power rooted in anti-imperialist and anti-colonial discourses. Questions surrounding religion took centre-stage, because these critiques challenged the hegemony of an underlying and unacknowledged ideological bias towards Western forms of Christianity and post-Christian secularism, even in the very tools philosophy employed.[21] This ideational imperialism can be traced back to the collusion of European philosophy of religion with the modern Western-style nation-state in the global spread of the capitalist system. Indeed, it is this very critique of modern philosophy of religion that led to the abandonment of the moderns (which this volume seeks to correct). As Asad writes,

---

[21] Thus, as Talal Asad tells us, many opponents to secularism in the Middle East have rejected the secular as specific to the Western mode of governance. Talal Asad, *Formations of the Secular: Christianity, Islam, Modernity* (Stanford: Stanford University Press, 2003), 2.

Secularism is not simply an intellectual answer to a question about enduring social peace and toleration. It is an enactment by which a *political medium* (representation of citizenship) redefines and transcends particular and differentiating practices of the self that are articulated through class, gender, and religion.[22]

The question the contributors to section two of this volume ask concerns the capacity for modern philosophy to be subtracted from its political medium and transformed (in the words of Laruelle) into a simple material for reconsidering secularity, both intellectual and political—that is, they ask about the possibility of turning philosophy of religion *against* secularism (or, at least, its historically instantiated forms). The next seven essays in the volume, under the heading "Reinterpreting the Secular", are representative of the recent impetus in Continental philosophy of religion to think beyond the failures of the moderns (while remaining within that tradition) so as to carry out a speculative inquiry into the very nature of the secular. While the *postsecular* event has for the most part occurred amidst Islamic thinkers (both orthodox and unorthodox), the task for Continental philosophy of religion now is *not* an Islamic turn (as a new insanitation of the Christian theological turn), but a thinking *from* that event in a secular way, allowing identities to proliferate without overcoding secular philosophical thought. At the moment when modern secularism has failed and the so-called return to the religious is on the precipice of failing, philosophers must be bold in putting forth a theory of secularity that is, in its very thinking, an abstract instance of that new secular.

Modern Philosophy of Religion and the Secular

We would be blind, however, if we did not acknowledge the failures of the moderns in their attempts to move to the secular via Christianity. The postsecular posture towards the history of thought and to our contemporary conditions, taken up by such diverse thinkers as Milbank and Hamid Dabashi, remains powerful because it is responding to a real failure in the history of the human world and, as a human failure, it is responding to real suffering. While, after the various periods of fits and starts of the European Enlightenment, Western thought often took the secular to be the highest social and political ideal as the most effective path to peace between nations and peoples, it also resulted in the erasure of identities, often at the barrel of a gun, in the Middle East, Africa, Asia, and South America (to say nothing of local indigenous cultures in North America and Europe).

---

[22] Ibid, 5.

We must distinguish, however, between the genuine postsecular event and its misappropriation and misuse at the hands of theologians. In the wake of the postsecular event, a distinction is necessary between the *infidelity* to that event attested in the "theological postsecular" and a potential *faithfulness* to it made possible through thinking the secular anew. The failure of "imperial secularity" criticised legitimately by genuine postsecular critiques is very different from that depicted in the orthodox theological response to the postsecular event. Phillip Blond describes this latter failure in the Introduction to the edited volume, *Postsecular Philosophy: Between Theology and Philosophy*:

> We live in a time of failed conditions. Everywhere people who have no faith in any possibility, either for themselves, each other, or for the world, mouth locutions they do not understand... Ever since Kant dismissed God from human cognition and relegated access to Him to the sphere of practical ethics and moral motivation, human beings have been very pragmatic indeed. They have found value in self-legislation and so see no reason for God.[23]

Blond contends that the failure of secularism (the postsecular event) does not constitute an event that demands new theories, but is rather an event that requires the darkening of reason (like Badiou's "obscure subject" unfaithful to the event), and so a return to transcendence—the transcendence of the Christian God.[24]

To this form of thinking—and to the political form of "Red Toryism" it has recently taken on in Britain (described by Žižek as "soft fascism")—this volume stands in defiant opposition.[25] As evidenced by Adam Kotsko's chapter, which engages with the genealogical work of Giorgio Agamben, we must remain faithful to the postsecular event without using

---

[23] Phillip Blond, "Introduction: Theology before Philosophy" in Phillip Blond ed, *Postsecular Philosophy: Between Theology and Philosophy* (London: Routledge, 1998), 1-2.

[24] See Alain Badiou, *Logics of Worlds: Being and Event II*, trans. Alberto Toscano (London: Continuum, 2009), 58-62. There he writes, this infidelity is "the descent of this present into the night of non-exposition... In the panic sown by [the event of] Spartacus and his troops, the patrician—and the Vendean bishop, and the Islamist conspirator, and the fascist of the thirties—systematically resorts to the invocation of a full and pure transcendent Body, an ahistorical or anti-evental body (City, God, Race...) from which it follows that the trace will be denied... and, as a consequence, the real body, the divided body, will also be suppressed." (59-60)

[25] Slavoj Žižek, "Dialectical Clarity versus the Misty Conceit of Paradox" in John Milbank and Slavoj Žižek, *Monstrosity of Christ* (London: MIT Press, 2009), 240.

it as an excuse for reactionary escapism. The response to the postsecular situation is not, *pace* Blond, to return yet again to the presecular (to theology), but (at least for Kotsko and Agamben) a radical messianic nihilism that dismantles the theo-political machine. In other words, what is required in the face of the postsecular event is a philosophy which takes up the modern emancipation of philosophy in the service of a new speculative construction of a true secular. This requires a reconsideration of discussions of the secular in modernity so as to take up what is most powerful therein, and recast it in a new critical form. Clare Greer's contribution to the volume constitutes one such reconsideration, turning to recent debates regarding Hegel's conception of the relationship between religion and the State. She argues that Gillian Rose's interpretation of the Hegelian absolute as a "broken middle" where neither State nor religion dominate challenges Milbank's postsecular rejection of Hegel.

Speculation and the Secular

When social theorists, philosophers and anthropologists began to investigate secular cultures using the same tools they had used to investigate religions, it was a true event in the history of thought comparable to Darwin's theory of evolution and Freud's discovery of the unconscious. It humiliated Western culture, casting it down from its central place in human history and exhibiting the relativity of its particular secular culture. Secularism was identified as the site of disciplines and forces. Just like religions (although the discipline of the secular was (and remains) more complicit in the rise of capitalism, in both its liberatory and oppressive aspects), secularism developed in Western nation-states as a social form necessary for capital to flow. In modern Britain, for example, the need for cheap labour after the neo-liberal destructuring of the 1980s meant that many immigrants from former British colonies and lands where British interests had historically dominated began arriving in the country. The need for this labour created a need for a multicultural society that placed (amongst many other markers of identity) different religious groups within the same social milieu. This, in turn, led to religious antagonisms that were also helpful to the functioning of capital, since they kept workers divided, giving rise to the current myth of a "deeply divided Britain". Many factors are at work here, including the attempt in the name of secularism to rebrand the immigrant communities and have them adapt a "secular lifestyle"—which, in reality, means collapsing their own identity into the identity of the majority population (White and post-Christian). At the global level this call to secularism has meant that Muslims (in particular) have no recourse to the Islamic tradition in their struggle against imperialism or, even, repressive Islamic states.[26] The secular in the hands of Western powers becomes an imperialist weapon, for the secular is always already interpreted as a *particularly Western and post-Christian secular, rather than* anything approaching a generic secular that can be located *equally* in all religious traditions.

Again, this gives rise to a distinction between the "imperial secularity" of the past and the genuine potential of the secular as a category to do justice to all religious particularities. This latter idea we designate "the generic secular". The task, then, a number of contributors undertake is the construction of a truly generic secular, a secularity that can sustain the particularity, and even proliferation, of all religious and post-religious modes of being. Unleashing both the religious and the secular for such a politics of resistance and positive rebellion is the challenge Daniel Colucciello Barber, for example, takes up. By subsuming both religion and the secular into immanence, Barber is able to refuse the attempt by both to assert themselves as the universal plane, casting the secular and the religious, instead, as *immanent sites of particularities*. John Mullarkey's essay follows a similar trajectory by means of Bergson's *The Two Sources of Morality and Religion*. Mullarkey argues through the Bergsonian notion of "creative emotion" for a "bellicose" (or, we might say, excessive) equality, the thought of which is equal in both form and content.

These essays are among the first to take up the thought of the "generic" secular within Continental philosophy of religion. Indeed, philosophy of religion's neglect of the speculative possibilities of diverse cultural materials is shocking. Over the last twenty years, there has been a serious failure to engage in any real way with this aspect of the postsecular event. Islam and the other non-Christian religions have not been taken seriously in the same way that Christianity has, and in consequence there has not been anything like an Islamic turn in philosophy, any more than there has been a Buddhist or Hindi turn. Alberto Toscano's contribution to the volume goes some way to remedying this lack. It is a stellar example of the practice of the generic secular, tracing particular instances of fanaticism through both Christianity and Islam. Such a genealogy does not have the well-worn goal of denouncing the fanatic (as one always finds in those pop attempts at philosophy of religion common to the opinion pages), but aims towards a fuller understanding of how fanaticism operates as a complex idea within both religious traditions and attempts to practice a "politics of truth".

---

[26] See Hamid Dabashi, *Islamic Liberation Theology: Resisting the Empire* (London: Routledge, 2008).

There has been a sense among many thinkers who try to inhabit a space between theology and philosophy that the Christian tradition could be cast in the role of victim at the hands of the secular. Such is the Radical Orthodox appropriation of the postsecular event—nothing but a philosophical manqué. Following that appropriation, there has been a persistent tendency to maintain that the truly radical response to the postsecular event is not only a return to the religious, but a return to the dominance of the religious over all other forms of thought. Theology—specifically *Christian* theology—would once again become Queen of the sciences. The return of the religious means, within the context of globalisation, a return to religious conflict, war, and violence, and, it is claimed, Christianity would uniquely respond to such events as the tradition that would best rescue the meaning necessary to resist the loss of identity following from *imperial* secularism. The choice given to us by these thinkers is not between freedom and imperialism, but between two imperialisms, both equally parochial. The postsecular has become not an event (as it had initially promised to be), but an obscure disaster that created nothing but fear, a fear utilised by theology to redirect attention to itself.[27]

A subtler response is required to the postsecular event than the reactionary proselytising of a few. Yes, it is true, that the tools used within Christian theology and the philosophical analysis of Christianity have a wider significance and can be employed in the analysis of post-religious phenomena (capitalism or the secular, for example). However, this is in no

---

[27] The attitude in Radical Orthodox circles to Spinoza is symptomatic. Conor Cunningham's dismissal of Spinoza reads like the worst sort of eighteenth-century heresy-hunting, claiming perversely and hyperbolically, "In the world of Spinoza there can be no difference between a Holocaust and an ice cream." (Conor Cunningham, *Genealogy of Nihilism: Philosophies of Nothing and the Difference of Theology* (London: Routledge, 2002), 68) Just like Blond, Cunningham attempts to bring about a return to the religious through inspiring fear and superstition in his readers. We should, it is implied, run screaming into the arms of the Church on encountering this nihilistic spectre. Apparently, this theology does not know the difference between scholarship and assertion, blindly referencing Spinoza scholars like Yovel and Deleuze out of context to support his own peculiar reading. For example, he claims Spinoza was trying to trick his readers by hiding behind Scholastic concepts and, as evidence for this view, quotes Deleuze: "It is for this reason that Deleuze says that 'the *Ethics* is a book written twice simultaneously'." (Ibid, 68) However, the point Deleuze is making (in *Spinoza: Practical Philosophy*, trans. Robert Hurley (San Francisco: City Lights, 1988), 28) has nothing to do with Spinoza's use of Medieval terminology, but is rather to do with the inextricably linked metaphysical and practical lines of thinking in the *Ethics*.

way proves that Christianity trumps all. Rather, it shows the importance of paying attention to the strategies and practices of discourse on religion for improving political analysis. Nina Power's essay proceeds in precisely this way, returning to one of the sources of Marxist theory (Feuerbach's *The Essence of Christianity*) so as to rejuvenate post-Marxist analysis of capital. By means of a reconsideration of Feuerbach's historical naturalism, Power is able to employ the same tools used to undermine religion in the service of a radical political critique of capitalism. She shows that this framework is already at work in mutated form in the philosophy of Paulo Virno. Power's essay demonstrates how the premise of all criticism (the criticism of religion) can be used in the service of the criticism of anti-humanist and anti-naturalist capitalism. Essential here too is Alex Andrews' bringing together of Hägglund's reading of Derrida and Bataille's theory of religion—a combination which also serves as a convenient hinge between sections two and three of this volume—to show how both areligious and religious politics may be organized in a secular project that seeks to alleviate human suffering in the here and now.

V. Contemporary Speculative Philosophy and Religion

Recent Continental philosophy of religion has been practiced primarily within the phenomenological and hermeneutical traditions. What sets this volume apart is the fact that the essays herein are (for the most part) unconcerned with these traditional ways of "doing" Continental philosophy of religion. These essays situate themselves in the *speculative tradition of philosophy*. This label has a threefold reference. First, it is one name among many for the above-mentioned liberative and mutative strategies open to Continental philosophy of religion. Second, speculation refers to the modern tradition of metaphysical speculation with which the first section of this volume engages.

The third—and at present most widespread—reference of the term "speculation" is to those contemporary philosophers who have situated themselves as heirs to modernity.[28] "Speculation" thus includes Badiou's

---

[28] Bryant, Harman and Srnicek sum up the affinities and tensions between these three references: "This activity of 'speculation' may be cause for concern amongst some readers, for it might suggest a return to pre-critical philosophy, with its dogmatic belief in the powers of pure reason. The speculative turn, however, is not an outright rejection of these critical advances; instead, it comes from a recognition of their inherent limitations. Speculation in this sense aims at something 'beyond' the critical and linguistic turns. As such, it recuperates the pre-critical sense of 'speculation' as a concern with the Absolute, while also taking into account the

reappropriation of "classical" (pre-Hegelian) modernity—ignoring the pathos of finitude so central to phenomenology, hermeneutics and deconstruction and, instead, prioritising the infinite. It also includes Meillassoux's return to the Cartesian project of a comprehensive account of reality grounded in mathematics. While the impact of "this new 'primordial soup' of Continental philosophy"[29] is beginning to be felt in philosophy of religion (especially Badiou's reading of Paul), there has been little extensive engagement with this new generation of Continental philosophers. It is this lack the present volume remedies.[30]

On first glance, however, the outlook for a rapprochement between speculation and philosophy of religion is not promising. A pervasive (even if often implicit) distaste for the "theological turn" can be discerned in much recent speculative philosophy. To take one example, the theological turn is extensively critiqued by Meillassoux in *After Finitude* under the label of "fideism". As Alain Badiou points out in his Preface to the work, Meillassoux's argument "allows thought to be destined towards the absolute once more, rather than towards those partial fragments and relations in which we complacently luxuriate while the 'return of the religious' provides us with a fictitious supplement of spirituality."[31] For Meillassoux, all recent philosophy is complicit in exacerbating the eruption of theological modes of thinking. It can be traced back through Heidegger and Wittgenstein (in equal measure) to Kant.[32] The legacy the Kantian settlement has bequeathed thought is one in which philosophy becomes once more the handmaiden of theology. "The end of metaphysics,"

---

undeniable progress that is due to the labour of critique. The works collected here are a speculative wager on the possible returns from a renewed attention to reality itself." "Towards a Speculative Philosophy", 3.

[29] Ibid, 1.

[30] Of course, this is not to say that this volume subscribes to any of the particular "schools" of contemporary speculative thought (Harman's "object-orientated philosophy", Brassier's "transcendental nihilism", Grant's "dynamicist naturalism" or Meillassoux's "speculative materialism"). Nor do we particularly subscribe to the idea of a "speculative *turn*" in Continental philosophy, if that is taken to imply speculative philosophy was not being undertaken prior to 2007. However, this volume is obviously indebted to the visibility that recent speculative projects have been given, and such a readjustment of focus onto the speculative is only to be welcomed.

[31] Alain Badiou, Preface to Quentin Meillassoux, *After Finitude*, trans. Ray Brassier (London: Continuum, 2008), xiii.

[32] Meillassoux, *After Finitude*, 41-2.

Meillassoux writes, "has taken the form of an exacerbated return of the religious."[33] And this is because, he continues, since Kant,

> It [has] become rationally illegitimate to disqualify *irrational* discourses about the absolute on the pretext of their irrationality... In effect, religious belief has every right to maintain that the world was created out of nothingness from an act of love, or that God's omnipotence allows him to dissolve the apparent contradiction between his complete identity and His difference with his Son.[34]

Philosophy's post-Kantian "renunciation of the absolute"[35] is an abandonment of the metaphysical structures which compelled talk about the absolute to submit before the tribunal of reason. This renunciation, then, is a divestment of reason's authority, and, in consequence, makes room for a "religionising of reason"[36]—a contemporary "fideism". Such fideism becomes most visible in the theological contamination of recent philosophy of religion.

Meillassoux's *After Finitude* is certainly (although not solely) an indictment of the current state of Continental philosophy of religion. However, this critique of the return of the theological and its prevalence in postmodern and postsecular philosophy of religion is *not*, we contend, a critique of philosophy of religion *tout court*. In fact, Meillassoux's critique of fideism could well be read as a call to practice *philosophy* of religion: to make rational claims on the absolute once again, in opposition to its theological colonisation by religious discourses. Speculative philosophy of religion is, therefore, a means of saving philosophy from religion.[37] A speculative philosophy of religion which risks thinking the absolute does not fall foul of Meillassoux's criticisms of contemporary fideism; it is, in fact, one of the only ways such fideism is to be countered and falsified. Meillassoux's critique of fideism is a call to arms against the forfeiture of the absolute to theological forms of thought.

The five essays collected in the third part of the volume consider this re-absolutising of philosophy of religion in a plurality of heterogeneous ways, but ways which all share a concern with the experimental nature of philosophical operations on religion. They perform experiments in thought which disrupt and mutate existing forms of Continental philosophy of

---

[33] Ibid, 45.

[34] Ibid, 41.

[35] Ibid, 42.

[36] Ibid, 47.

[37] Meillassoux's own work in progress on "divine inexistence", for example, could be read in this way. See Burns' essay for further exploration of this corpus.

religion. Within the speculative realm itself there can be no orthodoxy, only a practice of radical heresy. Even Meillassoux's call to arms does not guarantee one specific form of speculative materialism. As John Mullarkey has shown, Meillassoux's hyper-choas is prefigured, "ironically" in "the philosophy of Emile Boutroux, whose *De la Contingence des Lois de la Nature* (1874) argues for the same contingency as Meillassoux, only then in the interest of spiritualism (at that time meaning anti-reductionism), rather than materialism."[38] Michael Burns essay, the first reading of Meillassoux's philosophy with regard to philosophy of religion, contextualises Meillassoux's nascent divinology in his understanding of Cantorian set theory. In a debate with Hägglund's humanist philosophy of religion, Burns argues for a prioritisation of contingency within any materialism. This, Burns argues, has political power for resistance to dominant power structures because it shows that, at the ontological level, things could be radically otherwise. Clayton Crockett (to take another example) uses Catherine Malabou's reading of Hegel's dialectic as an antidote to current obsessions with Judeo-Christian messianism; Bradley Johnson, on the other hand, critically mutates Crockett's own earlier work on a theological sublime to produce a politically-orientated form of aesthetic practice. Thus, within the volume as a whole and this section in particular a nascent speculative debate opens up regarding the act of mutating theological practice. Already within this volume, a proliferation of heresies and experiments are in the process of being produced.

However, all such heresies must ultimately be assessed for their cogency and power, and one criterion recently proposed by Iain Hamilton Grant for so evaluating the recent spate of speculative experiments is the "extensity test". Central to both Daniel Whistler's and Anthony Paul Smith's chapters is such an "extensity test" of philosophy. Whistler demands of Grant's own reading of Schelling an explanation of those aspects of thought he is most critical of (language and religion). Through testing Grant's thought in this way, Whistler ultimately argues for a "geology of divine names", ending with the ultimatum that speculative philosophy account for the words of the Qur'an and the Nicene Creed, alongside Lovecraftian monsters and Okenian slime. Anthony Paul Smith's essay also subjects philosophy to a radical questioning. This time, however, it is Continental philosophy of religion which is interrogated from the point of view of Laruellean non-philosophy. Such interrogation

---

[38] John Mullarkey, "The Future of Continental Philosophy" in Beth Lord and John Mullarkey eds, *The Continuum Companion to Continental Philosophy* (London: Continuum, 2009), 274.

has a twofold purpose: first, to mutate philosophy of religion into a practice of non-theology which can cope with the trauma of religious violence; second, to mutate non-philosophy itself into a mode of thought which avoids the temptation of self-sufficiency in a more radical way.

Yet (by way of conclusion), the "extensity test" is not the only criterion by which to evaluate new experiments in Continental philosophy of religion, and in the Afterword to this volume, Philip Goodchild (and the personae which populate his piece) subjects the very practice of philosophy of religion to a far-reaching critique of its sincerity/hypocrisy. The volume thus ends with a number of questions: is speculation necessarily fabrication? How can heresies remain faithful to human living in the world? Questions which only further experiments in Continental philosophy of religion can hope to answer. This volume stands witness to this call to further experimentation.

Bibliography

Asad, Talal. *Formations of the Secular: Christianity, Islam, Modernity.* Stanford: Stanford University Press, 2003.

Anderson, Pamela Sue and Beverley Clack edited. *Feminist Philosophy of Religion: Critical Readings.* London: Routledge, 2004.

Anderson, Pamela Sue edited. *New Topics in Feminist Philosophy of Religion: Contestations and Transcendence Incarnate.* London: Springer, 2010.

Badiou, Alain. *Logics of Worlds: Being and Event II.* Translated by Alberto Toscano. London: Continuum, 2009.

Blond, Phillip. "Introduction: Theology before Philosophy." In Phillip Blond edited, *Postsecular Philosophy: Between Theology and Philosophy.* London: Routledge, 1998. 1-66.

Brassier, Ray. *Nihil Unbound: Enlightenment and Extinction.* Basingstoke: Palgrave Macmillan, 2007.

Bryant, Levi, Graham Harman and Nick Srnicek. "Towards a Speculative Philosophy." In Bryant, Harman and Srnicek edited, *The Speculative Turn: Continental Realism and Materialism.* Melbourne: re:press, 2011. 1-18.

Crockett, Clayton. *A Theology of the Sublime.* London: Routledge, 2001.

Cunningham, Conor. *Genealogy of Nihilism: Philosophies of Nothing and the Difference of Theology.* London: Routledge, 2002.

Dabashi, Hamid. *Islamic Liberation Theology: Resisting the Empire.* London: Routledge, 2008.

Deleuze, Gilles. "Seminar on Spinoza/Cours Vincennes 25/11/1980."
    Available at: <http://www.webdeleuze.com/php/texte.php?cle=17
    &groupe=Spinoza&langue=2>. Accessed on 10/02/2010.
—. *Spinoza: Practical Philosophy*. Translated by Robert Hurley. San
    Francisco: City Lights, 1988.
De Man, Paul. *Aesthetic Ideology*. Edited by Andrzej Warminski.
    Minneapolis: University of Minnesota Press, 1996.
Goodchild, Philip. "Continental Philosophy of Religion: An Introduction."
    In Philip Goodchild edited, *Rethinking Philosophy of Religion:
    Approaches from Continental Philosophy* (New York: Fordham
    University Press, 2002). 1-39.
—. "Why is philosophy so compromised with God?" In Mary Bryden
    edited, *Deleuze and Religion*. London: Routledge, 2001. 156-66.
Hanby, Michael. "Desire: Augustine beyond Western Subjectivity." In
    John Milbank *et al* edited, *Radical Orthodoxy: A New Theology*.
    London: Routledge, 1999. 109-26.
Israel, Jonathan I. *Radical Enlightenment: Philosophy and the Making of
    Modernity, 1650-1750*. Oxford: Oxford University Press, 2001.
—. *Enlightenment Contested: Philosophy, Modernity and the
    Emancipation of Man, 1670-1752*. Oxford: Oxford University Press,
    2006.
Janicaud, Dominique. "The Theological Turn of French Phenomenology."
    In *Phenomenology and the "Theological Turn": The French Debate*,
    translated by Bernard G. Prusak. New York: Fordham University
    Press, 2000. 3-103.
—. *Phenomenology "Wide Open": After the French Debate*. Translated
    by Charles N. Cabral. New York: Fordham University Press, 2005.
Le Doeuff, Michèle. *Hipparchia's Choice*. Second edition. Translated by
    Trista Selous. New York: Columbia University Press, 2007.
Löwith, Karl. *Meaning in History: The Theological Implications of the
    Philosophy of History*. Chicago: University of Chicago Press, 1949.
Meillassoux, Quentin. *After Finitude*. Translated by Ray Brassier. London:
    Continuum, 2008.
Milbank, John. "Knowledge: The Theological Critique of Philosophy in
    Hamann and Jacobi." In John Milbank *et al* edited, *Radical Orthodoxy:
    A New Theology*. London: Routledge, 1999. 21-37.
—. *Theology and Social Theory: Beyond Secular Reason*. Second edition.
    Oxford: Blackwell, 2006.
Mullarkey, John. "The Future of Continental Philosophy." In Beth Lord
    and John Mullarkey edited, *The Continuum Companion to Continental
    Philosophy*. London: Continuum, 2009. 259-76.

Žižek, Slavoj. "Dialectical Clarity versus the Misty Conceit of Paradox." In John Milbank and Slavoj Žižek, *Monstrosity of Christ*. London: MIT Press, 2009. 234-306.

PART I

THE CONTRIBUTION OF MODERNITY

CHAPTER ONE

THEOLOGY OF THE CHIMERA: SPINOZA, IMMANENCE, PRACTICE

ROCCO GANGLE

I. Spinoza's Strategy of the Chimera

François Zourabichvili locates a uniquely Spinozist art in the philosophical style of the *Ethics*. In a brief but highly suggestive passage, Zourabichvili identifies the dominant textual strategy of the *Ethics* as "a strategy of the chimera" that uses old terms in new ways such that a new "subversive notion" is created that "retains in spite of everything the prestige of its original signification."[1] When Zourabichvili speaks of Spinoza's "strategy of the chimera," it is above all with regard to Spinoza's use of traditional philosophical vocabulary. In the *Ethics* and elsewhere, Spinoza consistently employs philosophical terminology that has come to possess relatively precise and technical meanings across the sedimented histories of ancient philosophy and medieval Scholasticism, yet Spinoza uses these terms in ways that shift or distort their traditional senses, imposing unfamiliar meanings through new syntactical practices and systematically constructed relations. In many cases, a newly produced "chimerical" sense is directly opposed to the traditional sense of a given term, but this opposition itself becomes disclosed and available only to readers patient and careful enough to reproduce the steps of formal deduction comprising the *Ethics'* "geometrical method" (*more geometrico*).

Part lion, part goat, part snake, the chimera has long served as a philosophical figure of unreality and has done so in two distinct ways. On the one hand, philosophers summon the chimera to exemplify generally what can be thought but does not in fact exist, the false or unreal as such. On the other hand, the chimera is used to represent a specific form of the

---

[1] François Zourabichvili, *Spinoza: une physique de la pensée* (Paris: PUF, 2002), 112. Translation mine.

unreal, that which is cobbled together from really existing parts into the unity of an impossible whole. In this more specialized sense, the chimera draws together and individuates the unreal less in terms of matter than of form. There is nothing unreal in this latter sense of the chimera except the formal unity of its constituent parts. The *Ethics'* "strategy of the chimera" cuts across the difference between these two senses. Thus Zourabichvili's analogy of Spinoza's usage with the mythical beast is inexact—and thereby all the more perfect. Whereas the chimera is composed of the parts of separate real animals, the Spinozist chimera is a single, self-identical term whose relational context becomes altered. Its new sense is generated not internally or intensively but externally or practically through syntactical and formally deductive connections with other terms.

How exactly does the "strategy of the chimera" proceed? How does the *Ethics* elicit new coinages from well-worn terms, infused or burdened with specific histories and consensual meanings? Briefly put, the new sense of a term emerges out of the formal context of its systematic use. In other words, the way a traditional term is used in Spinoza's argumentation as a vehicle for specific logical deductions, inferences and implications relative to the *Ethics* as a whole retroactively imbues that term with a particular, system-dependent sense. A common term is made to circulate within a determinate logical and textual "economy," a self-consistent, immanently relational structure. This structure, or context, shapes the local meaning of the term in ways that may go against the grain of its historical sense. The new meaning of the term thus comes from its functional role in the network of logical inferences produced within the form of the text itself. Textual and argumentative form distorts or unmakes traditional content.

The most obvious and far-ranging example found in the *Ethics* is Spinoza's use of the term God (*Deus*), his famous *"Deus, sive Natura"*—God, or Nature. With this "impossible" equation, Spinoza formalizes the central metaphysical doctrine of the *Ethics*: monism, or the claim to real existence of exactly one substance of which all apparently discrete and independent entities are simply variant modes. Despite the formal identification of God, Nature and substance, however, Spinoza continues to privilege the term God in particular contexts throughout the text of the *Ethics* and does not shy away from setting his new "chimerical" sense in explicit confrontation with the sense of tradition, as with the claim in Part Five that "He who loves God cannot strive that God should love him in return."[2] Still, "God" is not the sole instance of Spinoza's strategy of the chimera. Similar chimerical transformations may be noted in many other

---

[2] Benedict Spinoza, *The* Ethics *and Other Works*, ed. and trans. Edwin Curley (Princeton: Princeton University Press, 1994), VP19.

traditional terms used in the *Ethics*: mind (*mens*), idea (*idea*), freedom (*libertas*) and so on. Even more strongly, the *Ethics* as a whole may be understood to perform a chimerical translation of this kind with respect to previous philosophical thinking in general insofar as it substitutes a new standpoint of radical immanence for previous traditional variants of philosophical correlation and transcendence (both explicit and implicit) and does so through a specific formal employment of traditional philosophical vocabulary and argument.

To make sense of this latter claim, it is first necessary to grasp the unity of the *Ethics'* logical form. A strictly formalist reading of the *Ethics* would strive as far as possible to bracket the inherited meanings of the terms Spinoza uses and to attend only to the complex network of relations established between them, as in any axiomatic system. In Euclid's geometry, for instance, the terms "point," "line" and "plane" obviously refer to ordinary and familiar concepts, yet in the rigour of Euclidean demonstration these words must be understood solely as "undefined terms," or empty variables whose meanings are grounded only in the relations established by the initial axioms of the system, such as "two points determine a line." A formalist interpretation of Spinoza's thought, following the *more geometrico*, would read the *Ethics* in a similar way, radicalising the indifference of Spinoza's thinking to the historically-embedded meanings of his natural language vocabulary. One might cultivate the habits of such a reading by substituting logical variables— mere placeholders—for the terms chosen by Spinoza himself. Call substance "X," attribute "Y," and the modes, or affections of a substance "Z." Propositions 4-7 of Part One would then read, proposition 4: "Two or more distinct things are distinguished from one another, either by a difference Y of X or by a difference Z of X." Proposition 5: "In Nature there cannot be two or more X of the same Y." Proposition 6: "One X cannot be produced by another X." Proposition 7: "It pertains to the nature of X to exist." As the examples multiply and an increasing number of terms are made substitutable in this way, the formal relations between the terms thus become clearer while the terms themselves—the relata— become indistinct, fading as it were into the background through the indifference of their diversity. As more and more propositions and demonstrations are enveloped or included by this method, the emerging complex structure of relations comes to take precedence over the meanings of the things related, and a unified form—the "structure" of the *Ethics*— takes shape in the mind of the interpreter. However, this form still remains pinned, as it were, to the background meanings of the utilized terms, which are transformed into indices of the new logical structure. At one level, then, the "esoteric" form may now be read off of and against the "exoteric" content, but, more profoundly, this distinction itself is undercut at a second level by the recurrence or one-sidedness of the formalist manoeuvre itself, the very *action* of the form on the content.

The attribution of an esotericist rhetorical strategy to Spinoza has been much more commonly made with respect to the *Theological-Political Treatise* than the *Ethics*. The readings of the *TTP* by Leo Strauss and Sylvain Zac in particular have been highly influential.[3] Along similar lines, André Tosel has argued that the intrinsic purpose of the *TTP*—its political "content"—conditions the form in which that message necessarily is conveyed and that this introduces an important distinction between the *TTP* and the *Ethics*. Tosel marks the difference between Spinoza's two texts by claiming that "the *Ethics* deduces true knowledge and its genesis," as opposed to the *TTP* which "seeks to form this knowledge practically from some true ideas that are already present, in minds that are also credulous and dominated by the ontotheological conception of the world."[4] In other words, the rhetorical structure of the *Ethics* would follow a strictly formal arrangement of its parts as determined solely by the matters themselves, (as in a mathematical or geometrical proof), while the *TTP* would necessarily take an "indirect path" of argument corresponding to the mixed state of its intended audience. Thus a purely *deductive* method characterizing the *Ethics* would be contrasted with a heterogeneous strategy of rhetoric in the *TTP*. Zourabichvili, with his analysis of the "strategy of the chimera", suggests that the deductive method of the *Ethics* may in fact be more mixed than it appears.

If Zourabichvili is right, the difference between the rhetorical strategies of the *TTP* and the *Ethics* is less clear-cut. The difference is more that of scope or scale than of kind. The application of a mixed strategy in the *TTP*

---

[3] Working within the framework of the problem of politically subversive writing in the context of a society of censorship, Strauss developed a theory of esoteric writing through examination of the writings of various thinkers in antiquity, the medieval period and early modernity including Plato, Aristotle, Maimonides and Spinoza. See Leo Strauss, *Persecution and the Art of Writing* (Chicago: University of Chicago, 1988), and *Spinoza's Critique of Religion*, trans. E.M. Sinclair (Chicago: University of Chicago, 1997). For Zac, in the *Ethics* "c'est la vérité philosophique qui se révèle elle-même," while in the *TTP* "c'est un homme qui s'adresse à d'autres hommes." Sylvain Zac, *Spinoza et l'interprétation de l'ecriture* (Paris: PUF 1965), 219.

[4] André Tosel, "Superstition and Reading," trans. Ted Stolze, in Warren Montag and Ted Stolze, eds, *The New Spinoza* (Minneapolis: University of Minnesota, 1998), 150.

as limited to Biblical and political hermeneutics would be generalized in the *Ethics* to a new textual practice of metaphysics, or thought itself, *as* ethics. Yet due to such greater universality, if the strategies of double writing and double reading in the *TTP* work to separate two planes or two discourses—theology and philosophy—even while seeming to deliver a single discourse, the *Ethics* would invoke a seemingly identical practice that would nonetheless operate on a single plane and in a single discourse (indeed, within discourse, meaning or thought as such). If the *TTP* makes use of an implicit but long-standing distinction between traditional theo-(mytho)-logy and critically enlightened philosophy, the *Ethics* invents an immanent and universal identity of thought through a new use of philosophical terminology and argument that demonstrates previous philosophy's own separation from itself. The form of this identity is the systematic unity expressed by the *Ethics* itself. Because the two strategic layers of the *TTP* are clearly distinguished in kind, the reading they call for remains relatively straightforward—a dissimulating, exoteric interpretation set against a genuine, esoteric one. The reading of the *Ethics*, however—based as it must be on the identity of immanence—requires a still more radical resituating of thought.

Because the strategy of the chimera expresses itself solely as a formal practice, it eludes any direct thematisation. Yet the rigor of the *Ethics* demands that immanence be made both *explicit* and *universal*. This means that the *Ethics* must somehow account for *itself,* even as one of its essential aspects remains the use of a rhetorical strategy that resists definitive expression. If the *Ethics* is to account for its own formal strategy, then, it must meet a seemingly impossible demand: there must be at once a diremption and a perfect coincidence of its content and its form. The solution to this problem is given indirectly through the *Ethics'* explicit theory of modal individuation. How shall the *Ethics* speak of its own practice, its peculiar usage of philosophical language consisting precisely in that language's transformation in the "context" of immanence? It must introduce a way of speaking that converts the very objectivity of the objects of speech into a field (and no longer an object) of affectivity. The theory of modal individuation pursues this course both thematically and methodologically. It thus serves at once as an exposition and an instance of the strategy of the chimera.

The following section should therefore be read simultaneously from two apparently distinct perspectives which, once the matter at hand is fully grasped, are to be experienced as ultimately identical. The "exoteric" perspective is that of an exposition of the doctrine of modal individuation in the *Ethics*, that is, the account of how particular modes of substance are to be understood in their distinctive unity. The "esoteric" standpoint—to which the reader ought to strive to remain attuned throughout—is that which attributes this exoteric doctrine directly to the unity of the thought of immanence as expressed by the *Ethics* itself, in particular inasmuch as its strategy of the chimera *works*.

II. Individuation and Affect

Certain propositions of the *Ethics* stand out as uniquely important, consolidating in a single claim multiple lines of Spinoza's thought and branching out deductively with far-ranging consequences. Taken together, these propositions – a mere handful scattered throughout the five Parts – determine through their various implications the salient features of Spinoza's ethical thought as a whole, like the peaks and valley floors of a topographical map or the hubs of a transportation network.[5] Among these crucial propositions must surely be counted Spinoza's so-called "parallel postulate" at IIP7: "The order and connection of ideas is the same as the order and connection of things."[6] With this claim Spinoza identifies the "order and connection" of individual ideas under the attribute of thought with that of bodies under the attribute of extension. In other words, the relations subsisting among ideas and the relations subsisting among extended things are conceived as one and the same set of ordered relations. In the scholium to IIP7 Spinoza goes one step further, claiming that "a mode of extension and the idea of that mode are one and the same thing, but expressed in two ways."[7] This further claim both clarifies and strengthens the sense of the original proposition – not only the *relations* between modes but *the modes themselves* considered under distinct attributes must be understood as identical in substance. Not only is the "order and connection" of ideas and bodies one and the same, but an individual idea and its corresponding body are considered to possess an identical particularity—to be a single mode.

---

[5] A purely heuristic candidate-list of these major propositions in the *Ethics* might include: IP14-15, IP29, IIP7, IIP13, IIP38, IIIP7, IIIP59, IVP36-37, IVP67, VP10, VP23, VP24.

[6] Spinoza, *Ethics*, IIP7. For one particularly influential reading of this proposition, see Jonathan Bennett, *A Study of Spinoza's* Ethics (Indianapolis: Hackett 1984), 127-135.

[7] Ibid. Spinoza goes on to note that "some of the Hebrews seem to have seen this, as if through a cloud, when they maintained that God, God's intellect, and the things understood by him are one and the same."

Our question is: How are we to understand the unity or individuality of such a mode (an "affection of substance"[8]) given the overarching monism of Spinoza's system? We note first that in the *Ethics* the general problem of individuation arises solely at the level of the finite modes. The attributes, infinite "each in its own kind" are not themselves properly individuated, but rather expressed. The infinite, immediate modes—the "idea of God" and "motion and rest"—are not individuals, but common natures. At the level of finite modes, however, apparently distinct and relational individuals must be accounted for. The passage from Part One to Part Two of the *Ethics* articulates this. Part Two, "Of the Nature and Origin of the Mind," involves a shift in focus from relations between substance and attributes (God, thought and extension) which structure Part One to relations subsisting among finite modes of whatever attribute.

We are thus led naturally in this context to examine Spinoza's understanding of the relation of minds and bodies (modes of thought and modes of extension). Strictly speaking, there is no proper *relation* between minds and bodies (or ideas and things) in Spinoza's view since (a) minds and bodies are conceived as identical and (b) the two attributes of thought and extension remain causally independent even as the "order and connection" of their causes is one and the same.[9] Importantly, in Spinoza's thought, the human mind as such has no foundational or otherwise privileged status in this regard. While Spinoza does begin with the particular case of the unity of the human mind and the human body,[10] he quickly clarifies that this unity of body and mind applies equally and in precisely the same way to bodies of all kinds: organic and inorganic; simple and complex; molecular, geological, galactic.[11] For Spinoza the human mind is thus not anomalous; it is not, as Spinoza says, "a kingdom within a kingdom," but rather merely one part of infinite Nature, or God.

In this light, Spinoza's way of answering the question of what constitutes an individual mind or body, human or otherwise, differs from the consciousness-based approach that develops out of Descartes and comes later to characterize phenomenology. For phenomenological method, an individual essence is precisely what appears as an individuated element of conscious experience, and the conscious apprehension of an

---

[8] Ibid, ID5.

[9] Ibid, IIP7.

[10] Ibid, IIP13: "The object of the idea constituting the human mind is the body, *or* a certain mode of extension which actually exists, and nothing else."

[11] See ibid, IIP13S: "For the things we have shown so far are completely general and do not pertain more to man than to other individuals, all of which, though in different degrees, are nevertheless animate."

object grasps the object in the unity of a synthetic intuition. Things are given to perception and knowledge as unities, and the unity of consciousness itself as the form of such appearance takes on a transcendental function for philosophical reflection. A phenomenological approach is correlated to our everyday perceptions of things. Individuals are first of all *objects* of egoic experience—in normal sensory perception these are constituted as continuous spatial forms. For Spinoza, on the contrary, individuation is conceived independently of any witnessing consciousness and without reference to any transcendental unity of experience. For Spinoza, individuation is an event immanent to the unique causal order of universal Nature, or God, and is not a function of any subjective-objective or noetic-noematic correlation or polarity.

Instead, the individuation of finite modes is expressed in the *Ethics* in terms of the dynamics of physical processes. The full elaboration of Spinoza's view is provided by the consideration of individual bodies that takes up a considerable portion of Part Two—following a break in the form of the *Ethics* just after IIP13S, often referred to as the "physical digression." Here, Spinoza addresses in detail the question of the unity of physical bodies and, by implication, that of ideas. He first briefly considers "the simplest bodies"—rigid bodies without complex parts—and then turns his focus to "composite bodies," for which the questions of unity and individuation are more problematic and philosophically interesting. Having identified the object of the idea that constitutes the human mind as the human body itself, Spinoza addresses the more general question: What constitutes *a body* as such?

Spinoza first claims that all individuals "though in different degrees, are nevertheless animate," but then qualifies this claim immediately by interpreting the "different degrees" of animation as different degrees of excellence determined by varying capacities to act.[12] Bodies are animated to a greater or lesser degree as they are capable of doing more or fewer things.[13] On this view a stone, for instance, does have a soul—this would be its idea or mind—but a stone's soul remains a quite simple one, capable of only limited kinds of internally determined action. What a stone does is, in fact, almost entirely exhausted in what is done *with* or *to* it by other things and forces, with the possible exception of gravitational attraction –

---

[12] Ibid, IIP13S.

[13] "In proportion as a body is more capable than others of doing many things at once, or being acted on in many ways at once, so its mind is more capable than others of perceiving many things at once. And in proportion as the actions of a body depend more on itself alone, and as other bodies concur with it less in acting, so its mind is more capable of understanding distinctly." Ibid.

perhaps a stone's single "active affect." A flower, on the contrary, has the potential to act in various ways: heliotropic movement, drawing nourishment from the soil, and so forth. A hare, to continue along the spectrum of increasing activity and complexity, is capable of many more ways of acting, including sense perception, movement and communication. Progressing in this way from the mineral to the vegetable to the animal, Spinoza recognizes variabilities in degrees of activity, not distinct ontological levels. In this respect Spinoza's view emphasizes the continuity of nature (differences in degree) over its discontinuity (differences in kind), and individuation within nature is conceived on the basis of relations immanent to material continuity and wholeness rather than presuppositions of separation and discreteness. There are various degrees of mind according to this view, corresponding to various degrees of bodily activity. Differences between the soul or mind of an insect and that of a human are not annulled by such a conception, but they are understood on the basis of an underlying continuity of nature.

What all the various degrees of animation share are how they constitute distinct individuality through the relative motions and affects of their component parts. Spinoza defines an individual in general as a composite of bodies which "communicate their motions to each other in a certain fixed manner." The complete definition is as follows:

> When a number of bodies, whether of the same or of different size, are so constrained by other bodies that they lie upon one another, or if they so move, whether with the same degree or different degrees of speed, that they communicate their motions to each other in a certain fixed manner, we shall say that those bodies are united with one another and that they all together compose one body or individual, which is distinguished from the others by this union of bodies.[14]

We see that bodies are united to one another and thereby "compose one body or individual" under two separate sets of criteria. On the one hand, bodies are united if they "are so constrained by other bodies that they lie upon one another." This, in effect, causes two or more bodies to move and act together in a fixed and rigid way, as if they were a single body, for all practical purposes such bodies thus function as simple bodies, like bricks mortared together.[15] On the other hand, more importantly, bodies may be said to unite to compose a single individual if and when "they so move,

---

[14] Ibid, IIP13A2'' (Definition of *individual*).
[15] What Spinoza calls the "simplest bodies" in distinction from composite bodies are described in IIP13A2''.

whether with the same degree or different degrees of speed, that they communicate their motions to each other in a certain fixed manner." In other words, what makes a body a single, unified or individual body would be in this case the relatively fixed set of relations of motion among the various smaller bodies of which it is composed. Instead of mortared bricks, we might imagine a village square dance, or the inner movements of a mechanical clock, or the living symmetries of a running horse. In each of these cases the movements of component parts (villagers; wheels, springs and cogs; bones, nerves and muscle tissues) do not exhibit randomness in their mutual relations but rather order, regularity and interdependence, and the many parts in their coordinated movements become capable of unified affects at the level of a new whole (here, keep in mind the second "esoteric" attribution of this doctrine to the work of the *Ethics* itself).

The individuality of a composite body is thus defined by Spinoza not simply through material or spatial continuity, but by means of formal and communicative relations of motion composing it as a singular, affective whole within universal Nature.[16] In other words, individual bodies are conceived as such not by virtue of continuous material extension, but rather on the basis of the relative unity of the movements of their parts, formal relations that themselves communicate affects.[17] Spinoza's description applies equally well to "parts" that are not contiguous in space, such as the parts of a flock of birds flying in formation. For the duration of their flight at least, the flock constitutes an individual. On this view, individuality is rhythmic and intrinsically relational, not substantive.

---

[16] Spinoza claims, reaffirming the ultimate unity of substance: "Bodies are distinguished from one another by reason of motion and rest, speed and slowness, and not by reason of substance." Ibid, IIP13L1.

[17] The text of the *Ethics* makes this clear in lemmas 4-7 of the "physical digression." Each of these lemmas asserts that an individual maintains its own "nature," even when its composite bodies are altered in some fashion. Lemma 4 states that if certain bodies replace the composite parts of an individual, the individual "will retain its nature, as before, without any change of its form," so long as the replacement parts possess the "same nature" as those they replace. Lemma 5 makes the same claim regarding the relative size of an individual. If its parts grow or shrink, as long as the ratios of motion and rest between those parts remain proportional, the individual as a whole retains the same nature. Lemmas 6 and 7 make similar claims regarding the sustained nature of an individual when it or its parts undergo motion in new and different ways. In these two lemmas, it is not the ratio of motions of parts that is emphasized (since this obviously changes), but rather the capacity of the parts to "communicate" their motions to each other in a fixed and continuous way.

How are we to understand the "certain fixed manner" of this rhythm? It is not so much a matter of a fixed proportion of movements, which would effectively define an individual in terms of an abstract stasis; it is rather the coordinated ability of composite parts to *communicate* their movements to each other in a regular and unified way that assures the consistency of a particular individual. Thus the very consistency of an individual is affective. It is defined in terms of the capacity of various bodies to consolidate their mutual relations of motion and rest into a coherent set of affective relations. As an important consequence, it follows that a significant "blurring" of essence must be understood to be constitutive of all finite modes other than simple or rigid bodies. The relations between component parts must be conceived as functioning within certain variable tolerances, since to communicate movements is to relate motions within variable zones of proximity and distance, acceleration and deceleration. The communication of movements can thus be clearly distinguished from a fixed ratio of motions.

Communication in this physical and active sense thus implies a range of possible values, a lower and upper limit of relation between which communication may be said to occur. We can now understand the importance of defining individuality on the basis of a capacity to communicate affects, rather than a fixed proportionality of simple movements: a tree would become a different individual every time the wind changed direction or blew harder, if what constituted the tree's individuality were only a single, fixed set of relations of movement between its parts (its leaves, branches, trunk and roots). If, on the other hand, the tree's essence is a matter of the capacity of those parts to communicate their motions in a regular way, it becomes obvious that the tree maintains its identity even in a strong and blustery wind, just so long as the tree's system of affects continues to function in a relatively ordered and consistent way.

For Spinoza the essences of individual, composite modes can only be conceived as complex, overlapping zones of relative elasticity, bordered by thresholds of rupture—critical points at which the communication of motions between their parts is broken off. For simple material objects, these thresholds are generally determined by physical continuity: a chair leg communicates its motion to the seat so long as the leg remains attached.[18] Yet for bodies with a higher degree of animation, such as

---

[18] In such cases, we are more appropriately referred to the "constraint" of parts that "lie upon one another" rather than the communication of movements. As explained above, this form of unfree or non-variable "communication" essentially repeats the "simple bodies" of IIP13A2.

bumblebees, the advent of perceptual organs and social behaviours makes the delimitation of these thresholds much more problematic. The social organization of a beehive, for example, certainly exhibits the movements of various bodies (drones, queen, pollen, honey, etc.) which could be said to "communicate their motions to each other in a certain fixed manner." In this fashion, as an individual mode increases in complexity, the essence it expresses tends to become internally differentiated at the same time that it becomes capable of acting externally in new ways.

The Spinozist account of individuation therefore helps us to understand more clearly the sense of *affects* in the *Ethics* as functioning both internally and externally to individuals. Spinozist affects are defined as capacities of bodies to affect and to be affected by other bodies in all specifically determined ways. The various ways motions may be communicated must therefore be interpreted on the basis of affects. The constitution of new affects and the conversion of passive to active affects by means of the common notions can be modelled in this way as a structural dynamics of individuation, emphasized thereby as a process, a constructive movement of self-differentiation or singularisation. It is impossible to distinguish what a thing is from what it does (how it affects and is affected by others), and the affects are thus determinative of individual natures in two ways—(a) the internal affects by which its component parts communicate their motions to one another; and (b) the ways the individual thus constituted affects and is affected by its environment of other bodies. The essence or nature of a thing, for Spinoza, becomes understood as the sum of its internal and external affects.

We may also now make better sense of Spinoza's notion of *common natures*. The *Ethics'* account of individuation, by making individuals themselves thoroughly relational, allows us to see how common natures are always necessarily implied by individuals who are capable of entering into particular forms of affective relation with one another. The *blurring* of essence described above implies that individuals with natures in common with others are never absolute particulars, but are always themselves relational components of other individuals. As Spinoza puts it, emphasizing here the overarching unity of nature, second-order individuals may be composed of parts that are themselves composite individuals, third-order individuals from second-order individuals, and so on, and "if we proceed in this way to infinity, we shall easily conceive that the whole of nature is one individual, whose parts, that is, all bodies, vary in infinite ways, without any change of the whole individual."[19] For Spinoza natures

---

[19] Ibid, IIP13L7S. This is the "infinite mediate mode" which Spinoza also names "the face of the whole universe."

common to finite individuals are both grounded in this ultimate unity of Nature and distinguish themselves partially from it by interacting in common at some specific level of organization. This is as true of the *Ethics* itself as of any other part of Nature. But the *Ethics* expresses this very fact, and it thus articulates a specific common nature cutting across the divisions or levels of individuated modes. In this way the formal architecture of the *Ethics* makes *use* of a language and commonsense ontology of discrete individuals in order to manifest a strictly unrepresentable field of immanent affectivity, that is, monism as such.

III. Immanence, or Theology

The affectivity defining individual modes for Spinoza is *only* affective, or practical. It cannot be reduced to one side of any pre-established duality or correlation. And to remain consistent this affectivity must, in turn, be exercised upon the thought of the *Ethics* itself. The immanence that Spinoza's *Ethics* displays or performs is thus not a philosophical thesis in any normal sense. Precisely *as* immanent, it does not position itself vis-à-vis other candidate theses, vying for dominance or exclusive correctness. Immanence does not have any contrary or other side, although, exactly because of this, it cannot obviate, contradict or deny the philosophical positionings (such as the various modalities of philosophical correlation and transcendence) that would oppose themselves *to it*. The genius of the *Ethics* is, instead of offering unto tradition yet another articulation of philosophy as a system, to have saturated the formal differentiation of philosophical articulation itself to the point of an absolute immanence, or monism.[20]

Spinoza's shift to affective individuation modifies the philosophical enterprise as such by disorienting philosophy away from the transcendental presupposition that has governed it in one way or another throughout its entire tradition, namely the very presupposition that thought is itself governed transcendentally. One essential aspect of the Western philosophical tradition has always been the idea that thought carries an intrinsic, structural relationality somehow determined in advance (whether to the true, the good, the one, to procedures of communicative rationality,

---

[20] The reading of the *Ethics* offered in this final section is heavily indebted to the auto-affective phenomenology of Michel Henry and especially to the practice of non-philosophy developed by François Laruelle, particularly the doctrine of the "cloning (*clonage*) of the One" laid out in *Principes de la non-philosophie*. See Michel Henry, *L'essence de la manifestation*, 2nd ed. (Paris: PUF, 1990) and François Laruelle, *Principes de la non-philosophie* (Paris: PUF, 1996), ch. 4-5.

or to something else, is here immaterial). This basis of thought is thoroughly destabilized by the strategies implemented in Spinoza's *Ethics*. This destabilization of thought's presupposed underlying relational structure holds consequences far more radical than Spinoza's well-known and more explicit rejection of teleology in Nature, since the latter merely excises one particularly obsolete philosophical interpretation among others, whereas the former wipes clear the interpretative and generally dialectical character of philosophical thought altogether.

Philosophies may be categorized, of course, and they live off such categorization. Where would the history of philosophy be without its great dualities—Stoics and Epicureans, Realists and Nominalists, Rationalists and Empiricists, and so on—as well as its grand synthetic visions—Pico della Mirandola promising to reconcile Plato and Aristotle, or Kant overcoming the division of Descartes and Hume? Immanence in the Spinozist sense mimics both these essential sides of philosophy (disjunctive and synthetic) but cannot be reduced to either.

The whole result of the *Ethics* consists precisely in *how* it is accomplished. It would be drastically insufficient merely to assert the essential affectivity or non-dialectical nature of thought. For such an assertion would, like any other philosophical assertion, implicitly (a) produce the more or less determinately articulated field of its alternatives or rivals, and (b) distinguish between a global sense and a local utterance, thus reproducing in a twofold way at the level of form the very conditions which the assertion itself is meant to unbind at the level of content. Indeed, it is any such possibility of a form/content distinction remaining practically relevant for thought that Spinoza's monist or immanent "thesis" undertakes to abolish. The difficulty and intractability of this methodological problem underlies the need both for an overarching "strategy of the chimera" in Spinoza's philosophical presentation and a doctrine of individuation and affectivity that forces a passage through the impossible when applied to the sense and reality of the text itself. Only the complex, formal rigour of a monist architectonic proceeding step by step through the ineluctable themes of the philosophical tradition—God, mind, body, reason, cause, desire, and so on—without ever once leaving (or, for that matter, entering) the absolute singularity of immanence, remains sufficiently "simple" to avoid falling back into the production of yet another philosophical model, thesis, interpretation, or point of view. It is a case of the simple or continuous mapping of a given map's own discrete articulations dissolving the latter's apparently objective territory. The *practice* of immanence here dissolves the inevitable transcendence or correlativity of representation (in the most general sense).

It could be objected that this Spinozist (dis)solution is at best merely formal—unlike, for instance, the Hegelian work of negation and historical struggle—but such an objection misconstrues the force of the *formal affectivity* of Spinoza's demonstrative method itself. What is meaningfully "proven" in and by the constructions of the *Ethics* are not the contents of discrete propositions, but rather the indissociable unity and simplicity of an absolutely open and universal affectivity of thinking. In light of such explicitly absolute universality (that is, a paradoxically articulated or "chimerical" monism), any attempt to refute Spinoza's "vision" (or strategy) by opposing some material or empirical counterexample or structural contrariety quite simply begs the question. A much more clear-sighted kind of objection comes from someone like the twentieth-century Hegelian Alexandre Kojève who does not dismiss the Spinozist project as an unreal formalism, but rather sees it as a potential rival—perhaps the only genuine rival—to Hegel's universal synthesis.[21] Yet Kojève takes Spinoza's project seriously only just up to and not, as it were, across its crucial limit. For Kojève, Spinozism remains strictly *impossible in time* and this is sufficient in itself to disqualify it from practical consideration. Yet not without a certain fascination and wonder proper to the speculative pathologist:

> Hegel *becomes* God by thinking or writing the *Logik*; or, if you like, it is by becoming God that he writes or thinks it. Spinoza, on the other hand, must *be* God from all eternity in order to be able to write or think his *Ethics*... And this, obviously, is the height of absurdity: to take Spinoza seriously is actually to be—or to become—mad.[22]

What Kojève here refuses is precisely the New Earth rendered visible by Spinoza's formal monist machinery, its untrodden immanence. Kojève is right—such immanence *is* impossible. But this is the case only because our pre-given conception of practical possibility has been reduced already in advance to the structurally relational presuppositions of philosophical thought and expression.

If the practice of Spinozist immanence cannot rightly be called philosophy, then, what shall we call it? Is Kojève correct to name it madness? Perhaps so, but there is a still stronger and more exact term, the

---

[21] Kojève treats Spinozism as one of the structurally possible permutations of relating the Concept to Time and/or Eternity, the others being Plato, Aristotle, Kant and, of course, the ultimate victor Hegel. See Alexandre Kojève, *Introduction to the Reading of Hegel*, ed. Allan Bloom and Raymond Queneau, trans. James H. Nichols, Jr. (Ithaca: Cornell University Press, 1980), 113-130.

[22] Ibid, 120.

use of which potentially deploys the strategy of the chimera today in all its possible fullness and precision. This term, buffeted historically from arrogance to humiliation and back, is *theology*. One possible application of the strategy of the chimera today would thus be to write: *Immanence*, or *theology*—in other words, to use the material of "theology" in a thoroughly immanent fashion. Spinoza's *Ethics* then becomes the work in and through which the philosophical as such "becomes" theology, theo-logos—except that there can be no question here of any becoming or *a posteriori* hyphenation. Because the *Ethics* demonstrates a transcendental dissolution of philosophical possibility, an "impossible" dissolution of philosophy *as* transcendental prior to any and every effectivity or act, the concrete work of the *Ethics* must be understood as effecting a conversion in thinking more radical than any Platonic or religious *metanoia*. The term "theology" is capable of bearing the signification of what thought becomes in the presence of such dissolution as the index of a new practice only because it has never named anything other than its own impossibility, its own performative contradiction—to speak *of* the Absolute Other, to say what strictly cannot be said. God, as Spinoza himself saw, is *the* singular term drawn from the Western tradition of thinking, the radical self-contradictoriness and inconsistency of whose "saying" lends it unique capacities to express immanence in the most powerful way.

The term "theology" has belonged first and foremost to the theologians themselves and has then been sounded secondarily in reactive modes by anti-theologians of various stripes. Yet the practice of theology itself has always harboured its own duality—*a* theology is everywhere represented, expressed, defended or attacked as *the* theology (theology as orthodox, as de-mythologized, as metaphysical, etc.). In this way theology has always expressed a partisanship for one tradition or subtradition among others—and this has been true not only historically and accidentally but transcendentally and for reasons of essence. To name immanence theology, then, or more exactly to use the term "theology" (and here the "thing" itself *is* the term—not just the one word, but all its corollary vocabularies, grammars and dynamisms equally fixed into the identity of a mere indeterminate index), according to an immanent strategic, is to convert its constitutive duality orthodoxy/heterodoxy into a new instrument of affectivity and a new employment of thought. Only a "theology" whose very practice would situate itself outside orthodoxy and heresy in equal measure, because beyond the possibility of any such opposition, could make free use of the opposition itself in this way. The irony of course is that from the standpoint of any given orthodoxy, such "theology" must appear as the worst and most extreme heresy, just as any self-proclaimed heresy will likely see it as the assertion of some new universalist orthodoxy. Yet both views depend upon a necessity of thematisation and objectivisation that immanent practice makes irrelevant.

The impossibility of immanence—an impossibility nonetheless *realized* by the *Ethics'* own strategies of the chimera—unconstrains language from the difference between the saying and the said. The representational function of language is then no longer constitutive, but becomes merely accidental for thought. Under the condition, or liberty of immanence, representation thus becomes simply one more affect, one more individuation, and in no way serves as a transcendental basis for truth. *Only* the practice of such thinking reveals its sense. Thus to call Spinozist immanence theology is by no means merely to appropriate the weight and prestige of the powerful affects that have accrued to the concepts of theology for particular theoretical or political ends—this would be no more than vulgar opportunism. It is a matter rather of disengaging the act of thought from its subservience to any and all pre-given ends and thereby throwing into relief how limited in scope and yet ubiquitous such subservience traditionally has been. This is particularly true to the extent that Thinking as correlation (*logos*) and Otherness as transcendence (*theos*) have determined one another historically through particular variations of disjunction and synthesis.

Immanence does not realize one possible figure of thought. It is not a framework, template or schema. It does not interpret. It unlocks. And thought's every real future remains foreclosed if thinking itself is not first made truly free.

Bibliography

Bennett, Jonathan. *A Study of Spinoza's* Ethics. Indianapolis: Hackett, 1984.

Henry, Michel. *L'essence de la manifestation.* 2nd edition. Paris: PUF, 1990.

Kojève, Alexandre. *Introduction to the Reading of Hegel: Lectures on the Phenomenology of Spirit.* Edited by Allan Bloom and Raymond Queneau. Translated by James H. Nichols, Jr. Ithaca: Cornell University Press, 1980.

Laruelle, François. *Principes de la non-philosophie.* Paris: PUF, 1996.

Spinoza, Benedict. *The* Ethics *and Other Works.* Edited and translated by Edwin Curley. Princeton: Princeton University Press, 1994.

Strauss, Leo. *Persecution and the Art of Writing.* Chicago: University of Chicago, 1988.

—. *Spinoza's Critique of Religion.* Translated by E.M. Sinclair. Chicago: University of Chicago, 1997.

Tosel, André. "Superstition and Reading." Translated by Ted Stolze. In Warren Montag and Ted Stolze edited, *The New Spinoza.* Minneapolis: University of Minnesota, 1998. 147-168.

Zac, Sylvain. *Spinoza et L'Interprétation de L'Ecriture.* Paris: PUF, 1965.

Zourabichvili, François. *Spinoza: Une physique de la pensée.* Paris: PUF, 2002.

CHAPTER TWO

JOHN TOLAND'S *LETTERS TO SERENA*: FROM THE CRITIQUE OF RELIGION TO THE METAPHYSICS OF MATERIALISM

JAMES C. BROWN

The thought of John Toland (1670–1722) is closely associated with intellectual movements of the seventeenth and early eighteenth centuries such as Deism and Republicanism. The polemical tone of his writings has long obscured the philosophical merit of the arguments underpinning his diatribe against arbitrary political authority and revealed religion. A prolific writer, a number of Toland's tracts and pamphlets may rightly be deemed circumstantial in nature. However, a more profound thought lurks underneath the heated engagements in the public arena. Despite his relatively humble origins in rural Catholic Ireland, Toland succeeded in making his mark in London intellectual circles that arose in the wake of the Revolution of 1688/89. Considered a "minute philosopher" by some (such as George Berkeley) and an enemy of religion by Tories and High-Church Anglicans, Toland was successful in placing the abuse of religious authority known as "priestcraft" at the centre of debates in his day. Works such as *Christianity not Mysterious* (1696) and *Letters to Serena* (1704) constitute the heart of Toland's philosophical critique of theological discourse which, for him, was the necessary prologue to reforming reason and establishing a more just political order. In this essay, I will present the main arguments of Toland's critique of religion in *Letters to Serena* and demonstrate how it prepares the way for theorising his materialist doctrine of the universe. I argue that Toland's metaphysical speculation articulates a philosophy of immanence that fundamentally refutes notions of divine transcendence.

Comprised of five letters, *Letters to Serena* is Toland's principal foray into metaphysics. Its objectives are not exclusively critical, such as may be found in contemporaneous works in historical criticism. Indeed, its aims are positive in nature, for it intends to liberate readers from ingrained prejudices and to win them over to a materialist conception of nature. For sure, this text often lends itself to confusion regarding its scope, since Toland writes the first three letters as a historian of ancient religions and pagan idolatry before donning the role of metaphysician in his last two letters. Whereas the first three letters echo familiar Deist charges against revealed religion, the last two letters are dedicated to honing a materialist doctrine whose cosmological implications allow us to better identify the frontier between pantheism and Deism. It is upon these foundations that Toland conceives a philosophical doctrine that privileges internal reflection on the law of nature (which can be compared to, but not identified with, the natural religion of many Deists). Drawing from the philosophical curriculum of classical philosophy, Toland places himself on the wrong-end of St Augustine's condemnation of Pelagianism. As a former student of theology and ecclesiology, he forged the concept of pantheism as someone who knew and previously adhered to the premises of theological discourse, but who eventually desired to rid himself entirely of its influence. He never expressly articulated a philosophy of religion as such since the problematic he addressed was otherwise. That is to say, given the way he identified the intellectual crisis of his day, Toland did not allow himself to step back and take a holistic approach, so as to examine the problem of theological discourse. Indeed, the crisis remained internal, afflicting reason prior to becoming articulated as a subject of philosophical enquiry.

The following study is divided into three parts. I shall first examine the historical background behind the writing of the five letters, most of which took place during Toland's prolonged sojourns to the courts of Hanover and Berlin from 1701 to 1704. His encounters with Leibniz and other eminent men of letters at the court of the Queen of Prussia, Sophie Charlotte (1666–1705) in Berlin were key factors in motivating him to communicate his views on speculative matters. As the title implies, *Letters to Serena* is comprised of missives addressed to correspondents with whom Toland exchanged and debated ideas relating to historical and metaphysical matters. Toland's rationalist theory of knowledge developed in *Christianity not Mysterious* is of particular significance for his "philosophical epistolography" and thus for the metaphysical argumentation in *Letters to Serena*.

The next part of this study will examine in closer detail the problem of superstitions and irrational beliefs, such as the doctrine of the immorality of the soul. Toland underlines the pernicious role of implicit belief which handicaps reason when theorising upon the first principles of the natural world. His correspondents in Letters IV and V fall prey to several aporia of thought, because they remain partisans of classical metaphysical notions (like active form and passive matter). According to Toland, they err in much the same way as Leibniz and Spinoza do (whose philosophical systems are equally subjected to criticism in the latter part of *Letters to Serena*). By basing their philosophies upon unquestioned and erroneous suppositions, they all ruin their systems from the outset.

The third part of this study will deal more specifically with the arguments of Toland's metaphysics (or "speculation" as he more commonly labels it), beginning with how he defines its methodology and subject matter. His metaphysical speculation touches upon the "principles" of the material universe and is articulated in the form of predicate logic. It is by speculative argumentation that Toland articulates his materialism which precludes any role to transcendence and any notion of divine activity in the natural world. The closing arguments of this last part of the essay shall be dedicated to explaining the intent and meaning of Toland's *Pantheisticon*. This excursion into Toland's last philosophical text is of great importance in order to clarify our understanding of the normative ends of his critique of religion. In a word, *Pantheisticon* builds upon *Letters to Serena* but is in no way meant to be a philosophical liturgy or a secularised version of a theological system. Rather, it is a work whose form and imagery invites the reader to further introspection and to philosophical knowledge of the good life.

I. Historical Background

Let us then first look at the historical context in which *Letters to Serena* arise. Contemporary historians have singled Toland out as a major figure in early modern Deism, even to point of considering him the "spokesman" of the Deist movement in his own time.[1] To this day, the Irish philosopher is best known for his first work published in 1696, *Christianity not Mysterious*, which purported to reconcile reason and Scripture but drew the ire of religious orthodoxy. However, the scandal surrounding this work did not damage Toland's reputation to the point of excluding him from influential Whig circles. Indeed, his hand in writing and publishing *Anglia Libera* (1701) was instrumental in getting him invited to join the English delegation headed by Lord Macclesfield at the court of Hanover in 1701. This diplomatic mission was sent in order to

---

[1] J.C.D. Clark, *English Society 1688-1832. Ideology, Social Structure and Political Practice during the Ancien Régime* (Cambridge: Cambridge University Press, 1985), 280.

present to the ageing dowager of Hanover the Act of Settlement which would later pave the way for the Hanover succession. Toland, however, quickly proved to be lacking the tact necessary for diplomacy but not before he had culled sufficient material to publish the five letters that comprise *Letters to Serena*.

He explains in the Preface to the work that the circumstances surrounding the first three letters are related to audiences he had had with Queen Sophie Charlotte, the daughter of Princess Sophia, Electress of Hanover (1630–1714). The occasion of the first letter stems from a passage taken from Cicero's discussion of the problem of prejudices. Sophie Charlotte admits that she too is not free from erroneous notions and solicits Toland to provide his opinion on the matter. The second letter results from a conversation between Toland and the Queen who is curious about the role Plato's *Phaedo* played in the decision of Cato to commit suicide. It surprises her to learn that the immortality of the soul was viewed as a historical question by many classical authors. According to Toland, the Ancients were indifferent to the question of immortality. Cicero, for instance, attached no importance to the proposal of Socrates in *Phaedo* and, Toland adds, he did not approve the teaching therein.[2] The third letter is likewise supposedly written at the request of the Queen who wished that Toland develop his opinion on the question of idolatry. The Irish philosopher obliges and, contrary to a well-known work of their day, he endeavours to explain the causes and the genealogy of idolatrous practices in Antiquity.[3]

The second part of *Letters to Serena* which comprises Letters IV and V likely originate from philosophical exchanges between Leibniz and Toland beginning with the latter's first voyage to Germany in 1701. Not long after the Irishman's arrival at the court, Leibniz transcribed a manuscript written originally by Toland entitled *Parallèle entre la raison originale ou la loy de la nature* which contains many of the ideas later developed in the third letter.[4] In July 1702, Toland returned to Germany this time on a personal invitation sent to him by the Queen at her residence in

---

[2] It should be noted, however, that Cicero was not at all indifferent on the subject of suicide which he deemed laudable in certain circumstances. Cicero, *De finibus* (Cambridge, MA: Harvard University Press, 1983), III.18, 279.

[3] Toland refers to the work of Antony van Dale, *Dissertiones de origine ac progressu idolatriae et superstitione*. Amsterdam, 1696.

[4] Tristan Dagron in his translation, *Lettres à Serena et autres textes* (Paris: Editions Honoré Champion, 2004), 35–38.

Lützenberg.[5] Among the topics of discussion broached during this trip was the soul's immortality. Ultimately, the debate between Leibniz and Toland revolved around the problems of the origin of activity and the movement of physical bodies. This problem harked back to the distinction made by Locke between spirituality and immateriality: according to Locke, only the latter can be demonstrated (or refuted). The question as he states is to know "whether Omnipotency has not given to some systems of matter, fitly disposed, a power to perceive and think...that God can, if he pleases, superadd to matter a faculty of thinking."[6] As witnessed by the questions raised at the court of Sophie Charlotte, the relationship between thought and matter remained as problematic as ever.

However, one cannot but note that letters IV and V of *Letters to Serena* deal with Spinoza's "system". According to Tristan Dagron, the correspondent in Letter IV may very well have been a certain Georg Wachter who would later pen *Elucidarius cabalisticus* in 1706. Such a hypothesis allows for a better appraisal of the several discrepancies which arise in Toland's description of Spinozism. For Wachter, Spinoza is the last representative in a long line of Jewish philosophers and succeeded where Greek philosophy failed in surmounting the problem of the duality of matter and thought.[7] The fifth letter is addressed to a different correspondent but was written at the request of Queen Sophie-Charlotte. According to Stuart Brown, the anonymous "noble friend" was Jakob Heinrich von Flemming.[8] He, too, would have participated in the philosophical discussions at Lützenburg. His philosophy, as presented by Toland, holds to the traditional theses on the activity of form and the passivity of matter. The fifth letter thus continues the theme developed in the fourth – the question of the motion essential to matter.

Despite the different subject matters of Letters I to III and Letters IV and V, both are written in the form of "philosophical epistolography". This is of greater significance than it may at first seem. Whereas the first three letters sprung from conversations with Sophie Charlotte, the last two are presented as part of an epistolary exchange initiated by Toland's

---

[5] F.H. Heinemann, "Toland and Leibniz," *The Philosophical Review* LIV.5 (1945): 441.

[6] John Locke, *An Essay concerning Human Understanding*, ed. Kenneth Winkler (Indianapolis: Hackett, 1996), IV 3.6, 241.

[7] Dagron, *Lettres à Serena*, 55.

[8] Stuart Brown, "Two Papers by John Toland: His 'Remarques Critiques sur le Système de M.Leibnitz...' and the last of his 'Letters to Serena'" in *John Toland torna a Dublin, Rivista I Castelli di Yale* IV (1999): 59.

correspondents. Toland thus presents his philosophy of nature not in treatise form or by means of theorems but rather in letters addressed to correspondents neither of whom is deemed a philosopher properly speaking.[9] Given the need to expel erroneous suppositions from philosophical discourse, the crucial area of experimentation is not that of the scientific laboratory but rather that of human discourse. Prior to its articulation in laws and mathematics, science is conditioned by the limitations on human knowledge arising from prejudice and from language itself.

The epistolary form is more apt to give rise to the sort of polite conversation suggested by Toland's responses to arguments submitted to him in previous letters. Insofar as Toland is both participant of the epistolary exchange and author of the five letters, he is more readily able to focus on the problems that interest him the most, namely the suppositions underlying his correspondents' metaphysical systems. Note that this form of philosophical exchange precludes the systematisation of philosophy. Indeed, Toland's philosophical method is expressly apophantic; that is to say, it identifies the statements possessing truth claims before proceeding to assent or reject the propositions contained therein. For him, the systematisation of an author's thoughts is one of the causes of its inevitable corruption.[10] Toland eschews the systematisation of philosophy or even adherence to an inherited philosophical system based on authority. Rather, he holds that it is better to identify and extract all erroneous notions in those philosophies which have been influential in the formation of one's own opinions. Instead of believing through authority and implicit belief, it is essential to examine the suppositions which are often in reality mere prejudices and not constitutive of true knowledge.

Let us take a look at the main tenets of Toland's rationalism, especially to the extent it leads to metaphysical speculation. Toland writes the latter part of *Letters to Serena* in light of the theory of knowledge he developed in *Christianity not Mysterious*. As indicated in the title, the author of *Christianity not Mysterious* endeavours to argue that Christian doctrine is in no way mysterious and that the Christian religion contains no mysteries. The articles of Christian faith are neither above reason nor against reason; indeed, they are within the grasp of human understanding. Contrary to Locke who argued for the reasonableness of Christianity, Toland argues

---

[9] Of all the persons encountered during his German voyages, Leibniz alone is considered to be a philosopher by Toland in *Letters to Serena*. John Toland, *Letters to Serena* (London, 1704), V.31, 238.

[10] Toland, *Letters to Serena*, IV.5, 136.

that Scripture is articulated in propositions that concur entirely with reason.[11] Indeed, he subjects Scripture to the purview of human reason which is, for Toland, a method of knowledge. Scripture is merely one means of information for reason, amongst many others. The objective of knowledge, according to Toland, is certainty. In his theory, any truth which is not immediately self-evident must be a truth acquired by means of a proposition, and thus by a demonstration. The judgments of demonstrative reason must in the end be made as evident as those of axiomatic or intuitive reason.[12] An idea, or a representative being, is necessarily a particular, and thus limited, thing whereas an axiom is always true.[13] There is a notable influence of Locke's empiricism in Toland's theory and the distinction he maintains between nominal and real essences. In keeping with empiricist premises, Toland holds that the origin of ideas arises from sensory contact with the natural world. Objects disposed to the senses are the exemplary causes of knowledge. According to Toland, knowledge of the nominal properties of things suffices to perceive intuitively the reality of things.[14] There is no knowledge of things *in se*, however.[15] Evidence, otherwise known as evident truth, is the immediate perception of objective reality and natural phenomena: to know and understand are two words which signify the same thing.[16]

The thesis at the heart of Toland's theory of knowledge runs thus: he who "knows" something is as certain of the truth of this object of knowledge as is the author who originated such an object of knowledge. To know the idea of a proposition is to know it as it was initially conceived by its author or, as Toland states: "He that comprehends a thing, is as sure of it as if he were himself the Author."[17] Comprehension of a

---

[11] Locke's work, *The Reasonableness of Christianity*, published in 1695 intends to extricate Christian faith from the hold of theological systems. He attempted to clarify the position of his rationalist epistemology vis-à-vis questions on faith and reason against both the orthodox clergy who accused him of atheism and Socinianism and Deists like Toland who drew from *An Essay concerning Human Understanding* in order to attack theology and to reject revealed religion as a whole.

[12] "So that though Self-evidence excludes Reason, yet all Demonstration becomes at length self-evident." John Toland, *Christianity not Mysterious*, ed. Philip McGuiness, Alan Harrison & Richard Kearney (Dublin: Lilliput Press, 1997), I.2.8.

[13] Toland, *Christianity not Mysterious*, I.2.5-7.

[14] Ibid, III.2.20.

[15] Ibid, III.2.9.

[16] Ibid, III.2.10.

[17] Ibid, II.1.9.

proposition embedded in a text is knowledge of this object as it exists ideally and as it was initially conceived. The importance of philosophical epistolography lies in the fact that Toland invites the reader to understand his propositions just as he, the author, originally understood them.

II. Critique

Throughout the course of history outlined in *Letters to Serena* the tribulations reason undergoes stem from its acquiescence to statements that were not, and indeed could not be, understood. The first three letters are typical of the Deist diatribe against priestcraft.[18] Their titles give a clear indication as to their subject matters. The first letter, "The Origin and Force of Prejudices", is followed in kind by Letter II, "The History of the Soul's Immortality among the Heathens", and then by Letter III, "The Origin of Idolatry, and Reasons of Heathenism". Toland owes much to the "histoire critique" of French authors such as Jean Le Clerc and Richard Simon. In reference to Herodotus, the "father of history", his historiography is a secular rejection of a providential historiography.[19]

According to Toland, the first letter, "Of the Origin and Force of Prejudices" can be considered the key to all his later works.[20] Of the first three letters, it is this letter that is the least dependent on historical sources. From earliest infancy, Toland contends, one's understanding is handicapped by the superstitions and prejudices transmitted by parents and one's immediate social environment. The individual plays not only a passive role as the receiver of prejudices but is also to be considered a vector actively transmitting notions to other members of the same socio-linguistic milieu.[21] Socially conditioned limits to the understanding become a permanent fixture of one's intellectual development. According to Toland, prejudice and superstition have influenced human understanding of the natural world since the most ancient times. What were at first seemingly harmless practices and expressions of piety are later transformed into the

---

[18] For more on the subject of Toland and the Deist critique of institutional religions, see Justin Champion, *The Pillars of Priestcraft Shaken: The Church of England and its Enemies (1660-1730)* (Cambridge: Cambridge University Press, 1992).

[19] Toland, *Letters to Serena,* II.8, 34.

[20] John Toland, "Letter to Hohendorf, 23 December 1709", BM Add. MS 4465, folio 7.

[21] Pierre Lurbe, "Individuo e società in John Toland" in Antonio Santucci ed, *Fonti e connessioni Continentali John Toland e il deismo* (Bologna: Il Mulino, 2001), 384.

most aberrant doctrines which preclude men from critical inquiry. This problem results from the transition from informal expressions of religiosity to the creation of doctrines and the institutionalisation of religious practices under the aegis of a priestly cast. The priests are not the originators of superstition, rather they serve "not to undeceive, but to retain the rest of the People in their Mistakes."[22]

Toland's analysis of historical religious practices is rooted in his conception of human nature whose development precedes and finally accompanies the recorded practices of ancient religions. For him, the human mind is not primarily driven by curiosity or bewilderment in the face of nature but rather by the recognition of one's own personal mortality. Fear of death is the predominant passion and lies at the root of men's continuous oscillation between fear and hope. Elaborate systems were developed to palliate such fears; astrology, for instance, convinced men that they lived in a fixed order of time.[23] Custom and education inculcated individuals to conform to the social order which was rendered coherent and predictable thanks to a symbolical theology. The priestly orders were thus all the more able to take advantage of their position as intermediaries between the celestial and terrestrial.[24]

The dogma of the immortality of the soul is the most prosaic, as well as the most crucial, case of superstitions which were meant to alleviate the anguish of those fearful of their eventual death. Toland adheres to the thesis, first proposed by Herodotus, that this dogma originated with the Egyptians.[25] The point he makes clear, at the beginning of Letter II through a reading of Aristotle, is that the most ancient Greek philosophy is devoid of an organizing principle or:

> ...actuating Spirit in the Universe it self, nor more than in any of the Parts thereof: but [it] explain'd all the Phaenomena of Nature by Matter and local Motion, Levity and Gravity or the like, and rejected all that the Poets said of the Gods, Daemons, Souls, Ghosts, Heaven, Hell, Visions, Prophecys, and Miracles as Fables invented at pleasure, and Fictions to divert the Readers.[26]

---

[22] Toland, *Letters to Serena*, I.8, 8.

[23] Ibid, III.4, 80.

[24] Ibid, III.14, 104.

[25] *Ibid*, II.6, 30-31. The thesis of Egypt as the font of science ran counter to the widely-held view that privileged Jewish antiquity, especially the Mosaic inheritance, as the source of philosophy, notably ancient Greek physiology. Ralph Cudworth, *A Treatise concerning eternal and immutable morality* (Cambridge: Cambridge University Press, 1996), 39.

[26] Toland, *Letters to Serena*, II.3, 22.

The problem of the erroneous suppositions pertaining to passive matter and active form arose from philosophers who introduced into their systems notions (such as *nous* or a presiding intelligence over the universe) which were originally the invention of poets. Toland's historical inquiry into to the transmission of dogma resembles the history of metaphysical doctrines elaborated by Aristotle in his *Metaphysics*. Citing ancient sources, Toland notes that Anaxagoras was the first "who added Mind to Things."[27] Philosophers have since been led into error when discoursing upon matter. Worse, the force of authority and the prevalence of implicit belief have assured that Anaxogoras' aporia would never be questioned. It easily lent itself to be included in religious doctrines and philosophical systems which conceptualised the immortality of the soul. "The People begun it, from them their Children learnt it, at last it became a part of all mens Education...and so the Learned themselves believed it before they had a reason for it."[28]

The third letter is an account of the consolidation of erroneous doctrines and superstitions. For Toland, the role of fables and symbolical theologies has been nefarious for the development of natural philosophy. The priestly casts and secular authorities cemented a relationship which reinforced the hold of superstitions on the people. Formal censure and the risk of persecution impeded movements to rectify popular beliefs. The obscure language of many philosophers is to be ascribed to the risks many incurred at any sort of "general Reformation".[29] Their recourse to fables or mythological language was, at best, a means to transmit their doctrines to those able to read between the lines. However, fables inherently obscure the truth and ensure that not only the greater number of unlearned but also the smaller number of philosophers will hold to erroneous suppositions that cloud a genuine understanding of nature. Toland's position in this regard contrasts with that of Leibniz who believed that fables could be a useful means of communicating doctrines to the greatest number. In his *Nouveaux Essais*, the German philosopher broaches this topic in a conversation between the characters Philalèthe and Théophile. The latter wonders about the moral identity of a human soul which passes into the body of an animal, such as in the case of Lucius in Apulaeus' *Metamorphosis*.[30] According to Leibniz, Lucius retains his personal identity whether he be in his original body or in a donkey's body.

---

[27] Ibid, II.4, 27.
[28] Ibid, II.13, 53.
[29] Ibid, III.18, 114.
[30] G.W.Leibniz, *Nouveau essais sur l'entendement humain* (Paris: Flammarion, 1966), II.XXVII, 199–201.

Toland's materialism, for which there is nothing but figure and movement in nature, undermines not just the idea of the soul's immortality but the very definition of personal identity and selfhood. For him, Leibniz's monadology relies on the invention of fabulists and poets but in no way can be adhered to by philosophers. Immortality and the personal identity of a soul can only be asserted as an article of faith and not natural reason. The soul's immortality simply cannot be schematised as a problematic in philosophical speculations whose concerns are the first principles of nature. Toland's rejection of the self, or personal identity, stems from his rejection of immateriality and immortality of the soul. His Materialism is seen as a corrective of the corrupt philosophical systems which since Antiquity have integrated ideas originating in poetry and mythological fables. Toland insists that the existence of an afterlife, such as that described by Socrates in *Phaedo*, is recounted as myth and not in a philosophical demonstration. The problem of the soul's immortality for Toland is, at bottom, a historical problem and not a matter of speculation.

The second part of *Letters to Serena* comprises Letter IV, "A Letter to a Gentleman in Holland, showing Spinosa's System of Philosophy to be without any Principle or Foundation", followed by Letter V, "Motion essential to Matter; in Answer to some Remarks by a Noble Friend on the Confutation of Spinosa". The transition from the first three letters to these latter two is coherent so long as one remembers that the former treat the weaknesses menacing any endeavour in natural philosophy. Prejudice and superstitions are the common lot of humans; they are most pernicious for philosophers in the form of assumptions and presuppositions that go unquestioned. The most significant case in point is that of passive matter and the idea of an organizing principle distinct from the material matrix of the universe. A reading of the last two letters will show that Toland dedicates much, if not most, of his time to criticizing these theses. This is a crucial step, since *speculation proceeds in step with dialectical critique.*

Toland holds that the erroneous presuppositions of both Spinoza and Leibniz undermine the "systems" they attempt to construct. It causes them to dismiss the very first elements of philosophy – the exemplary causes which arise from sensory contact with the material world.[31] Spinoza and Leibniz share the same presupposition according to which thought is distinct from the determinations of body and the soul has a nature *in se.* For Spinoza, thought is one of the attributes of the unique substance. In a text contemporaneous to the *Letters to Serena*, Toland criticizes Leibniz

---

[31] Toland endeavours to refute Spinoza not article by article but by showing his entire system is groundless.

for asserting that "L'Esprit est l'unique substance, et...la Matière est seulement modale."[32] For Toland, experience shows that mind and matter are not two distinct substances. Thought is a physiological effect resultant from the composition and arrangement of matter. That is to say, Toland understands thought in a way which explains it from the determinations of body, and not from a metaphysical schema tying it to an attribute of substance.[33]

The two philosophers are also criticised by Toland for supposing that an idea of the absolute must be posed outright in order to render intelligible the phenomena of nature. That is, they pose as a principle something which, for Toland, could only be the result of a logical inference. As for Spinoza's system, Toland cannot accept that one should consider the nature of God first. In line with the initial common notions first received in childhood, one only knows God by means of relative, and truncated, ideas of His useful and necessary properties. Toland throws back at Spinoza his critique of empiricist methodology developed in Part II of the *Ethics*, writing,

> Every man at the beginning stands on the same ground with the Vulgar, receiving the same Prejudices and Impressions, and however he may extricate himself from many Errors, yet if he leaves any in possession unexamined, he shall always reason himself into Contradictions of Aburditys from that Principle, tho otherwise justly reckon'd a wise and able Person.[34]

Whereas, on the one hand, Spinoza's "system" is groundless since it has no principles, on the other, the terms utilised by Leibniz are not reconcilable with propositional reason. For Toland, therefore, the metaphysics of both Spinoza and Leibniz do not have an object of study, properly speaking. The supposition that matter is inert leads to innumerable errors, such as the divisibility of matter, a non-immanent cause for movement, the existence of a void and the idea of "a kind of extension that can penetrate another kind."[35] In general, the false suppositions that result are, thus, of the sort that take an abstract idea for a real being or to falsely think that a relative idea is an absolute one. Indeed, to take a relative being for an absolute one is like considering comparisons and similarities to be solid and precise proofs. In metaphysical speculation,

---

[32] John Toland, *Remarques critiques*, in *Lettres à Serena et autres textes*, annexe 6, 306.

[33] Dagron, *Lettres à Serena*, 49.

[34] Toland, *Letters to Serena,* V.21, 205.

[35] Ibid, V.24, 216.

however, the idea of any sort of modification of matter *cannot but be* a relative idea, compared to the absolute subject.

III. Toland's Materialist Speculation

We shall begin the third and final part of this study by examining more closely the metaphysical propositions of *Letters to Serena*. If, according to Toland, metaphysics cannot discourse upon the essence of things *in se*, or being *qua* being, what then does metaphysical speculation signify for him? His definition of speculation is that it is the domain of philosophy that attempts to discover the truths of nature.[36] It is the pure search for truth free of the prejudices that handicap human reason. Speculation does not concern itself with the definition of things nor does it deal with the words that comprise them. Nature's truths are constituted by the law of nature which is known immediately and intuitively, as opposed to other laws (such as those of science) which are known through the intermediary of human language.[37] To be a true science, speculation must thus have a subject matter that is not a mere accident, just as the basic elements of its study must be commensurable with propositional reason.

What, then, is the subject matter dealt with by speculation and what is the methodology necessary to grasp the basic elements that constitute this subject matter? Metaphysical speculation deals with a subject matter anterior to that of the explanation of the "Origin of the World, its present Mechanism, or the Affections of Matter", that is to say, the cause of movement.[38] For the cause of movement cannot be explained by mechanical philosophy or the experimental sciences. Toland understands the domain of physics in light of the advancements made by Newton; "...indeed all Physicks ought to be denominated from the Title he has given to the first Book of his Principles, viz. *of the Motion of Bodys*."[39] Physics studies the attributes of matter three of which are, according to Toland, essential to it: extension, solidity and action.[40] However, as he is

---

[36] "Authority is to decide matters of Fact, but not to determine Truths of Nature." Ibid, V.1, 164.

[37] Toland states: "...car les autres loix dependent d'un certain language, soit mort il y a long temps ou subsistent encore, ne sauroient estre entendues de tout le monde." John Toland, *Parallèle entre la Raison ou la Loy de la Nature*, in *Lettres à Serena et autres textes*, I.9, 244.

[38] Toland, *Letters to Serena*, IV.9, 141.

[39] Ibid, V.20, 202.

[40] "I won't say that Matter has no other essential Propertys but these three of Extension, Solidity, and Action: but I am persuaded that from the due and joint

careful to note, these three attributes are three ideas of matter and not three different things.[41]

For Toland, *the goal of speculation* is to discover the axioms of nature which can allow such physics to better study the phenomena of nature. It is thanks to speculation that human reason can identify certain ideas which, though particular and limited, are nonetheless always true. Axiomatic ideas are not predicates because they do not depend on any subject other than themselves. The unique source of ideas is the world of material objects, or nature. Despite an inability to know the real essences of things, human understanding can immediately perceive their nominal essences. However, ever since Anaxagoras, most philosophers have accepted the traditional aporia which omits from matter its essential attribute of movement, or more precisely "action". Others have erred by taking local movement for essential movement, or action, which is akin to confusing cause and effect.[42] According to Toland, nobody contests that movement is the cause of change in matter.[43] What is in question is the idea of movement as a "principle" which must not only be supposed but also "proved and explained".[44] Note that there is no mention of causation or a causal chain in Toland's speculation beyond that of exemplary causes. The "real subject" of metaphysical speculation, the material universe as one and absolute, is known by principles.

In contradistinction to this real subject, the three principles are known intuitively and are axiomatic ideas whose logical validity is dependant on nothing but themselves. In Toland's thought, a principle is not held to be something that is cause of itself, rather it is deemed to be something without cause. Such principles are the basic materials of Toland's metaphysical speculation. It is these which are able to construe the truth of those propositions of relation which assert that the real subject exists. The idea of a "real subject" is a logical inference whose predicates are the axiomatic ideas of solidity, extension and action. Indeed, it is the sole subject which possesses reality without regard to any abstract ideas, for it is the only thing whose existence can be derived solely from itself. With this identification of the sole real being (the one material universe) and the

---

Consideration of these alone, a world of its Phaenomena may be better accounted for than hitherto." Ibid, V.29, 229.

[41] Ibid, V.29, 230–231.
[42] Ibid, IV.8, 140.
[43] Ibid, IV.8, 141.
[44] Ibid, IV.9, 141.

three principles which are immanent to it, the physical sciences would be in a position to explain natural phenomena.[45]

Toland is adamant that one cannot dismiss these axiomatic principles, since they are the first building blocks for correct speculation on nature. A principle is, for him, indissoluble from the element, the "matter", by which it comes to be known. It is very likely that Toland inherits this notion of element, or "arché", as the principle of becoming from ancient atomists.[46] It is also useful to point out the influence of Giordano Bruno and his doctrine of participation (according to which the "universal form" is an immanent principle, for it manifests itself as much at the level of the whole as in its parts).[47] The exemplary cause resultant from sensory contact with the material world is the very vehicle by which such principles are known. The primary materials of Toland's speculation are ideas, and not the words or names of things meant to represent them. For Toland, it is not a matter of separating the "world of things" from the "world of representation and discourse" (as in the case of Hobbes), but rather of distinguishing things from their representative beings, or ideas.[48]

The truth of an idea is a function of predicative judgement. A simple idea is the representative being of an exemplary cause. A simple axiomatic idea can be said to be true because, when put into the form of a predicative proposition, it affirms (or denies) only the existence of the thing it represents and not its essence or intrinsic nature. For Toland, it is a matter of distinguishing predicative propositions which are proper to intuitive reason from propositions of relation which are proper to demonstrative reason. As we saw with *Christianity not Mysterious*, Toland argues that all demonstrations must ultimately become self-evident. In other words, a true proposition of relation is that wherein the predicate (the predicative judgment) affirms the existence of one of the determinations of the subject which it evokes. Aside from axiomatic, or intuitive, ideas, all discourse

---

[45] Ibid, V.29, 230.

[46] In Lucretius, bodies are partly original elements of things and partly those which are formed of a combination of those elements. Lucretius, *On Nature*, ed. M.F. Smith (Indianapolis: Hackett, 1981) I.480-485, 37.

[47] In *De la causa*, Bruno examines the implications of the identity of cause and principle. If the soul of the world is both cause which engenders particular forms and the principle which lies intrinsically within the constitution of things and remains within the effect, it must thus be considered the universal form of the whole as well as the particular form of natural realities. Tristan Dagron, *Unité de l'être et dialectique: l'idée de philosophie naturelle chez Giordano Bruno* (Paris: Vrin, 1999), 267.

[48] Yves-Charles Zarka, *La décision métaphysique de Hobbes* (Paris: Vrin, 1999), 134.

dealing with the attributes of matter are propositions of relation. The truth of these propositions is thus a function of their logical validity and not a function of their reference to things.[49]

The relationship which exists between real conceptions and relative conceptions is that of the relationship between subject and predicate. This logical relationship corresponds to the relationship between an absolute representative being and an abstract notion which represents it in a limited and relative way. An example of such a logical relation is that of an idea of matter and one of its modifications. The subject has a logical priority vis-à-vis its predicate because the idea of the latter only includes one of the determinations, or attributes, of the former. A principle is thus logically anterior to its modification because, as real, it subsists in and of itself.[50] A principle cannot be reduced to an exemplary or particular cause, for such a cause is but a mere determination of a principle. An example would be that of action which is "always in the Whole, and in every Part of the same, and without which it cou'd not receive any Modifications."[51] Principles are modifications, or abstract parts, of the one real subject. Toland, for sure, hardly seems concerned to distinguish the sense of terms such as "mode" from other terms such as attribute, property or nominal essence. Be that as it may, a mode does not subsist in and of itself, but rather depends upon another subject, one of the determinations of which it is the abstract representation.[52]

Toland endeavours to "prove" that the abstract idea of action is necessary to matter; in other words that action is a necessary predicate of the unique real subject, or the one material universe. It is thus at the level of the logical necessity of a principle, and of the identification of action as a principle, that Toland bases his argument. The apophantic procedure of argumentation developed by Toland consists in first identifying solidity and extension as predicates of the unique real subject. Solidity and extension are axiomatic ideas which cannot be defined for they are

---

[49] Toland, like Hobbes before him, separates out propositions of identity from any reference to the real existence of things.

[50] Toland supposes that the properties of solidity, extension and action "...have a real existence, and tho seemingly opposite, they are but the Affections of the same Subject under various Considerations." *Letters to Serena*, V.25, 215.

[51] Ibid, IV.16, 159.

[52] For Spinoza, a mode is to be distinguished from an attribute (*Ethics*, ID5). Such is not the case with Toland. His conception is that of the relationship between two terms, one of which is dependent upon the other. It is thus more akin to Locke's definition whereby a mode is dependent upon a substance. John Locke, *Essay Concerning Human Understanding*, II 12.4, 88.

immediately perceived as such.[53] All of these "properties" are principles because they have "certain modes which are conceiv'd to belong immediately to it self".[54] Contrary to the principle of movement, the truth of these propositions of relation is agreed upon by Toland's correspondents. For example, the logical necessity of extension and of one of its determinations, infinity, has no need to be demonstrated.[55] The "real Existence" of solidity and extension stems from the fact that they are logically consequential to an antecedent whose existence they confirm.[56]

Such is the case too for action according to Toland. His argument can be summarised thus: if movement is a simple idea which is not reducible to merely exemplary causes, it is axiomatic. Insofar as it is an axiom, its existence is not a result of particular accidents, indeed it is the cause of such accidental effects. It is consequently an attribute as well. In other words, it is a principle. If all principles are necessary, then action is necessary. Since a principle is a conceptual limitation; it is the expression of something absolute. It is thus by logical inference that Toland conceptualises the "real subject", or the one and infinite matter.

The noble friend of the fifth letter deduces that from Toland's thesis of "admitting the Activity of Matter, there seems to be no need of a presiding intelligence."[57] Indeed, that is precisely the point of Toland's argument. The organizing principle of the universe is not transcendent but rather an immanent quality of it. This fundamental position of natural philosophy obviously has consequences for revealed religion and those philosophical systems and theologies which support it. The movement and activity of matter has no beginning nor end: there is no creation *ex nihilo* or impulsion of active form into passive matter. Toland admits that the notion of an infinite matter does not exclude a "pure Spirit or Immaterial Being".[58] This, however, is not a positive assertion drawn from speculation. Following his theory of knowledge, Toland's metaphysics is written in such a form as that we may understand his propositions as he originally understood them. He never confirms or attempts to argue for such a state of affairs because the notion of immateriality has no reality in metaphysical speculation.

---

[53] Toland, *Letters to Serena,* V.28, 225.
[54] Ibid, V.29, 230.
[55] Ibid, V.24, 213.
[56] Ibid, V.25, 215.
[57] Ibid, V.30, 234.
[58] Ibid, V.30, 236.

This last point is of importance since it serves to clarify the pedagogical ends of Letters IV and V which are lacking in his last work, *Pantheisticon*. Toland's Pantheism is discursive by nature, meaning that it is meant to rest on the merits of its propositions and not on the invocation of an authority other than that of the reason of the individual. For Toland, that which we cannot conceive can in no way induce us to acquiesce to its truth. *Pantheisticon* is not meant to argue for a cosmology that results from Toland's materialist conception of the natural world. Indeed, Toland's last philosophical text supposes the truth of pantheist positions without supporting arguments.[59] The objective of *Pantheisticon* is, instead, to induce the reader to further inward reflection, not by the force of argumentation but rather by means of suggestion through the utopian image of a Socratic society whose "Formula" will render the reader "better and wiser".[60] Toland composes the imaginary setting of a philosophical banquet that brings together peers and kindred spirits. The Formula's incantations are evocative of the *"monstrare"* typical of rhetoric rather than the *"demonstrare"* which is proper to philosophical argumentation. Though devoid of argumentation, the work is nevertheless intelligible. The Irish philosopher endeavours not to transmit the doctrinal content of pantheism but to influence the disposition of readers so that they will seek out the way of truth. The world of words and representations that compose *Pantheisticon* obliges readers to reflect upon themselves and to see that their own bodies are situated in a material universe in constant movement without limits or centre. The core interest of *Pantheisticon* is indeed matter, more specifically that of the human body. The "physics" to which the author refers is that of *De Diaete*, meaning the physiology of the Hippocratic tradition which supposes knowledge of the *phusis* of nature.[61] The end goal of this work is therapeutic in nature, since contemplation of the law of nature, the true route to wisdom, implies a continuous effort to rid oneself of erroneous ideas which instil the fear of death.

In conclusion, we may note that the complementary relationship of *Pantheisticon* to *Letters to Serena* for Toland's philosophical enterprise

---

[59] This position stands in contrast to the thesis of Tristan Dagron who proposes that *Pantheisticon* is a continuation of Toland's materialist theorisation in which he hones an architectonic perspective for his philosophy of immanence first laid out in *Letters to Serena*. Tristan Dagron, *Toland et Leibniz: l'invention du néo-spinozisme* (Paris: Vrin, 2009), 405-409.

[60] John Toland, *Pantheisticon,* ed. and Italian trans. Onofrio Nicastro and Manlio Iofrida (Pisa: ETS, 1996), Preface, 129.

[61] Ibid, XIV, 203.

was both critical and pedagogical in nature. In his critique of religion, his theses describe the socio-linguistic mechanisms that favour the predominance of common notions, prejudices, superstitions, and most importantly, theological discourse. From his position at the margins of philosophical heterodoxy, Toland was sensitive to the formal institutions and informal practices that served to impede criticism and the reform of reason. The author of *Letters to Serena* believes that the theological discourse which communicates doctrines such as that of a transcendent deity, passive matter and the immortality of the soul hinders a truer understanding of the natural world, which he in turn conceptualised as being structured immanently and composed exclusively of matter. Questions such as that of the soul's immortality and the participation of a transcendent God in His creation are of no interest for the pantheist who rejects them. However, insofar as Toland saw himself as a philosophical and political reformer, the predominance of such notions in ordinary discourse was of grave concern. The principles which constituted the law of nature were of importance not as disinterested speculations on the universe but because understanding them, for Toland, opens the way to knowing the good life, shorn of the fear of an eventual death.[62]

Bibliography

Brown, Stuart. "Two Papers by John Toland: His 'Remarques Critiques sur le Système de M.Leibnitz...' and the last of his 'Letters to Serena'" in *John Toland torna a Dublin, Rivista I Castelli di Yale* IV (1999): 55-79.

Champion, Justin. *The Pillars of Priestcraft Shaken: The Church of England and its Enemies (1660-1730)*. Cambridge: Cambridge University Press, 1992.

Cicero. *De finibus*. Cambridge, MA: Harvard University Press, 1983.

Clark, J.C.D. *English Society 1688-1832. Ideology, Social Structure and Political Practice during the Ancien Régime*. Cambridge: Cambridge University Press, 1985.

Cudworth, Ralph. *A Treatise concerning Eternal and Immutable Morality*. Cambridge: Cambridge University Press, 1996.

Dagron, Tristan. *Unité de l'être et dialectique: L'idée de philosophie naturelle chez Giordano Bruno*. Paris: Vrin, 1999.

—. *Toland et Leibniz: L'invention du néo-spinozisme*. Paris: Vrin, 2009.

---

[62] Toland, *Parallèle entre la Raison ou la Loy de la Nature*, I.6, 242.

Heinemann, F.H. "Toland and Leibniz," *The Philosophical Review* LIV.5 (1945): 437-57.

Locke, John. *An Essay concerning Human Understanding*. Edited by Kenneth Winkler. Indianapolis: Hackett, 1996.

Leibniz, G.W. *Nouveau essais sur l'entendement humain*. Paris: Flammarion, 1966.

—. "Considérations sur la doctrine d'un esprit universel unique (1702)."In *Œuvres de Leibniz* vol. I. Edited by Lucy Prenant. Paris: Aubier Montaigne, 1972.

Lucretius. *On Nature*. Edited by M.F. Smith. Indianopolis: Hackett, 1981.

Lurbe, Pierre. "Individuo e società in John Toland." In Antonio Santucci edited, *Fonti e connessioni Continentali John Toland e il deismo*. Bologna: Il Mulino, 2001. 371-89.

Toland, John. *Letters to Serena*. London, 1704.

—. "Letter to Hohendorf, 23 December 1709." BM Add. MS 4465, folio 7.

—. *Pantheisticon*. Edited and Italian translation by Onofrio Nicastro and Manlio Iofrida. Pisa: ETS, 1996.

—. *Christianity not Mysterious*. Edited by Philip McGuiness, Alan Harrison and Richard Kearney. Dublin: Lilliput Press, 1997.

—. *Lettres à Serena et autres textes*. Translated by Tristan Dagron. Paris: Editions Honoré Champion, 2004.

Zarka, Yves-Charles. *La décision métaphysique de Hobbes*. Paris: Vrin, 1999.

CHAPTER THREE

PANTHEISM AND ATHEISM IN SCHELLING'S *FREIHEITSSCHRIFT*

ASHLEY U. VAUGHT

I. Introduction

In this essay I argue that Schelling's *Philosophical Investigations into the Essence of Human Freedom* (1809) constitutes his response to F.H. Jacobi's critique of philosophy during the *Pantheismusstreit*, but that while his response effectively undermined the presuppositions of that critique, he inadvertently confirmed Jacobi's conclusions.

Although the *Pantheismusstreit* largely took place during the mid-1780s, its effects were felt throughout the rest of that century and into the beginning of the next. Jacobi crudely claimed that philosophy's commitment to demonstrative reason undermined its capacity to comprehend freedom and, consequently, morality. In its most famous articulation, Jacobi claimed that in its systematic pretensions all philosophy is ultimately pantheism, and that pantheism is atheism. In short, pantheism's systematicity contradicts freedom and morality.

Though Jacobi's argument was perhaps simplistic, this did not mute its persuasive force within the intellectual and philosophical community. Various figures felt the need to respond to this polemic. Even Kant, who belittled the dispute in correspondence,[1] engaged with it both explicitly in his essay "What is Called Orientation in Thinking?" (1786) and implicitly in the purpose behind the *Critique of Judgment* (1790). Schelling's early

---

[1] In his April 7th, 1786 letter to Marcus Herz, Kant writes, "The Jacobi [-Mendelssohn] controversy is nothing serious; it is only an affection of inspired fanatics trying to make a names for themselves and is hardly worthy of a serious refutation. It is possible that I shall publish something in the *Berliner Monatsschrift* to expose this fraud." Immanuel Kant, *Philosophical Correspondence*, trans. and ed. Arnulf Zweig (Chicago: University of Chicago Press, 1967), 123.

work makes reference to Jacobi at various points,[2] but only the *Freiheitsschrift* engages substantially with the latter's intellectual legacy. In the introductory remarks to the *Freiheitsschrift*, Schelling interrogates the concept of pantheism. Brashly contradicting conventional intellectual wisdom, he argues that pantheism not only *does not* quash human freedom, but that in fact *only* pantheism can rescue the concept of human freedom.[3]

Schelling thinks freedom as the capacity for good and evil, the possibilities for human character that are rooted in (but not reducible to) a unique, two-fold metaphysical pantheism. That is, Schellingian pantheism conceives a distinction between the co-constitutive principles or powers of God's existence and of the ground for God's existence. The principles provide evil with a positive, real basis. However, as a consequence of the centrality accorded to human freedom, God becomes subject to the vicissitudes of human history. That is, if human freedom forms the most complex and complete development of God's revelation in nature, God suffers human history.

In conclusion, Schelling's response to the Jacobian polemic presents a dramatic dialectical movement in the philosophico-historical transformation of the concept of pantheism *vis-à-vis* morality: pantheism initially opposes freedom, negating its possibility and that of morality; pantheism is then reconceived to centralize freedom, such that thinking either concept is impossible without the other; but this revision of pantheism and freedom, although giving morality a metaphysical basis for both good *and* evil, reduces God to a hapless observer. Ironically, in showing that freedom and pantheism do not contradict one another, contra Jacobi, Schelling leads metaphysics towards a certain form of atheism.

---

[2] In the "Philosophical Letters on Dogmatism and Criticism" (1795), Schelling refers to Jacobi's account of Spinoza as "*a nihilo nihi fit*" and then claims "I believe that the very problem of the transition of the nonfinite to the finite is the problem of *all* philosophy." F.W.J. Schelling, "Philosophical Letters on Dogmatism and Criticism" in *The Unconditional in Human Knowledge*, ed. And trans. Fritz Marti (Lewisburg: Bucknell University Press, 1980), 177. F.W.J. Schelling, *Sämmtliche Werke*, ed. K.F.A. Schelling (Stuttgart and Augsberg: J.G. Cotta, 1856-61), 1: 313.

[3] F.W.J. Schelling, *Philosophical Investigations into the Essence of Human Freedom*, trans. Jeff Love and Johannes Schmidt (Albany: SUNY Press, 2006), 12; *Werke*, 7:340.

II. Jacobi's Critique of Pantheism, "and Matters Connected Therewith"

Histories of the *Pantheismusstreit* frequently mention F.H. Jacobi's opportunism in publishing *Concerning the Doctrine of Spinoza in Letters to Herr Moses Mendelssohn* (1785).[4] Pretending to the unique confidence of G.E. Lessing's latent Spinozism, Jacobi appeared as the heir to a powerful cultural figure. But the force of the argument he made in those pages cannot be limited to the trifling question of intellectual lineages. Jacobi's critique, though hyperbolic and crude, troubled German thinkers for at least the next 25 years.

The debate was precipitated by Jacobi's claim that Lessing had admitted to him, shortly before his death, that he was a Spinozist, but ultimately this revelation was the stage for a broad critique of philosophy and the *Aufklärung*. Although Jacobi had drawn Moses Mendelssohn into the debate, as the erstwhile defender of the *Aufklärung* in the absence of Lessing, in fact, it was largely a one-man show. Jacobi perceived Lessing's Spinozism as a symptom of the impotence of philosophical cognition and as a certain reckless disregard for its metaphysical consequences. Lessing's Spinozism was not a regrettable, merely individual (as it appeared at the time) intellectual orientation, but characteristic of the eminence of demonstrative reason. In one part of the conversation with Lessing that Jacobi retells, Lessing says, supposedly: "There is no other philosophy than the philosophy of Spinoza. I [Jacobi]: That might be true. For the determinist, if he wants to be consistent, must become a fatalist: the rest then follows by itself."[5] In this passage we observe the key concerns motivating Jacobi: that philosophy is inseparable from Spinoza's system, and that Spinoza's system is a "consistent" determinism that ends in the abolition of freedom. That is, Spinoza employs demonstrative logic to its final necessary conclusions. Philosophy at large fails to be as consistent as Spinoza, but if it were, it too would deny human freedom and affirm fatalism.

Absent from the above passage is the metaphysical valence of this critique. Spinozism (and philosophy's epistemological systematicity)

---

[4] Frederick Beiser, *The Fate of Reason* (Cambridge MA: Harvard University Press, 1987), 65.

[5] F.H. Jacobi, *The Main Philosophical Writings and the Novel* Allwill, ed. and trans. George di Giovanni (Cambridge: Cambridge University Press, 2002), 187. Beiser and Henry Allison doubt the authenticity of this confession. Beiser, *Fate of Reason*, 65. Henry Allison, *Lessing and the Enlightenment* (Ann Arbor: University of Michigan Press, 1966), 73.

demands, on Jacobi's account, a metaphysics of immanence, or pantheism:

> This immanent infinite cause has, as such, *explicite*, neither understanding nor will. For because of its transcendental *unity* and thorough-going absolute infinity, it can have no object of thought and will; and a faculty to produce a concept before *the concept*, or a concept that would be prior to its object and *the complete cause of itself*, or so too a will causing the willing and thus determining itself entirely, are nothing but absurdities.[6]

Substance cannot bear either thought or volition, as Jacobi sees it. Thought is denied because it requires objects and the capacity to form concepts—neither of which obtains. Volition is impossible for the same reasons. The infinity of substance obliterates any possible finite being. This is effectively the acosmist critique, namely, that God's actuality does not allow for the self-subsistence of any finite being. To put this differently, finite being is dependent on God for its actuality, but that dependency prioritises and actualises God, making the finite being unreal. Pantheism cannot abide the existence of finite beings, as much as it cannot allow for the possibility of intellection or will.

The next step in Jacobi's series of propositions seems not to follow: pantheism is atheism.[7] That is, how can one deny the existence of God if God is so real, on this account, that He cannot suffer finitude? This is a question that Jacobi does not answer. At least two reasonable explanations exist, although on my view the latter is more so. First, in the seventeenth century atheism had been primarily an indictment implying the departure from the orthodox conception of God. Some of Spinoza's first critics attacked him for attributing extension to God's essence.[8] In the same way, when Jacobi calls Spinoza an atheist, he could be drawing on that sense of the term, insofar as Spinoza's views dispossess God of thought and will. But against this explanation, Jacobi does not defend the traditional views of God whatsoever, and this sense of the word "atheism" belonged more properly to the end of 17th and the beginning of the 18th century. As George di Giovanni claims, "Jacobi's religiosity was thoroughly secular in nature", and this would correspond to his disinterest in defending orthodox revelation (or revelation whatsoever).[9]

Second, the opposition between pantheism and religion slowly lost its

---

[6] Jacobi, *Main Philosophical Writings*, 188.

[7] Ibid, 233.

[8] In his article on Spinoza, Pierre Bayle's first target is the materiality of God. Pierre Bayle, *Historical and Critical Dictionary: Selections*, trans. Richard H. Popkin (Indianapolis: Hackett, 1965), 302.

[9] George di Giovanni, "Introduction" to Jacobi, *Main Philosophical Writings*, 43.

meaning during the eighteenth century, in part because of the repeated gestures of philosophers—like Lessing and Mendelssohn—to separate religion from revelation. Lessing was famous for his quite heterodox views of Christianity. He once stated that revealed doctrine corresponds only to the "state's natural and fortuitous condition" whereas natural religion was religion's "inner truth."[10] Thus, the charge of atheism gains traction insofar as it was addressed to natural religion and to its condition, human freedom. Although Jacobi doesn't speak of natural religion explicitly, it seems safe to assume that freedom is as vital—and certainly not wholly separate from—as faith (*Glaube*) to such natural religion. What is more, freedom and faith are both expressed by a kind of immediate, non-discursive intuition of existence: "I must assume a source of thought and action that remains inexplicable to me."[11] Thus, for Jacobi the fatalism of pantheism leads to atheism, not by undermining the doctrines of Christian revelation, but by its abolition of human freedom, which was the means by which our morality and knowledge of God was assured.

Because of its resonance in the *Freiheitsschrift*, it is worth saying a few words about Jacobi's notion of belief, or *Glaube*. Jacobi did not think of belief in the contemporary sense of "justified belief." Instead he conceived this belief as the unacknowledged, unconditional ground for the interminable syllogistic propositions of demonstrative reason. Jacobi thought that reason's logic pursued an infinite path. As Terry Pinkard explains: "The basic idea is that if one believes something, then one must be able to justify that belief, and one can justify it only if one can show that it follows logically from some other true belief or proposition."[12] Ironically, despite his critique of Spinoza, Jacobi intimates that the latter inspired this notion of belief. When referring to third-order knowing in Spinoza, he calls it "insight" and refers directly to a passage from the *Ethics*.[13] The source for the idea of belief—which is Jacobi's solution to

---

[10] G.E. Lessing, *Philosophical and Theological Writings*, trans. and ed. H.B. Nisbet (Cambridge: Cambridge University Press, 2005), 36.

[11] Jacobi, *Main Philosophical Writings*, 193.

[12] Terry Pinkard, *German Philosophy: 1760-1860* (Cambridge: Cambridge University Press, 2002), 94.

[13] Jacobi claims that he clings to "the light, of which Spinoza says that it illuminates itself and the darkness as well." Jacobi, *Main Philosophical Writings*, 193. The source for this quotation comes from the end of part two, "Of Mind", in which Spinoza describes third-order knowing: "What can there be which is clearer and more certain than a true idea, to serve as a standard of truth? As the light makes both itself and the darkness plain, so truth is the standard both of itself and of the false." Spinoza, *Ethics* (in *The Collected Works of Spinoza* vol. 1, trans. and ed. Edwin Curley (Princeton: Princeton University Press, 1980), IIP43S.

the problems of philosophy—is such a form of knowing, even though Spinoza's system is also supposedly the paradigm of demonstrative rationality gone amok.

Despite the crudity and ostensible internal contradiction of Jacobi's critique, it was incredibly persuasive. Although Moses Mendelssohn was Jacobi's primary interlocutor in the *Pantheismusstreit*, several others felt the need to respond to Jacobi, including both Herder and Kant. Later Jacobi engaged Fichte in debate in an exchange of letters, and finally Jacobi even argued with Schelling, after the publication of the *Freiheitsschrift*. Some scholars even believe that figures as late as Kierkegaard were influenced by Jacobi.[14] It is difficult to determine why Jacobi could be such a vital figure, especially since Jacobi was writing as the same time as the epoch-making appearance of the Kantian critical philosophy, which was both sympathetic to certain elements, but ultimately critical, of his critique. How, in proximity to an eclipsing figure like Kant, could Jacobi's polemic have left its mark? In neither its account of demonstration nor its insistence on belief had Jacobi anything to offer the Kantian critique. Yet, there is a vague resemblance between the opposition that Jacobi establishes between philosophy and morality and the separation in Kant between theoretical and practical philosophy. If Jacobi's argument is glossed as the failure of demonstrative logic to account for moral principles, then the "immense gulf" between theoretical and practical philosophy, which Kant addresses in his introduction to the *Critique of Judgment* and then tries to overcome,[15] appears as an example of that failure. Of course, Kant would bristle at the idea that the critical philosophy is a form of *pantheism*, but for Jacobi, pantheism was merely the model of consistent philosophical reason.

Hegel breathed new life into Jacobi's critique of pantheism in the *Phenomenology of Spirit* (1807). The target of this critique was Schelling and his philosophy of identity, not philosophy *tout court*. The philosophy of identity included texts such as the *Presentation of My System of Philosophy* (1801) and the *System der gesammten Philosophie* (1804). In those texts, Schelling describes a pantheistic system in which self-identical reason takes the place of Spinozist substance. In the following passage, Hegel describes the limitations of the "divine life" of self-identical reason.

---

[14] See Anders Moe Rasmussen, "The Legacy of Jacobi in Schelling and Kierkegaard", in Joachim Hennigfeld ed, *Kierkegaard und Schelling: Freiheit, Angst und Wirklichkeit* (Berlin: DEU, 2002).

[15] Immanuel Kant, *Critique of Judgment*, trans. Werner S. Pluhar (Indianapolis: Hackett, 1987), 14.

> That life is indeed one of untroubled equality and unity with itself for
> which otherness and alienation, and the overcoming of alienation, are not
> serious matters. But this in itself is abstract universality, in which the
> nature of the divine life to be for itself, and so too the self-movement of the
> form, are altogether left out of account.[16]

Such "equality and unity" betrays an incapacity of "divine life" to achieve
the "alienation" of finite life. Schelling's system lacks the negativity
necessary to overcome alienation and for the "divine life to be for itself."
God does not create himself in finite life, and, without the action of
creation, God's own essence remains merely formal and unactualised.
Hegel's critique actually has two parts. The first part is the acosmist
critique, or the failure of non-derivative finite life to emerge from the
infinite. This part of the critique is consistent with what we observed in
Jacobi's critique of Spinoza. Finite beings lack actuality because they are
merely modifications of the infinite essence. The second part of the
critique follows dialectically from the first. An account of God that cannot
bring finite life into being, namely, acosmism, is ultimately not even God,
and is therefore atheism. Jacobi skipped the second step of this critique
and merely claimed that the failure to account for belief was atheism. But
for Hegel not all philosophical reason is stigmatised by an abstract inner
life. Thus, for Hegel, philosophy is not cursed by this abstract inner life—
only the "monochromatic formalism" of Schelling's philosophy of
identity.

Now it is true that Hegel is not criticizing pantheism *per se*. But it is
clear that the same indictment of pantheism by Jacobi is now being
directed towards Schelling. The fact that this critique is renewed by
Schelling's former friend and colleague only sharpens its sting.[17] Schelling

---

[16] G.W.F. Hegel, *Phenomenology of Spirit*, trans. A.V. Miller (Oxford: Oxford
University Press, 1977), 10-11.

[17] Alan White denies that Schelling was concerned with Hegel's critique, citing the
continuity of the concerns of the *Freiheitsschrift* with earlier work as evidence.
Alan White, *Schelling: An Introduction to the System of Freedom* (New Haven:
Yale University Press, 1983), 104-106. In his last letter to Hegel, Schelling even
says that he could not have assumed himself the target of this critique—that it was
meant for his disciples. Yet Schelling also says that he wishes Hegel would have
made that distinction. F.W.J. Schelling, *Aus Schellings Leben in Briefen*, ed. G.L.
Plitt (Leipzig: Hirzel, 1869-70), 2:124. Tilliette thinks, however—and I follow him
on this issue—that Schelling couldn't have failed to have noticed that he was
intended as the target of this critique and that in the *Freiheitsschrift* Schelling
attempts to show that Hegel is mistaken. Xavier Tilliette, *Schelling: Une
Philosophie en Devenir* (Paris: Vrin, 1970), 1:513.

does not refer directly to Hegel in the *Freiheitsschrift*, but he does refer explicitly to a contemporary critique of pantheism made by Friedrich Schlegel in *Über die Sprache und Weisheit der Indier* (1808). In correspondence Schelling expresses a desire to engage Schlegel in debate. Although there are personal reasons for this state of affairs,[18] Schlegel had condemned the *hen kai pan* of pantheism as reducible to all is nothing, and claimed that pantheism could not account for evil.[19] Thus, Schlegel also continues the acosmist critique of pantheism, but adds something new to these charges.

In summary, we may say that there is a certain intellectual momentum to the critique of pantheism, and it is this generalized critique that Schelling seeks to overturn. First, Schelling sees the *Freiheitsschrift* as overturning the platitude that system and freedom are mutually contradictory concepts, and as such responding to Jacobi. Second, Schelling wants to show that human freedom is not merely a moment of the "system" of the *Freiheitsschrift*, but precisely what makes the "system" what it is. In such fashion, Schelling emphasizes the finite life of the divine, overcoming Hegel's critique. Third, human freedom is conceived as the capacity for good and evil, and as such, this pantheistic system responds to Schlegel's comments. These are the intentions of the *Freiheitsschrift*.

III. Human Freedom Suspends the Divine Will

From the opening pages of the *Freiheitsschrift* onwards, the explicit task is to show not merely that system and freedom do not contradict one another, but that freedom and system can only be thought insofar as they are thought together. Yet Schelling begins by asserting the fact of freedom, "the feeling of which is imprinted in every individual", and the givenness of its existence within the whole of creation: "Individual freedom is surely connected in some way with the world as a whole... [and thus] some kind of system must be present, at least in the divine understanding, with which freedom coexists."[20] The task for Schelling is *not* to prove that freedom and system do not contradict one another—for the fact of created existence is the proof—but merely to explain how that is the case.

---

[18] Schlegel claimed that Schelling had plagiarized his work. Tilliette, *Schelling*, 1:499.

[19] Joachim Henningfeld, *F.W.J. Schellings* Über das Wesen der menschlichen Freiheit (Darmstadt: Wissenschaftliche Buchgesellschaft, 2001), 38.

[20] Schelling, *Inquiries*, 9; *Werke*, 7:336-337.

Nonetheless, the introduction to the text is devoted to examining the platitude that pantheism cannot sustain human freedom and that this is because the concepts of system and freedom contradict one another.[21] Schelling considers three interpretations of pantheism. The first contends that pantheism means the "complete identification of God with things."[22] God is nothing more than the aggregate of all finite things and the unity of the infinite could not obtain. As such, pantheism is atheism. In response, Schelling claims that this interpretation fails to even approach Spinoza's system, the paradigm for it, because the latter insists upon the most "total differentiation of things from God." This distinction appears in the generic difference between substance and modes, namely that the former exists in itself and that the latter exist through another. Rather than effecting ontological indistinction, Schelling here seems to think that Spinozism protects the infinity of God by separating Him from the realm of singular things.[23] The second interpretation is that "in Spinoza [or pantheism] the individual thing is equivalent to God."[24] Pantheism implies the unmediated sameness of the finite and infinite beings. Schelling responds: this is merely a failure of basic propositional logic. Even the most fundamental logical proposition, that of identity, never implies that both the subject and predicate are identical in precisely the same sense.

In the third interpretation Schelling finally broaches pantheism's supposed acosmism, namely, "that things are nothing, that this system abolished all individuality."[25] Nothing other than God exists, because the existence of all finite beings is derived from God's existence. As derivative

---

[21] Ibid, 9-25/7:333-355. Buchheim introduces these textual distinctions in the Meiner edition of the *Freiheitsschrift*. F.W.J. Schelling, *Philosophische Untersuchungen über das Wesen der menschlichen Freiheit*, ed. Thomas Buchheim (Hamburg: Felix Meiner Verlag, 1997), v-vii.

[22] Schelling, *Inquiries*, 12; *Werke*, 7:340.

[23] On this point, Bracken comments that for Schelling, Spinoza is only "apparently pantheistic", but not really. Joseph Bracken, *Freiheit und Kausalität* (Freiburg: Verlag Karl Alber, 1972), 37. That being said, Schelling's dismissal of this interpretation is premature. Even if Spinozism is the model for this interpretation and this resemblance is misleading, that does not justify moving on. The fact remains that this interpretation of pantheism is provisionally valid: pantheism may result in atheism insofar as divine unity is displaced by the plurality of finite beings. To this Schelling might reply that the notion of a plurality of finite beings is incoherent except on the presupposition of an infinite, unified being, against which their plurality and differentiation is possible. Nevertheless, as we will see in our conclusion, Schelling's pantheism errs—if it errs—in this direction.

[24] Schelling, *Inquiries*, 13; *Werke*, 7:341.

[25] Ibid, 15/7:343.

beings, they lack actuality. Here Schelling abandons Spinoza to acosmism, yet he notes that it applies as much to Leibniz as to Spinoza.[26] On my view, Schelling's reaction to this interpretation is his acknowledgement of the problem he must address in his essay. Acosmism is *the* critique of pantheism that sticks. To be clear, however, acosmism does not posit the insufferable contradiction of system and freedom *per se*, but that of ontological infinity and actualised, non-derivative finitude. As we saw above, this is implied by Hegel's critique in the *Phenomenology*. Here we see that Schelling is quite conscious of the challenge posed.

At the end of the introduction, Schelling introduces the principle that will allow for the possibility of human freedom in God, without reducing human freedom to an expression of God's will. That "principle" is the "dark ground," which is equally the condition for human freedom as it is the condition for creation altogether. By the dark ground Schelling thinks of something like the Platonic *khora*; the ground is a mass of dynamic forces that are bound by no rules yet are perpetually in motion. Schelling will say of the ground that it is what is *in* God, which is not God. The dark ground will be the "material" of creation, which the "light" of the divine understanding shall successfully bring into a fragile equilibrium as a "bond of forces," giving birth to corporeal nature.[27] This is the "first creation." This creation is repeated, as we shall see, in the act by which each individual "decides" his essence. In other words, it might be said that there are two creations.

The "first creation" is the production of corporeal nature, which is directed by a "universal productive will" that teleologically organizes nature's development. The "will of the understanding," which Schelling will also call a "universal productive will" also divides this "bond of forces" and informs the body with a soul. Primitive organic natural forms develop vegetable souls in plant life, and then irritable, sensible souls in animal life. All throughout corporeal nature and in each of its created beings, however, the will of the understanding dominates the will of the ground. But the process of division and evolution continues until the soul of the human being is created and both the will of the understanding and the will of the ground coexist in equal parts in this soul.[28]

The wills of the understanding and of the ground, as they appear in the soul of the human being, are the basis for human freedom. Whereas the

---

[26] Ibid, 16/7:345. One cannot help but wonder how, if the generic difference between substance and modes is so great, acosmism stigmatizes Spinozism (if the first interpretation of pantheism does not). Schelling does not think this is an issue.

[27] Ibid, 30-31/7:361-362.

[28] Ibid, 31/7:362.

life of all non-human life is always directed by the teleological principle of the will of the understanding, in the human being it is equalled by the will of the ground. The will of the ground had been necessary for the life of all creatures, but it had always been subordinated to the will of the understanding. At the rare moments in natural history when the will of the ground surpassed the limits of the will of the understanding, disease struck natural life.[29] In the human being the wills of the ground and of the understanding are called the self and universal wills, respectively. Human freedom, in its eternal aspect, concerns the decision that makes one of these wills into a leading principle. If the universal will assumes domination, this will is ordered according to the teleological ends that the divine understanding established within nature, and it therefore exists in harmony with the whole of nature. This is a good will. But human freedom also consists in the possible affirmation of the self will. The latter would be evil and would pervert the natural order of forces. "Self-will can strive to be as a particular will that which it is only through identity with the universal will; to be that which it only is, insofar as it remains in the *centrum* (just as the calm will in the quiet ground of nature is universal will precisely because it remains in the ground), also on the periphery".[30] Whichever will is chosen, the other will is made subordinate to it in a "bond of forces," which he refers to as an "identity" in the passage above.

The "decision" between these two wills constitutes what Schelling calls the "second creation." The likeness of these two creations consists in the fact that in both creations—in the creation of corporeal nature and in the decision producing the human soul—both wills stand at equal power. Moreover, in both creations a bond of forces is established. In the first creation, the bond of forces is the equilibrium obtaining between the will of the understanding and the will of the ground in corporeal nature. In the second creation, the bond of forces is the identity of the universal and self wills as "spirit," when one of these two wills has been selected as the dominant principle.

A second respect in which these two creations resemble one another appears in their temporal modality. Both creations occur eternally. Strictly speaking, of course, the first creation, the creation of corporeal nature, must be an eternal act insofar as creation brings temporality into being. The second creation is also an eternal act, because this is the decision that determines the moral character of the person throughout his life.[31] "This

---

[29] Ibid, 38/7:371.
[30] Ibid, 33/7:365.
[31] "First" and "second" do not, it should be clear, indicate temporal demarcations, since both creations are eternal.

sort of free act, which becomes necessary, admittedly cannot appear in consciousness to the degree that the latter is merely self-awareness and only ideal, since it precedes consciousness just as it precedes essence, indeed, first produces it."[32] If the decision occurred in human life, it would be overdetermined by a plurality of forces. In order to be free it occurs in eternity, although this is a strange eternity that "precedes" both consciousness and essence. This decision is essentially one of self-actualisation. The individual determines his own essence and the decision that he makes is his own act, although the individual is produced by this decision.

The last and most vital respect in which these two creations repeat one another comes in the function of the dark ground. We must remember that the ground is the condition for God's existence in creation. The ground is what is *in* God, which is not God. It is only because there is something that is *in* God which is not God that it is possible for independent, non-derivative finite beings to emerge. All created beings share in the dark ground as a co-constitutive principle of their existence. But only in human being is the will of the ground brought forward and given potential autonomy. The equality of the will of the ground in human being is what truly makes human being free. All created beings are independent in part, but the freedom of the human being is its own act. To put this a different way, if throughout non-human nature, a teleological principle directs the evolution of those created beings, only in human being does that teleology reach its suspension. This means that human freedom expresses the possibility by which that "universal productive will" can be affirmed or perverted. The dominance of that will is by no means assured.

And yet.

This teleology reaches its suspension, in part, because human freedom is the final end of God's creation, and it is through human freedom that God is finally and completely revealed. But human freedom, as we have presented it so far, has been conceived solely in its eternal dimension, whereas human freedom would be nothing without a moral life by which the essence each person has chosen is affirmed in their life. That is, human freedom is not merely the eternal, non-conscious decision of self-actualisation; it is also the life that affirms the will of the individual human being. Similarly, Schelling says of God, "God is a life, not merely a Being."[33] This passage expresses the fact that the eternal essence of God must experience its revelation in the history of creation in order to become what it is. Created nature achieves its finest production in the freedom of

---

[32] Ibid, 51-52/7:386.
[33] Ibid, 66/7:403.

the human being, and the self-actualisation of the human being repeats the act whereby God gave birth to himself in creation. Just as God must be revealed and live this life, human freedom is revealed in the moral life of the individual.

"All life has a destiny, however, and is subject to suffering and becoming."[34] But not all life is the same. The revelation of God, the life of God, occurs through creation and in particular through the gift of freedom in human being, whereby creation reaches its apotheosis. Thus, God suffers human freedom and the vicissitudes of human history. All of the evil and glory that human life produces is a spectacle for God. Human life suffers and becomes only the individual essence that it selected and it must affirm only that essence. For the human being, the moral life he lives is his action. God, by contrast, suffers the life of another. There is still another difference between divine and human suffering. The human life is an end in itself[35] and thus human becoming is an irreducible aspect of human being. The end of divine suffering is not that suffering itself, but the completion, the exhaustion of that suffering, "when God will be in all things, that is, when he will be finally realized."[36] And this means that God may never affirm the suffering and evil of human history, unlike the human being whose life is a celebration of the moral character for which he has decided. Human life is affirmation; the divine life is the suffering of what cannot be affirmed, but at best can be distinguished from the ends of the will of the understanding[37]—the principle that the divine understanding attempted to realize in nature. To put this differently, in his zeal to give non-derivative life to human being, to overcome the acosmist critique of pantheism, Schelling has inadvertently submitted God to a fate that cannot be affirmed. Schelling has directed his pantheistic account of God and the freedom of human life to certain atheism.

IV. The Meaning of this Atheism

In the preceding I argued that the account of human freedom in the *Freiheitsschrift* and its consequences for God amounts to a form of atheism. In my concluding remarks I want to consider what precisely this

---

[34] Ibid.

[35] By "end in itself" I am referring to the fact that human freedom for good *and* for evil may affirm its own action as *not* being instrumental to another purpose.

[36] Ibid.

[37] "For this is the final purpose of creation, that, whatever could not be for itself, should be for itself insofar as it is raised out of the darkness into existence as a ground that is independent of God." Ibid, 67/7:404.

may mean. By making this judgment I clearly do not mean to intimate that Schelling "does not believe in God", according to the facile understanding of this term. As it was in Spinoza's time, so it is today: atheism is a term that marks violence done to a traditional concept of God. Spinoza's critics denounced the *Deus, sive Natura* because it attributed materiality to the divine essence, which clearly contradicted the traditional identification of God with the immaterial, non-perishable transcendent being. This constituted the first meaning of Spinoza's atheism, as his earliest readers saw it. Only later did readers thematise and condemn his fatalism.

The question about atheism needs to be framed in terms of Jacobi's critique and its extension by Hegel. For Jacobi, the atheism of Spinozism was the elimination of will and thought within the system of immanence. Atheism meant the failure of Spinozism to account for the two fundamental characteristics of human being, as well as of the divine being. On these terms, Schelling has masterfully overcome the principles of the critique. Human and divine being find a common basis for their will in the dark ground, and the *Freiheitsschrift* describes the genesis of the divine understanding. While the *Freiheitsschrift* does not detail the state of human knowing, it certainly does not eliminate human knowing.

In fact, if the key component of Jacobi's alternative, belief (*Glaube*), denotes an immediate "knowing" of existence, then Schelling has in fact integrated this into his account. One of the four forms of moral character he describes is the individual possessed by "religiosity": "For God is the clear cognition in us or the spiritual light itself in which everything else first becomes clear... it is conscientiousness or that one act in accordance with what one knows and [does] not contradict the light of cognition in one's conduct."[38] Religiosity signifies the most "clear" form of knowing, and this knowing is inseparable from the most resolute moral action. This inspired person is blessed by a radical clarity. We cannot help but notice the resonance of this passage with Jacobi's description of Spinozist insight—the inspiration for his notion of belief—as the light that illuminates itself and the darkness. Not only does Schelling manage to account for Jacobi's notion of belief, but also he refines it.

These are the reasons why Schelling explicitly concludes, at the end of the *Freiheitsschrift*, that system and freedom do not contradict one another:

A system that contradicts the most holy feelings, character and moral consciousness, can never be called, at least in this respect, a system of reason, but rather only one of non-reason. To the contrary, a system in

---

[38] Ibid, 56-57/7:392.

which reason really recognized itself would have to unify all demands of the spirit as well as those of the heart and those of the moral feeling as well as those of the most rigorous understanding.[39]

By the "most holy feelings [*Gefühlen*]", perhaps Schelling means the character of "religiosity" that we encountered above. In this respect, as the divine understanding constitutes the universal will towards which the religious person is wholly oriented, these "holy feelings" coincide with the "system of reason." As Schelling writes elsewhere, God is not merely a system, but a life.[40] The divine understanding represents God *qua* system.

However, in my lead to the passage excerpted above, I slipped in the word "freedom", so as to present the connection with Schelling's brief treatment of three interpretations of pantheism in the introduction to the *Freiheitsschrift*. Schelling actually writes "moral feeling", not freedom. This slippage is not accidental. For freedom is the capacity for good *and* for evil. Could the sinner, could the evil individual, be said to possess "moral feelings"? Is the conduct of the sinner in concert with the "system of reason"? Let us suspend this question for the time being and turn to Hegel's renovation and extension of Jacobi's critique. Schelling has dispatched the general charge of the latter.

Hegel, by contrast, emphasizes the acosmist failure of the philosophy of identity, and moves from this acosmism to the conclusion that any divine life, for which created beings are dependent and un-actual, cannot be a divine life. Here too we find that Schelling has successfully overcome this critique. Human freedom in its eternal dimension, as the self-actualisation of the individual, constitutes an account of finite life that is not merely derivative in relation to the divine understanding. Only through the notion of the ground is this individuated, "alienated" finite life possible. Thus, Schelling reveals an alternative to the function of negativity that dominates the unfolding of the *Phenomenology*.

Now we may return to question of evil and system, and we cannot help but recall Schlegel's critique of pantheism, that it cannot account for evil. Schelling addressed this critique too by making human freedom the capacity for good and for evil. Yet as we have seen above, the "destiny" of the divine life requires that evil be cast out and that the tragedy of human history be left unaffirmed. Evil cannot be integrated into the "system of reason." As such, God never wholly overcomes the alienation that Hegel recommends for an actual, authentic divine life. While Schlegel's complaint about pantheism may have been addressed in the design of this

---

[39] Ibid, 74-75/7:413.
[40] Ibid, 62/7:399.

system, it was ultimately left unanswered in the execution of the final purpose of creation.

Bibliography

Allison, Henry. *Lessing and the Enlightenment*. Ann Arbor: University of Michigan Press, 1966.

Bayle, Pierre. *Historical and Critical Dictionary: Selections*. Translated by Richard H. Popkin. Indianapolis: Hackett, 1965.

Beiser, Frederick C. *The Fate of Reason*. Cambridge MA: Harvard University Press, 1987.

Bracken, Joseph. *Freiheit und Kausalität*. Freiburg: Verlag Karl Alber, 1972.

Di Giovanni, George. "Introduction: The Unfinished Philosophy of Friedrich Heinrich Jacobi." In Jacobi, *Main Philosophical Writings*, 1-167.

Hegel, G.W.F. *Phenomenology of Spirit*. Translated by A.V. Miller. Oxford: Oxford University Press, 1977.

Hennigfeld, Joachim. *F.W.J. Schellings* Über das Wesen der menschlichen Freiheit. Darmstadt: Wissenschaftliche Buchgesellschaft, 2001.

Jacobi, F.H. *The Main Philosophical Writings and the Novel* Allwill. Edited and translated by George di Giovanni. Cambridge: Cambridge University Press, 2002.

Kant, Immanuel. *Philosophical Correspondence: 1759-99*. Translated and edited by Arnulf Zweig. Chicago: University of Chicago Press, 1967.

—. *Critique of Judgment*. Translated by Werner S. Pluhar. Indianapolis: Hackett, 1987.

Lessing, G.E. *Philosophical and Theological Writings*. Translated and edited by H.B. Nisbet. Cambridge: Cambridge University Press, 2005.

Pinkard, Terry. *German Philosophy, 1760-1860: The Legacy of Idealism*. Cambridge: Cambridge University Press, 2002.

Rasmussen, Anders Moe. "The Legacy of Jacobi in Schelling and Kierkegaard." In Joachim Hennigfeld edited, *Kierkegaard und Schelling: Freiheit, Angst und Wirklichkeit*. Berlin: DEU, 2002. 209-222.

Schelling, F.W.J. *Sämmtliche Werke*. 14 vols. Edited by K.F.A. Schelling. Stuttgart and Augsberg: J.G. Cotta, 1856-61.

—. *Aus Schellings Leben in Briefen*. 3 vols. Edited by G.L. Plitt. Leipzig: Hirzel, 1869-70.

—. "Philosophical Letters on Dogmatism and Criticism." In *The Unconditional in Human Knowledge*, edited and translated by Fritz

Marti. Lewisburg: Bucknell University Press, 1980.
—. *Philosophische Untersuchungen über das Wesen der menschlichen Freiheit und die damit zusammenhängenden Gegenstände.* Edited by Thomas Buchheim. Hamburg: Felix Meiner Verlag, 1997.
—. *Philosophical Investigations into the Essence of Human Freedom.* Translated by Jeff Love and Johannes Schmidt. Albany: SUNY Press, 2006.
Spinoza, Benedict. *Ethics.* In *The Collected Works of Spinoza,* edited and translated by Edwin Curley. Princeton: Princeton University Press, 1980.
Tilliette, Xavier. *Schelling: Une philosophie en devenir.* 2 volumes. Paris: Vrin, 1970.
White, Alan. *Schelling: An Introduction to the System of Freedom.* New Haven: Yale University Press, 1983.

CHAPTER FOUR

A PHILOSOPHY OF LIFE: BERGSON'S *CREATIVE EVOLUTION*

MICHAEL KOLKMAN

I. Life and Death

Creative Evolution [*CE*] (1907) is Henri Bergson's third major and probably best-known work. It is here that he applies his philosophy of duration to the problem of life. This philosophy he had developed in his second work, *Matter and Memory* [*MM*] (1896). In that work, Bergson unequivocally affirmed the reality of duration, and with it the productivity of time itself. The opposition of matter and spirit is demonstrated to be, not an extrinsic difference, but the result of an intrinsic differentiation within duration itself. Existence consists of various degrees of a temporal form of organisation named duration, ranging from the almost completely closed and predictable circuits of action-reaction found in brute matter, to the integrative and adaptive action-reaction circuits found in the spiritual. That is to say, reality tends in two directions: towards matter and towards spirit, and everything consists of varying degrees of these two tendencies.

The philosophy of duration allowed Bergson to demonstrate a monism of substance. All of existence, be it matter or spirit, is made of the same stuff; the difference now lies between action-reaction circuits that are more closed, repetitive and predictable and those that are more inclusive, adaptive and novel. But having thus demonstrated the continuity of matter and spirit, it is the question of *life* that forces him to rethink this unity. The problem with the account given in *MM* is that, although allowing us to understand the fundamental continuity of existence, from the perspective of life, there is a vital and irreducible difference between the living and the non-living. The account of degrees of contraction and of rhythms of duration as an explanation of the continuity of body and soul cannot, at least *prima facie*, account for the very real difference there is between the organic and the anorganic or between a body with a soul and a body without one. Although Bergson displays a real reluctance to speak of death, it is precisely the death of an organism that reveals most clearly the difference between matter and spirit and body and soul. Between a dead body and a living body there seems to be no apparent material difference yet all that is left for a dead body is "a letting go". Can we say that, while a dead body falls completely under the laws of entropy and dispersion, a living body falls under these laws of dispersion *but also under another law*, a law of life and of progressive or vital organisation?

The question of death in Bergson's philosophy has received little attention thus far. This is unfortunate as it could very well shed a whole new light on his philosophy of life. Hyppolite, in his "Du Bergsonisme à l'existentialisme", writes that the absence of a meditation on human mortality is precisely what constituted the breaking-point between Bergsonism and existentialism, and ultimately between Bergsonism and Christianity.[1] For Bergson a *"sérénité finale"* is even more than a possibility but will be a reality once we give ourselves over to, or return to, our original participation in the Whole.[2] But for existentialism (in agreement here with Christianity, according to Hyppolite), man must be seen as ultimately a failure and an impassable limit, a being who can only be saved through the mystery of faith and by the grace of God. Where Bergson believes in the transcendence of the human condition, existentialism feels itself *"impuissant"*, other than through faith, to transcend this condition. Because faith cannot be philosophically justified, existentialism signals a profound crisis of philosophy.[3] Hyppolite wrote this after the Second World War, a war of which Bergson saw the beginnings but not its end (Bergson died in 1941). The horrible experiences of this war lie as an almost unbridgeable gulf between Bergson and post-war philosophy. Although I do share this sense of lack, I think that the question of death should not be posed without a meditation on life, and here there is still much to learn from the study of Bergson.

The question of death within Bergson's philosophy of life will only figure in the background of our discussion. Without an exploration of what is specific about life this question would be maladdressed. What we will focus on are the two concepts of spirituality and materiality. As I have indicated above, Bergson needed to rethink the relations between the two. While, on the one hand, existence must be understood as composed of essentially the same stuff, on the other hand, a radical difference between

---

[1] Jean Hyppolite, "Du Bergsonisme à l'existentialisme" in *Figures de la pensée philosophique* (Paris: PUF, 1971), 448.
[2] Ibid, 453.
[3] Ibid, 458.

the organic and anorganic must equally be maintained. This tension, as we will discuss presently, is made manifest in Bergson's problematic equivocation in *CE* between the terms inversion and interruption. On the one hand, materiality and spirituality are said to be merely inverted degrees of each other. From this perspective Bergson is able to claim a fundamental continuity of matter and mind. Yet, on the other hand, they act as though they were forces that aimed to "interrupt" each other. The body is an obstacle for the soul, for the body is constantly threatening to fall apart, whereas the soul or the spirit works against material decline. The solution, bluntly put, will be to appeal to two modes of thought, and to the movement between these two modes. There is a speculative or contemplative mode of thought, and a practical mode of thought. What we shall start to see is that when we do not separate the two clearly and when we are not adequately receptive to the shifting from one mode to the other that constantly takes place, this will inadvertently lead us to pose some of the "big questions" that Bergson tries to help us do without, like why is there something rather than nothing?

Although it is in his last work *The Two Sources of Morality and Religion* [*TSMR*] (1932) that Bergson is most explicit about religion, *CE* is no less relevant to the philosophy of religion because of its rigorous and sustained attempt to think the relation of matter and spirit in both a non-reductive and non-epiphenomenal manner. Bergson clearly prioritises spirit over matter. But this does not mean that matter is reduced to the status of mere manifestation. Materiality must also be seen as a form of organisation, hence in essence as a positive phenomenon. But *as a form of organisation* (and organisation can only be understood temporally for Bergson) it is not extrinsic to spirituality. Hence a monism of substance is retained. Whether this attempt is judged successful or not, the persistent pursuit of the issue make it stand out above the crowd. Indeed, before judgement is passed, the question of whether full systematicity is attainable within philosophy needs also to be addressed, and here too Bergson provides much insight.

II. Inversion and Interruption

Bergson, on his own admission, does not "feel qualified to settle the question" of life and death.[4] The difference that he feels needs to be

---

[4] Henri Bergson, *Oeuvres* (Paris: PUF, 1959), 509. Translation: *Creative Evolution*, ed. Keith Ansell Pearson, Michael Kolkman, and Michael Vaughan, trans. A. Mitchell (Basingstoke: Palgrave Macmillan, 2007), 12. All further

discussed lies rather between "the organised" and "the unorganised".[5] In the fascinating opening section to Chapter Three of *CE* on "The Method in Philosophy", Bergson criticises two types of philosophy, exemplified by two philosophers he "happened to have just brought together", Herbert Spencer and Johann Fichte:

> Between the organized and the unorganised they do not see and they will not see the cleft. Some [i.e., Spencer] start from the inorganic, and, by compounding it with itself, claim to form the living; others [i.e. Fichte] place life first, and proceed towards matter by a skilfully managed decrescendo; but, for both, there are only differences of degree in nature—degrees of complexity in the first hypothesis, of intensity in the second.[6]

The accidental meeting of the two is not really that arbitrary because we know that in his younger years Bergson was an enthusiastic follower of Spencer's evolutionary determinism.[7] But he soon parted ways. Bergson writes towards the very end of *CE*: "The usual device of the Spencerian method consists in reconstructing evolution with fragments of the evolved."[8] Spencer's fault, says Bergson, lies in not seeing the difference in nature between "the evolved" and evolution, between the *ready-made* individual and that which is always *en train de se faire*, namely, life itself. Spencer attempts to reconstruct life by adding complexity to simple terms, an undertaking that is bound to fail in Bergson's eyes. For Fichte, Bergson displays a bit more sympathy. Fichte too Bergson studied intently.[9] Fichte pays "more respect to the true order of things, [though this] hardly leads us any further".[10] Bergson writes: "Fichte takes thought in a concentrated state, and expands it into reality."[11] Fichte starts with consciousness and then aims to deduce matter, where this deduction is seen as a movement of descent (*descresendo*). Bergson writes that Fichte starts from *life*. Yet Fichte's failure is similar to Spencer in that between life and matter he too

---

references to Bergson's work will cite the page number from the *Oeuvres* followed by that from the English translation (where available).

[5] Ibid, 656/122.

[6] Ibid, 656/122-3.

[7] See Jean de la Harpe, "Souvenirs personnels d'un entretien avec Bergson" in Albert Béguin and P. Thévanez eds, *Henri Bergson. Essais et témoignages recueillis* (Neuchatel: Éditions de la Baconnière, 1943), 358-9.

[8] Bergson, *Creative Evolution*, 802/232.

[9] See Henri Bergson, "Fichte (cours inédit)" in Henri Bergson and Octave Hamelin, *Fichte* (Strasbourg: Presses Universitaires de Strasbourg, 1988).

[10] Bergson, *Creative Evolution*, 656/122.

[11] Ibid.

sees only a difference of degree—be it one of *intensity* in the case of Fichte or one of *complexity* in the case of Spencer.

For Bergson, an intensification of complexity can never produce "the simple", whereas the simple *can* lead to complexity (the movement of life is a differentiation, as Deleuze also stressed[12]). The simple or undivided movement of my hand, looked at purely from the outside may be broken down into separate positions, and an external relation between these positions. So, at least as far as it concerns a choice between complexity and intensity, Bergson will have to side with Fichte. But Fichte also does not start with a homogeneous kind of intensity. His key concept of the *Tathandlung* as found in his Jena *Wissenschaftslehre* is both simple (or "one movement") *and* internally differentiated.[13] It takes place at once but it is only for reflection that it is broken up into separate stages.[14] Fichte's "deduction" is not a gradual descent into increasingly less intense forms of life but a constant navigation of quantitative and qualitative difference. For all its shortcoming, the descent Bergson criticises comes closer to his own account from *MM* than it does to Fichte's. Perhaps this is why it was convenient for Bergson to pass-over the question of the alleged equivalence of intensity and complexity as evinced in this passage.

One of the questions for *CE* concerns the specificity of life. There is a real difference, a "cleft", between the organised and the unorganised. We do not get from the organised to the unorganised through a simple difference in degree. As Bergson will repeatedly stress in *CE,* life and matter *interrupt* each other:

> All our analyses show us, in life, an effort to remount the incline that matter descends. In that, they reveal to us the possibility, the necessity even of a process the inverse of materiality, creative of matter by its interruption alone... It has not the power to reverse the direction of physical changes, such as the principle of Carnot determines it. It does, however, behave absolutely as a force would behave which, left to itself, would work in the

---

[12] Gilles Deleuze. "Lecture Course on Chapter Three of Bergson's Creative Evolution" in *SubStance* 114.3 "Henri Bergson's *Creative Evolution*" (2007), 74

[13] See the analysis in Chapters I-III of my *Towards a Philosophy of Freedom: Fichte and Bergson*. University of Warwick, Ph.D. Thesis, 2009. This article is an abbreviated version of the third of three chapters on Bergson that make up the second half of the thesis.

[14] Johann Gottlieb Fichte, *Foundations of Transcendental Philosophy (Wissenschaftslehre) novo methodo (1796/99)* (Ithaca: Cornell University Press, 1992), 84

inverse direction. Incapable of stopping the course of material changes downwards, it succeeds in retarding it.[15]

There are two powers, or two forces, spirituality and materiality, and each strives to undo the work of the other. The living organism is the equilibrium that results from this conflict.[16] Life is a work of progressive organisation, of higher levels of contraction, of being able to synthesise more and more influences, and this, as Bergson also demonstrated in *MM*, indicates the extent of its freedom. But this work takes place in a living body and it is the material aspect of the body that works against it. The body is subject to Carnot's law of the degradation of energy, of entropy. The material world is on a downward slope towards heat-death and interestingly it is here that we find the footnote on death alluded to previously. Here Bergson disputes the idea that everything tends towards death. Matter is a descent into inertia and stasis and life is incapable of stopping. What it *can do* is delay it.[17]

This *Manichean* account of two opposed forces seems a regression from the previous account given in *MM*. In that work, duration was the highest *degree* of contraction; matter had the lowest *degree* of duration. The *unity* of body and soul was made possible because we pass by "imperceptible stages" from the one to the other. In that work it was the concept of memory that allowed Bergson to demonstrate degrees of difference between matter and duration. But although it might seem otherwise, Bergson does not renounce the results of *MM*.[18] As he writes at the start of the section entitled "The Ideal Genesis of Matter": it "was necessary to show how the real can pass from tension to extension and from freedom to mechanical necessity by way of inversion."[19] The dynamic monism of *MM* is reaffirmed in this passage. If spirituality and materiality are two wholly distinct and opposing forces, each possessing its own positivity, then we would be in want again of a middle term. It was precisely duration-as-memory, with its different degrees of contraction all internal to each other, that served to unify spirituality and materiality. As Deleuze rightly claimed, "Memory is the coexistence of degrees of difference... The meaning of memory is to give the virtuality of duration

---

[15] Bergson, *Creative Evolution*, 704/158.

[16] Ibid, 706/160.

[17] In that footnote Bergson goes on to suggest that perhaps life *wills* death (ibid).

[18] See Vladimir Jankélévitch, *Henri Bergson* (Paris: PUF, 1999), 169.

[19] Bergson, *Creative Evolution*, 696/152.

itself an objective consistency."[20] *CE* does refer to this earlier work on memory, but memory no longer plays anything like the role it had before.[21] In fact, it is not really easy to see where exactly Bergson stands on all this. Taken at face value, interruption and inversion refer to two quite different types of relations. Interruption is something that causes a rupture, something that breaks up a previous continuity, whereas inversion constitutes a change in direction. Inversion seems to imply monism and interruption dualism. The two then cannot simply be equated, *yet this is precisely what Bergson intends to show*—that inversion means interruption:

> Behind "spirituality"... and "materiality"... there are then two processes opposite in their direction, and we pass from the first to the second by way of inversion, or perhaps even by simple interruption, if it is true that inversion and interruption are two terms which in this case must be held to be synonymous, as we shall show at more length later on.[22]

Contrary to what Bergson claims we find no explicit discussion of either the precise difference between interruption and inversion or of how they are supposed to be seen as synonymous. This does not mean the solution is not there but it is, as Jankélévitch suggests, "indicated" rather than made explicit.[23]

A comprehensive understanding of the problem of inversion and interruption can only unfold as our reading of *CE* progresses. But what can we already say to clarify this problem? A part of the problem with inversion/interruption is the problem of monism and dualism. On the one hand, Bergson cannot and does not renounce the monism attained in *MM*. Between body and soul, between the material and the spiritual, there are certainly differences but these do not lie between a material and an immaterial world. The traditional material-immaterial distinction is reconfigured by Bergson as one of *forms of temporal organisation*. Indeed, even the more fundamental distinction between matter and time is redefined. Matter as such is inscribed within duration. The material has become and will remain a degree of the temporal. There are different degrees of contraction which are degrees of action, and they range from

---

[20] Gilles Deleuze, "Bergson's Conception of Difference" in John Mullarkey ed, *The New Bergson* (Manchester: Manchester University Press, 1999), 55.

[21] On memory in *Creative Evolution*, see 498-9, 508/3-4, 11.

[22] Bergson, *Creative Evolution*, 666/129. See also 672-3, 681, 683, 696, 703/134-5, 140, 143, 152, 157-8, where Bergson repeatedly uses the two in a single sentence without clear distinction.

[23] Jankélévitch, *Bergson*, 175.

freedom to (near) necessity. There is no epiphenomenalism or any doubling of reality. Perception is not a copy of the world but a part of, because *selection* of, the world.[24] Although Bergson speaks of the difference between the spiritual and the material, the spiritual is not immaterial and the material is not aspiritual. Rather, both exist as tendencies and not as separate worlds.

The problem of monism and dualism first came up in an article from 1912 by the Rev. Joseph de Tonquédec entitled "M. Bergson, est-il moniste?"[25] De Tonquédec asked whether there is a place in the philosophy of Bergson for God as a reality distinct from that of the world. To this he answers in the negative: "Nowhere do we perceive a creative act as heterogeneous to what it creates".[26] Because, according to De Tonquédoc, Bergson denies transcendence, Bergsonism is a form of monism.[27] Interestingly Bergson did not agree and responded that a free and creative God was rather a *consequence* of *CE*: God may be seen as that out of which both matter and life spring forth.[28] However, a spiritual world, or God, or *duration,* as existing alongside the material world in some quasi-material parallel world clearly is not Bergson's position. Hence the idea of a Creator-God as both a separate reality and at the same time active in this world would have to be denied. All action and all movement, be they of matter or of life, take place in one and the same world. Although Bergson was of Jewish origin, he later came to believe in Catholicism as a more perfect form of faith. In his last work *TSMR*, Bergson discussed the great Catholic mystics. It is in active participation within the creativity of existence itself that the mystic becomes one with

---

[24] This is developed by Bergson in *MM*. Here too, see chapter V of my aforementioned thesis.

[25] Partially reprinted in the supplements to the *L'évolution créatrice,* edition: "Le choc Bergson", ed. Frédéric Worms (Paris: PUF, 2008), 618-33.

[26] Ibid, 627.

[27] Ibid, 620.

[28] In a private letter to De Tonquédec that was later published with Bergson's permission (in ibid, 632). Also reproduced in Henri Bergson, *Mélanges* (Paris: PUF, 1972), 964. Note that this exchange took place prior to Bergson's later adherence to Catholicism. Although he never converted, because (as he said in the last years of the life and leading up to the Second World War) he wanted to "stay among the persecuted", he did ask for and was granted the Catholic funeral rites. See Philip Soulez and Frédéric Worms, *Bergson: Biographie* (Flammerion, 1997), 227.

God. God indeed is the mystery of creation, but this creation takes place everywhere within the very heart of life.[29]

Although all is movement or action or duration, this does not mean that all actions are of the same kind. To return to the passage discussed above, Bergson is insistent that there is a real difference between the organised and the unorganised. Jankélévitch writes: "What Bergson denounced and pursued without relent, both with the Spencerians as with the Romantics [think here again of Fichte—MK], is the idea of a single or unique science, whether this be grounded on the notion of life, or on the notion of a mechanistic causality."[30] Although all actions take place in the same world, there are different kinds of causes at work in the organised and the unorganised, working in diverging directions. On the one hand, there is the interminable degradation of "downward" material changes; on the other hand, there is true creation of the forms of life. Both these developments or tendencies are real, different, and opposed to one another. Hence Bergson now also refers to them as forces. There are two forces and they are both "absolute".[31] Hence materiality is also an absolute. Where in *MM* Bergson understood materiality as the lowest degree of duration and space a mere intellectual abstraction effected by us on the world, now materiality attains its own positivity. This allows Bergson to address a problem that appeared in his account from *MM*. If materiality is a true tendency of the real, then the abstraction we effect on it and that from which results our schema of space is not *ins Blaue hinein*. This then allows him to account for mathematics. But if materiality is also an absolute, how can it at the same time be *a mere degree* of spirituality? This, then, is the problem that inversion/interruption aims to address.

III. Spirituality and Materiality

Bergson criticises science and philosophy for having assumed the unity, or we could say *univocity,* of existence. From his Doctoral Thesis on "the immediate data of consciousness" onwards[32], Bergson consistently

---

[29] Bergson, *Oeuvres* 1162. Translation: Henri Bergson, *The Two Sources of Morality and Religion*, trans. R.A. Audra and Cloudsley Brereton (New York: Henry Holt, 1935), 209.

[30] Jankélévitch as cited approvingly by Canguilhem. See Georges Canguilhem, "Commentaire au troisième chapitre de *L'Évolution créatrice*" in *Annales bergsonienne* 3 "Bergson et la science" (2007), 130.

[31] Bergson, *Creative Evolution*, 664/128.

[32] This is the original title of *Time and Free Will* [*TFW*].

stressed that conscious phenomena, which include life, have a form of organisation different from that claimed to exist in a deterministic system. There is a rupture between the organised and the unorganised and as long as we do not see this as a qualitative difference we will inadvertently turn it into one of degree—which then leads us to posit no real difference between the deterministic, repetitive movements as perceived in the material world and the creative and unique actions of the living world. Not seeing this rupture means reconstructing the simplicity and totality of the *being-made* with fragments of the *already-made* (like Spencer or Fichte).

Life is the *modus vivendi* that results from two "currents" or two forms of organisation[33]: spirituality and materiality.[34] Although each strives to undo the work of the other, a delicate and dynamic balance is struck, and this is the living or "organised" body.[35] The spiritual force, as we know, is duration itself. It is a constant work of integrating the present into the past and of pushing the concentrated experience of the past into the future. Duration, which is of the temporal order, is not restricted in the way that matter would be: being essentially continuous, all actions reverberate throughout the system. And all these actions continue all the actions of the past. Hence it is a Whole that swells in its entirety, one gigantic memory. Therefore, life conceived as duration is irreversible, cannot be repeated and is unique *de jure*. Life as duration is an *ascent* to ever higher integration and concentration.

The material tendency constitutes a *downward* change. The second law of thermodynamics states that physical changes tend to degrade into heat and that heat is distributed in a progressively uniform manner throughout the system. "It tells us that changes that are visible and heterogeneous will be more and more diluted into changes that are invisible and homogeneous, and that the instability to which we owe the richness and variety of the changes taking place in our solar system will gradually give way to the relative stability of elementary vibrations continually and perpetually repeated".[36] Materiality is a tendency towards homogeneity and repetition. Such a tendency Bergson sees as an *unmaking of matter itself*.[37] This is something life cannot stop or reverse; it cannot even free itself from it: "Incapable of *stopping* the course of material changes downwards, it succeeds in *retarding* it".[38] In Chapter Two, Bergson shows

---

[33] Bergson, *Creative Evolution*, 706/160. See also 784-5/218-9.
[34] Ibid, 666/129.
[35] Ibid, 704/158.
[36] Ibid, 701/156.
[37] Ibid, 702-4 *passim*, 725/157-9, 174.
[38] Ibid, 703/158.

how life strives to store some of the Sun's dissipated heat through the chlorophyllian function of plants. The leaves of plants thus created in turn serve as energy to animals, recycling the Sun's energy even further.[39] Life recycles entropic heat-loss, passing it from organism to organism.

Living organisms are the dynamic result of the two processes. On the one hand, life is the constant creation of form; it is a "generative force".[40] Life is an *élan vital*, a vital impulse.[41] On the other hand, life is "attached to matter"[42]; it undergoes the resistance of matter[43] and is continually threatened to be *unmade* by matter. Because life needs matter, life is a *limited* force.[44] Because the living organism is the result of a tendency towards spirituality and a tendency towards materiality Bergson writes:

> For, as soon as we are confronted with true duration, we see that it means creation, and that, if that which unmakes itself endures [se qui se défait dure], it can only be because it is inseparably bound to what is making itself.[45]

The *enduring of what is being unmade* is the living body and this is something that is *making itself* against its constant "unmaking". The "self-making" aspect is the spiritual tendency, the "unmaking" aspect the material one. The living organism uses or reorganises matter. But this matter is a constant dissipation of organisation. The living organism needs to constantly repair the entropic damage of materiality.

Most of the effort of the organism will be spent in maintaining a fine balance between destruction and creation. But as Bergson remarks in the footnote on death to which I have already alluded, life is not interested in any particular individual, but only in the whole.[46] It hopes that somewhere along the line a *surplus* might be created[47], and this is the true purpose of life. This surplus is the aim of the true *creative* effort of life; the moment it not only overcomes obstacles but is truly free.

The living organism should not be seen as an individual thing but as (part of) a process, again part of other, higher-level processes of species-life, etc. Or rather, the living organism is the *modus vivendi* of *two*

---

[39] Ibid, 585-609/69-88.

[40] Ibid, 636/107.

[41] See, for example, ibid 569-78/57-63.

[42] Ibid, 703/158.

[43] Ibid, 578, 592-3/64, 75.

[44] See, for example, ibid 504, 602, 618, 621-2/8, 82, 92, 96, 97

[45] Ibid, 785/219 (translation modified). See also 666/129.

[46] Ibid, 704n/158n.

[47] Ibid, 629/102.

processes: a making and an *unmaking*. As an *unmaking*, the living organism is no different from matter with its entropic tendencies. But clearly it is not in its *unmaking* that the organised differs from the unorganised, or that life differs from inert matter: it is its "making of itself", its *se faisant*, that sets it apart. It is this self-making that Bergson constantly tries to explain. As we know this involves memory, duration, creation.

Although Bergson rejects all notions of intrinsic finality (i.e. taking the individual organism as purpose, rather than the whole of life), he does end this remarkable section on "Mankind" by speaking of the destiny of life as the conquest of matter, and "perhaps even death".[48] We may speculate that the overcoming of death (as well as his remarks at the closing of his very last work, *TSMR*, concerning the universe as a "machine for the making of gods"[49]) has everything to do with this surplus. It is the surplus which life (perhaps wholly unwittingly) creates, that allows a creature to appear that is able to *reflect* on its own conditions. Such reflection, pursued in a mystical direction, contains the potential that life overcomes its differentiation to become one again with itself.

We know that for Bergson materiality is a tendency towards homogeneity, repetition and dispersion. An analogous state, he writes, is what we find when we let go of effort, when we detach from the past and future to reach a state without will or memory. At its limit "we get a glimpse of an existence made of a present which recommences unceasingly—devoid of real duration, nothing but the instantaneous which dies and is born again endlessly".[50] Although we might think that for Bergson to relax from past and future would lead one to experience true duration, instead the opposite occurs. For Bergson, duration is not a static *hic et nunc*; duration is continuity, effort and action, a point he will extensively develop in *TSMR*. When we detach ourselves from will and memory, we detach ourselves from duration, and what we then experience is not duration but materiality within us. Materiality is a "letting go".[51]

We see here that for Bergson existence is not simply action, but *creation*. Life is not merely *l'évolution créative*, a "creative" or innovative evolution, but *l'évolution créatrice*, a "creating" (as in *productive*) evolution.[52] This partly explains his later judgement that Buddhism did not

---

[48] Ibid, 721-5/171-3.

[49] Bergson, *Two Sources*, 1245/306.

[50] Bergson, *Creative Evolution*, 666/129.

[51] See, for example, ibid 675/137.

[52] I want to thank Frank Chouraqui for having pointed this difference out to me.

attain the highest spirituality.[53] For Buddhism life indeed is *créatrice,* but it is not interested in its *créative* side, for productive creativity is seen as the very source of suffering. Life maintains its *individuality* because of its incessant effort to create. Such creation is both a source of pleasure and of suffering, but even this pleasure is never true pleasure because it is always bound up with instrumentality—that is, with the attaining of a result. This, for Buddhism, cannot but lead to more suffering. That is why it ignores the *creative* or innovative side. For Buddhism individuality is tantamount to suffering and only a return to the Whole can bring true joy.[54] Although Bergson too stresses that we should let go of our practical attitude to become one again with the cosmos, he cannot let go of the idea of action as production. For Bergson true joy always remains bound up with growth.[55]

IV. A Manichean Opposition

Life as a *modus vivendi* of a spiritual force and a material force leads to a rather Manichean account of existence. It sees life as composed of Good and Evil. We can never completely root out Evil as all things partake of Evil, but we must constantly strive to rid ourselves of it and aim to ascend to the Good alone. Bergson:

> Consciousness and matter appear to us, then, as radically different forms of existence, even as antagonistic forms, which have to find a modus vivendi.[56]

Vladimir Jankélévitch, probably the most erudite of Bergson's commentators, clearly takes this line when on two occasions he speaks of matter and intellect as a necessary evil.[57] For him life in essence has no need for a

---

[53] Bergson, *Two Sources,* 1165-9/213-7.

[54] My profound gratitude goes out to the Ven. Ajahn Khemadhammo for all his generous *dhamma* during my years at the Warwick Buddhist Society. For a reading that explores Bergson's similarities with Zen-Buddhism, see M. Yamaguchi, *The Intuition of Zen and Bergson* (PhD Thesis: University of Fribourg, 1969). For a Buddhist inspired exploration of the notion of immediate experience in Bergson see Jan Bor, *Bergson en de onmiddelijke ervaring* (Amsterdam: Boom, 1990).

[55] See Bergson, *Oeuvres,* 832-3. Translation: Henri Bergson, "Life and Consciousness" in *Mind-Energy,* ed. Keith Ansell Pearson and Michael Kolkman, trans. H. Wildon Carr (Basingstoke: Palgrave Macmillan, 2007), 22-3.

[56] Ibid, 824/13.

[57] Jankélévitch, *Bergson,* 169, 177.

body and the only true reality is the creative effort of life itself.[58] The body is there and needs to be dealt with, but it is really only a negative reality: "The body represents a partial interruption of life, in the same way as the idea is a negation of thought and rest is a negation of movement."[59]

But does this not conflict with the account given in Chapter IV of *MM*, he asks?[60] No, because there is also an essential form of cooperation between the two. The answer as to how this is supposed to work exhibits an ambiguity that is quite particular to the issue we are after. Matter, or incarnation, has an important function to play in bringing out an important quality of life, but at the same time it should not be seen as a thing—rather as a tendency that opposes life.

Matter is not only a necessary evil; it also makes that life *pour soi* and not just *en soi*.[61] Matter constitutes an obstacle or a resistance and it is this that makes life into the creative effort that it is: "*Elle provoque l'effort*".[62] We could say that life without the resistance of matter would be unlimited or absolute. Bergson:

> For we feel that a divinely creative will or thought is too full of itself, in the immensity of its reality, to have the slightest idea of a lack of order or a lack of being.[63]

Such an unbounded will would lack any exteriority or, to speak with Fichte, it would lack an *Anstoß*. As Jankélévitch states, life could have been possible without matter or body but then there would have been no *élan* and no evolution.[64] Matter thus calls forth the creative effort of life and forces life to focus itself.[65]

But, Jankélévitch notes, Bergson also affirms monism, and this question of monism and dualism, he writes, is one of the most complex of questions within Bergsonism.[66] Only life is real, and matter endures solely through its "solidarity" with life. As Canguilhem says in language strongly reminiscent of Fichte: "The only positivity is that which can posit [*poser*], which means to create, and this is spirit. Matter is nothing but the fatigue

---

[58] Ibid, 168
[59] Ibid.
[60] Ibid, 170.
[61] Ibid.
[62] Ibid, 171.
[63] Bergson, *The Creative Mind*, 1304/62-3.
[64] Jankélévitch, *Bergson*, 172.
[65] Ibid, 171.
[66] Ibid, 173.

[*défaillance*] of this creation."[67] The two are not opposing principles, but two inverse *movement* or tendencies, and this is the second aspect that Jankélévitch mentions. Matter and space do not exist as such; they only have their existence in duration or spirituality. There is, Jankélévitch writes, a monism of substance and a dualism of tendencies.[68] Yet, hardly having written this down, Jankélévitch seems immediately to contradict himself: the material tendency is an "anti-vital" tendency, that "goes against", "reverses", or "resists", the effort of consciousness, and this tendency *is* something.[69] To make matters even more confusing, although there is a monism of substance, both the vital and the anti-vital tendency must have the same dwelling (*foyer*): "because the tendencies only exist in a will in which they have their source."[70] If this is a monism, then how to explain the, at least *prima facie,* positive nature of the two tendencies? Jankélévitch concludes that there is a "transactional" solution, which Bergson was "only able to indicate", that shows life always torn asunder (*dechirée*) and incessantly turning between (*tourbillonne sur place*) the two tendencies of life and death, good and evil.[71]

Georges Canguilhem, lecturing on Chapter III of *CE* during the Second World War, discusses in more detail what such a transactional account might be. The problem is made more difficult because, as we know, Bergson claimed to have written each book while forgetting the others. Canguilhem quotes from "Introduction: Part II", where Bergson writes that, because each problem demanded a unique effort, the theory of body and soul as presented in *MM* could not have been extracted from the theory on the immediate data of consciousness, as equally the theory of evolution could not have been extracted from that of body and soul.[72] Canguilhem concludes:

> If, therefore, it is impossible to reduce the matter of CE to the matter of MM, it is in the relation between matter and the evolution of life that we must search for its justification. In MM it is the relation between the matter of the individually organised body and the individual consciousness that is studied. In CE it is the relation between cosmic matter and universal consciousness in its organisational effort that is studied.[73]

---

[67] Canguilhem, "Commentaire", 150.
[68] Jankélévitch, *Bergson*, 174.
[69] Ibid.
[70] Ibid.
[71] Ibid, 175.
[72] Canguilhem, "Commentaire", 139. See Bergson, *The Creative Mind*, 1329-30/89-90.
[73] Canguilhem, "Commentaire", 139.

In *MM* it was the body that was said to limit the totality of the soul. The soul, or the spiritual, is what participates in duration. Duration is a totality of action-reaction. From this totality the body selects what is of interest to the organism. It is the body that brings the spirit to focus. In order to demonstrate this, all Bergson needed was a body and its needs. But to show the *unity* of body and soul Bergson, in the second part of that work, then changes perspective. Duration and space are shown to allow for degrees of contraction and relaxation and this made it possible to solve the triple opposition of the extended and the unextended, of quantity and quality, and of necessity and freedom. These two accounts in *MM*, a practical one and a contemplative one, are not harmonious. On the first account the individual body must be assumed as already given. In that work it is said that it is life *itself* that effects a primary discontinuity between the living organism and that which may serve to satisfy it. But *how and why* this happens was left unanswered by Bergson. Why are there "centres of action", why does life display an essential lack? Nor did the second account help answer this question. Different degrees of contraction may be said to give us general conditions for individuation, but not specific, and certainly not *vital* conditions for individuation.

We have seen that this is what *CE* set out to demonstrate. In contrast to *MM*, Bergson no longer assumes the existence of an individually organised body but, as Canguilhem indicates in the quote above, Bergson now asks after the relations between a *cosmic* materiality and the organisational efforts of *universal* consciousness. How, and more especially, *why* does life organise itself into bodies? What is the relation between the individual and the species, between the individual and society? How is materiality both an obstacle to be overcome and the essential embodiment for life?

We start to see more clearly that the question of the *role and function* of the body and the question of the *unity* of body and soul consist in two different gnoseologies. The first gnoseology, "with a view to action", is a practical perspective, the other, we could say, a contemplative perspective. From a practical point of view, body and soul serve different functions and consist of different realities. From a contemplative point of view, body and soul express different degrees of one unifying principle of duration. The problem of interruption and inversion is not simply that of reconciling the unitary and oppositional aspects of life (one world but with real difference between the organised and the unorganised, the One and the Many, different multiplicities), but it also involves the reconciliation of two ways of understanding and interacting with the world (action and contemplation). The difference between *MM* and *CE* lies not between conflicting accounts of reality. Rather, the problem in *CE* is how to unify two accounts of body and soul with two modes of understanding and interacting with the world, a dual account that, in fact, was already implicit in *MM*.

Bergson wants to show how interruption and inversion mean the same thing. But when I quoted him above I omitted the sentence that follows. Here Bergson goes on to say: "This presumption [that inversion means interruption—MK] is confirmed when we consider things from the point of view of extension, and no longer from that of duration alone."[74] The solution to the question of interruption and inversion lies in seeing reality, not from the perspective of duration *alone*, but *also* from the point of view of *extension*. It is not a case of showing that inversion by itself means interruption, but that we may understand reality under two aspects, or that we interact with the world in two different ways, ways that correspond to two aspects of reality itself. On the one hand, there is the point of view of action ("extension") for which matter and spirit are oppositional, and, on the other hand, there is the point of view of contemplation or intuition for which matter and spirit are two degrees of difference within one world of duration. It is when we consider reality from both points of view and when we contemplate the difference between action and contemplation that we understand how interruption means inversion. Although Jankélévitch and Canguilhem both intimate this "transactional" solution, they do not pay enough attention to the constant and subtle *movement between* the two perspectives that an understanding of life requires. For Bergson, the truth lies neither in pure intuition, nor in conceptual explication, but in a constant going backwards and forwards *between* them.

V. Action and Contemplation

In distinguishing between two aspects of reality and two modes of knowing and interacting with the world, Bergson continues the transcendental project of understanding life. "We necessarily express ourselves by means of words and we usually think in terms of space".[75] These were the very first lines that Bergson wrote. Although "thinking in space" is completely legitimate for the practical domain, when "the habits formed in action find their way up to the sphere of speculation... they create fictitious problems, [and so] metaphysics must begin by dispersing

---

[74] Bergson, *Creative Evolution*, 666/129.
[75] Bergson, *Oeuvres*, 3. Translation: Henri Bergson, *Time and Free Will*, trans. F.L. Pogson (London: Allen and Unwin, 1959), xix.

this artificial obscurity".[76] This oldest and most persistent of Bergsonian themes is an appropriation of the critical distinction between knowledge and philosophical reflection. Where knowledge concerns *what we know*, philosophy after Kant asks, how is this knowledge possible? It asks after the conditions for the intelligibility of knowledge. This question cannot be asked by empirical knowledge itself, since this would only result in a description, or enumeration, of various ideas, and not in a thinking through. It would not give us *a priori* conditions. Bergson, writing at the start of the twentieth century, makes essentially the same point when he writes that we are doomed to repeat the contingencies of human culture and history if we do not reflect critically on how understanding has come about.[77]

In all his works, there are certain misunderstandings that Bergson never fails to criticise. These misunderstandings, in fact, share the same root which lies in not properly distinguishing between the practical perspective and the contemplative perspective. Thus arise the confused ideas of the primacy of the possible over the virtual, the trajectory over movement, disorder over order, the complex over the simple, absence over presence, and space over duration. These ideas all have the same origin, namely, "that we import into speculation a procedure made for practice".[78]

Our perceptive and cognitive faculties are not given to us without purpose. In *MM*, Bergson shows that perception really is part of our action on things. A substantial part of *CE* is devoted to showing how our intellect cannot but reduce real becoming to stable states, movement to trajectories and the living to the inert. For Bergson the intellect is a faculty of action; it helps us survive and as long as it restricts itself to its task it may be said to "touch the absolute", i.e. be adequate to the object at hand.

But if we want to understand how life, not from its "fragments" but the constant and progressive effort that is life, we will have to break away from the habits of practical thought in order to think anew. To truly know life we must make thought participate in life—something Bergson names: being in intellectual sympathy with life.[79] This perspective, which unfortunately I will not be able to fully develop here, allows us to

---

[76] Bergson, *Oeuvres*, 168. Translation: Henri Bergson, *Matter and Memory*, trans. N.M. Paul and W.S. Palmer (New York: Zone Books, 1991), 16. Translation modified.

[77] Bergson, *Creative Evolution*, 492/xxxvii.

[78] Ibid, 726/175.

[79] Bergson, *Oeuvres*, 1421. Translation (of the 1903 edition): Henri Bergson, *An Introduction to Metaphysics*, ed. John Mullarkey and Michael Kolkman, trans. T.E. Hulme (Basingstoke: Palgrave Macmillan, 2007), 40

understand the fundamental continuity, interpenetration and participation of all things living in life understood as duration. Yet, as we have seen in Bergson's criticisms of Spencer and Fichte, we normally reduce life to the *ready-made* of the living body. We thus transpose the categories of practical thought into the sphere of speculation. Practical thought is oriented towards the fulfilment of needs. Hence it starts from a perceived situation of lack and works towards the presence of the desired object. But when this schema of the primacy of lack is transposed onto the nature of reality itself, the question becomes: What was there before there was duration? What was there before life? Why is there something rather than nothing? The perceived primacy of nothingness, disorder, the inert, and the immobile results from confusing a schema adequate to action with what is proper to contemplation. Although from a practical point of view we understand that first there is nothing before there can be something (it first needs to be created), all the analyses of conscious phenomena and life show the undeniable and irreducible positivity or spontaneity of these phenomena. But this is precisely what we cannot see from a practical perspective. Hence a (methodical) effort is required, a going against the normal habits of thought. If we do not keep the two well apart, then we will surreptitiously be lead to assume that what is appropriate to practical thought is applicable to the speculative.

The influential Swiss Catholic theologian Hans Urs von Balthasar noted the same disparity between these two accounts within Bergson's thought. In an extraordinary six-page article "La philosophie de la vie chez Bergson et chez les allemands modern", written on Bergson's death in 1941, he discusses the difficulty a philosophy of life has in accounting for values and Spirit.[80] A philosophy of life, Balthasar writes, must be at the same time both monist and dualist. It must be monist in that only Life can be its first principle; yet it must be dualist in relation to Value and Spirit. On the one hand Value and Spirit are seen by a philosophy of life as mere limits, as a mere alienation of life. Balthasar quotes Nietzsche: "There where life petrifies, the Law erects itself."[81] Values are secondary and parasitical and must be criticised from the point of view of Life which alone holds truth. And so we have seen Bergson appealing on numerous

---

[80] Hans Urs von Balthasar, "La philosophie de la vie chez Bergson et chez les allemands modernes" in Béguin and Thévanez eds, *Henri Bergson*, 264-70. It is the only entry by von Balthasar found in P.A.Y. Gunter, *Henri Bergson: A Bibliography* (Bowling Green, Ohio: Philosophy Documentation Center, 1986).
[81] As quoted in Balthasar, "La philosophie de la vie", 266.

occasions to the experience of duration as the only true arbiter.[82] Value and Spirit must subject themselves *to life* and not the other way around.

On the other hand, the "vital necessities" of Life reserve for themselves the right to reformulate a new "kingdom of values" that better express Life's values. Indeed, it is only in this way that a philosophy of life escapes its reduction to a form of "brutal amoralism".[83] Although Life is the only court of appeal, Life does not speak to us directly, but only ever *through us*. Because the only sense we can make of things is the sense that *we make*, we must express Life through Spirit and Value. It must be expressed through both Spirit and Value if we do not want our lives reduced to life's basest instincts. A philosophy of life is thus bound to a "hybrid couple" of Force and Value, Life and Spirit.[84] It is a hybrid couple because Value and Spirit are always secondary to Life, yet Life cannot do without Value and Spirit.

The ambiguous relation of Life and Value that one finds in the German philosophers of life, one also finds in the Jewish philosopher Bergson, writes Balthasar. We find in Bergson two diametrically opposed systems.[85] The first one has as its centre the intensity of duration and creation. It is only at its periphery that we find matter. We may think here of the interruption thesis. The other, writes Balthasar, is found in *MM*—this sees the maximum of intensity in pure perception, in a plane of action purified of memory and with maximum detension in pure memory. Pure memory and pure perception are brought to one single focal point in the present action. This present is what is most intense, whereas detension increases as we move up in memory.

When we approach the two systems from the side of the nature of action, the opposition becomes clearer, writes Balthasar. The first system sees true authentic action residing in the effort of the creative mind. Here the practical is merely "an indirect and distant reflection" of it.[86] It is Life that is true reality and Form, Value and Matter are only derivative. These we have come to understand as so many relatively closed circuits of action-reaction, of habit and of the loss of interest. But in the second system it is practical life itself; it is the present that is itself the centre of action.[87] Both in the theory of pure perception, as in the continuity of duration in the second part of *MM,* the present is *the* reality and this is a

---

[82] See, for example, Bergson, *The Creative Mind*, 1329-30/89-90.
[83] Balthasar, "La philosophie de la vie", 267.
[84] Ibid, 268.
[85] Ibid, 268-70.
[86] Ibid, 269.
[87] Ibid.

continuity and holism of action and reaction. Matter here is the effect of selection, of a cutting-up of continuity under the exigencies of need.

If we dig even deeper, we find that behind the two lie two forms of *ressentiment*: the action-as-effort of the first system displays hostility to the "geometric rationality" that "empties" life of its intelligible and teleological structures.[88] The confusion of duration with space reduces life and creativity to mechanism and determinism. The second system, action-as-present-totality, displays hostility to "pure spirit" that impedes the full immersion in the Whole of life and action. The two are opposed, writes Balthasar, as mystic contemplation and action.[89]

These triple pairs appear to be presented to line up as follows:

From the point of view of *intensity* there is an opposition between:
(a) creative effort as the most intense; matter is a letting-go, an unmaking (*interruption*).
(b) continuity of duration in the present is most intense; extensity and space are homogeneous and discrete (*inversion*).

From the point of view of *action* there is an opposition between:
(a) the true action that is creative effort; the practical a *derivative* perspective.
(b) practical reality itself that is true action; space a mere *abstraction*.

From the point of view of *resentment* there is a:
(a) hostility to geometric rationality that makes life *unintelligible* (*contemplation*).
(b) hostility to pure spirit that impedes *immersion* in Life (*action*).

Although there is much that is profound in what Balthasar writes, and although I fully recognise the limitations on any article of this length, a feeling of confusion seems irrepressible when we line the three pairs up in this way.[90] From a practical or creative perspective, matter is both an obstacle and the very material with which I work. Matter is assumed as that what is both given to and distinct from myself. The true creative effort is to make something new with the old. The practical and the habitual must be unmade for novelty to appear. This requires effort. But when I want to understand life, I see that life is spontaneous, continuous and wholly positive. The present is a continuity and it is from this perspective that I see that the divisions to which we cling are so many effects of the practical

---

[88] Ibid.
[89] Ibid, 270.
[90] A confusion I will readily admit to be my own when this is shown.

nature of life itself. Matter as ready-made and distinct is an effect both of how I am inclined to see things and of the need for life to create habits for itself. True action is *here,* is *everything,* and it makes itself whether I actively take part in it or not.

But then Balthasar seems to be saying that the second, speculative attitude, the one that sees the continuity of duration as true reality, is hostile to the pure spirit that impedes my *immersion* into the totality of Life, *and that this is the attitude of action.* The first one, the one I claimed was a practical and creative attitude, the effort *against* habit, would, on Balthasar's account, be hostile to the confused geometric rationality that makes life *unintelligible*—and this is the attitude of *contemplation.* Yet it seems to make little sense to say that the practical, creative attitude concerns contemplation and that the speculative concerns action.

Yet there is a sense to this. Although the speculative mind *sees* or understands the continuity and totality of life, it remains unable to immerse itself in life. Although intellectually it understands its embeddedness in life, it remains thoroughly detached from life; life considered as *action.* Hence the speculative mind is *alienated* from itself. The creative mind, on the contrary, sees or knows nothing of the continuity of all action; it sees only obstacles and habits which lie in the way of creation. Yet, in unmaking what was made and making it into something new it is profoundly one with life. But creating does not mean taking part in Spirit and Value. Participation does not entail reflection. When it does reflect on Life (which inevitably it must), it remains locked in the practical attitude. It attempts to raise itself to the speculative, but being unable to detach itself from the practical, it is unable to unmix what is proper to the practical and what is proper to the contemplative. It is unable to make the effort to go against the habits of thought and ends up with a ratiocination of Life. In desiring to understand Life, it raises the practical to the Ideal and hence comes to desire the Truth of Life as One, Immobile, Unchanging and Transparent. The practical attitude, now as a *form of understanding,* and aimed at oneness with life, desires the end of life, the nothing or nihilism.

Where the philosopher's mind, in contemplating life, is detached from the creative *élan* of life, it wants to *immerse* itself in life, because it feels alienated from creative life. It thus reacts against itself, against the "pure spirit" that impedes its own immersion. Being contemplation it *desires action.* The creative mind, being action but not yet Spirit, wants to *understand* Life, but finds itself unable to contemplate Life without mixing in its practical attitude. It creates for itself the geometric rationality that reduces life to a Truth One and Unchanging. Being essentially action it desires contemplation and reacts against the pseudo-contemplation it has created for itself. Balthasar saw very clearly that this opposition of action and contemplation can never be solved in "pure contemplation" alone.[91] Indeed as Bergson himself said later in his life: "One must act as a man of thought, and think like a man of action".[92]

Bibliography

Balthasar, Hans Urs von. "La philosophie de la vie chez Bergson et chez les allemands modernes." In Béguin and Thévanez edited, *Henri Bergson*. 264-270.

Béguin, Albert and P. Thévanez edited. *Henri Bergson. Essais et témoignages resueillis*. Neuchatel: Éditions de la Baconnière, 1943.

Bergson, Henri. *The Two Sources of Morality and Religion*. Translated by R.A. Audra and Cloudsley Brereton. New York: Henry Holt, 1935.

—. *Time and Free Will*. Translated by F.L. Pogson. London: Allen and Unwin, 1959.

—. *Oeuvres*. Paris: PUF, 1959.

—. *Mélanges*. Paris: PUF, 1972.

—. "Fichte (cours inédit)." In Henri Bergson and Octave Hamelin, *Fichte*. Strasbourg: Presses Universitaires de Strasbourg, 1988.

—. *Matter and Memory*. Translated by N.M. Paul and W.S. Palmer. New York: Zone Books, 1991.

—. *The Creative Mind*. Translated by M.L. Andison. New York: Citadel Press, 2002

—. *An Introduction to Metaphysics*. Edited by John Mullarkey and Michael Kolkman. Translated by T.E. Hulme. Basingstoke: Palgrave Macmillan, 2007

—. *Creative Evolution*. Edited by Keith Ansell Pearson, Michael Kolkman, and Michael Vaughan. Translated by A. Mitchell. Basingstoke: Palgrave Macmillan, 2007.

—. *Mind-Energy*. Edited by Keith Ansell Pearson and Michael Kolkman. Translated by Carr, H. Wildon. Basingstoke: Palgrave Macmillan, 2007.

—. *L'Évolution créatrice. Le choc Bergson*. Paris: PUF, 2008.

Bor, Jan. *Bergson en de onmiddelijke ervaring*. Amsterdam: Boom, 1990.

---

[91] Ibid.
[92] Bergson, *Mélanges*, 1537.

Canguilhem, Georges. "Commentaire au troisième chapitre de L'*Évolution créatrice*." *Annales bergsonienne* 3 "Bergson et la science" (2007): 113-160.

Deleuze, Gilles. 1999. "Bergson's Conception of Difference." In John Mullarkey edited, *The New Bergson*. Manchester: Manchester University Press, 1999. 42-65.

—. "Lecture Course on Chapter Three of Bergson's Creative Evolution." *SubStance* 114.3 "Henri Bergson's *Creative Evolution*" (2007): 72-90.

Fichte, Johann Gottlieb. *Foundations of Transcendental Philosophy (Wissenschaftslehre) novo methodo (1796/99)*. Ithaca: Cornell University Press, 1992.

Gunter, P.A.Y. *Henri Bergson: A Bibliography*. Bowling Green, Ohio: Philosophy Documentation Center, 1986.

Harpe, Jean de la. "Souvenirs personnels d'un entretien avec Bergson." In Béguin and Thévanez edited, *Henri Bergson*. 357-364.

Hyppolite, Jean. "Du Bergsonisme à l'existentialisme." In *Figures de la pensée philosophique*. Paris: PUF, 1971. 443-458.

Jankélévitch, Vladimir. *Henri Bergson*. Paris: PUF, 1999.

Kolkman, Michael. *Towards a Philosophy of Freedom: Fichte and Bergson*. PhD Thesis: University of Warwick, 2009.

Soulez, Philip, and Frédéric Worms. *Bergson, Biographie*. Flammerion, 1997.

Yamaguchi, M. *The Intuition of Zen and Bergson*. PhD Thesis: University of Fribourg, 1969.

CHAPTER FIVE

FROM THE REVOLUTION IN THINKING TO THE RENEWAL OF THINKING: THE SYSTEMATIC TASK OF *THE STAR OF REDEMPTION*

KARIN NISENBAUM

When *The Star of Redemption* was published in 1921, Franz Rosenzweig was profoundly disappointed by the reception of the book that was the culmination of his lifetime engagement with philosophy.[1] *The Star of Redemption* was initially read as a "Jewish book"[2] showing the way back to the old law. Yet in 1925 Rosenzweig writes "The New Thinking," an essay responding to the amicable "echo" the book had aroused during the first few years of its publication and explaining the content and structure of *The Star* in terms that would be more accessible to the layman. He makes it clear that *The Star* is not, at least in any straightforward sense, a "Jewish book," and it does not "claim to be a philosophy of religion." Instead, Rosenzweig insists that we understand his book as a "system of philosophy". He situates his greatest work at the end of a trajectory that begins with Kant's "Copernican Revolution" in philosophy and progresses through German Idealism, fulfilling the objectives of both movements by bringing about a "total renewal of thinking."[3]

What is the ancient task that Rosenzweig inherits from Kant and the German Idealists? Why does he hope to fulfil this task in the modern form of a philosophical system? And how can a modern system find meaningful

---

[1] I am grateful to Rick A. Furtak, Paul W. Franks, Benjamin Pollock, Ulrich Schlösser, and Sue Sinclair for perceptive comments and hospitable conversations, and to Stan Erraught for general support and encouragement.
[2] Franz Rosenzweig, "The New Thinking," in *Philosophical and Theological Writings,* trans. and ed. Paul W. Franks and Michael L. Morgan (Indianapolis: Hackett, 2000), 109.
[3] Ibid, 109-10.

expression through "old Jewish words"?[4] I wish to address these questions by taking seriously Rosenzweig's claim regarding the systematic nature of *The Star of Redemption*.[5] Sections I and II of my paper show that Rosenzweig inherits from Kant and the German Idealists the grounding task of metaphysics, and from the German Idealists the commitment that knowledge and experience be grounded through a holistic and monistic philosophical system. Sections III and IV focus on Hegel's discussion of morality in the *Phenomenology,* clarifying the conversion in our self-understanding in relation to the world and to others that Hegel holds to be necessary if we are to attain absolute knowledge. The movement of reconciliation between the acting conscience and the beautiful soul leads us to a new conception of the nature of knowledge, determining everything that is included in human experience through its role within a relational whole. Section V considers Rosenzweig's critique of Hegel's philosophical system; in Rosenzweig's view, Hegel's system fails to take into account the particularity of each being and divorces knowledge from our human vocation. Sections VI, VII, and VIII clarify how Rosenzweig hopes to remedy this failure. Rosenzweig takes as his starting point the threefold "nothing of our knowledge"[6] corresponding to the traditional three sciences of supersensible beings: theology, psychology, and cosmology, and shows how God, human beings, and the world secure their being by entering into reciprocal relations. The event of revelation names the "conversion"[7] that God, human beings, and the world undergo when entering into reciprocal relations. In the event of revelation, the freedom of each human being turns into the humble recognition that he or she is sufficiently loved; this recognition becomes manifest insofar as each

---

[4] Ibid, 131.

[5] By stressing the systematic nature of Rosenzweig's magnum opus, my reading of *The Star of Redemption* differs from existentialist and postmodern readings. Yet if it is important to situate Rosenzweig's thought within the Kantian and German Idealist traditions, it is also important to clarify his relation to existentialism and postmodernism. Rosenzweig shares with Kant no less than with Kierkegaard a concern about the different ways in which we can fail to inhabit our finitude, either by stepping beyond our boundaries or by becoming too complacent within them. My reading of *The Star* therefore differs from Benjamin Pollock's insofar as he wishes to distance Rosenzweig from these two families of philosophical positions. See Benjamin Pollock, *Franz Rosenzweig and the Systematic Task of Philosophy* (Cambridge: Cambridge University Press, 2009), 315.

[6] Franz Rosenzweig, *The Star of Redemption,* trans. Barbara E. Galli (Madison: University of Wisconsin Press, 2005), 29.

[7] Ibid, 98.

human being turns into redemptive relations with others and the world, taking his or her place in a relational whole.

I. Kant's Commitment to Dualism

Kant's "revolution in the way of thinking" seeks to address a complex set of problems that can be encompassed under the task that Kant first announces in the second edition Preface to the first *Critique*: to set metaphysics on the "secure path of a science."[8] Traditionally, the central task of metaphysics was to show that philosophy is a universal "science of truth"[9] capable of providing a reason or grounded explanation for everything that human experience includes: all beliefs, facts, and events. In order to provide a grounded explanation, everything that is conditioned must end in an unconditioned, absolute ground. The human soul, the cosmos, and God, the objects of the three rational sciences: psychology, cosmology, and theology[10], served distinct and indispensable explanatory roles in a scientific philosophical system.

Kant inherits from Leibniz this conception of the nature of reasons. The "principle of sufficient reason"[11] turns into the *Monistic Demand* that "every genuine grounding participate in a single systematic unity of grounds, terminating in a single absolute ground."[12] Yet like Leibniz, Kant also inherits the modern commitment to explain all phenomena naturalistically, through necessary physical laws. This issues in the *Dualistic Demand* that "physical grounding and metaphysical grounding be kept rigorously separate."[13] The world of nature must form a closed sphere. We can easily see why the modern commitment to naturalism threatens the possibility of metaphysics, at least as traditionally conceived. For how can we genuinely ground human experience if physical laws condition phenomena, and if we cannot ground physical phenomena in

---

[8] Immanuel Kant, *Critique of Pure Reason,* trans. and ed. Paul Guyer and Allen W. Wood (Cambridge: Cambridge University Press, 1998), Bxii.

[9] Aristotle, *Metaphysics,* trans. Hippocrates Apostle (Des Moines: Peripatetic Press, 1979), Book α 1, 993b20–32.

[10] Kant, *Critique of Pure Reason*, A335/B392.

[11] G.W. Leibniz, *Philosophical Essays,* trans. Roger Ariew and Daniel Garber (Indianapolis: Hackett, 1991), 217.

[12] Paul Franks, *All or Nothing: Systematicity, Transcendental Arguments, and Skepticism in German Idealism* (Cambridge, MA: Harvard University Press, 2005), 20.

[13] Ibid.

metaphysical substances and ultimately in God, the sole unconditioned or absolute ground?

Kant's critique of speculative metaphysics seeks to preserve the central explanatory task of metaphysics through a commitment to dualism or to "two orders of grounding."[14] This is his revolutionary insight. Insofar as the *phenomenal* world is grounded in and conditioned by necessary physical laws, it is finitely intelligible.[15] Yet we need to make positive claims about the *noumenal* so as to avoid entering into conflict with reason's unavoidable demand for the unconditioned. If we try to explain the nature of moral action, which presupposes the ability to freely determine our will through maxims that are in conformity with the moral law, although we are empirically determined by natural laws, reason legitimately demands that we think of ourselves as transcendentally real, free agents:

> Yet we are conscious through reason of a law to which all our maxims are subject, as if a natural order must at the same time arise from our will. This law must therefore be the idea of a nature not given empirically and yet possible through freedom, hence a supersensible nature to which we give objective reality at least in practical respect, since we regard it as an object of our will as pure rational beings.[16]

As rational beings conscious of the moral law within us, we can legitimately think of ourselves as unconditioned causes, providing a genuine grounding for moral action.

II. The German Idealist Commitment to Holistic Monism

If we turn our attention to the philosophical programs of German Idealism, we discover an entirely different conception of the nature of reasons and hence a different conception of how to fulfil the explanatory task of metaphysics. In the wake of the Spinozism controversy initiated by Friedrich Heinrich Jacobi in 1785, the German Idealists hold that Spinoza, rather than Leibniz or Kant, showed what is required if philosophy is to be capable of providing a grounded explanation for human experience: a

---

[14] Ibid, 9.
[15] See Paul W. Franks, "All or Nothing: Systematicity and Nihilism in Jacobi, Reinhold, and Maimon," in Karl Ameriks ed, *The Cambridge Companion to German Idealism* (Cambridge: Cambridge University Press, 2000), 101.
[16] Immanuel Kant, *Critique of Practical Reason,* trans. and ed. Mary Gregor (Cambridge: Cambridge University Press, 1997), 5:44.

genuine philosophical system must be *holistic* and *monistic*. Holistic Monism names a commitment to the view that everything included in human experience be determined through its role within a relational whole, and that the whole be grounded in an absolute principle that is immanent, not transcendent. This absolute principle is a principle of unity that makes a domain of objects intelligible.

Although the German Idealists commit to this view, they also take seriously Jacobi's claim that a philosophical system that is holistic and monistic leads to nihilism, for it denies the existence and independent subsistence of individual entities: "To be an entity is to be the individual locus of organic activity, determined both in contrast with other entities and in terms of some positive internal nature."[17] If *all properties* of empirical items are determined through a relational framework, and if we no longer have at our disposal the distinction between the phenomenal and the noumenal, no room is left for anything like a positive internal nature, which was held to be requisite for the exercise of freedom.[18] Thus, Jacobi argued that a holistic and monistic system would "annihilate the individuality of any person who actually came to believe it and live according to it."[19] His solution was to take a *"salto mortale"*[20] or life-risking leap to faith, to renounce the philosophical urge for comprehensive explanations and return to one's natural conviction that a personal God exists and that we are free.[21] The German Idealists do not follow Jacobi's

---

[17] Franks, "All or Nothing: Systematicity and Nihilism", 98.

[18] See Franks, *All or Nothing*, 140: "Holistic Monists see no role for intrinsic properties *whatsoever*...Thus, Fichte and Hegel undertake to show that one could have neither intellect nor will—neither theoretical nor practical reason—unless one were conscious of oneself as situated within a relational framework of objects other than one's body and of subjects other than oneself."

[19] Ibid, 10.

[20] Friedrich Heinrich Jacobi, *The Main Philosophical Writings and the Novel Alwill,* translated and edited by George di Giovanni (Montreal: McGill-Queen's University Press, 2009), 195.

[21] See ibid, 193: "I love Spinoza, because he, more than any other philosopher, has led me to the perfect conviction that certain things admit of no explication: one must not therefore keep one's eyes shut to them, but mast take them as one finds them. I have no concept more intimate than that of the final cause; no conviction more vital than that *I do what I think,* and not, *that I should think what I do.* Truly therefore, I must assume a source of thought and action that remains completely inexplicable to me." Although Jacobi's contemporaries understood him to be an irrationalist, urging a return to Christian faith and opposing reason, Paul W. Franks argues that Jacobi invokes a conception of *reason* that is in opposition to *rationalism*. See Franks, "All or Nothing: Systematicity or Nihilism", 99.

solution, yet they are concerned to construct a holistic and monistic philosophical system that does not end in nihilism. We will see that Rosenzweig's critique of German Idealism, and particularly his critique of Hegel's philosophical system, diagnoses the failure of this family of philosophical programmes to meet this internal criterion for success. Yet before we can understand Rosenzweig's critique, we need to understand how Hegel hopes to ground knowledge.

III. Absolute Knowing in Hegel's *Phenomenology of Spirit*

Hegel considered the *Phenomenology of Spirit* to serve as the introduction or propaedeutic to his philosophical system, arriving at an understanding of the nature of absolute knowledge and articulating a principle of unity between thought and being that would finally enable philosophy to "lay aside the title '*love* of knowing' and be *actual* knowing."[22] We are held out the promise of arriving at this point by following the path of "phenomenal knowledge"[23], which Hegel also calls the "movement of cognition"[24] or the "experience of consciousness."[25] Each shape or pattern of consciousness replicates a general schema, including a subject-object relation and a criterion of truth that the subject upholds as a standard grounding its claim to know an object.[26] In the Introduction to the *Phenomenology,* Hegel characterizes this general schema as follows: "For consciousness is, on the one hand, consciousness of the object, and on the other, consciousness of itself; consciousness of what for it is the True, and consciousness of its knowledge of the truth". Each shape or pattern of consciousness "tests" its criterion or standard of knowledge against the object that it tries to know, attempting to bridge the gap between subject and object: "Testing is not only a testing of what we know, but also a testing of the criterion of what knowing is." Through this process each shape of consciousness discovers that its standard of knowledge contradicts or fails to correspond to the object of knowledge, so the object itself does not "stand the test."[27] When each shape of consciousness renews this endeavour, its new standard includes and overcomes the contradiction from its previous attempt. This "dialectical

---

[22] G.W.F. Hegel, *Phenomenology of Spirit,* trans. A.V. Miller (Oxford: Oxford University Press, 1977), §5.
[23] Ibid, §77.
[24] Ibid, §802.
[25] Ibid, §88.
[26] Ibid, §89.
[27] Ibid, §85.

movement which consciousness exercises on itself and which affects both its knowledge and its object"[28] is what Hegel calls the experience of consciousness.

Hegel shows that the difference of knowledge and Truth, the gap between the subject and object of knowledge, can only be bridged when all attempts to determine the subject and object of knowledge in distinction from each other are revealed as self-contradictory, until the attempt is given up. Hence, the argument implicit in the experience of consciousness has the form of a *reductio ad absurdum*. It is worthwhile to pause and explain this idea, as Michael Forster does in *Hegel and Skepticism*:

> The thesis which Hegel sets out to reduce to absurdity in the *Phenomenology* concerns the distinctness of subject and object in general—or equivalently for Hegel, the distinctness of concept and instance in general… The demonstration in the Phenomenology… exhibits in serial fashion that each possible way in which the distinctness of a subject and object might be articulated (each shape of consciousness), and hence each way in which the distinctness of a concept and its instance might be articulated, is self-contradictory… proceeding to the self consistent viewpoint of Philosophical Science, at the point where the attempt to articulate a distinction between subject and object, and hence a concept and its instance, is given up.[29]

The attempt to uphold and articulate the thesis that a subject and object can be determined independently is given up when the parade of shapes of consciousness and shapes of Spirit[30] reaches its end and we arrive at the concept of absolute knowledge, which Hegel defines as the "concept in its truth, viz. in unity with its externalisation"[31] or "realization".[32] The prospect of arriving at this conception of the nature of knowledge is the promise that Hegel holds out to us in the *Phenomenology*. Let us recall how, in Hegel's account, we arrive at the last shape of consciousness.

---

[28] Ibid., §86.

[29] Michael Forster, *Hegel and Skepticism* (Cambridge, MA: Harvard University Press, 1989), 144.

[30] While each shape of consciousness replicates the general schema including a subject-object relation and a criterion of truth or standard of knowledge, each shape of Spirit attempts to fix the relation that holds between an individual and the community to which he or she belongs.

[31] Hegel, *Phenomenology of Spirit*, §795. Although Miller translates the term "Begriff" as "Notion", I follow Terry Pinkard's forthcoming translation and translate it as "concept".

[32] Ibid., §798.

"Absolute Knowing," the final chapter in the *Phenomenology,* summarizes the critical moments and transitions in the path of phenomenal knowledge, reminding us one last time how we arrived at the true concept of absolute knowledge. This final chapter takes us back to the section from the chapter on "Morality", entitled: "Conscience. The 'beautiful soul,' evil and its forgiveness," for Hegel believes that the movement of confession and delayed forgiveness between the acting "conscience"[33] and the "beautiful soul"[34] captures a conversion in our self-understanding in relation to our actions that applies to our self-understanding in relation to the world and to others,[35] and he believes that this conversion is the best way to explain the movement from what he calls the "simple unity of the concept" of absolute knowledge to the "true concept, or the concept that has attained its realization."[36] In the following section I wish to clarify the nature of this conversion.

IV. Acting Conscience and the Beautiful Soul: The Movement of Confession and Delayed Forgiveness

The section from the chapter on "Morality" entitled: "Conscience. The 'beautiful soul,' evil and its forgiveness" emerges directly out of the tensions and contradictions that are inherent in the Kantian moral view of the world. In Hegel's account, the most significant among these tensions are those between pure duty and moral action, between the transcendental realm of morality and the empirical world, and between universality and particularity. Morality requires that the moral law be the sole and supreme incentive of our actions, and that the intentions of our actions conform wholly to pure duty; it requires that morality be efficacious in a world governed by mechanistic laws of nature, and it requires that the maxims of our actions conform wholly to universal laws of pure reason. Exhausted by the attempt to resolve these tensions, moral conscience finds a solution by withdrawing into itself and finding the required adequation between pure duty and action in its own conscience, in the personal conviction or *immediate certainty* that what it does is right: "Duty is no longer the universal that stands over against the self; on the contrary, it is known to

---

[33] Ibid, §646.
[34] Ibid, §795.
[35] See Robert Pippin, "The 'logic of experience' as 'absolute knowledge' in *Hegel's Phenomenology of Spirit,"* in Dean Moyar and Michael Quante ed, *Hegel's Phenomenology of Spirit: A Critical Guide* (Cambridge: Cambridge University Press, 2008), 211.
[36] Hegel, *Phenomenology of Spirit,* §795.

have no validity when thus separated."[37] Moral conscience falls into its own, internal contradictions; what is significant is that it can only secure itself against the tensions and contradictions inherent to the moral worldview by withdrawing into its conviction, inuring itself against the judgment of others: "In the strength of its own self-assurance it possesses the majesty of absolute autarky, to bind and to loose. This self-determination is therefore without more ado absolutely in conformity with duty."[38]

The "beautiful soul," too, attempts to resolve the tensions and contradictions inherent in the moral view of the world. Yet it finds a solution by refraining from action. The "beautiful soul," Hegel shows us, "lacks the power to externalise itself, the power to make itself into a Thing, and to endure [mere] being. It lives in dread of besmirching the splendour of its *inner being* by action."[39] This does not keep it from judging the acting conscience and "holding fast to the disparity of the action with itself." Its beauty is maintained only through its critical stance.

The opposition between the acting conscience, which acts but does not subject its actions to the judgment of others, and the beautiful soul, which judges but does not act, begins to dissolve when the acting conscience perceives its identity with the beautiful soul. They are each in their own way attempting to resolve the tensions inherent to the moral view of the world. The attempt to meet the demands of morality has enfeebled both of them and opened a gap between them. The acting conscience confesses that it is "wicked", for this is what it means, from the moral worldview, for an action to result from an intention that is not wholly in conformity with moral duty. Yet it confesses with the expectation that the beautiful soul will reciprocate immediately and "put [itself] on the same level". It is only in the moments when the beautiful soul does not reciprocate that the acting conscience experiences the magnitude of the disparity between the intention and the action, and experiences this as a "loss of its own self."[40] In these moments, too, the locus of the disparity shifts; it is no longer experienced as the disparity between intention and action, but as the disparity in understanding that two persons can have of the meaning and scope of an action.

It is worthwhile to clarify why the experience of this disparity amounts to a loss of selfhood. Before and during its encounter with the beautiful soul, the acting conscience acts and understands its actions through the

---

[37] Ibid, §639.
[38] Ibid, §646.
[39] Ibid, §658.
[40] Ibid, §78.

"standard or default understanding of the distinction between actions and events in the modern Western tradition," where actions are conceived as events resulting from a particular, specifiable intention, and where the "proper focus for any explanation of an action is on this causally efficacious, determinate, prior mental state or intention, whether a passion or maxim."[41] An action is different from an event insofar as we can lead it back to our own self as the individual locus of agency. Starting from this understanding of the nature of action, we experience the unforgiven disparity between our intention and the action as a loss of selfhood, for what we lose is the authority or exclusive ownership of the explanation for our own actions.[42]

Hegel shows that it is only after the acting conscience endures this loss of selfhood and after the beautiful soul, too, "surrenders the being-for-self to which it so stubbornly clings"[43], that both come to see this loss as the "true *realization* of…subjectivity."[44] Hegel's terms are more precise: because what is recovered is not the modern *self*, he says that the movement of reconciliation between the acting conscience and the beautiful soul heals the wounds of *Sprit*.[45] The disparity between intention and action can only be bridged when the proper locus of explanation is no longer the prior mental state or intention, but a conversation between two persons, or between a person and the community to which he or she belongs, which determines the meaning and scope of the action.[46] The movement of reconciliation enables each of those involved to arrive at a new conception of the nature of knowledge, grounding the unity of thought and being on "reciprocal recognition", and determining everything that is included in human experience through its role within a relational whole.[47]

In my concluding remarks to the previous section, I claimed that the movement of confession and delayed forgiveness captures a conversion in our self-understanding in relation to our actions that applies to our self-understanding in relation to the world and to others. By taking us back to this movement in the chapter on absolute knowing, Hegel shows that he believes this to be the best way to explain what it means for the true concept of absolute knowledge to be in unity with its externalisation or

---

[41] Pippin, "Logic of Experience", 220.
[42] See ibid, 223.
[43] Hegel, *Phenomenology of Spirit*, §668.
[44] Pippin, "Logic of Experience", 223.
[45] Hegel, *Phenomenology of Spirit*, §669.
[46] Ibid, §667-8.
[47] Ibid, §668-70.

realization, what it means to move from the "simple unity of the concept" of knowledge to the "concept in its truth."[48] Let us now turn to Rosenzweig's critique of Hegel's system.

V. Rosenzweig's Systematic Renewal of Thinking

Between 1916 and 1918, the years preceding his composition of *The Star of Redemption*, Rosenzweig wrote a series of letters articulating his conception of a philosophical system in contradistinction to the German Idealist conception of systematicity, specifically directing his critique at Hegel's philosophical system. The critique is complex and easily misinterpreted. Rosenzweig does not relinquish the aspiration to comprehensive knowledge that accompanies metaphysics from its inception. Rather, he is critical of the manner in which a specific conception of systematicity succeeds in grasping the conceptual identity of all beings insofar as they are known, but fails to grasp the particularity of each known being. And he is critical of the manner in which a specific conception of systematicity becomes "a mere logical playing-around,"[49] divorcing knowledge from our human vocation.

On 18th November 1917, Rosenzweig wrote a letter to his cousin Rudolf Ehrenberg, later entitled the "Urzelle" to the *Star of Redemption*, in which he describes having found the "perspicuous interconnection of thoughts"[50] that is required if knowledge is to have systematic unity.[51] Yet he immediately qualifies his claim, stating that his conception of the "systematic" interconnection of thought follows that of his friend Viktor Freiherr von Weisäcker, rather than the conception of a philosophical system articulated by Kant or Hegel. In a follow-up letter to the "Urzelle," written on 1st December 1917, Rosenzweig defines his and Weisäcker's conception of a philosophical system:

---

[48] Ibid, §795.
[49] Franz Rosenzweig, "'Urzelle' to the Star of Redemption," in *Philosophical and Theological Writings*, 55.
[50] Ibid, 51.
[51] Let us recall that in the "Architectonic of Pure Reason," Kant holds that a philosophical system is one in which the "manifold of cognitions" are unified under one idea. This idea is the "rational concept of the form of a whole insofar as through this the domain of the manifold as well as the position of the parts with respect to each other is determined *a priori*." Kant, *Critique of Pure Reason*, A833/B861.

> System is *not architecture*, where the stones assemble the structure and are there for the sake of the structure (and otherwise for no reason); rather, system means that every individual has the drive and will to *relation* to all other individuals... In the Hegelian system, each individual position is anchored only in the whole and indeed (therefore) with two others, with one according to the immediately preceding and with one according to the immediately following position.[52]

This passage is critical of the "architectonic" formulation of a philosophical system insofar as it suggests that each particular being, each "stone," is taken into account only as a *means* to build a complete structure, and not also as an *end*. Against this formulation, Rosenzweig holds that a genuine philosophical system must show how and why each individual being "has the drive and will to *relation* to all other individual beings." This passage opposes the Hegelian system specifically, because, by anchoring all individual beings in an all-encompassing whole, Hegel reduces the diversity and multiplicity of all beings to one form, overlooking the uniqueness of each individual.

We have seen that in the *Phenomenology of Spirit* absolute knowing culminates in a conversion in our self-understanding in relation to our actions that applies to our self-understanding in relation to the world and to others, such that everything included in human experience is determined through its role within a relational whole. By claiming that this conception of absolute knowledge cannot yield knowledge of particular beings, Rosenzweig raises anew the spectre of nihilism, questioning whether Hegel's philosophical system meets its own criteria for success. As we have seen, Jacobi had argued that, although a genuine philosophical system should be holistic and monistic, such a system would annihilate the individuality of any person who came to "believe it and live according to it."[53] For this reason, the German Idealists were concerned to construct a philosophical system that would determine all things through their position within a whole, while taking into account their particular being.

This is the aim that Rosenzweig adopts. Further into the follow-up letter to the "Urzelle," Rosenzweig announces that he still retains the aspiration to absolute knowledge: "Where then does the Absolute remain, without which philosophy cannot do? ... The totality of the system is no longer objective, but rather subjective ... The *philosopher* is the form of philosophy."[54] Rosenzweig suggests that philosophy can only uphold its

---

[52] Rosenzweig, "Urzelle", 51 (note 11).

[53] Franks, *All or Nothing*, 10.

[54] Rosenzweig, "Urzelle", 51 (note 11).

claim to be a universal science of truth, whose ultimate aim is absolute knowledge, if this aim can be shown to be relevant to the philosopher, as the particular human being that he or she is.

This precondition for philosophy finds fuller expression in Rosenzweig's "Urzelle" itself. After mentioning that he has found a "systematic" interconnection of thoughts, Rosenzweig characterizes the independence that philosophy attains in the German Idealist tradition and the satisfaction of knowledge that this independence yields:

> Thus, I say: philosophising reason stands on its own feet, it is self-sufficient. All things are grasped in it, and ultimately it grasps itself (the only epistemological act, against which nothing can be said because it is the only one that occurs not according to the form A=B, which is the form of knowing actuality and of actuality, but rather according to the form of *logical* knowing A=A). After it has thus taken up everything within itself and has proclaimed its exclusive existence, man suddenly discovers that he, who has long been philosophically digested, is still there.[55]

We have seen that in Hegel's *Phenomenology* each shape of consciousness represents an attempt to bridge the gap between subject and object, attaining epistemological satisfaction. And we have seen that, for Hegel, this satisfaction is attained when we discover in others the condition of possibility for the true realization of our own subjectivity or Spirit. Rosenzweig is questioning whether the movement that Hegel describes can amount to more than a conversion *in thought*, whether grasping the true nature of knowledge is enough, without also grasping how true knowledge is knowledge of *actuality*. Rosenzweig will argue that true knowledge can be knowledge of actuality only if we can grasp how and why each *being* must undergo a conversion in order to secure its own being, but we are getting ahead of ourselves. Here, Rosenzweig is claiming that as the culmination of the phenomenology of *mind*, philosophy can arrive at the epistemologically secure status of logical knowing, represented by the equation A=A, but that this security is gained "at the cost of giving up any claim to knowledge of actuality, including any claim to knowledge of the actual philosophising subject."[56] Knowledge of actuality takes the form of the equation A=B.

In order for philosophy to become more than a "mere logical playing-around", philosophers must raise anew the question of the relation between thought and being. If thus far we have succeeded in showing how thinking, as self-knowledge, can "ground itself," Rosenzweig contends

---

[55] Ibid, 52.
[56] Ibid (note 12).

that we haven't yet succeeded in showing that the "self-grounding of thinking is ... necessary only for the sake of *willing* the thinkability of being."[57] Apart from this relation to volition and hence to our own being, Rosenzweig protests, philosophy is mere child's play or "a sophist's whirling-stick,"[58] sufficient to pass time, but incapable of healing the wounds in our spirit, and unable to help us meet the small, at times exceedingly small, demands of each day.

Hegel concludes the chapter on "Morality" in the *Phenomenology* by remarking that the "reconciling *Yea*" uttered between the beautiful soul and the acting conscience is "God manifested in the midst of those who know themselves in the form of pure knowledge."[59] As if looking back to this sentence, Rosenzweig states in the "Urzelle" that it is still necessary to separate the "'being' of God... from his concept (self-sufficiency)," and it is still necessary to separate the "actuality of reason... from its concept (self-consciousness, *noesis noeseos*)."[60] Rosenzweig concludes the letter to his cousin by telling him that his philosophical system can be depicted in a "triangle of the sciences", with philosophy occupying the right side of the triangle and theology occupying the left side of the triangle, the base completed through a practical movement from left to right and through a theoretical movement from right to left, engendering a third science, "theosophy".[61]

Thus, Rosenzweig's philosophical system does not ultimately disown Hegel's, but urges us to actualise the self-transformation or conversion that is already at least partly captured in its logical form. Hegel's philosophical system holds out the promise of grounding knowledge through a conversion *in thought,* and Kant's Copernican revolution holds out a similar promise through a "revolution in the way of thinking". Rosenzweig's system redeems these two promises, contending that we must "bring about a total *renewal* of thinking"[62], leading to the understanding that each *being* must undergo a conversion in order to ground or determine its own being. It is in this manner that Rosenzweig's philosophical system takes into account the uniqueness and particularity of each being. In the following section we will see that, in Rosenzweig's view, the possibility of articulating this alternative conception of a

---

[57] Ibid, 55.
[58] Franz Rosenzweig, *God, Man, and the World,* trans. and ed. Barbara E. Galli (Syracuse: Syracuse University Press, 1998), 38.
[59] Hegel, *Phenomenology of Spirit*, §671.
[60] Rosenzweig, "Urzelle", 55.
[61] Ibid, 70.
[62] Rosenzweig, "The New Thinking", 110.

philosophical system hinges on finding a genuinely presuppositionless starting point.

VI. From the One and Universal Nothing towards the Threefold Nothing of Knowledge

In the Preface and Introduction to the *Phenomenology of Spirit,* Hegel promises to found a genuinely presuppositionless philosophical science by showing how the concept of absolute knowledge emerges as a determined concept only at the end of the *Phenomenology,* as the result of the complete movement of cognition or experience of consciousness.[63] Rosenzweig questions the presuppositionless character of Hegel's philosophical science. He opens *The Star of Redemption* by stating that it is "from death" and "from the fear of death ... that all cognition of the All begins."[64] In Rosenzweig's view, this is where we must begin if we are to arrive at a systematic conception of absolute knowledge that is tied to our vocation as human beings.

Rosenzweig encourages us to agree with him that, for each of us, the reality of death is "not nothing, it is something"[65]; it is the erasure of our particular memories, the conclusion of our particular hopes, the absence of our place in a family, in a relationship, or in a friendship. Each life is unstable, "wavering between nothing and something"[66] in a manner that is not replicable. Rosenzweig wants to show that the nothing-something character of death "holds out the promise of definability."[67] It promises to redeem the promise of German Idealism, that of arriving at a philosophical system capable of grounding everything that is included in human experience while taking into account the individuality of each being.

In the Introduction to *The Star,* Rosenzweig takes pains to make such a promise seem viable. In mathematics, he says, we can find a guide instructing us "how to recognize in the nothing the origin of the something."[68] Hermann Cohen's 1883 *The Principle of the Infinitesimal Method and Its History* showed the fruitfulness for philosophy of the discovery of the differential, enabling us to understand how something can be derived from a "definite nothing"[69] by considering how the relation

---

[63] See Hegel, *Phenomenology of Spirit,* §20.
[64] Rosenzweig, *Star of Redemption,* 10.
[65] Ibid, 11.
[66] Pollock, *The Systematic Task,* 154.
[67] Rosenzweig, *Star of Redemption,* 29.
[68] Ibid.
[69] Ibid, 28.

between infinitely small differences yields an actual number.[70] Thus, Rosenzweig explains, "The differential combines in itself the properties of the nothing and of the something"; its fruitfulness for thought consists in determining "two paths that go from the nothing to the something, the path of the affirmation of that which is not nothing, and the path of the negation of the nothing."[71]

The central task of *The Star of Redemption* is to derive a complete list of categories that provide comprehensive knowledge of the nature of particular beings and clarify the relation between knowledge and our human vocation. This task can be fulfilled by starting from a "threefold nothing of knowledge"[72] corresponding to the traditional three sciences of supersensible beings: theology, psychology, and cosmology, and showing how God, human beings, and the world attempt to secure their being, first by embarking on two paths from their particular nothing, and ultimately by entering into reciprocal relations with each of the other two kinds of beings, in three interrelated temporal dimensions. Because in Rosenzweig's view the philosophical tradition that culminates in German Idealism fails to provide us with such comprehensive knowledge, he intends to restore God, human beings, and the world as "irrational" objects, using "the prefix *meta*" to indicate that we will discover the nature of each kind of being only by stepping "outside the boundaries of philosophy's traditional scope."[73] By starting from the threefold nothing of knowledge, Rosenzweig promises to lead us towards the metaphysical God, towards the metalogical world, and towards the metaethical human being.

Although tracing each of these trajectories would require a separate monograph, in the remainder of this paper I want to trace at least part of the trajectory of the metaethical human being, which first arrives at the elemental stability of the isolated Self, and through the reversal of freedom into humility, culminates in an understanding of each human being as a soul.

---

[70] See Pollock, *The Systematic Task*, 152. See also Kant's discussion of the concept of nothing in "On the Amphiboly of Concepts of Reflection". Kant, *Critique of Pure Reason*, A 292.

[71] Rosenzweig, *Star of Redemption*, 28.

[72] See Pollock, *The Systematic Task*, 147: "In the *Critique of Pure Reason,* Kant had determined God, world, and the human soul to be 'nothings' for human knowledge insofar as he deemed them to be transcendental ideas to which no sensible objects correspond, and insofar as he deemed their objectivisation in the history of philosophy to be the result of the improper, transcendent use *of* reason itself."

[73] Ibid, 145.

VII. Metaethics and the Elemental Self

We have seen that Rosenzweig points to Cohen's work on the principle of the infinitesimal method to show that we can determine two ways in which something, an "element of our world"[74], can emerge from its determinate nothing: through the negation of nothing and through the affirmation of something which is not nothing. Employing Rosenzweig's formal language, "Yes" designates the path of affirmation and "No" that of negation.[75] Each element attains a measure of stability, securing its being against its particular nothing, when both paths are joined through the conjunction "And." In addition, the two paths of affirmation and negation correspond to two attributes characteristic of each element: "'Yes' always corresponds to a certain quality of 'substantiality' or 'being'... 'No' always corresponds to an 'active' quality."[76]

Let us begin with the determinate nothing of a human being: each human being secures its own being through the affirmation of its character: "Yes" affirms the "lasting being" or "lasting essence" of our character.[77] Equiprimordially, each human being secures its being through a "newly renewed action"[78], the finite freedom to will. Human freedom is finite, giving it its particular quality of proud "defiance", since its "immediate origin" is in "the denied nothing".[79] When this defiant free will takes the affirmed character as its content, each human being attains the measure of stability sufficient for selfhood:

> The defiance remains defiance; formally it remains unconditional, but it takes the character as content: the defiance defies the character. This is the self-consciousness of man, or, more briefly: it is the Self. The 'Self' is that which springs up in this encroachment of the free will on the attribute, as And of defiance and character.[80]

---

[74] Rosenzweig, *Star of Redemption*, 93.
[75] Rosenzweig adopts this formal language from Schelling's *The Ages of the World*. Schelling devotes a large part of *The Ages of the World* to an account of the dialectical unfolding of the three "potencies" that compose God: the eternal Yes and eternal No, and the unity of both Yes and No. See F.W. J. Schelling, *The Ages of the World*, trans. Jason M. Wirth (Albany: SUNY, 2000).
[76] Pollock, *The Systematic Task*, 159.
[77] Rosenzweig, *Star of Redemption*, 74.
[78] Ibid, 38.
[79] Ibid, 75-6.
[80] Ibid, 77.

Through the "And" conjoining the will of defiance and character, the self is "configured"[81] into a "whole".[82]

Yet we can see that this uneasy union of defiance and character places human selfhood in a precariously stable condition, requiring constant vigilance against falling back into nothingness. The "mythical God" and the "plastic world"[83], the elemental forms that God and the world attain when they are similarly generated out of their own determinate nothings, are also precariously stable. In their elemental form, God, human beings, and the world, only attain "hypothetical" being.

In the "Transition" between Parts One and Two of *The Star of Redemption*, Rosenzweig articulates two main reasons why God, human beings, and the world, are unstable in their elemental form. First, while explaining what it means for each of these beings to attain merely hypothetical being, Rosenzweig states that the elemental forms do not correspond to our experience of God, human beings, and the world: "The hypothetical—this word explains to us that strange aspect of the pieces of the All. None of these pieces has a sure, unalterable place; above each of them an 'if' is secretly written."[84] Rosenzweig is here asking whether we can explain our experience of freedom in its uneasy union with character. Yet this phenomenological point is not central to the trajectory from the threefold nothing of knowledge to threefold being that Rosenzweig is tracing.

A more significant reason is that there is an internal contradiction in each element's claim to be whole. Calling to mind the dialectical movement of Hegel's *Phenomenology,* in which each shape or pattern of consciousness progresses to a more comprehensive stage of knowledge through an internal contradiction that is exposed by the phenomenologist's questions, Rosenzweig writes: "Before your questions, the three elements could very possibly seem to co-exist in a tranquil solidity, each of them caught up in the feeling of One and the All, a feeling, blind to the outside, of their own existence." Yet as soon as we expose the fact that three wholes cannot coexist, for they cannot mean what they say when they each claim to be All, we need to "ask the question of their relationship."[85] Ultimately, Rosenzweig shows that it is only by entering into reciprocal relations with each other, relinquishing the security that is attained in elemental form, and discovering that an "aspect of [their] self rests in the

---

[81] Ibid, 78.
[82] Ibid, 94.
[83] Ibid, 93.
[84] Ibid, 94.
[85] Ibid, 93-4.

domain of others"[86], that God, human beings, and the world, can attain the "unequivocal certainty"[87] of being that they each seek through separate means.

We have seen that for Hegel, absolute knowing is only possible though a conversion in our self-understanding, which enables us to see that others are essential to the realization of our own subjectivity. And we have seen that for Hegel this conversion is the condition of possibility for the realization of freedom and hence the condition of possibility for the actuality of moral action. At first blush, Rosenzweig is making similar claims. Revelation, the cognitive heart or "Archimedean point"[88] of Rosenzweig's system, names the "conversion" or "inversion"[89] that each of the three elements undergoes when it enters into reciprocal relations, and this conversion is necessary if each of the three elements is to secure its being with "unequivocal certainty".[90] Yet, Rosenzweig shows that the Revelation of the "inner nature" of each of the three elements not only brings about a conversion in our understanding of the nature of knowledge. We can only ground our knowledge of God, human beings, and the world, through reciprocal relations, but this grounding ultimately transforms our fundamental categories.

VIII. From Freedom to Humility

In what manner is a self transformed when he or she enters into relations with God and the world? In *The Star of Redemption*, the concept of Revelation does not only name the conversion or inversion that each element undergoes when it enters into reciprocal relations. Along with Creation and Redemption, Revelation is a particular temporal dimension, the dimension in which God and the self enter into relation. In this section, I want to show how the inversion of the inner nature of the human self when it enters into relation with God secures the realization of freedom, through the conversion of freedom into humility.

We know that the elemental self gains a measure of stability when, through the two paths that go from its definite nothing to something ("Yes" and "No"), the essential attribute of the self, its character, is joined to the active attribute of the self, its freedom to will. The elemental self is

---

[86] Pollock, *The Systematic Task*, 186.
[87] Rosenzweig, *Star of Redemption*, 95.
[88] Rosenzweig, "Urzelle", 48.
[89] Rosenzweig, *Star of Redemption*, 98.
[90] Ibid, 95.

unstable because human freedom is both "finite" and "unconditional".[91] The unconditional, unlimited freedom to will is limited in its realization, for unlike God's freedom, human freedom is not the freedom to act. It is "not free power, but free will."[92] How can this tension be resolved when and if a self enters into reciprocal relation with God?

Although we have not traced the path through which the elemental God is formed, all we need to know here is that His essential attribute, which is attained through the affirmation ("Yes") of something in God's definite nothing, is the attribute of "Being".[93] In Revelation, God's essential attribute reverses into the active and eventful force ("No") of love: "Now being... must reveal itself in a corresponding reversal... his eternal essence [turns] into—love at every waking moment, always young, always first... God, as a No, as a perpetually new self-negation."[94] We may ask: does not the elemental God lose the security of His essential, unconditional being through this reversal? Rosenzweig characterizes divine love in precisely these terms, as a perpetually new *self-negation.* Yet, by entering into reciprocal relation with human beings, God first *secures* the unconditional nature of his being, through our recognition of this *self-negation.*[95]

When the human self is awakened to divine love in the event of Revelation, the active ("No") and "defiant pride of free will" reverses into a different form of pride. Through the assurance of God's love, the *soul* is "tranquil... like a child in the arms of its mother"; this assurance is a "pride that is simply there, in which man is silent and by which he lets himself be carried; [it] is therefore the exact reverse of the defiance that constantly explodes anew. It is humility." Through the event of revelation humility becomes the enduring, essential attribute ("Yes") of the soul. Since humility has its origin in the defiant will of the elemental self and so "is nothing other than the defiance coming out if its mute enclosure", it is not purely passive but has "the strength of... faithfulness". Humility, Rosenzweig wants to show, is at the same time the power to continue to recognize, and so to have faith in, the unconditional nature of divine love. This notion enables us to understand why God secures the unconditional nature of his being only through human recognition:

---

[91] Ibid, 75.
[92] Ibid, 75.
[93] Ibid, 36.
[94] Ibid, 173.
[95] See Pollock, *The Systematic Task,* 206: "Might God first realize the unconditional nature of his being through recognition in revelation?"

> There emerges from the beloved a strength, not a strength of endlessly new impulses, but the silent brightness of an immense Yes, where the love of the lover, which always denies itself, finds that which it could not find within itself: affirmation and duration... The faith of the soul testifies, in its faithfulness, to the love of God, and it gives to it permanent *being*.[96]

By entering into reciprocal relation with human beings, God regains the unconditional nature of His being, which he had lost through self-negation in the event of Revelation. Through human recognition, God is the One whose love is unconditional.

Yet what becomes of human freedom? What does our active, endlessly renewed power consist in, now? Humility has become the essential attribute of the human soul. When the *"dialogue* of love comes to an end"[97] and the human soul moves beyond Revelation and enters into redemptive relations with the world, the essential attribute ("Yes") of the elemental self, character, reverses into the active ("No") renewed, the "momentary... surmounting" or self-negation that is required in order to turn towards one's neighbour. Love for the neighbour is not grounded in an unconditional freedom; it does not "reside in the will alone". This distinguishes love for the neighbour from moral action. Its necessity and unconditional quality "presupposes" the recognition of the unconditional nature of divine love: "Only the love received from God makes the act of love on the soul's part more than a mere act." The actuality of love for one's neighbour, the self-negation that is required to attend to the physical, emotional, and intellectual needs of the individuals that surround us, requires the gratitude and humble recognition that we have been taken into account and are sufficiently loved. Humility, then, rather than "autonomy", is what enables us to fulfil the "unambiguous" commandment of love.[98] If and when we recognize that our ability to fulfil the commandment of love depends on our ability to recognize divine love, that free recognition turns into the "living *anamnesis* of the concept of freedom."[99] Storing that free recognition in memory, we each enter into clear and necessary relations with others and the world, taking up our place in a relational whole.

---

[96] Rosenzweig, *Star of Redemption*, 180-5.

[97] Ibid, 200.

[98] Ibid, 230-1.

[99] Rosenzweig, *Philosophical and Theological Writings*, 60.

IX. Conclusion

My central aim has been to clarify Rosenzweig's insistence in "The New Thinking" that we read and understand *The Star of Redemption* as a "system of philosophy". Like Kant and the German Idealists, Rosenzweig seeks to revive the traditional task of metaphysics, to show that philosophy is a science capable of grounding human experience. Like the German Idealists, he holds that a modern philosophical system must be committed to the view that everything included in human experience be determined through its role within a relational whole, and that the whole be grounded in an immanent absolute first principle. Rosenzweig is critical of Hegel's philosophical system, for he believes it cannot take into account each individual being. By grounding his philosophical system on the event of revelation and our recognition of divine love, Rosenzweig hopes to tie the systematic task of philosophy to the vocation of each human being, bringing about a "total renewal of thinking". Through the use of "old Jewish words", Rosenzweig leads us to a renewed understanding of the concept of freedom, turning it into faithfulness and humility. Although Rosenzweig insists that *The Star of Redemption* is not in any straightforward sense a "Jewish book," nor a book on "philosophy of religion", perhaps we can let him lead us to a renewed understanding of the significance of leading an observant life, and to a renewed understanding of the reasons that still compel us to "struggle for religion"[100] in the twenty-first century.

Bibliography

Aristotle. *Metaphysics.* Translated by Hippocrates Apostle. Des Moines: The Peripatetic Press, 1979.

Forster, Michael. *Hegel and Skepticism.* Cambridge, MA: Harvard University Press, 1989.

Franks, Paul W. "All or Nothing: Systematicity and Nihilism in Jacobi, Reinhold, and Maimon." In Karl Ameriks edited, *The Cambridge Companion to German Idealism.* Cambridge: Cambridge University Press, 2000. 95-116.

—. *All or Nothing: Systematicity, Transcendental Arguments, and Skepticism in German Idealism.* Cambridge MA: Harvard University Press, 2005.

---

[100] Rosenzweig to Hans Ehrenberg, 26th September 1910. Cited in Rosenzweig, "Urzelle", 45 (note 13).

Hegel, G.W.F. *Phenomenology of Spirit.* Translated by A.V. Miller. Oxford: Oxford University Press, 1977.

Jacobi, F.H. *The Main Philosophical Writings and the Novel Alwill.* Translated and edited by George di Giovanni. Montreal: McGill-Queen's University Press, 2009.

Kant, Immanuel. *The Critique of Pure Reason.* Translated and edited by Paul Guyer and Allen W. Wood. Cambridge: Cambridge University Press, 1998.

—. *The Critique of Practical Reason.* Translated and edited by Mary Gregor. Cambridge: Cambridge University Press, 1997.

Leibniz, G.W. *Philosophical Essays.* Translated by Roger Ariew and Daniel Garber. Indianapolis: Hackett, 1989.

Pippin, Robert. B. "The 'Logic of Experience' as 'Absolute Knowledge' in *Hegel's Phenomenology of Spirit.*" In Dean Moyar and Michael Quante edited, *Hegel's Phenomenology of Spirit: A Critical Guide.* Cambridge: Cambridge University Press, 2008. 210–227

Pollock, Benjamin. *Franz Rosenzweig and the Systematic Task of Philosophy.* Cambridge: Cambridge University Press, 2009.

Rosenzweig, Franz. *God, Man, and the World.* Translated and edited by Barbara E. Galli. Syracuse: Syracuse University Press, 1998.

—. *Philosophical and Theological Writings.* Translated and edited by Paul W. Franks and Michael L. Morgan. Indianapolis: Hackett, 2000.

—. *The Star of Redemption.* Translated by Barbara E. Galli. Madison: University of Wisconsin Press, 2005.

Schelling, F.W. J. *The Ages of the World.* Translated by Jason M. Wirth. Albany: SUNY, 2000.

Chapter Six

Existence, Anxiety and the Moment of Vision: Fundamental Ontology and Existentiell Faith Revisited

George Pattison

I. Introduction

In this paper I shall examine Kierkegaard's presence in *Being and Time*. In large part this will mean focussing in detail on the text of Heidegger's early masterwork. However, the topic has a wider significance, not least with regard to the question as to *whether* and *how* phenomenology might contribute to the interpretation of religious existence or, more generally, how the kind of fundamental ontology that Heidegger regards as coterminous with phenomenology actually does illuminate the everyday circumstances of life as it is lived. In other words, it is a question as to the kind of understanding of existence at which *Being and Time* aims or which it in the event achieves. We shall see Heidegger running into a number of problems in pursuit of his aims and consider the extent to which he takes these into account and succeeds (or not) in addressing them. Of course, the question of faith does not stand or fall with Kierkegaard any more than the question of phenomenology stands or falls with Heidegger. Nevertheless, both of them are eminent representatives of their respective discourses and their encounter in the pages of *Being and Time* is not without significance for the subsequent history of the philosophy of religion in the Continental tradition. Whilst they cannot foreclose on how we may address the relationship between phenomenology and faith today, our consideration of the question stands within a trajectory that continues to be shaped by Heidegger's reading of the Danish thinker.

At the same time, and as my closing comments in particular make clear, this is also a striking case of the intersection of historical and systematic ways of reading and of how systematic approaches may, from a historical point of view, play fast or loose with or significantly distort the texts that they incorporate—and yet in so doing bring out possibilities in those texts that historical study alone will never elicit. Yet the converse is also true and historical study may in its own way retrieve possibilities of interpretation that are obscured in the great systematic readings, of which *Being and Time*'s treatment of Kierkegaard provides such a striking example.

II. The Problem of Kierkegaard and *Being and Time*

The role of Kierkegaard in the genesis and argument of *Being and Time* has been discussed many times. A broad consensus—at least among Kierkegaard scholars—is that the three footnotes in which Heidegger specifically mentions the Dane scarcely do justice either to the scope of Kierkegaard's presence in this phase of Heidegger's path of thinking nor to Kierkegaard himself. We remind ourselves that they mention Kierkegaard (a) as "The man who has gone farthest in analysing the phenomenon of anxiety... in the context of a 'psychological' exposition of the problem of original sin"[1]; (b) as having "explicitly seized upon the problem of existence as an existentiell problem, and thought it through in a penetrating fashion" although "the existential problematic" was "alien" to him and "as regards his ontology, he remained completely dominated by Hegel and by ancient philosophy as Hegel saw it"; (c) (in the same footnote) as the author of a number of edifying writings from which "there is more to be learned philosophically... than from his theoretical [works]— with the exception of his treatise on the concept of anxiety"[2]; and, finally, (d) as "probably the one who has seen the existentiell phenomenon of the moment of vision with the most penetration," although "this does not signify that he has been correspondingly successful in Interpreting it existentially". This is because "He clings to the ordinary conception of time, and defines the 'moment of vision' with the help of 'now' and 'eternity'" and so, when he speaks of temporality, "what he has in mind is man's Being-in-time". Nevertheless—and in case we are tempted to read this as a kind of intellectual put-down—Heidegger adds that although "within-time-ness" knows only the "now" and "never knows a moment of vision", "if... such a moment gets experienced in an existentiell manner,

---

[1] Martin Heidegger, *Being and Time,* trans. John Macquarrie and Edward Robinson (Oxford: Basil Blackwell, 1962), 492/190. In all references, the English text pagination will be followed by the German first edition pagination.
[2] Ibid, 494/235.

then a more primordial temporality has been presupposed, although existentially it has not been made explicit".[3] This last reference also refers the reader to Karl Jaspers' *Psychologie der Weltanschauungen* for further comment both on the moment of vision and on Kierkegaard.

Taken together these remarks suggest that the "points of contact" between Heidegger and Kierkegaard are focussed on the topics of existence, anxiety, and the moment of vision. These are, of course, by no means trivial or merely incidental topics in a philosophy of *Existenz* that gave special prominence to the phenomenon of angst and for which the moment of vision provided a synthesizing centre point for all it has to say about time—and what this particular work says about time, we may add for completeness' sake, is rather generally regarded as perhaps its most distinctive contribution to modern philosophy. Quantitatively, then, these footnotes do not say much but they seem to do enough to place Kierkegaard at the heart of the innovative philosophical programme announced to the world in *Being and Time*.[4] Nevertheless, those who know their Kierkegaard as well as their *Being and Time* have often felt that these few comments do not go nearly far enough in acknowledging Kierkegaard's role in shaping Heidegger's interpretation of human existence.

Firstly, they note the rather grudging tone in which, whilst conceding Kierkegaard's "penetrating" approach to the named issues, Heidegger simultaneously declares that the existential problematic was alien to the Danish thinker (a point made twice, on the second occasion with specific reference to the question of time), that his philosophical writings are less interesting than his edifying ones (and, note, less interesting philosophically!), that his ontology is undeveloped and remains within the Hegelian paradigm, and that, like other theological thinkers such as Augustine and Luther, his approach is "psychological" and therefore, by implication, not genuinely philosophical. All of this, however, is seen by some Kierkegaard commentators as eminently contestable. Even if Kierkegaard does not have the tools of Husserlian phenomenology, they claim, he does set in motion a genuinely phenomenological analysis of existence and, moreover, one that, like Heidegger's, is oriented towards a

---

[3] Ibid, 497/338.
[4] Werner Brock, Heidegger's assistant in the early 1930s, makes clear that it was to Kierkegaard that contemporary German philosophy owed its most characteristic concept: existence. See Werner Brock, *Contemporary German Philosophy* (Cambridge: Cambridge University Press, 1935), 73.

fully ontological interpretation.[5] Or, conversely, it can be argued that it is precisely Heidegger who has headed off down an intellectual cul-de-sac by attempting to force material derived from religious life into the framework of phenomenological thought. On this basis, it is Kierkegaard who is the more consistent and ultimately more satisfying thinker.[6]

In addition to questioning in this way the legitimacy of Heidegger's reservations, Kierkegaard's advocates have, secondly, pointed out that, important as they are, the topics of existence, anxiety and the moment of vision do not exhaust the points of contact between Kierkegaard's thought and that of his German interpreter. Idle talk, the "one" (*das Man*), guilt, nothingness, the confrontation with death, resoluteness, and repetition are all well-attested Kierkegaardian themes that recur in *Being and Time*. Thus the Kierkegaardian influence is not limited to establishing the lynch-points of Heidegger's argument but can more accurately be said to pervade its whole development. When grafted on to the previous criticism of Heidegger this might lead to a sense that the existential thinker is suffering from a certain anxiety of influence vis-à-vis the Christian psychologist.

These are significant objections to Heidegger. However, it is also possible to sense a certain over-enthusiasm amongst at least some of those who have taken up Kierkegaard's cause. Undoubtedly, Kierkegaard was a more important part both of the internal argument of *Being and Time* and

---

[5] See, for example, Arne Grøn, *Subjektivitet og Negativitet* (Copenhagen: Gyldendal, 1997); Jörg Disse, *Kierkegaard's Phenomenology of the Experience of Freedom* (Freiburg: Karl Alber, 1991), Calvin O. Schrag, *Existence and Freedom: Towards an Ontology of Human Finitude* (Evanston IL: Northwestern University Press, 1961).

[6] This was the argument of Lev Shestov. See Natalia Baranova-Shestova, *Jiizn" L"va Shestova,* Vol. 2 (Paris: La Presse Libre, 1983), 17. It is also essentially the argument of my article "Ethics, Ontology and Religion: Reflections on Kierkegaard's Upbuilding Discourses" in *Topos* (*Journal of the European Humanities University, Minsk*) 1.6 (2002), 51-64, repeated in my forthcoming article "Kierkegaard and Phenomenology" in Jeffrey Hanson ed, *Kierkegaard as Phenomenologist* (Evaston IL: Northwestern University Press, 2010). In a different vein, John D. Caputo comments that "Heidegger's parsimonious references to Kierkegaard in the published sections of *Being and Time* are not the main problem. The more astonishing thing is how profoundly Kierkegaard had both anticipated and set in motion the deconstruction of the history of ontology that Heidegger had not yet addressed. It would take more than a footnote on Heidegger's part to fix his relationship to Kierkegaard. It took the full force of his turning in his later writings to get as far as *Repetition.*" John D. Caputo, "Kierkegaard, Heidegger, and the Foundering of Metaphysics" in Robert L. Perkins ed, *International Kierkegaard Commentary: Fear and Trembling and Repetition* (Macon GA: Mercer University Press, 1993), 201-24.

of Heidegger's development in the decade preceding its publication than these notes allow us to see. For example, Michael Theunissen has persuasively argued for the role of Kierkegaard's edifying discourse entitled "At a Graveside" in relation to Heidegger's notion of Being-towards-death and has also pointed to the likely paper-trail for Heidegger's knowledge of it—even though no trace of this intertext is found in *Being and Time* itself.[7] More broadly, the second two decades of the twentieth century were perhaps the high-point of Kierkegaard-reception in the German-speaking world, which Heidegger acknowledged in the preface to an edition of his early writings, where he singles out Kierkegaard and Dostoevsky as two especially prominent non-philosophical sources in this cultural moment.[8] Nevertheless, even a cursory survey of Heidegger's development in this period reveals an extraordinarily broad range of sources feeding the formation of his mature thought. Of course, he is reading Kierkegaard, Dostoevsky, Hölderlin, Rilke, and other influential writers of the period as well as such religious thinkers as Augustine, Luther and Schleiermacher (and not forgetting Paul and the New Testament!). But he is also reading them in the context of a philosophical development dominated by Husserl and Aristotle.[9] If Heidegger's literary and religious sources provide him with a certain view of the human condition, it is clear that Aristotle-read-phenomenologically and phenomenology-read-à-la-Aristotle are generating the methods by which philosophy can lay hold of and clarify this condition in its own distinctive way. This is not a matter of concealing his sources or acknowledging them only begrudgingly but of a basic methodological orientation: once a certain view of the human condition has been achieved, these same

---

[7] See Michael Theunissen, "The Upbuilding in the Thought of Death: Traditional Elements, Innovative Ideas, and Unexhausted Possibilities", trans. George Pattison, in Robert L. Perkins ed, *International Kierkegaard Commentary: Prefaces and Writing Sampler* and *Three Discourses on Imagined Occasions* (Macon GA: Mercer University Press, 2006), 321-58.

[8] See Martin Heidegger, *Frühe Schriften* (Frankfurt am Main: V. Klostermann, 1972), ix-x. Earlier appearances of Kierkegaard in Heidegger's work include the few but important references in the lectures on historicity in *Phänomenologie des religiösen Lebens*, Gesamtausgabe Vol. 60 (Frankfrut am Main: V. Klostermann, 1995), 192, 268. For discussion of these references see my, "Heidegger, Augustine and Kierkegaard: Care, Time and Love" in Craig de Paulo ed, *The Influence of Augustine on Heidegger: The Emergence of an Augustinian Phenomenology* (New York: Edwin Mellen Press, 2006).

[9] See Theodore Kisiel, *The Genesis of Heidegger's Being and Time* (Berkeley CA: University of California Press, 1993); for Aristotle see especially Chapters 5 and 6.

sources are no longer relevant to the next stage of the process and do not need to be further debated.[10]

Nevertheless, questions remain. For even on Heidegger's own terms, we might ask whether the apparently clear distinction he draws between Kierkegaard's existentiell approach and a thorough existential analysis (which, as the footnotes themselves suggest and the text makes clear at many points, is alone capable of leading to an adequate ontological interpretation of existence) is in fact sustainable. It would, after all, seem to fundamentally misconceive what Heidegger says about the existentiell and the existential and about the ontic and the ontological to imagine that he was talking about two levels or realms of Being (such as a world of appearances and a thing-in-itself). It is not that an existential approach looks away from what is given or laid bare by such "penetrating" analyses as those of a Kierkegaard toward some modern correlate of a world of ideas. Precisely the role of Aristotle in the genesis of *Being and Time* should forewarn us that if there is a dualism in early Heidegger, it is not a dualism of that kind. Rather, "form"—what is to be understood in philosophical analysis—is not to be found elsewhere than in the concrete existence of substantive entities. To use a phrase that will become formulaic in Heidegger's later thought, it is a matter of Being-in-beings.

But if philosophical investigation is not directed towards a class of objects to be found anywhere other than in what is manifest in the human condition itself, what is it directed towards or in what way is it different from penetrating psychological exposition? The simple answer is, of course, that the difference is found precisely in the philosopher's concern for Being. Where Kierkegaard might be read as asking "What might it mean for me to become a Christian?", the existential phenomenologist asks, "What is the kind of Being or the relation to Being that is at issue in the question—any question—about what I might become?" Put like this, it should be clear that such a question does not so much require leaving the Kierkegaardian question behind but looking at it from a different point of view.

---

[10] In this sense it might seem entirely appropriate that the comments on Kierkegaard and other religious thinkers are assigned to footnotes just as, on another occasion, Kierkegaard will be cited in relation to lectures on Aristotle—but only in the motto (see below for further discussion).

III. The Existentiell, the Existential,
and the Question of Method

Of course, it isn't that simple, because (we might think) Being is already at issue in the Kierkegaardian question. When the subjective thinker described in the *Concluding Unscientific Postscript* or the representative figures who populate both the pseudonymous and upbuilding writings ask what is going on in their lives, they seem to testify that it is precisely they themselves, it is their very life, their existence, their to-be-or-not-to-be that is at issue. Not least is this so when they meditate upon their ineluctable death and the infinite difference it will make for their self-understanding if they believe themselves to be headed for annihilation rather than eternal life. But we might say this kind of religious self-questioning is irrelevant to the philosopher who needs to ask about structures of Being—that are equally determinative whether the existentiell question is becoming a Christian, converting to Islam, joining a political party, or changing one's life-style. For the particular individual concerned the question will hinge on the truth of the Bible, the Qur'an, or the cause, but why should this concern the philosopher? Yet Heidegger does not wish to abandon the kind of arousal or unrest that is specific to individuals facing such life-choices that are also always specific with regard to their content. On the contrary, Part One of *Being and Time* begins by telling the reader that "We ourselves are the entities to be analysed", that "That Being which is an issue for the entity in its very Being, is in each case mine", and he calls this the character of "mineness" that is intrinsic to Dasein and that demands the use of the personal pronoun (67-8/ 41-2).[11] It is the same individual who asks, "What must I do to inherit eternal life?" or "What is my life if there is no eternal life?"(to paraphrase the question of Kierkegaard's *Postscript* in its twofold aspect), who is to be interrogated with regard to its relation to Being—this same individual, and not another. Heidegger himself marks this interdependence of existentiell and existential in the Introduction, when he writes that "the roots of the existential analytic, on its part, are ultimately *existentiell*, that is *ontical*. Only if the inquiry of philosophical research is itself seized upon in an existentiell manner as a possibility of the Being of each existing Dasein, does it become at all possible to disclose the existentiality of existence and to undertake an adequately founded ontological problematic".[12]

---

[11] Heidegger, *Being and Time*, 67-8/41-2.
[12] Ibid, 34/13.

In this sense, Kierkegaard's religious subject is also the subject of Heidegger's existential enquiries and what Heidegger is asking about is not to be found otherwise than as revealed in the self-questioning of this subject. The existentiell and the existential are to be distinguished, as are the ontic and the ontological, but they are also given to us rather like the two natures of Christ according to the formula of Chalcedon: neither to be confused, nor divided, nor separated, nor changed by virtue of being united. However, before we are misled by the implications of an essentialist understanding of persons in terms of their "nature",[13] we should examine in more detail how Heidegger himself understands not just the difference but also the intertwining of the existentiell and the existential, the ontic and the ontological.

At the beginning of II.3, 300 pages into his enquiry, Heidegger makes what might seem like a rather extraordinary admission. "Up till now," he states, "except for some remarks which were occasionally necessary, we have deferred explicit discussions of method. Our first task was to 'go forth' towards the phenomena. But *before* laying bare the meaning of the Being of an entity which has been revealed in its basic phenomenal content, we must stop for a while in the course of our investigation, not for the purpose of 'resting', but so that we may be impelled the more keenly."[14] This pause gives Heidegger the opportunity to sum up and restate—somewhat repetitively, it has to be said—where the enquiry has now got to. In the previous two chapters (II.1 and II.2) he has analysed Dasein's striving to be-as-a-whole, the modulation of this striving into a being-towards-death, and the anticipatory resoluteness in which, in conscience, Dasein takes upon itself the guilt of its own nothingness. All of this represents a situation with which readers of Kierkegaard (and for that matter of Luther, Pascal and Russian literature) will be familiar. But that is entirely in keeping with Heidegger's aim, which, he tells us, has been to attest to "an authentic existentiell possibility"[15], that is, a possibility for becoming authentically resolute that is attested in Dasein's own existentiell life in the world. Only on the basis of such an authentic

---

[13] This is the objection made by Schleiermacher, who regards the failure to revisit this formula in the context of the Reformation as an item of unfinished business it is now time to address. See F. D. E. Schleiermacher, *The Christian Faith*, trans. and ed. H. R. Mackintosh and J. S. Stewart (Edinburgh: T. & T. Clark, 1928), 391. Others may, of course, argue that it is precisely an attempt, enduringly successful, to overcome the pre-Christian limitations of such categories by using them in new and paradoxical ways.

[14] Heidegger, *Being and Time*, 350/303.

[15] Ibid, 312/268.

breakthrough to authentic existence will Dasein be in a position to become clear about its relation to its own Being. Having established this existentiell possibility—or, at least, provided adequate attestation to it— the task now is to "project" the possibilities of anticipation and resoluteness in their *existential* aspect, i.e. as bearing a relation to Dasein's way of Being, onto the existentiell scenario and "'think these possibilities through to the end' in an existential manner".[16] Only so, only by showing that the ontological claims about an authentic understanding of Being can, as it were, be "lived" by real life human beings, will these claims "lose the character of an arbitrary construction".[17]

Method, Heidegger now tells us, involves "viewing in advance in an appropriate way the basic constitution of the 'object' to be disclosed"[18] and he now sets out to view in advance how the phenomenon of anticipatory resoluteness might also be understood as revealing the true nature of temporality and therewith also of care "in a phenomenally primordial way".[19] Yet, as he moves into ¶62 this involves him in (once more) explicating anticipatory resoluteness "as the way in which Dasein's Potentiality-for-Being-a-Whole has *Existentiell* Authenticity".[20]

We seem to be going round in circles. Which comes first, the existentiell achievement of authentic resoluteness or the existential "projection" onto existence of authentic resoluteness as also authentically revealing Being? If we start with the former, it seems, this will never of itself lead us on to ontological interpretation and we might, like Kierkegaard *et al.*, remain at that level in our self-understanding, whether this takes on a more religious or a more psychological colouring. Only by bringing to bear the hypothesis that such resoluteness is also ontologically significant can we, in fact, make it ontologically productive. But is this not open to the charge that it is a case of "projection" in a negative sense, i.e. the projection onto existence of a kind of interest and a kind of understanding that is essentially alien to it? Such resistance to the further step of existential interpretation is acknowledged by Heidegger in terms of the charge that such interpretation "has the character of doing violence, whether to the claims of the everyday interpretation, or to its complacency and its tranquillized obviousness".[21] This might even mean "following the opposite course from that taken by the falling ontico-ontological tendency

---

[16] Ibid, 350/303.
[17] Ibid.
[18] Ibid.
[19] Ibid, 351/304.
[20] Ibid, 352/305. My emphasis.
[21] Ibid, 359/311.

of interpretation".[22] Yet, at the same time, "Unless we have an existentiell understanding, all analysis of existentiality will remain groundless".[23] But how are we ever to know whether the particular existentiell understanding we have (let's say Christian or psycho-therapeutic) really is capable of grounding an ontological interpretation that is to be unconditionally valid for Dasein as such? How can we be sure that the particular existentiell scenario set out in the preceding chapters is not something more or less accidentally "pounced upon"?[24]

It might, I think, fairly be said that ¶61-¶63 are distinctly repetitious, not to say sluggish. It seems as if Heidegger is constantly trying to move forward to the next stage of his argument only to be repeatedly led back to the stage before. He puts forward his "advance" view as to the existential significance of resoluteness and proposes "thinking through to the end"[25] what this might involve. But how do we ever know when we have got to the end? What could possibly assure us that the goal had been reached and that our interpretation of Being was not so much the projection of an ontological possibility onto a certain existentiell understanding of human existence—of a kind attested by Kierkegaard's Western European, Lutheran anthropology but quite alien to Chinese Daoists? Attempting to think the matter through to the end, Heidegger seems to succeed only in going round in circles, each time tightening the knot still further and rendering his own procedure all the more problematic. Nevertheless, he is not unaware of this and it is no coincidence that he recalls his earlier discussion of the unavoidability of the hermeneutical circle. "We cannot ever 'avoid' a 'circular' proof in the existential analytic," he reminds us, "because such an analytic does not do any proving at all by the rules of the 'logic of consistency'."[26] This is because: "What common sense wishes to eliminate in avoiding the 'circle', on the supposition that it is measuring up to the loftiest rigour of scientific investigation, is nothing less than the basic structure of care."[27] What matters is to be able to bring the issue to language, letting it "put itself into words for the very first time"[28] so that Dasein can decide for itself in the light of its care for its own Being whether or not the account that will have been given is adequate. The answer, in other words, cannot be given except as Dasein's own free

---

[22] Ibid.
[23] Ibid, 360/312.
[24] Ibid, 361/313.
[25] Ibid, 353/305.
[26] Ibid, 363/315.
[27] Ibid.
[28] Ibid, 362/315.

affirmation with regard to its own way of being that, yes, this is how it *is*. But this shows from yet another angle how the existentiell and the existential, the ontic and the ontological are inseparably yet unconfusedly joined in Dasein's self-questioning since we are now back in the domain of the personal pronoun, of mineness, where I must freely take responsibility for the understanding of my own way of Being according to where my thinking through of the question has led me. Kierkegaard, we recall, was credited (twice) with having considered existence in an exceptionally "penetrating" manner although he seems not to have penetrated beyond what we have recently heard Heidegger call the ontico-ontological kind of understanding. Yet this expression itself seems to suggest that we are not, in the event, dealing with a simple duality between "ontic" and "ontological", "existentiell" and "existential" ways of understanding but rather with a kind of continuum, a process that is not divided up into distinct levels but is measured by how far we have "penetrated" the matter at issue (in each case, remember, the Being that we ourselves are) or how far we have thought it *through* and whether we have been able to attain or draw near to the "advance view" that we have projected onto our existentiell self-understanding. Does how we are thinking succeed in "exhibiting the phenomena in their primordiality"?[29] Does it achieve "ontological transparency"?[30] Does it "lay bare" "the meaning of the Being of care"?[31]

The metaphorics of illumination and revelation that shape such questions return us to the early pages of *Being and Time* and to Heidegger's reflections on the concept of the phenomenon and the nature of phenomenology. In a now well-known characterization of these terms, he himself underlines the original invocation of luminosity embodied in them. Tracing *phainomenon* back through the verb *phainō* to the root *pha-* he reminds his readers of its connection to *phōs*, light, so that "the expression '*phenomenon*' signifies *that which shows itself in itself*, the manifest". And, he continues, "the *phainomena* or 'phenomena' are the totality of what lies in the light of day or can be brought to the light—what the Greeks sometimes identified simply with *ta onta* (entities)."[32] Of course, as he immediately notes, it is always possible that such entities can show themselves as what they are not, that what appears is not the thing itself but a semblance (*Schein*). Against this background, phenomenology means "to let that which shows itself be seen from itself in the very way in

---

[29] Ibid, 359/311.

[30] Ibid, 361/313.

[31] Ibid, 364/317.

[32] Ibid, 51/29.

which it shows itself from itself"—which as Heidegger immediately comments, is simply another formulation of the Husserlian slogan "To the things themselves!".[33]

In the context of an enquiry into the place and role of Kierkegaard in *Being and Time*, it is perhaps germane in this connection to note the two quotations from Kierkegaard that Heidegger took as the "motto" to his 1921/22 lecture course on "Phenomenological Interpretations of Aristotle/Introduction to Phenomenological Research", lectures that give an early airing to some of the key issues that will achieve fuller treatment in *Being and Time* itself. The first, quite lengthy, quotation is taken from *Training in Christianity*. In it Kierkegaard accuses contemporary philosophy of making things look too easy in one of two ways. Either it facilitates an unearned assurance that the would-be philosopher has passed through the cauldron of doubt and emerged the other side, or else it has brought about the "semblance" (*Schein*) that human beings can "get out of their skin and speculate themselves into pure semblance (*Schein*)".[34] This is immediately supplemented by a shorter quotation from *Either/Or*, "What, on the other hand, is difficult for philosophy and for the philosopher is to stop"—to which Heidegger comments: "Stopping at the genuine beginning!"[35]

Reading these quotations in the context of *Being and Time*, they suggest that Heidegger might have seen in Kierkegaard an ally in redirecting philosophy away from semblance towards the things themselves, in letting "that which shows itself be seen from itself in the very way in which it shows itself from itself". However, precisely because this can only occur as a process, as a sustained and continuing act of holding open the view towards the things themselves and letting that view get ever clearer, it is also possible to see that Heidegger might quite consistently have seen Kierkegaard as falling short of all that might be required for a "phenomenology" worthy of the name—and recall that, as Heidegger makes very clear, the kind of phenomenological view onto the things themselves that he is counselling is intrinsically directed at the Being of entities, at what they *are*: phenomenology is ontology.[36]

---

[33] Ibid, 58/34.

[34] Martin Heidegger, *Phänomenologische Intepretatationen zu Aristoteles/Einführung in die phänomenologische Forschung*, Gesamtausgabe Vol. 61 (Frankfrut am Main: V. Klostermann, 1984), 182

[35] Ibid.

[36] I am not suggesting here that Heidegger's idea that philosophy needed to disentangle itself from semblance and find its way back to a genuine beginning derives from Kierkegaard, since his preoccupation with Plato, Aristotle, and

As in the (much) later reflections on "method", there is frequent mention in these early pages of how the access to Being sought in phenomenological investigation is, paradoxically, *hidden*. "What is it that phenomenology is to 'let us see'? What is it that must be called a 'phenomenon' in a distinctive sense? What is it that by its very essence is *necessarily* the theme whenever we exhibit anything explicitly?" Heidegger asks. As has just been stated, his answer is the surprising one that "Manifestly, it is something that proximally and for the most part does not show itself at all: it is something that lies *hidden*, in contrast to that which proximally and for the most part does show itself." However, he immediately adds—and the pattern is one with which we are now surely familiar—"at the same time it is something that belongs to what thus shows itself [i.e. what shows itself proximally and for the most part], and it belongs to it so essentially as to constitute its meaning and its ground."[37] In such "hiding", semblance is offered as and is mistaken for true being, so that the phenomenologist—let us say, simply, the philosopher—will have to engage in a continuous struggle to distinguish what really is from what merely seems to be so. This, as Heidegger notes, means that the philosopher needs a "proper method" in order not only to begin but also to gain access to the phenomenon and to work his "passage through whatever is prevalently covering it up".[38] Yet, as we have seen, he himself will have to acknowledge 300 pages later that he has proceeded rather far along the way without actually making explicit his methodological presuppositions. His difficulty in doing so is, however, precisely tied up with his difficulty in making a clear distinction between what is going on in existentiell and existential "thinking through".

These comments, of course, also bear on one of the most influential redefinitions of terms found in *Being and Time*, namely, the interpretation of the Greek word for truth, *alētheia*, as "unconcealment". Truth is arrived at when—shall we say in a "moment of vision"?—we arrive at a view onto what we are in our own first-person existence which is sufficient for us to decide whether this view itself is adequate to what we find ourselves to be.

But what is it that is "prevalently" covering up our view onto who we are? As a first step towards answering this question, we note that

---

Husserl in this period more than adequately provided him with the materials for such a thought. Nevertheless, nor is it simply a matter of finding a good "quote" to serve as a motto. The particular duality of Kierkegaard's role may, once again, be noted in terms of this reference standing, in a sense, "outside the text" of the lectures themselves (see also note ten above).

[37] Heidegger, *Being and Time*, 59/35.

[38] Ibid, 61/36.

immediately prior to his programmatic statement concerning the nature of phenomenology, Heidegger has completed or supplemented his definition of the phenomenon with some remarks on *logos* or discourse (*Rede*). In continuity with what has just been said about the phenomenon, *logos* too is said to mean "to make manifest what one is 'talking about' in one's discourse".[39] *Logos* is *apophansis*, "letting-something-be-seen"[40] and, as such, functions very similarly to a genuinely revelatory phenomenon, so that "*what* is said is drawn *from* what the talk is about, so that discursive communication, in what it says, makes manifest what it is talking about, and thus makes it accessible to the other party."[41] However, not all discourse has this character. As well as true discourse there is false discourse, characterized by Heidegger as "*covering up*: putting something in front of something (in such a way as to let it be seen) and thereby passing it off *as* something which it is *not*".[42] The parenthetical remark that when false discourse covers up the truth it does so by letting it be seen points back once more to what we have already encountered in relation to semblance. The problem besetting our attempts to get clear about the truth of our Being, to attain "ontological transparency", is not that this truth is far off or on another level but that we are encompassed by a world of semblance that seems to us "proximally and for the most part" to be true. Thus deceived (or "tranquillized") we typically never even make a start on putting these semblances to the test.

What is crucial to note here, however, is that all this is being said with reference to discourse as the pre-eminent mode in which what is to be made manifest in a genuinely phenomenological view of beings and that both truth (the genuine manifestation or unconcealment of beings is revealed as they are) and falsehood (the covering-up of beings by a mere semblance of truth) occur in and as discourse. This then prepares us for all that Heidegger will say in ¶34 and ¶35 about discourse and especially about the *Gerede*, the "idle talk", the kind of discourse that "has lost its primary relationship-of-Being towards the entity talked about, or else has never achieved such a relationship" and which therefore "does not communicate in such a way as to let this entity be appropriated in a primordial manner, but communicates rather by following the route of

---

[39] Ibid, 56/32.
[40] Ibid, 56/33.
[41] Ibid, 56/32.
[42] Ibid, 57/33. For the background to these definitions, see Heidegger's lectures on *The Sophist* (Martin Heidegger, *Plato's Sophist*, trans. R. Rojcewicz and A. Schuwer (Bloomington: Indiana University Press, 1997)) and also his lectures on Aristotle (see note 34).

gossiping and passing-the-word-along", whether in speaking or writing, private conversation or public discourse.[43]

IV. *Gerede*, "Chatter" and the Task of Philosophy

Secondary literature has on a number of occasions assimilated what Heidegger is saying here to Kierkegaard's critique of the "chatter" that he regards as symptomatic of the moral degeneracy of "the present age" and, in connection with this, has been seen as reflecting the degradation of discourse in the mass society of the twentieth century, a degradation furthered by newsprint, radio, television and other media of mass communication.[44] However, at this point at least, there does seem to be a real difference between Kierkegaard and Heidegger, even if their approaches are not incompatible. For whilst Kierkegaard is every inch the moralist in his acidic mockery of his contemporaries' vacuous chatter, Heidegger states clearly at the outset of ¶35 that "The expression 'idle talk' is not to be used here in a "disparaging" signification. Terminologically, it signifies a positive phenomenon which constitutes the kind of Being of everyday Dasein's understanding and interpreting."[45] In fact, the record of Heidegger's lectures show that the background of his account of *Gerede* is less Kierkegaard and more Aristotle, particularly the view mediated through his reflections on Aristotle's *Rhetoric* that the "everyday" discourse of the Greek agora provided the pre-philosophical *sitz-im-leben* out of which philosophy itself emerged, specifically as a counter-movement to the manipulation of discourse by the professional rhetors and their facility in substituting semblance for a true view of the matter at issue.[46] *Gerede* is not degenerate, it is just how people get on with talking to each other about whatever might be at issue—local gossip, politics, the nature of things—without regard to whether what is being said is truly manifest in the saying of it. In this sense, *Gerede* is the way in which the assumptions that prevail in a given society about what is good and what is bad, what is worth striving for and what is to be shunned, who's in and who's out are collectively mediated. It is the medium of the self-understanding and world-view of an age. As such, what is said in *Gerede*

---

[43] Heidegger, *Being and Time*, 212-3/168-9.
[44] See, for example, Peter Fenves, *"Chatter": Language and History in Kierkegaard* (Stanford: Stanford University Press, 1993), 248-9.
[45] Heidegger, *Being and Time*, 211/167.
[46] See Martin Heidegger, *Grundbegriffe der aristotelischen Philosophie*, Gesamtausgabe Vol. 18 (Frankfurt am Main: V. Klostermann, 2002), especially Part One (45-268).

is not necessarily false in a conventional sense. I believe it to be true that the earth goes round the sun, but, actually, I only know this on the basis of having been told it by others: I do not myself understand fully the astronomical calculations that would let me see why this has to be so. I know it because, in Heidegger's phrase, this item of knowledge has been "passed along" to me. Nevertheless—and as in fact this example also suggests—even if *Gerede* is not formally untrue, to the extent that my world is in fact constituted by it, my ability to hold myself open to things as they are and to see myself as what I truly am is diminished and becomes progressively atrophied. I perish in what George Steiner would call "secondariness".[47]

Here, then, is where the "covering-up" that is currently prevalent is most likely to be found. Nevertheless, it is, as such, also the only material with which philosophy itself is able to begin: philosophy must fight its way through to a true view of things precisely by contesting the claims of what gets said about human being in the *Gerede* of an average everyday understanding shaped by the words, images and ideas about human beings that are currently passed on and passed around among us, including "philosophical" and even "scientific" words, images, and ideas. Heidegger the philosopher, then, can himself begin only with what is said about human beings in the general *Gerede* of his time: this is the material that he must counter-intuitively interpret in order to bring forth and to validate the "advance view" he has taken as to the possibility of a genuine and adequate understanding of Being.

These comments suggest two possibilities for understanding Kierkegaard's role in *Being and Time* and, I suggest, these help clarify the ambivalence of Heidegger's relation to this "penetrating" existentiell thinker. In the first place, Kierkegaard himself or, more precisely, a certain reception of Kierkegaard—the Kierkegaardianism of the crisis-ridden post-War years, we might say—is to be taken as the currently paradigmatic instance of *Gerede*. In this cultural moment, we surmise, everybody (or everybody Heidegger thought worth talking with) more or less took it for granted that "we" had become alienated, isolated individuals, left alone to anxiously await our death and therefore all the more prone to lose ourselves in the distractions and "tranquillizing" remedies offered by the age. In the second place, and by way of contrast, Kierkegaard is rather to be seen as one of those whose penetrating analyses of this situation enabled them to pierce the tranquillizing fog of modern alienation and start on the way towards seeing the world in its true light.

---

[47] See George Steiner, *Real Presences* (London: Faber, 1989).

But are these views mutually exclusive? Or are they perhaps complementary? Of course, everything we have heard Heidegger say about Kierkegaard, little as it is, might be taken as pointing towards the second. Wasn't it Kierkegaard who back in 1921-2 had provided the motto for a phenomenological project that would disillusion philosophy of its absorption in semblance and lead it once more towards the things themselves? However, just as we have seen something of the difficulties that Heidegger encountered in trying to draw a clear line between existentiell and existential thinking and the consequent circularity of their complex interrelationship, so too I am suggesting that comparable difficulties await any attempt to make a firm decision as to the boundaries between genuine thinking and *Gerede*. There is Kierkegaard—and there is Kierkegaardianism, and the adherents of Kierkegaardianism will in all likelihood use the same words as Kierkegaard himself and sometimes maybe use them both aptly and beautifully; at the very least they will be able to use them seductively. Angst can become fashionable. It has happened. Once the Kierkegaardian word has been passed along, it too is subject to the power of *Gerede* and can perhaps only be rescued (if Heidegger is right) by the "violent" intervention of a thinker who understands him better than he himself. In these terms, the presence of Kierkegaard in *Being and Time* can be interpreted in a Hölderlin quote that Heidegger (and many others, including C. G. Jung) would use in relation to the crisis of modernity, that "where danger is, there grows the saving power".[48] That is to say, Kierkegaardianism—a certain kind of subjectively accentuated pessimism—is the danger, but Kierkegaard himself offers a way of penetrating beyond this and orienting us towards genuine thinking.

Might this explanation satisfy the complaining Kierkegaard scholars from whom we heard at the start of these reflections, if we could say that there is nothing said in *Being and Time* against Kierkegaard, but only against allowing Kierkegaard to be deployed as an instrument in the service of *Gerede*? Unfortunately, there is nothing in the text to suggest that Heidegger himself drew this kind of distinction, although we perhaps detect something similar in Karl Barth's disavowal of a certain Kierkegaardianism[49] and Heidegger would certainly make an analogous move later with regard to the popular appropriation of his own philosophy of existence (and, for that matter, with regard to the distinction of his own position from what is "mostly called" National Socialism). Heidegger

---

[48] The quotation is from the opening lines of Hölderlin's Hymn *Patmos*.
[49] See Karl Barth, "Kierkegaard and the Theologians" in *Fragments Grave and Gay*, trans. Eric Mosbacher (London, Collins, 1971), 102-4.

seems to believe that the limitations he places on Kierkegaard are, in fact, intrinsic to Kierkegaard's own work and not merely to the misreadings of his epigones.

But there is a third possibility that comes into view if we understand the possibilities under discussion neither as mutually exclusive nor even as complementary but as interconnected at a very fundamental level, blending into each other and conditioning each other at every step. For just as existential analysis has to work its way through existentiell self-understanding and therefore bears within itself the marks of that same self-understanding, so too must existentiell self-understanding bear within itself the marks of the *Gerede* out of which it has had to fight its way, even when it penetrates so far as to be able to lay hold of itself in authentic resoluteness. Its origin in and its continuing proximity to *Gerede* means that even authentic self-understanding is always prone to slip back into "idle talk".[50] But this would also seem to mean that, via its intercalation with existentiell thinking, not even existential phenomenology that has been successful in thinking its way through to the end can deliver a "result" that would be secure against being degraded back into such "idle talk". In its anxiety to distinguish itself from a merely ontic, psychological or existentiell kind of thinking, such a phenomenology reveals a still deeper anxiety, namely, the anxiety that it too will revert to *Gerede*—a "jargon of authenticity", we might say.

It seems as if Heidegger himself came to understand this, at least implicitly, as he continued to change the vocabulary and style of his path of thinking, abandoning the quest to lay a basis for human self-understanding that would, as such, provide a secure ground for scientific research in all fields of enquiry. Instead, his later thought seems to move towards a more poetic, meditative, and, we might say with hindsight, "weak" understanding of its task and responsibilities, culminating in the *Gelassenheit* in which it becomes content just to let beings be. This seems to take him ever further from Kierkegaard, but if the argument of this paper holds, then it may also be understood as a response to the anxieties that come to the surface in his earlier attempts to forge a sustainable distinction between the existentiell and the existential, which, as we have seen, was central to how he himself understood his relation to Kierkegaard.

---

[50] This is argued in the case of Kierkegaard by Peter Fenves. See his *Chatter*, 243.

V. Conclusion

I do not presume to have exhausted the issues generated by Kierkegaard's presence in *Being and Time*. One may, for example, consider whether Heidegger's pursuit of ontology at the expense of a more extensive analysis of the existentiell situation of the human subject, including its moral as well as its religious obligations, is well conceived.[51] What I hope to have shown, however, is that we should not be too quick to take umbrage at the slight to Kierkegaard that the three footnote references might be taken as implying. Not only do they acknowledge his relevance to three of the most central topics of *Being and Time* (existence, anxiety, and the "moment of vision"), Heidegger's own reflections on the existentiell/ existential distinction reveal his understanding of their ultimate inseparability and his view that the relationship between them is better construed in terms of the hermeneutical circle than as one of different levels or even a kind of "sublation" à la Hegel. Nor, finally, should we reproach Heidegger with not having been more assiduous in providing further textual references for the multiple Kierkegaardian topics that appear throughout *Being and Time*, including, as previously noted, such central issues as death, guilt, and nothingness. For even though I concluded that Heidegger need not be reproached for confusing Kierkegaard with the Kierkegaardianism of the post-War years, it was entirely in accordance with his understanding of the starting-point of philosophy that the "Kierkegaard" who shaped the way in which his contemporaries "proximally and for the most part" talked about themselves and their existence should provide initial guidance in determining the direction of his own phenomenological enquiries. Whether or not *this* "Kierkegaard" faithfully represents what a more historically-informed or philosophically-sensitive interpretation of the Danish writer than that provided by the 1920s Kierkegaardians is, in an important sense, not relevant to Heidegger's project and so he does not

---

[51] I have argued elsewhere that Heidegger has not, in fact, chosen the better part. In an interesting article on Lévinas' interpretation of Kierkegaard, Samuel Moyn has argued that Kierkegaard served Lévinas as a way of securing a place for the "other" over against Heidegger's entire absorption of Dasein's essential interest in the purely immanent transcendence of a Being that is already in some sense interior to Dasein itself, i.e. that draws out and explicates a self-understanding already implicit in Dasein (one is also put in mind at this point of Kierkegaard's own critique of recollection/anamnesis in *Philosophical Fragments*). See Samuel Moyn, "Transcendence, Morality, and History: Emmanuel Levinas and the Discovery of Søren Kierkegaard in France" in *Yale French Studies* 104 "Encounters with Levinas" (2004), 22-54.

need to give chapter and verse for each Kierkegaardian allusion he makes. The point is precisely that this way of understanding the human situation is already prevalent amongst his contemporary readers and he does not need to spell it out for them. In its proximity to *Gerede*, such a "Kierkegaardian" view of life easily becomes a "semblance" obstructing our access to the things themselves. At the same time, thanks to Kierkegaard's own success in "penetrating" many of the prevailing semblances, his thought is able to provide a preliminary orientation to those, like Heidegger, who are hopeful of being able to think the matter through "to the end". But, as we have seen, philosophy seems doomed to a Sisyphean labour and, without the secure scientific outcome for which the Heidegger of the 1920s had some hopes, it finds itself once more, even after *Being and Time*, having to go back to the beginning and start over with attempting to make sense of the *Gerede* of its time.

However, having just indicated that, in his own terms, Heidegger was justified in not engaging in a more textually or historically thorough study of Kierkegaard it does not follow that such study—whether of Kierkegaard or of other decisive figures of the past who have in their various ways shaped the "average everyday" understanding of existence that prevails in our own time—may not be a means to releasing new possibilities for helping us think our way out of the *Gerede* that permeates our own attempts to work out just who we are and just what existence is asking of us. As so often, when the path ahead is blocked, it is often necessary to retrace our steps in order to move forward. The Kierkegaard scholars may be consoled, but they are also challenged to remember that their concern with the textual deposit bequeathed us from the past is also to be read in the light of our concern for the present and the future.

Bibliography

Baranova-Shestova, Natalia. *Jiizn" L"va Shestova*. 2 Vols. Paris: La Presse Libre, 1983.

Barth, Karl. "Kierkegaard and the Theologians." In *Fragments Grave and Gay*, translated by Eric Mosbacher. London: Collins, 1971.

Brock, Werner. *Contemporary German Philosophy*. Cambridge: Cambridge University Press, 1935.

Caputo, John D. "Kierkegaard, Heidegger, and the Foundering of Metaphysics." In Robert L. Perkins edited, *International Kierkegaard Commentary: Fear and Trembling and Repetition*. Macon GA: Mercer University Press, 1993.

Disse, Jörg. *Kierkegaard's Phenomenology of the Experience of Freedom.* Freiburg: Karl Alber, 1991.

Fenves, Peter. *"Chatter": Language and History in Kierkegaard.* Stanford: Stanford University Press, 1993.

Grøn, Arne. *Subjektivitet og Negativitet.* Copenhagen: Gyldendal, 1997.

Heidegger, Martin. *Being and Time.* Translated by John Macquarrie and Edward Robinson. Oxford: Basil Blackwell, 1962.

—. *Frühe Schriften.* Frankfurt am Main: V. Klostermann, 1972.

—. *Phänomenologische Intepretatationen zu Aristoteles/Einführung in die phänomenologische Forschung.* Gesamtausgabe Vol. 61. Frankfurt am Main: V. Klostermann, 1984.

—. *Phänomenologie des religiösen Lebens.* Gesamtausgabe Vol. 60. Frankfurt am Main: V. Klostermann, 1995.

—. *Plato's Sophist.* Translated by R. Rojcewicz and A. Schuwer. Bloomington: Indiana University Press, 1997.

—. *Grundbegriffe der aristotelischen Philosophie.* Gesamtausgabe Vol. 18. Frankfurt am Main: V. Klostermann, 2002.

Kisiel, Theodore. *The Genesis of Heidegger's Being and Time.* Berkeley CA: University of California Press, 1993.

Moyn, Samuel. "Transcendence, Morality, and History: Emmanuel Levinas and the Discovery of Søren Kierkegaard in France." *Yale French Studies* 104 (2004): 22-54

Pattison, George. "Ethics, Ontology and Religion: Reflections on Kierkegaard's Upbuilding Discourses." *Topos (Journal of the European Humanities University, Minsk)* 1.6 (2002): 51-64

—. "Heidegger, Augustine and Kierkegaard: Care, Time and Love." In Craig de Paulo edited, *The Influence of Augustine on Heidegger: The Emergence of an Augustinian Phenomenology.* New York: Edwin Mellen Press, 2006.

—. "Kierkegaard and Phenomenology." In Jeffrey Hanson edited, *Kierkegaard as Phenomenologist.* Evanston IL: Northwestern University Press, 2010.

Schleiermacher, F.D.E. *The Christian Faith.* Translated and edited by H. R. Mackintosh and J. S. Stewart. Edinburgh: T. & T. Clark, 1928.

Schrag, Calvin O. *Existence and Freedom: Towards an Ontology of Human Finitude.* Evanston IL: Northwestern University Press, 1961.

Steiner, George. *Real Presences.* London: Faber, 1989.

Theunissen, Michael. "The Upbuilding in the Thought of Death: Traditional Elements, Innovative Ideas, and Unexhausted Possibilities." Translated by George Pattison. In Robert L. Perkins edited, *International Kierkegaard Commentary: Prefaces and Writing*

Sampler and *Three Discourses on Imagined Occasions*. Macon GA: Mercer University Press, 2006.

PART II

REINTERPRETING THE SECULAR

CHAPTER SEVEN

SECULARISM, IMMANENCE, AND THE PHILOSOPHY OF RELIGION

DANIEL COLUCCIELLO BARBER

Philosophy of religion operates in the vicinity of the unconditioned. This is easy enough to see when philosophy of religion affirms religion, for religion asserts its capacity to articulate what is beyond conditions. But this is also the case in the more widespread scenario whereby philosophy of religion adopts a critical stance toward such an assertion, for even then it must become entangled with the unconditioned—if only to nullify it. There is, additionally, the scenario in which it is philosophy that invokes the right to think the unconditioned, in order to then pose it against religion. The analysis I am presenting, however, cannot be aligned with any of these three approaches. It does not directly offer a discourse on the unconditioned, but instead looks at the conditions produced by religion. What is religion? This is to ask, what conditions does religion engender, and under what conditions is it engendered? Only by addressing these questions can philosophy of religion construct a point of view that aims at the essence of its own operation.

My essay will commence by addressing these questions, and in doing so it will follow the thesis that the concept of religion is a Christian invention. I will then proceed to look at the concept of the secular. While the secular may seem to provide a means of escape from the limitations imposed by a concept of religion that is made in the image of dominant Christianity, this is not ultimately the case. In order to make such an argument, I delineate how the installation of a secular plane does not liberate the world so much as it finds a new way of transcending the world. Accordingly, I claim, the secular must be seen in many ways as a continuation of rather than a departure from the conditions set by the Christian invention of religion. It is in view of this continuity that I turn to the concept of immanence. Only immanence, I contend, allows us to get beyond the conditions involved in Christian religion and the secular plane.

First, then, I look at Spinoza's account of immanence, focusing specifically on two paradoxes intrinsic to his thought. Second, as a way of finding a potential power of innovation within these paradoxes, I propose an account of immanence that is both secular and religious, but in such a manner that secularity and religion evade the restrictions of Christianity and the secular plane.

I. The Christian Invention of Religion

I will begin with the argument, as it has recently appeared in the work of Daniel Boyarin, that the concept of religion is a Christian invention. Boyarin follows the thesis that the exigency of being able to name something as religion arises with the emergence of Christianity.[1] This is not, of course, to claim that what are now called religions were not practiced prior to Christianity. The point, more specifically, is that such practices were not understood as modes of belonging to something called "religion."[2] Why, then, does such a shift occur? What is it about Christianity that forces into existence something called religion? What matters here is not so much what Christians believe so much as the characterization of Christianity itself in terms of belief. To be a Christian is to believe the right things, such that one who does not believe rightly cannot be called a Christian—which is to say that the invention of Christianity is inseparable from the invention of heresy. According to Boyarin, "the question of who's in and who's out became the primary way of thinking about Christianicity. ... 'In' was to be defined by correct belief; 'out' by adherence via an alleged choice to false belief."[3] Concomitant to this characterization of Christianity in terms of belief is the insistence that one's identity is achieved rather than given. The connection between these is not obscure: if one is a Christian by virtue of

---

[1] Daniel Boyarin, in *Border Lines: The Partition of Judaeo-Christianity* (Philadelphia: University of Pennsylvania Press, 2004), notes the work of Seth Schwartz, whose thesis he describes as "claiming that the production of Christianity is, itself, the invention of religion as such—a discrete category of human experience" (11). One of the central insights that Boyarin adds to this thesis is that heresiology is intrinsic to the double production of Christianity and religion.

[2] Boyarin remarks: "The production of this category does not imply that many elements of what would form religions did not exist before this time, but rather that the particular aggregation of verbal and other practices that would now be named as constituting a religion only came into being as a discrete category as Christianization itself" (Ibid, 11).

[3] Ibid, 17.

belief, then it is necessary for one to *become* a Christian; to be a Christian is not something given by corporeal genealogy or cultural inheritance, it is something achieved by conversion to and incorporation within a group, defined by right belief, that transcends the marks of pre-established identity. After all, it was Paul who proclaimed that, in Christ Jesus, "There is no longer Jew or Greek, there is no longer slave or free, there is no longer male and female."[4]

What is this thing into which the believer in Christ enters? It is easy enough to say Christianity, or even the church, but this is only to push the question one step further along, such that we must now ask: What sort of thing is Christianity? Boyarin's answer—with which I am in agreement— is that Christianity is a religion.[5] But this is not to say that Christianity found itself conforming to a pre-existing category of religion. On the contrary, the significant novelty of Christianity, with its emphasis on right belief and on identity as achieved rather than given, rendered it unrecognisable within pre-established categories. Christianity found it necessary to invent a category to which it could properly belong. Thus it is no accident that when religion is conceived, it is conceived in the image of Christianity. A religion is determined according to an identifiable set of beliefs, and by adhering to these beliefs one achieves a properly religious identity. Religion, then, is the means by which Christianity recognizes itself. Christianity invents itself by inventing religion.

Such an invention effects a discontinuity—one between a time before and a time after religion—that is easy to overlook or underestimate. This is perhaps due to the (by now) widespread success or naturalization of what was invented, which allows philosophy of religion generally to presume that even as religions change, come into and leave existence, there have always been religions. But this is simply not the case. Not only has religion not always been with us, it has entered into existence by way of an essentially Christian operation. For instance, while there were obviously Jewish people prior to the emergence of Christianity, there were no practitioners of something called "Judaism." In fact, according to Boyarin, the religion of Judaism itself arises only in relation to the invention of Christianity. Similarly, while we could say that pagans exist prior to the Christian invention of religion, "Paganism" is a decidedly post-Christian

---

[4] Galatians 3:28. For an account of the limits of the universalism involved in this Pauline proclamation, see Daniel Boyarin, *A Radical Jew: Paul and the Politics of Identity* (Berkeley: University of California Press, 1994).

[5] Boyarin remarks: "This notion that identity is achieved and not given by birth, history, language, and geographical location was the novum that produced religion" (*Border Lines*, 17).

phenomenon—indeed, the very affirmation that pagans pre-exist Christianity involves one in an act of retroactive constitution, for the term "Pagan" is a product of Christianity. To make the emergence of Judaism and Paganism dependent upon an operation of Christianity is not to suggest that they lack agency, or that they do not creatively resist the character that Christianity seeks to give to them. Boyarin shows, for example, that Judaism defines itself in opposition to Christianity, that even though Christianity seeks to make Judaism conform to the model of a religion, Judaism refuses to be a religion homologous to Christianity.[6] The point, then, is not that resistance is not possible; it is rather that the conditions that are (or are not) resisted are first installed by Christianity, or by the Christian invention of religion.

But why does Christianity install these conditions? To answer this question, we need to return to the question of heresy. Christianity, because it defines itself in terms of right belief, constantly confronts the question of boundaries. It must incessantly draw and redraw the lines between itself and its outside—or, more exactly, the lines that bring about an inside and an outside. Right Christian belief emerges only in tandem with wrong belief; Christianity dialectically constitutes itself by constituting heresies. Properly Christian belief is not a measure that, already possessed (even if inchoately), can be used to straightforwardly identify heresies. Such orthodoxy only comes into possession through the act of negating—which is to say, defining something as—a heresy. Christian orthodoxy is necessarily post-heretical. One identifies oneself as having properly Christian belief—one achieves one's Christian identity—insofar as one identifies others as having heretical beliefs. For instance, there can be Christians precisely because there are Gnostics. In this sense, the invention of Christian orthodoxy presupposes the invention of its outside—and it is not enough for this outside to be indeterminate. There must be a determinate other, a determinate outside, if there is to be a determination of a Christian inside.

I have just spoken of Christianity's line-drawing, its classificatory operation, primarily with a view towards heresiology. Christianity defines itself by defining the heresies that, while purportedly aiming to achieve identification as Christian, fail to do so. But more important for my purposes is the way in which the classificatory production found in heresiology persists in the concept of religion. Just as the identity of Christianity is achieved by way of the invention of heresies, so the identification of Christianity as the one true religion is achieved by way of

---

[6] Judaism, on Boyarin's reading, resists its Christian interpellation as religion through its refusal—at least ultimately, if not initially—of heresiology, and through its insistence on identity as given rather than achieved.

the invention of religion (and the invention of religion entails the invention
of other religions). Religion functions not simply as another name for
Christianity, even if proper religion is found in Christianity. There can be
no proper religion unless there are improper religions, or no perfect
incarnation of religion unless there are imperfect religions. If religion is
just another name for Christianity, then religion, or Christianity, is a
singularity. Christianity thus determines its relation to religion not only by
conceiving religion, but also by conceiving other religions. Such a field of
religion/religions is necessary if Christianity is to be something other than
an incommensurable singularity, if it is to be what it claims to be: the one
true religion.

Christianity, in order to be true, must achieve something that others
aspire to achieve. It needs common aspirants, which is to say competitors
that are involved in the same game. This game is religion, and these
competitors are other religions (notably Judaism and Paganism, though
there will of course be others as history proceeds). It does not matter
whether these others sense themselves as belonging to a religion, for the
sense that they are given is the sense that Christianity needs them to have.
Of course, Christianity's ability to enforce and reproduce such a
classificatory scheme of religion—its ability to interpellate—rests on the
political power that it achieves by way of its becoming-Constantinian (i.e.,
on the establishment of Christendom). But awareness of this dependence
must not obscure the nature of the theoretical power that such political
power legitimates. What is of concern, especially when the philosophy of
religion is in question, is Christianity's—or religion's—conceptual power,
its power to produce and classify realities.

It is necessary, before proceeding from the question of Christian
religion to the question of the secular, to observe that what is at stake is a
peculiar sort of universalism. Christianity, of course, is a universal
discourse, for it asserts that it, particularly and especially, reveals the
fullness of the Logos. This is widely noted. Less noted, however, is the
way in which Christian universal discourse is inseparable from the
invention of religion. If Christianity is to be the particular revelation of the
universal, it must be possible to conceive, or to name, the universal it
reveals—and religion is this universal. All discourse on religion, even
when it no longer proceeds from a particularly Christian vantage, must
address this inheritance. For Christianity, the universal identity of religion
is refracted according to divisions occasioned by multiple religions. These
many religions are analogous, insofar as they are all meaningfully
denominated as religion, but the Christian religion—fitting into the

lineaments of a logic of sovereignty—figures as the primary analogue. It is one of many religions, but it is also the model of religion itself.[7]

This is to say that the invention of religion amounts to the installation of a new plane. The plane of religion is universal, but it is also populated and carved up by particular religions. It maintains a degree of immanence insofar as it is thus populated, but it is ultimately transcendent insofar as religion functions as an ordering, hierarchalising principle. Religions are named from above, even if this above has its origin in the particular interests of Christianity. Indeed, it is precisely the installation of this universal plane of religion that enables Christianity to occlude its particular, constructed character and to present itself as originate rather than derivative.

II. The Installation of the Secular Plane

It is possible to discern, embedded within the normative discourse of Christian religion that I have just sketched, something resembling a philosophy of religion. But this would not be philosophy of religion as we now imagine it. Thus, while contemporary philosophy of religion may address the claims of Augustine, Aquinas, and Anselm, it addresses them only as objects within a larger field. To treat such figures not as objects within a pre-constituted field, but instead as determinative of philosophy of religion—as any classically Christian philosophy of religion must do—would be to betray the purportedly secular aspirations of contemporary philosophy. From our vantage, it seems accurate to say not that Augustine, for instance, provides a philosophy of religion, but rather that he presents a religious philosophy, or a philosophically-oriented religion. All of this indicates that a break has occurred, that a significant discontinuity has been effected. My aim, I should make clear, is not somehow to contravene the reality of such a discontinuity. It is instead to examine the nature and

---

[7] Also worthy of observation is the specific relationship that is produced between Christianity and Judaism. Such a relationship has peculiar import due to Christianity's Jewish roots. Christianity wants to articulate itself as the primary analogate, but it is apparently secondary with regard to (what will later be named) Judaism. Christianity understands itself as logically originate, but precisely because of this it finds itself threatened by its historically derivative status. Accordingly, whenever we interrogate the universalism of Christian religion—as well as any universalism that maintains some relation, whether positive, negative, or qualified, to Christian religion—we must foreground the way in which such universalism functions to cast the secondary as primary, to occlude the derivative status of the origin.

degree of this discontinuity. In what ways does the obviousness of this discontinuity shift attention from certain implicit lines of continuity between Christianity and the secular? The secular is certainly not Christian, but we already know this. What we do not know, or in any case what we do not foreground, is the possibility of seeing the secular as a repetition—a differential repetition no doubt, but a repetition nonetheless—of Christian religion.

To gain such a vision, one can do no better than to turn to the work of Talal Asad, who has provided exemplary analyses of the basic operations of the secular. These analyses are for the most part varied and essayistic, but they are not without a basic thesis. This thesis is that the secular is improperly understood when conceived as responding to an eternal or ahistorical problem, or as referring to a universal, natural state that exists prior to particular and diversified religious modes of signification. The secular may very well promote itself along these lines, but as long as such a self-description is accepted we fail to attend to the fact that the secular is "an enactment."[8] To say that the secular is an enactment is to say something banal—what is not an enactment? But what matters here is the way that the secular's enactment cuts against its appearance as something natural, universal, and ahistorical, or as a response to a problem that is natural, universal, and ahistorical. "Secularism," Asad remarks, "is not simply an intellectual answer to a question about enduring social peace and toleration."[9] It is much more—it is a disciplining of bodies and affects, Asad certainly would add. But even then, it is still more, for what the secular by and large conceals is not only its dependence on various bodily modes of empowerment and disempowerment. It also conceals, even at the level of the "intellectual"—the level that most explicitly concerns the philosophy of religion—the way in which the questions it poses, and of course the answers it supplies, belong to an irreducibly particular form of life.

Central here is that the concept of the secular, even as it claims to have named something universal in scope, remains ensconced in a particular vantage. The necessity of its enactment marks that it is not a referential denotation of something already existent, that it is not, in fact, universal, but that it calls forth a universality to-come, and that it does so from a decidedly non-universal perspective. Drawing Asad's claims into my own ambit, and putting it rather directly—such that the point of continuity between Christianity and the secular might be made manifest—it can be

---

[8] Talal Asad, *Formations of the Secular: Christianity, Islam, Modernity* (Stanford: Stanford University Press, 2004), 5.

[9] Ibid, 5.

said that the conception of the secular aims not to address overarching questions about difference, religion, and common life, but rather to install a new plane. If the secular is universal, it is not because it responds to a problematic that is universal, it is because it proclaims itself as universal at the same moment that it conceals its particularity. Secular universality belongs to a particularity that effaces itself, or to a particularity that best conforms to a standard of universality set by that very particularity.

What I am proposing, then, is that the secular is an "enactment" in the same sense that the Christian invention of religion is an enactment. At stake in each instance is the installation of a plane that is universal, insofar as it presents itself as normatively encompassing, and transcendent, insofar as it provides a point of reference that stands outside and above every particular formation of life. This is not at all to deny that such a point of reference is engendered from one of these many particular formations, or that this universality is *de jure* rather than *de facto*. It is simply that the particular character of Christianity, or of the secular, is effaced by its exemplary instantiation of the universal—and this effacement is facilitated, of course, by the fact that the character of the universal is a product of Christian, or secular, particularity.

This poses a special difficulty for the secular, since the secular, if we are to take it at face value, wants to grant attention to the world, rather than to anything that transcends the world, or that would determine the world from a point beyond the world. But if the secular weds itself to a plane that it has installed, then it has not wedded itself to the world. This must be the case, unless we presuppose an isomorphism between the particular secular formation of the world and the world itself—but if this is the condition for being worldly, then how does such a secular presupposition meaningfully distinguish itself from a non-secular (which is to say religious) presupposition, whereby the truth of the world is isomorphic with the truth articulated by religion? Consequently, it must be affirmed that the secular formation of life is not life itself, that the secular is not the world, or simply that the secular is not secular.

Perhaps this assertion remains contentious. After all, one might observe, the secular, even if it diverges from an affirmation of the world itself, maintains the imperative to affirm the world. Whatever flaws the secular may involve, they can be overcome by way of the demand intrinsic to secularity. It is this imperative that makes the discontinuity with Christianity, or with religion in general, more basic then any degree of continuity. Now, while there is something to such a rejoinder—in fact, I will later pursue something like this line of thought—it still evades the mediatic character of the secular. What I mean by this is that the secular, even as it can be seen to issue such an imperative, never does so without simultaneously setting forth the proper mediations for becoming secular— and these mediations are always mediations that invoke the secular plane, which is transcendent to the world itself. In other words, the scenario set forth by the secular is not one in which secularity is differentially constituted by particular forms of life in the world. On the contrary, the secular is always already instantiated by the particular form of life named as "the secular," such that to become-secular is not to immediately become worldly from whatever particular form of life, it is instead to mediate all (non-secular) particular forms of life through the (always already) secular form of life.

We have, once again, a repetition of Christian religion, in which every becoming-religious must amount to becoming-Christian, for religion is mediated by Christianity. Similarly, there is a difficulty in posing secularity against the secular, for secularity is mediated by the secular. The plane of the world, of secularity beyond the secular, is mediated by the plane installed by the secular. In this regard, it may additionally be noted that the secular is, in a certain sense, more insidious than Christianity. This is because Christianity maintains a conceptual distinction between itself and religion. For this reason, the sheer assertion of identity between Christianity and true religion remained somewhat apparent, and the possibility of turning the essence of religion against Christianity, so as to say that Christianity is not true religion, or that all religions are equally religious, remained open. Indeed, it could be said that the secular pursues these very possibilities. This is not to say that the secular does not privilege Christianity, or at least the so-called "monotheistic" religions. It repeats these Christian presuppositions, but it does so as part of a larger articulation in which the dialectical opposition is no longer one between Christian religion and non-Christian religions, but instead becomes one between the secular and religion(s). So in what sense is the enactment of the secular more insidious than the enactment of Christian religion? It is because the secular presents no conceptual distinction between its particular formation and the plane it installs. One who wants to oppose secularity against the secular finds his desire instantaneously, yet strangely, recognized—does not the secular always already want the secularity that one poses against the secular? So, what is—or, more appositely, was—the problem?

The conflation of a particular secular formation of life and a transcendent, universal plane of the secular has a twofold function. On the one hand, it makes the particular formation of life normative, such that a proper inhabitation of this plane finds its ideal instantiation. On the other, the excess of the plane to the particular secular form of life provides something at which non-secular forms of life can aim. The plane's excess to the particular sets forth the mediations by which non-secular forms of life mime the secular's particular form of life. Thus Saba Mahmood notes that the aim of the secular is not to preclude religion as such so much as it is to induct religious forms of life into a process of secularisation.[10] It is as if the secular says, we don't want you to become like us, we simply want you to become secular—you do not need to obey us, you need to obey the universal that we are obeying. This is akin to a matter of translation, where becoming-secular does not require one to trade one's own particular language for another, particularly secular language. It requires something less, or something more: to translate one's particular language onto a universal, secular plane, the cipher of which is nonetheless provided by a particularly secular language. Thus Asad, in an attempt to resist what I am calling the mediations of the secular plane, recommends that anthropologists "learn to treat some of their own Enlightenment assumptions as belonging to specific kinds of reasoning—albeit kinds of reasoning that have largely shaped our modern world—and not as the ground from which all understanding of non-Enlightenment traditions must begin."[11] This is essentially to deny that the translation between particular forms of life be mediated by the secular plane. Here the secular becomes yet another particularity, and in this way the incommensurability between particularities is brought to the foreground.

III. Spinoza's Paradoxes

I have thus far articulated the dominant conditions that structure contemporary thought about the philosophy of religion. The point of this articulation, however, is to move beyond such conditions, to expel them. Precisely, what must be expelled is what has been installed: a transcendent, universal plane. It is therefore not a matter of posing the planes of

---

[10] Mahmood remarks that "secularism has sought not so much to banish religion from the public domain but to reshape the form it takes, the subjectivities it endorses, and the epistemological claims it can make. The effectiveness of such a totalising project necessarily depends upon transforming the religious domain through a variety of reforms and state injunctions." See Saba Mahmood, "Secularism, Hermeneutics, Empire: The Politics of Islamic Reformation," *Public Culture* 18 (2): 326.

[11] Talal Asad, *Genealogies of Religion: Discipline and Reasons of Power in Christianity and Islam* (Baltimore: The Johns Hopkins University Press, 1993), 200.

Christian religion and the secular against one another, of balancing them, or even of seeing some manner of teleological development in their succession. Both planes must be expelled, along with the various theories about the relation of philosophy and religion that presuppose and circulate within them. It is therefore not enough simply to cast philosophy of religion in secular terms. This certainly allows possibilities of thought that exceed those made available by Christianity, but it does not fundamentally escape the very plane of transcendence that limits the possibilities of thought in the first (Christian) instance. The movement from the Christian plane of religion to the plane of the secular is still too conservative.

If there is to be a break with the conditions that structure philosophy about—or within, or against—religion, then the capacity to think without a transcendent plane must be pursued. It is in this sense, and in this sense alone, that philosophy of religion must become secular. Already, however, a qualification is necessary: the secularity thus required is one that is utterly opposed to the secular as I have already articulated it. In what follows, then, I will argue for a secularity that is intrinsic to immanence. Only the rigor of immanence provides the possibility of a secularity that has nothing to do with a transcendent plane. I will argue, furthermore, that an immanent secularity provides a new way of thinking about religion—one that evades Christianity's interpellative invention of religion as well as the secular's dialectically oppositional relation to religion. In this regard, the way forward lies with Spinoza. This is not because Spinoza directly articulates the theory I am proposing. What matters here are certain paradoxes produced by Spinoza's work, paradoxes that harbour the potentiality for the sort of immanent secularity and immanent affirmation of religion that I am advancing.

The first of these paradoxes lies in his insistence on speaking of "God or Nature."[12] This is, of course, a notoriously enigmatic statement. Is it that these two terms are reversible, where they name the same thing but from different vantages? Is the distinction between these terms meant to preserve a real difference in signification, or is the distinction primarily strategic, in which only one term designates the real (the other then being strategically preserved yet remaining ultimately derivative or epiphenomenal with respect to the real)? To give attention to the ambiguity of "God or Nature" is in no way to disavow the ontological import of Spinoza's thought: that there is one substance, and that this substance is fully

---

[12] Benedict de Spinoza, *Ethics*, trans. G.H.R. Parkinson (Oxford: Oxford University Press, 2000), 226; Part 4, Preface. I have chosen to render this phrase, "*Deus, seu Natura*," as "God or Nature," rather than as "God, i.e. Nature," as Parkinson does.

expressed by modes. The cause of existence (substance) does not pre-exist its effects (modes), for substance is expressively constituted by these modes. They remain immanent to one another—or, we could say, they are mutually constitutive. The cause does not exist outside of the effects, and the effects differentially compose their cause. For this reason, immanence precludes the installation of every transcendent plane—or, equally, it dissolves each pre-established transcendent plane, making it inconsistent or multiply incommensurable (this, I would contend, is what is at stake in Asad's recommendations with regard to translation). As Gilles Deleuze and Félix Guattari have remarked, "Immanence is immanent only to itself."[13] There is no immanent realm *for* the transcendent, nor is there something beyond immanence *to* which immanence belongs. Immanence refuses anything other than its own immanent operation.

If all of this is the case, then in what sense is the ambiguity of "God or Nature" relevant? It comes into view insofar as it is impossible not to name immanence—for immanence, even if it has no proper name, must be called. This, essentially, is what Spinoza recognized when he called it "God or Nature." Immanence is prior to signification because of its ontological character. There can be no proper name of existence, no theological denotation (apophatic or otherwise). Yet at the same time signification is inescapable. The ontological priority of immanence runs into the mediatic priority of signification. This is to say that signification can never be done away with—not due to some tragic flaw, but simply because there is no immediacy to immanence, there is always mediation. The purely historical explanations of Spinoza's statement miss this when they claim that the invocation of God was an attempt to minimize controversy. It may very well have been this, or at least have been this, but that is not the key point. What is most noteworthy about Spinoza's statement is the way it foregrounds the paradoxical necessity of signifying that which has no proper name.

It is not that it is wrong to recognize a historical element in "God or Nature," it is just that history is unable to address the properly philosophical insight that signification of the nameless is necessary. That said, it is important to emphasize that philosophy too has its own means of

---

[13] For this reason, Deleuze and Guattari continue, immanence "consequently captures everything, absorbs All-One, and leaves nothing remaining to which it could be immanent. In any case, whenever immanence is interpreted as immanent *to* Something, we can be sure that this Something reintroduces the transcendent." See Gilles Deleuze and Félix Guattari, *What is Philosophy?*, trans. Hugh Tomlinson and Graham Burchell (New York: Columbia University Press, 1996), 45.

evading the problem of the signification of immanence. This evasion consists in identifying Nature, rather than God, as the proper name of immanence. Such an error is understandable. After all, God—especially as conceived in the Christian and Jewish traditions that Spinoza faced— would seem to involve a denial of immanence. Therefore Nature, not God, must provide the signification of immanence. Nature, on this reading, names immanence as such, immanence once it is stripped—as, definitionally, it must be—of its transcendently religious clothing. The denial of a theologically named immanence thus advances Nature as immanence's "true" name. Here we find the presupposition behind the purely strategic interpretation of "God or Nature": God is signified only to stave off theopolitical persecution, but what Spinoza "really meant" was Nature. Yet this evades the question of why Nature is not subject to the same denial to which God is subject. Immanence is properly nameless, and Nature is a name, even if what it names is something stripped of theological propriety. In other words, Nature is still signification, and at this level it is ultimately indistinguishable from God, which is also signification.

The consequence of this is that we must remain critical of attempts to ally immanence directly with naturalism, and particularly with a naturalist mode of explanation. What I have in mind here is the tendency to recast manifestly fabulous descriptions in straightforwardly naturalist terms. Take, for instance, a case in which an individual describes the Virgin Mary appearing on a wall, but the naturalist claims that what is really appearing is a water stain—it is just that the reality of this water stain signifies, for the religious individual, the Virgin Mary. It is true, there is no Virgin Mary without signification—but equally, there is no "real" water stain without signification. Restriction of religious signification occurs not in the name of immanence, but instead in the name of the signification of Nature— which is to say that there is no restriction without construction, or that the constructive power of signification is always at work, even when what is signified is Nature. I contend, for these reasons, that any interpretation of "God or Nature" be conditioned by the paradoxical necessity of signifying immanence. Immanence refuses both theological and natural interpretation to the degree that each tends to make immanence immanent *to* something called God or something called Nature. In each case, immanence has been subjected to a transcendent plane. But immanence remains irreducible to such subjection. In this sense, immanence stands against both the Christian interpellation of religion (which subjects immanence to the signification of God) and the installation of the secular plane (which subjects immanence to the signification of Nature).

The second paradox of Spinoza's thought can be located in his claim that immanence is without teleology. "Nature," he says, "has no end which is pre-established for it."[14] There is no purpose to existence, in the sense of an end after which existence strives. Immanence cannot be immanence if it has an end, for any end installs a *telos* outside of the immanent power of existence. Immanence, once again, would be made immanent to something else, this time an end. For the same reasons, there can be neither right nor wrong, neither just nor unjust. Immanent causality collapses final causality into efficient causality. An individual is its degree of power, and right is coeval with such power—one has the right to do whatever one has the power to do. Such power can be neither just nor unjust, for either would require the imposition of a point of view that transcends the immanent exercise of power. It would, in other words, require that one stand outside the exercise of power in order to judge it as just or unjust—but this standing-outside is precisely what immanence refuses.

Of course, this is not the entire story, as it is well known that Spinoza also claims that the aim of any individual is to preserve its existence, to seek its own advantage (which means, some would add, to increase the degree of power of its existence).[15] It is here that the paradox emerges, for any account of this preservation of existence or increase of power requires a means of evaluation—a means, in other words, that involves the imagination of ends. One must imagine that *this* will preserve or increase one's power (it will be to one's advantage), but that *that* will destroy or decrease one's power (it will not be to one's advantage). It may very well be said that this is no moralism, no judgment of justice and injustice, that it is merely a question of things being good or bad. But such a response changes nothing, for what matters is not the difference between moral judgment and ethical striving, but rather the maintenance, even in the latter, of a means of evaluation—and there is no evaluation without the imposition of an end. It is therefore not enough to assert that this end is immanent, for the very emergence of an end is what calls immanence into question.[16]

---

[14] Spinoza, *Ethics*, 108; Part 1, Appendix.

[15] "A free man," Spinoza says, "desires to act, live, and preserve his being on the basis of seeking his own advantage" (*Ethics*, 276; Part 4, Proposition 67).

[16] A. Kiarina Kordela, in the same vein, observes the incapacity of pure immanence to give any direction to decisions. She looks at Spinoza's account of God's warning to Adam that if he eats of the tree of the knowledge of good and evil, he will die. Spinoza suggests a transposition of religious signification into natural signification. God, in other words, is not issuing a moral command whereby eating from the tree must be punished. God is simply making manifest,

Connecting this second paradox to the first, we could say that the production of an end belongs to signification. Immanence itself is atelic, but the impossibility of escaping signification is simultaneously the impossibility of not producing ends (even though these ends may be revisable). Just as one calls immanence "God or Nature," so one calls an event good or bad, an increase or decrease of power, a preservation or destruction of individual existence/power. Once again, what we must be on guard against is the presumption that because religious signification (as judgment) is precluded, we have somehow discovered a proper signification of immanence. From this perspective, it makes little difference whether, for example, Adam's eating of the tree of knowledge of good and evil was a matter of sin (theological judgment) or a matter of health (natural preservation), for in either case it is a matter of signification.

All of this is further complicated by the fact that it is impossible to determine something as good or bad for one's existence/power in any ultimately decisive manner. What appears beforehand to be a decrease of power may afterwards come to be understood as an increase of power. This is due not simply to a certain finitude of anticipation, but more essentially to the non-necessity of any particular mode of signification, and to the impropriety of every mode of signification. One finds explicit instances of this in conversions (Paul reversing the significance of the early Christian movement, or Malcolm X changing the signification of his very self), but these mutations of significance happen quite broadly. The notion of an immanent *telos* of self-preservation falls apart in the face of signification: what is destruction according to one mode of signification may come to be a radical increase of power once another mode of signification is adopted. To say, then, that beneath these changes in signification there is the constant *telos* of self-preservation is not only to betray the atelic character of immanence, it is also to evade the vagaries of signification. Let us recall Spinoza's famous contrast between the tyrannical state in which, through the means of religion, people "fight as

---

through the fictive vehicle of religious signification, the natural consequence of eating from the tree. It is not a matter of judgment, then, but a matter of natural causality. Yet, Kordela asks, on what basis is Adam to make a decision? Why should he locate his own advantage in not eating? He cannot decide without locating himself within a mode of signification that gives meaning to and thus motivates his choice. "For the decision to eat or not from the tree, even if one hears the commandment not as a moral but as a scientific truth, presupposes a choice of a *telos*—a knowledge of what is good for oneself—which, in turn, as Spinoza rightly argues, presupposes a fiction. But without such a fiction, one cannot decide whether to eat or not to eat the fruit." See A. Kiarina Kordela, *$urplus: Spinoza, Lacan* (Albany: State University of New York Press, 2007), 8.

bravely for slavery as for safety," and "a free state" in which "no more mischievous expedient could be planned or attempted."[17] Why do such people fight for their servitude? Furthermore, from what perspective is Spinoza able to properly identify the distinction between servitude and freedom? Answers to these questions must lie in the impossibility of not signifying: what appears as servitude in one mode of signification appears as freedom in another (or the very opposition of servitude and freedom appears only in one mode of signification). There is servitude or freedom because there is signification, but neither of these can be a proper naming of the event unless immanence is forestalled—that is, unless freedom, for instance, names the (now transcendent) aim of immanence. In order for an individual's servitude to be evaluated as inferior, there must be a final cause of freedom. But immanence collapses the final cause into the efficient cause. In this sense, an individual's servitude is no less improper than a little fish being eaten by a bigger fish, for they proceed according to the same immanent necessity.

Let me make clear that I am not seeking to disqualify signification, or the production of ends, as such. More precisely, my point is that signification must be subjected to the rigors of immanence, even—or especially—when signification claims to name a properly immanent causality. But this does mean that signification as such is a betrayal of immanence. Given what I have thus far argued, this may seem counterintuitive, so let me clarify: signification betrays immanence when it makes immanence immanent to what is signified, but, at the same time, immanence must be signified. Only by insisting on this double necessity do we evade the lure of apophaticism. Immanence exceeds signification not because it belongs to a plane beyond signification—this would turn immanence into yet another mode of transcendence. Immanence exceeds signification because it produces signification, and because this signification is within immanence. The necessity of immanence produces the necessity of signification. The aim, then, is not (as it is in apophaticism) to go beyond signification, it is rather to restore signification to immanence, to signify immanently. When it comes to signification, it is less a matter of iconoclasm than a matter of polyiconicity—and this is to say that the constructive power of a multitude of incommensurable particularities must be posed against the restrictive universality of Christian religion and the secular.

---

[17] Benedict de Spinoza, *A Theologico-Political Treatise*, trans. R.H.M. Elwes (New York: Dover Publications, 1951), 5.

IV. The Improper Secularity of Immanence

I am now able to provide a positive account of what I am proposing, which is essentially a two-sided approach to immanence. One side foregrounds immanence's resistance to any proper signification of itself (though it does not deny the necessity of signification). What is central here is the nameless and atelic character of immanence. Accordingly, the special enemy of immanence, in this regard, is religion, for it is religious signification that tends to introduce ontological transcendence, and that tends to proclaim the proper ends for individuals. In this sense, Nature is valorised over against God. This is, furthermore, to valorise the secular, in the strict sense whereby secularity affirms the world. The world is immanent to itself, there is no signification that properly forms the world, for the world's existence is its own justification. Clearly, then, this is to oppose a plane of Christian religion. But it is also to oppose a secular plane, insofar as the secular plane is not the world itself, and as the secular plane imposes a proper form on the world. Indeed, it is here that we confront the lure of immanence's opposition to a theologically proper name, for in affirming this genuine opposition we expose ourselves to the identification of immanence with the signification of Nature. What I am arguing, then, is that to call immanence Nature is to pose the secularity of immanence against religion's proclamation of a proper name, but it is not to identify the name of Nature with immanence, for in doing so we make immanence immanent to signification—which is, after all, precisely what secularity opposes in the denomination of immanence as God.

Accordingly, the second side of my approach affirms the necessity of signification. To affirm the necessity of signification is to unmask the significative aspect even of Nature, and the perdurance of *teloi* in naturalistic—or secular—signification. There is, then, something of a flattening effect here, since to foreground the signification involved in Nature is to give attention to the concealed nonidentity between natural signification and immanence—that is, the very nonidentity that Nature finds concealed in God, or that the secular finds concealed in religion. This equivalence having been effected, however, certain determinations may be advanced. The immanent character of signification has to be maintained against the transcendence of religion. Yet once this condition is set, religious signification may be affirmed—for the problem with religion lies in its tendency towards transcendence, not in its introduction of signification, which is necessary, and which in any case is equally present in the naming of Nature. If the necessity of signifying immanence thus liberates a certain potentiality in religious signification, beyond the plane of Christian religion, then it also poses a criticism against any installation of a secular plane. This is because it highlights the way that the irreducibly significative character of the secular contravenes its claim to immediately reveal immanent secularity. In this sense, an avowedly immanent signification of God is valorised over against Nature, insofar as the latter can conceal the impropriety of its signification. To say that even God may become subject to immanent signification is to refuse the dialectical opposition between the secular and religion—that is, the opposition installed by the secular plane—and it is to affirm the radically improper power of signification that belongs to a rigorously immanent secularity.

Religion, like all signification, is fiction. Yet fiction is necessarily produced by immanence. What is necessary, then, is to make fiction into an immanent power of fabulation. Religion, or God, names the capacity of immanence to produce beyond all limits of propriety. As long as the secular proceeds iconoclastically, as long as it attempt to restrict the fabulation that religion signifies, it imposes a restriction on immanence— which is also to say that it imposes a restriction on the secular power of immanence. The very innovation of the secular gets lost in its dialectical— perhaps heresiological—identification of itself over against religion, in its sovereign self-identification as the liberator of the world from religion. The secular may very well liberate the world from the transcendent God, but it does so only by reinstituting a new transcendence of natural signification, of the fiction of Nature. The failure here is not that the secular is a fiction, but that it is fiction that does not recognize itself as fictive. There is, to be sure, a difference between the fiction of religious signification and the fiction of natural signification, but this difference is epiphenomenal to the difference between immanence itself and whatever fiction. It is thus imperative to inhabit the difference between immanence itself and the fictions it intrinsically produces, to know that there is necessarily this difference, and to weave an immanence between the namelessness of immanence and the production of fiction, to make them immanently co-constitutive.

Immanence is productive, and for this reason it is excessive. Its excessiveness is marked by the fact that it doubles itself by way of signification. Immanence is, to borrow a term from Kordela, "surplus."[18] But I want to take this surplus in a direction that differs from that followed by Kordela. This surplus, she rightly observes, exceeds every measure of the true and the false. It is for this reason that she makes axiomatic Spinoza's assertion that "truth is the standard both of itself and of the

---

[18] Kordela, of course, renders it as "$urplus."

false."[19] Truth and falsity derive from an excess that is captured by a mode of signification. Such a mode of signification, precisely because it has assumed the capacity to name the excess, can then refract immanence into the true and the false—the true becomes that which conforms to the dominant mode of signification, while the false becomes that which does not conform. This, I would add, is exactly what takes place in the interpellative invention of Christian religion and in the installation of the secular plane. The excess of immanence, though it is properly nameless, is captured by the fictive imposition of a proper name—first as religion (or God), and second as the secular (or Nature).

What Kordela does not pursue, however, is the way in which the excessiveness of immanence, or the necessity of an immanent production of fiction, can be turned against the capture of immanence that is effected by its purportedly proper naming. Surplus is always already signified, of course, so it is not a matter of arguing that Christian religion or the secular is not a signification of the surplus of immanence. They can and do name immanence because immanence can and must be named. Nor is it a matter of arguing that these significations are simply false, for this is to ignore that when it comes to immanence we encounter a production that exceeds any propriety of truth and falsity. So what, then, is the way forward? It is not to not name immanence, but to keep naming it. It is not to say that the dominant signification is false, but to exercise what Deleuze calls "the powers of the false," the capacity to turn the falsity of the necessarily produced fiction of immanence against immanence's capture by the purportedly true fiction.[20] Once again, this is to say not that everything is merely fictive, but rather that it is true that the fictive is produced. In other words, while it is true that the truth presents itself as the standard of both the true and the false, and that such fictive presentation is produced by the surplus of immanence, it is equally true that the false can ally itself with this surplus in order to produce beyond the boundaries signified by the fiction that presents itself as the true One.[21] Surplus is secular insofar as it

---

[19] Qtd. in Kordela, $urplus, 9. See Spinoza, Ethics, where Parkinson translates it as follows: "truth is the standard both of itself and of falsity" (150; Part 2, Proposition 43 Scholium).

[20] See Gilles Deleuze, Cinema 2: The Time-Image, trans. Hugh Tomlinson and Robert Galeta (Minneapolis: University of Minnesota Press, 1989), 126-155.

[21] We can draw similar conclusions with regard to the question of ends. Immanence is without teleology, but insofar as it is necessarily significative it always produces (fictive) ends. To orient immanence around these ends is to fall back into transcendent signification, and this is the case even when the end is freedom. Or this is at least the case when freedom presents itself in dialectical opposition to servitude, and as the proper name of immanent existence. The end of

is immanent, but it is religious, which is to say fictive, insofar as it expresses itself through always improper signification. The surplus of immanence is God or Nature.

Bibliography

Asad, Talal. *Genealogies of Religion: Discipline and Reasons of Power in Christianity and Islam*. Baltimore: The Johns Hopkins University Press, 1993.
—. *Formations of the Secular: Christianity, Islam, Modernity*. Stanford: Stanford University Press, 2004.
Boyarin, Daniel. *A Radical Jew: Paul and the Politics of Identity*. Berkeley: University of California Press, 1994.
—. *Border Lines: The Partition of Judaeo-Christianity*. Philadelphia: University of Pennsylvania Press, 2004.
Deleuze, Gilles. *Cinema 2: The Time-Image*. Translated by Hugh Tomlinson and Robert Galeta. Minneapolis: University of Minnesota Press, 1989.
Deleuze, Gilles and Félix Guattari. *What is Philosophy?* Translated by Hugh Tomlinson and Graham Burchell. New York: Columbia University Press, 1996.
Kordela, A. Kiarina. *$urplus: Spinoza, Lacan*. Albany: State University of New York Press, 2007.
Mahmood, Saba. "Secularism, Hermeneutics, Empire: The Politics of Islamic Reformation." *Public Culture* 18.2: 327-347.
Spinoza, Benedict. *A Theologico-Political Treatise*. Translated by R.H.M. Elwes. New York: Dover Publications, 1951.
—. *Ethics*. Translated by G.H.R. Parkinson. Oxford: Oxford University Press, 2000.

---

liberation is a fiction—a fiction that, recognized as such, must be placed within the surplus of immanence. Liberation must be understood, then, not as the proper end betrayed by the impropriety of servitude, but rather as the power of the impropriety proper to immanent surplus. If there is to be liberation, then it will be less a matter of restricting a dialectically opposed servitude that believes in "mere" fictions, and more one of constructing fictions that exceed the regnant fictions. To speak of liberation, then, it is necessary to recognize that it is an end only because it is first a fiction. Yet it is necessary, furthermore, to recognize that liberation's power lies not in the signification of itself, but rather in the capacity to signify or to construct new fictions. It is for this reason that liberation remains religious.

CHAPTER EIGHT

A BELLICOSE DEMOCRACY:
BERGSON ON THE OPEN SOUL
(OR UNTHINKING THE THOUGHT
OF EQUALITY)

JOHN MULLARKEY

Objections occasioned by the vagueness of the democratic formula arise
from the fact that the original religious character has been misunderstood.
How is it possible to ask for a precise definition of liberty and of equality
when the future must lie open to all sorts of progress, and especially to the
creation of new conditions under which it will be possible to have forms of
liberty and equality which are impossible of realization, perhaps even
conception, today.[1]

I. Introduction

Amongst the increasingly politics-hungry forms of Continental
philosophy presently in circulation, classical questions still abound,
especially ones concerning the key concepts of any politics—equality,
universality, representation, state, sovereignty, and subjectivity. The
question of equality, perhaps, is unique in its implications for understating
all the others. What is equality, if it is not simple sameness? What are its
origins, and the origins of inequality? Does it exist in some kind of
sovereign property or power, a possession (Singer), or in the lack of or any
such power (Levinas)? Must it be an axiom (Badiou), or can it be
"materially (or sensually) positioned"? Is it a concrete excavation into the
past and present (in the underworld of the autodidact, as Rancière shows,

---

[1] Henri Bergson, *The Two Sources of Morality and Religion*, trans. R. Ashley
Audra and Cloudesley Brereton, with the assistance of W. Horsfall Carter (Notre
Dame: University of Notre Dame Press, 1977), 282.

for example), rather than an inquisitive projection into the future? In short, how do we answer the "fundamental problem of the *location* of equality"?[2]

What I would like to do in this essay is to consider whether, in fact, it is actually the *thought* of equality that is most important in this set of questions (at least for a certain kind of philosopher). In the way they are usually posed, it is a rigorous, *consistent* thought of equality that is being sought. A thought that is firstly equal to itself (in the immanent, performative thinking of its "object"), but also equal to what it supposedly represents, namely, a fundamental concept in ethics and politics.

There is a connection between this question of equality and *any* self-consistent thought. "Don't read this sentence", "I am mute", "I am asleep", "everything is a lie". These performative contradictions, the source of the many paradoxes that have kept philosophers distracted for centuries, are one major point of entry into the performative aspects of philosophical thought. Speech-act philosophers like J. L. Austin, John Searle, and Jürgen Habermas would see such paradoxes in terms of the lack of fit between the content and the execution of an utterance—*saying* "I am asleep" does not fit well with *being* asleep (unless, of course, one happens to talk in one's sleep). The misfit (inconsistency) between the *saying* and what is *said* is also important with respect to the performance of philosophies *as a whole*, and not just particular speech acts. In Emmanuel Levinas' case, for example, the ethical message found in his first major work, *Totality and Infinity*—concerning the inability of anything in the objective world to totalise our infinite ethical responsibility to the Other—seems to be contradicted by the very writing of *Totality and Infinity*, which is all too adept at conveying its message *objectively*. Hence, the sequel to that text, *Otherwise than Being or Beyond Essence*, plays a far more complex game with language, between content and performance (or "the said" and "the saying") in order to scupper any false impression that Levinas' book has *something* it wants to say. Likewise, Søren Kierkegaard's whole panoply of rhetorical devices in his philosophical writing—irony, indirect discourse, the use of pseudonyms, parables, and so on—was ranged against performatively contradicting his message that Truth is Subjectivity, a message that could never be conveyed objectively through a traditionally written book. But note the emphasis for both of these figures on using performance to *avoid* contradiction, to assure *consistency*. Jacques Derrida, for instance, is famed for supposedly having stopped arguing for his quasi-concept of *différance* in the 1960s in favour of actually

---

[2] Nina Power, "Which Equality? Badiou and Rancière in Light of Ludwig Feuerbach" in *Parallax* 15.3 (2009), 64.

performing it in the 1970s (in books like *Glas*) *in order to be consistent* with his message regarding the futility of self-present arguments (logocentrism). Yet, one might say that neither Derrida, nor Levinas, nor even Kierkegaard, abandoned all argument in their work; rather, they simply adopted a higher-order, meta-argument in order to salvage their consistency, the *coherence* of their message. If *in-consistency* (alterity, *différance*, multiplicity) is the content of one's philosophy, of one's message or argument, then one must invent new ways of *consistently* arguing, new forms of argument or even of thought.[3]

Now a parallel problem arises in respect to the thought of equality. How might one execute that thought *equally*? And why *must* one do so— be equitable—anyway? Must one be equal to it, be *rigorous* or *consistent* in its performance? Or can one *invent a thought* of equality as one goes along, a consistent inconsistency in implementing it? Such would be a creative politics. This is what, I will argue, Bergson offers us in response to the problems of equality in his *Two Sources of Morality and Religion*. Or rather, he offers us a new model of thinking called "creative emotion" that responds to the problems created by new forms of equality. Positing any *ready-made basis* for equality—sentience, vulnerability, Number, or agonistics, for example—is too preemptive for Bergson. Equality, to be equal to itself, must be invented (or thought) anew within each and every situation, immanently. *The Two Sources* is an exercise in sociobiology, of course, but it grounds both ethics and religion in an open conception of life, one that is necessarily incomplete and indefinite—there is no *reduction* of the *socius* to a determining *bios*, but quite the opposite: the indetermination of all social forms on account of their immanence within a creative life. There is a "radical democracy" inherent within Bergson's metaphysics of life, one that Conor Cunningham has dubbed "*bellicose*". But the volume of its advocacy (too loud for some, no doubt) is grounded in a simultaneously moral and metaphysical emotion, which Bergson also calls the "open soul".

II. The Inadequacy of Consistent Thoughts of Equality

Before looking at Bergson, however, we should look at four of the most radical contemporary thinkers of equality, if only in order to show the depth of the problem of thinking consistently about equality: Alain Badiou, Jacques Rancière, Peter Singer, and John Llewelyn.

---

[3] See John Mullarkey, "Performative Metaphysics" in *Frankcija* 49 (2009), 143-7.

It is ironic that, according to Alain Badiou and his apologists, the "animal philosophy" of Gilles Deleuze is supposedly useless for politics because there is no feasible programme ensuing from the notion of creativity it inherited from Bergson. There is such a programme, however, in Badiou's thought of equality (at least according to these Badiouians). But, we must ask, how is it implemented—equally or partially? Clearly, it is partial.[4] Badiou shuts down the political processes of transformation (the event) at an arbitrary stage, human emancipation, even though his notion of the universal is *unqualified* precisely because its impetus is mathematically grounded: through *pure* quantity or Number. As Slavoj Žižek puts it, "The limitation of Badiou is nowhere more perceptible than in his positive political program, which can be summed up as unconditional fidelity to the 'axiom of equality'."[5] Badiou individualises his theory in the direction of an unnecessarily anthropocentric dogmatism that also covers over a highly dubious induction, to wit, that animals cannot think mathematically. Being equals counting (ontology equals mathematics), and so animals (and everything non-human) are discounted from being equals because they cannot count, supposedly. Badiou determines our mathematical power simply through the definition or axiom of all humanity, "generic humanity", as *mathematically gifted*.[6] In actuality, of course, mathematical power comes in degrees.

In contrast to this abstract equality, the egalitarianism found in Jacques Rancière's conception of the political is much more actual: it emerges in the struggle between an established social order and its excluded element, a democracy of the "part which has no part". A genuine political transformation is only inaugurated when a previously ostracised group requires a transformation of the rules of political inclusion, given that the group was so radically excluded beforehand. Genuine politics is a democracy *of absolute, agonistic, equality*.[7] Dissent, disagreement, or dissonance are not obstacles to democratic enfranchisement, but lie at its very essence. In this respect, we might say that Rancière has made

---

[4] See John Mullarkey, *Post-Continental Philosophy: An Outline* (London: Continuum, 2006), 117-121 for the full version of this argument.
[5] Slavoj Žižek, *Organs Without Bodies: On Deleuze and Consequences* (London: Routledge, 2003) 104.
[6] See Alain Badiou, *Being and Event*, trans. Oliver Feltham (London: Continuum, 2005), 353.
[7] See Jacques Rancière, *Disagreement: Politics and Philosophy*, trans. Julie Rose (Minneapolis: University of Minnesota Press, 1998) and Todd May, *The Political Thought of Jacques Rancière: Creating Equality* (University Park, PA: Penn State University Press, 2008) for more on the politics of absolute equality in Rancière.

inconsistency, this internal agon, the axiom or principle of equality (a move we will see Bergson prefigure in part). But to *state* it as such—as a *principle* of agonistics—would be to "thwart" it (to use Rancière's own language): one doesn't enter Monty Python's "Argument Clinic" *in order to* have a *real* argument, but only, at best, a meta-argument (an argument for, or against, having arguments).[8] Being "thwarted" might well be only another variation of agonistics, of course (and so a kind of consistency), yet we can still ask whether such a performative contradiction is *the right kind* of inconsistency in order to think equality consistently: in as much as it remains at a *recognisably* conceptual level, is it different enough, is it contradictory enough? I will argue later that Bergson can be seen to take Rancière's agonistic performance to its limit, a limit of actions that are both unrecognisable as thought, and thereby more adequate to thinking different equalities *equally*.

Singer's Love of Consistency

Peter Singer is one of the most rigorous thinkers of ethical and political equality. He borrows the leitmotif for his expansive theory of equality from W.E.H. Lecky's *The History of European Morals*:

> At one time the benevolent affections embrace merely the family, soon the circle expanding includes first a class, then a nation, then a coalition of nations, then all humanity, and finally, its influence is felt in the dealings of man with the animal world.[9]

Having ethical standards (as opposed to behaving ethically inadvertently) implies the ability to forward a justification of a certain type: the argument must be universalisable. Singer's contention is that universalisability, the principle that each individual is deemed *equal* by counting for one and none for more than one, is a feature of all true ethical thinking. In the modern era, of course, we all adhere to the principle of equality *amongst humans* (at least in theory). But what does that mean in practice? Not that we are all the same: clearly, there are differences between us in physical and mental endowment (be the latter genetically or culturally determined) that no one deems morally significant. Equality has a different sense here. But what is it? Singer's proposal is that there is no need to establish the

---

[8] See Jacques Rancière, *Film Fables (Talking Images),* trans. Emiliano Battista (Oxford and New York: Berg, 2006).
[9] Cited in Peter Singer *The Expanding Circle: Ethics and Sociobiology* (Oxford: Clarendon Press 1981), xiii.

principle of equality on the basis of either an *empirical* equality (everyone being a certain colour, gender, or whatever) or an *a priori* equality (being a member of a certain species irrespective of one's individual empirical properties); all that is required to ground a genuine ethic is the notion of *equality of interest*. The chief pre-requisite for any ethical behaviour for Singer is that we treat all sectional interests on a par with our own, no matter whose interests they are: "Ethics requires us to go beyond 'I' and 'you' to the universal law, the universalisable judgement, the standpoint of the impartial spectator or ideal observer."[10] No empirical fact or *a priori* principle (such as the "sanctity of human life") can be used to exclude any interest: only those or that without interests at all can justly be excluded. In part, of course, any ethics depends on reason and not just on the perception of interests. And Singer does concede to Hume's view that reason alone "cannot give rise to action", but he adds that love of reason and consistency can be motivating in itself. [11]

Giving equal consideration to every interest, however, need not always lead to equal treatment: where there are significantly different interests at hand, commensurably different treatment ought to follow. As Singer writes in the essay, "All Animals are Equal": "Since a man cannot have an abortion, it is meaningless to talk of his right to have one. Since a pig cannot vote, it is meaningless to talk of its right to vote."[12] To allow only certain interests to abide within a theory of equality, on the other hand, is simply inconsistent. Its most radical inconsistency indicates "a prejudice or attitude of bias in favour of the interests of members of one's own species and against those of members of other species". It is this that Singer famously labels "speciesism".[13] The principle of equality leads to some startling implications, and Singer is never fearful of pursuing these ideas to their logical conclusion. Consistent with his view is the stipulation that no species should receive preferential treatment for its members' interests simply on the basis of they being members of that species. This leads Singer to compare and often *equate* the lives of human animals and

---

[10] Peter Singer, *Practical Ethics*, 2nd ed. (Cambridge: Cambridge University Press, 1993), 12. That ethics must be universalisable gives us good reason, Singer believes, for favouring a broadly utilitarian position. Singer's reasoning is that, in conflict situations, impartiality demands that one *weigh up* the opposing *interests* and "adopt the course of action most likely to maximise the interests of those affected." (13)
[11] Singer *Expanding Circle*, 96-99, 106, 113, 142.
[12] Peter Singer, "All Animals are Equal" in Tom Regan and Peter Singer eds, *Animal Rights and Human Obligations* (Englewood Cliffs: Prentice-Hall, 1989), 2.
[13] Peter Singer, *Animal Liberation*, 4th ed. (London: Pimlico, 1995), 6. The term was first coined by Richard Ryder.

non-human animals. Significantly, the most important interests possessed by individuals are independent of the categories "human" and "non-human": pain, for example, is suffered and avoided by all regardless of colour, gender, or species. If we are ever forced to favour one individual's interests when they are in conflict with those of another, it can only be on the basis of those of their respective properties which *affect the interests either might have.*

Yet this begs the question of how "we" learn of these interests. According to Singer, if members of a species can indicate a preference for the avoidance of suffering or continued existence, then the onus is on us to respect that desire. *But how do we recognise this "indication"?* Is it not already anthropocentric (and so speciesist) to rest values *on how things appear to us*? How consistent is that with being objective?

Llewelyn's Aporia of Equality

It is in order to avoid the subject-centred aspect of Singer's stance that John Llewelyn adopts a position close to that of Emmanuel Levinas. Part of Llewelyn's rejection of an ethics such as Singer's is its Lockean reliance on properties enjoyed by a subject: consciousness, sentience, memory, expectation, and so on. Indeed, following Levinas, Llewelyn asks that ethics transcend the ego and its supposed powers and seek a *passive* principle of *responsibility* towards the other in its vulnerability.

What he agrees with Levinas is that ethics cannot value the human or any other entity as something of greater comparative worth (for example, an ape), for that is to measure an infinite value as though it were a commodity—to objectivise it and thereby transform ethics into economics. There should be no comparative evaluation of the other: in saying—as both Levinas and Llewelyn do—that the other counts "more" than myself, one should not understand that "more" comparatively, but as a structural claim about ethics itself.[14]

Yet Llewelyn reads this contentless otherness as a licence to view animals, plants, and even the inanimate as others too. Each and every being has a claim on me on account of the "that it is" rather than the "what it is" of each; the ontological rather than the ontic. There need be no qualitative similarity (having consciousness, sentience) between us, and yet there remains an ethical responsibility all the same. Moreover, there is no need for sympathy for this other to maintain my ethical obligation. Yet, Llewelyn is not extending political rights to animals and stones (correctly

---

[14] John Llewelyn, *The Middle Voice of Ecological Conscience* (Basingstoke: Macmillan, 1991), 260, 249-50.

or incorrectly), but simply showing where the *primordial* basis of any notion of "right" lies: the idea of exclusive human rights, in fact, is a restriction of the term "right" in general.[15]

So where does this proto-ethical responsibility leave us: respect towards the foetus, the cancer virus, the gas chamber? Yes, Llewelyn answers, and to all. Ethics is not about simplicity, but difficulty, and, through this hyperbolic egalitarianism, he has simply exposed how difficult ethics really is.[16] Yet Llewelyn's charity to all leads to such an *aporia*, an impasse for any ethical action at all (*aporia*, "difficulty of passing", from *aporos*, "impassable"), that, as with Zeno's excessive focus on the minutiae of walking, all movement is rendered impossible. In Bergson's notion of the "open", however, we will see a model of ethics that is able both to keep all that might be interested in sight, while still being able to move in actuality, because any ensuing conceptual aporias, its own impossibilities, are dissolved (side-stepped) by *creative moral action*.

III. From the Closed to the Open

"In order to speak of 'all citizens' it is necessary that somebody not be a citizen of said polity." So writes Etienne Balibar when formulating a rigorous concept of equality:

> Equality in fact cannot be limited. Once some x's ('men') are not equal, the predicate of equality can no longer be applied to anyone, for all those to whom it is supposed to be applicable are in fact 'superior,' 'dominant,' 'privileged,' etc. Enjoyment of the equality of rights cannot spread step by step, beginning with two individuals and gradually extending to all: it must immediately concern the *universality* of individuals … This explains … the antinomy of equality and society for, even when it is not defined in 'cultural,' 'national,' or 'historical' terms, a *society* is necessarily *a* society, defined by some particularity, by some exclusion, if only by a *name*.[17]

With this attempt to counter any "limited equality", Balibar also rediscovers Bergson's concept of the "closed society" from *The Two Sources*. According to Bergson, every form of group identity implies "a choice, therefore an exclusion." The most salient trait of social obligation

---

[15] Ibid, 254-5, 257, 261.
[16] Ibid, 263
[17] Etienne Balibar, "Citizen Subject", in *Who Comes After the Subject?*, eds. Eduardo Cadava, Peter Connor, and Jean-Luc Nancy (London and New York: Routledge, 1991), 50.

is that it immediately installs a "closed society, however large". It is in its nature to form social groupings like the family, the nation, the race and so on, each of which acts as an intermediary reinforcement of habitual social mores. Within each grouping, all are regarded in an equal light and all are allowed equal rights and freedoms. What is essential about such bounded domains, however, is that they are more or less closed to the outside. A social formation may be very broad, and even continue to grow broader by incorporating previously ostracised minority groups; no matter, they remain closed in the type of movement they instantiate: "Their essential characteristic is nonetheless to include at any moment a certain number of individuals, and exclude others."[18] But here's the rub: *even humanity in general only occupies the broadest and most abstract of these concentric circles surrounding the self.* And yet, from Aristotle to John Rawls, most theories of politics maintain their systems of justice on the basis of some type of opposition: be it towards the non-political animal or the non-reciprocating animal, something must be excluded.

The closed society (and its internal, closed morality) consists in a fixed set of rules and balances, pressures and obligations, that bear down on the individual, homogenising him or her.[19] Given this rigidity, therefore, how might a closed society transform itself into a genuinely open one rather than simply enlarge itself, still at the expense of some *new* outside? It cannot, according to Bergson—or at least it cannot do so *conceptually*: it is impossible for abstractions such as "universal love", for example, to change a movement of closure into one of openness. Universal love cannot raise any social egoism to a genuine altruism, for the goal is as daunting as any of the infinite tasks in Zeno's paradoxes. The closed and the open are no less different than the catching-up steps of Achilles are different from his overtaking steps.[20]

Behind the command to "love all" lies something else, according to Bergson, the desire for openness, specifically the desire to be open towards openness. Bergson talks of the "extreme limit" of this desire as follows:[21]

> The other attitude is that of the open soul. What, in that case, is allowed in? Suppose we say that it embraces all humanity: we should not be going too far, we should hardly be going far enough, *since its love may extend to*

---

[18] Bergson, *Two Sources*, 32, 18-19, 30, 31.
[19] Ibid, 39, 205, 207.
[20] Ibid, 36. See John Mullarkey, *Bergson and Philosophy* (Edinburgh: Edinburgh University Press, 1999), 14.
[21] Bergson, *Two Sources*, 33-34.

animals, to plants, to all nature. And yet no one of these things which would thus fill it would suffice to define the attitude taken by the soul, for it could, strictly speaking, do without all of them. Its form is not dependent on its content. We have just filled it; we could as easily empty it again. 'Charity' would persist in him who possesses 'charity', though there be no other living creature on earth.[22]

"All humanity" is not enough. Pure openness sympathises "with the whole of nature", but it is also a contact with a principle of nature which expresses itself in quite a different attachment to life than that found in a sympathy for the other members of one's group (and hence, it is not a simple extension). It is described as an *objectless* emotion that loves who or what it does only "by passing through" rather than aiming for them.[23] With respect to metaphysics, this openness is reflected in the *advocacy of every event*: it is found in the idea that "each and every locus is as real as any other as a resting place, but equally as unreal as any other as the bearer of an evolutionary movement", that, in other words, "each point is *equally new*".[24]

It is this radical, metaphysical, democracy that Conor Cunningham calls *"bellicose"*. Cunningham sees this egalitarianism as part of a "meontotheology", that, strangely enough, eliminates the particularity of the particular by prioritising the uni-vocity of the new—everything is said to be, or even shouted out as, equally new. Though Bergson's critique of nothingness in *Creative Evolution* might be seen as a potential ally in Cunningham's general project to displace a nihilistic logic with a Trinitarian one, he sees Bergson's positivism as merely the opposite extreme to nihilism, and one that results in the same outcome: an affirmation of homogeneity that eliminates particularity.[25] Yet Cunningham misses the point of process metaphysics completely (no less than Bachelard and Badiou did in their respective critiques of it in the 1930s and 1990s): *the new is not a definite, defined property to be distributed homogeneously or heterogeneously*, but what we might call a meta-property that *undoes* any such definite properties—it is the very particularity or singularity that entirely *undoes* the notion of property. And

---

[22] Ibid, 38. My emphasis.

[23] See ibid, 52, 39, 254-5.

[24] See Mullarkey, *Bergson*, 72 and Henri Bergson, *Creative Evolution*, trans. by Arthur Mitchell (Basingstoke: Macmillan, 1911), 30. I quote my own text here only because it is the basis of Conor Cunningham's critique that I discuss in the next paragraph.

[25] Conor Cunningham, *The Genealogy of Nihilism: Philosophies of Nothing and the Difference of Theology* (London: Routledge, 2002), 249.

it is this undoing that the thought of equality has itself to perform, to ad-
vocate, if it is to think it adequately.

As a consequence, therefore, it is not by a process of mere conceptual
extension that we pass from the closed to the open; indeed, Bergson
brands as "intellectualist" the idea that it is. An "open morality" is not
about re-calculating the *distribution* of justice: it is a "disposition of the
soul".[26] Such a relative, distributive justice is, in fact, only a matter of
reciprocity and equivalence—a mathematical balancing act of quantity
with quantity, quality with quality. This relative justice merely creates a
form of equality that remains set against the outsider.[27] An *absolute* justice
has another source altogether: it refuses to let even one individual suffer
for the good of the group. The welfare of "all humanity" would not be
enough.

Evidently, none of this tallies well with those discourses that place the
emphasis on political emancipation through conceptual reformation.
Bergson has no confidence in the value of increasing the boundaries of
enfranchisement through winning larger and larger associations, so much
as dissolving the *spatialised* discourse of "boundaries" altogether. What
we need is another, processual, metaphysics, and, with that, another *kind*
of discourse, advocacy, or metaphysical thinking to enact or perform this
new politics of equality.

IV. The Open and the Vague

It is usually said that Bergson offers a religious formula—"dynamic
religion"—to explain such radical transformations of society—the shift
from closed to open. Yet Bergson's religious formula is used only as one
place-holder for an indefinite, nature-less, movement in his thought.
Openness is a necessarily vague formula that requires continual creativity
to complete its content in any one situation; it is a moving position with no
fixed content. The basis of equality in sentience (Singer), vulnerability
(Llewelyn), the abstract concept of Number (in Badiou) or agonistics (in
Rancière) remain too presumptive for Bergson. Despite their apparently
"universal" nature, their content remains all too substantive in contrast
with Bergson's necessarily indefinite formulation. The form open morality
takes "is not dependent on its content". Its "aim" is only to pass through its
object. In other words, the evolution *to* openness is not teleology strictly

---

[26] See Bergson, *Two Sources*, 32, 38, 59.
[27] See ibid, 69-79.

speaking but, in a self-referential manner, an evolution that places itself at issue, that performs itself.

In political terms, democracy is the name given to this vague evolution. The idea of democracy, for Bergson, rests in the attempt to reconcile liberty and equality. But this can only be achieved each time, not by reason, but through what *The Two Sources* at one point calls "fraternity" or love. The vagueness of the democratic formula provides latitude for the moral creativity that will work empirically to reconcile concepts of freedom and equality that are presently unforeseeable, and perhaps even inconceivable too. After all, any new particular liberty for one individual or group of individuals must encroach on the liberty of others. But *how* the two conflict cannot be determined *a priori,* for others in the community may adapt their behaviour in recognition of this new liberty, that is, through a reflexive, feedback mechanism that subverts any possible algorithm for political change.[28] The contemporary idea of a democracy "to come", therefore, re-invents Bergson's idea of a vague democracy perfectly. As Simon Critchley puts it in his study of Derrida and Levinas:

> Democracy is an indeterminate political form founded on the contradictions of individual freedom versus ... [amongst other things] complete uniformity ... *Democracy does not exist*; that is to say, starting from today, and every day, there is a responsibility to invent democracy, to extend the democratic franchise to all areas of public and private life.[29]

Democracy is an ongoing invention that cannot be predicted (even through a notion of "extension" as Critchley implies). Now read Bergson:

> Objections occasioned by the vagueness of the democratic formula arise from the fact that the original religious character has been misunderstood. How is it possible to ask for a precise definition of liberty and of equality when the future must lie open to all sorts of progress, and especially to the creation of new conditions under which it will be possible to have forms of liberty and equality which are impossible of realization, perhaps even conception, today.[30]

This notion of the vague should not be seen as contingent on Bergson's social philosophy. The vague, or indefinite, is a technical idea at work

---

[28] See ibid, 79-80.
[29] Simon Critchley, *The Ethics of Deconstruction: Derrida and Levinas* (Oxford: Blackwell, 1992), 209, 240.
[30] Bergson, *Two Sources*, 282.

throughout Bergson's writings. *Contra* the disputes amongst philosophers of finitude and the infinite, Bergson forwards the idea of the "indefinite" as an ongoing, creative, abeyance of both the finite and the infinite as two static poles. Evidence of indefinites (or "dynamic definitions") are throughout Bergson's work. Reality as a whole, he says, is neither finite nor infinite but "indefinite". The infinite, by contrast, would be the substantialisation and ontologisation of the indefinite. The indefinite captures best the processual moment at issue. By contrast, to say that *x* is infinite is to *decide* its being; but to say that it is indefinite is to *leave it open*, to let it be beyond the finite or infinite as states or things. Finite and infinite are not reconciled through dialectical negation, but through an inherent and irreducible *layering*: the *constant* creation of types of finitude.[31] Returning to the specific realm of ethics, then, though it is generally true that liberty and equality are always in tension for Bergson, how they are reconciled each time cannot be anticipated but only created by what Bergson names "moral creators".[32]

V. The Affective Creation of Politics

Bergson also calls these creators "mystics", though the notion of an ascetic contemplative is far from what he has in mind. These mystics are creators, transgressing the boundaries of life, mind, and society through their very real and active politic advocacies and interventions. As one of his earlier essays put it, their "inventive and simple heroism" is "the great success of life", being at once its "culminating point" and most primitive "source".[33] In crossing all frontiers, mysticism goes "beyond the limits of intelligence", the ultimate end of mysticism being to establish a partial coincidence with the creative effort of life. Such inherent creativity can appear to society as a mental pathology (no less than Deleuze and Guattari's "schizos"), and Bergson does indeed take care to spell out the differences between the symptoms of mystic acts and those of insanity.[34] Insanity is regarded by Bergson as an *excess* of mental power rather than a deficiency: the usual restrictive role of the brain has been weakened to allow a greater degree of consciousness flood the subject. But the

---

[31] See Bergson, *Creative Evolution*, 89, 90, 111-112; Henri Bergson, *The Creative Mind: An Introduction to Metaphysics*, trans. Mabelle L. Andison (New York: Philosophical Library, 1946), 211; Bergson, *Two Sources*, 296.

[32] See Bergson, *Two Sources*, 80.

[33] Henri Bergson, *Mind-Energy: Lectures and Essays*, trans. H. Wildon Carr (Westport: Greenwood Press, 1975), 32.

[34] See Bergson, *Two Sources*, 220, 228.

weakness of a mental disorder lies in an inability to restore a new equilibrium between this surplus and the surrounding environment.[35] The mystic has travelled the same route as the madman but has also discovered a way back to society in order to change that society.[36]

So what are the hallmarks of this kind of open thinking and action as embodied by these mystics? Oddly enough, their actions are described in terms of a radical passivity by Bergson. They entail "the complete and mysterious gift of self".[37] What is termed "complete mysticism" is wholly for the other, an advocacy of the other, rather than self-absorbed: "True, complete, active mysticism aspires to radiate, by virtue of the charity which is its essence."[38] How it radiates is through the contagious properties of a genuinely "creative emotion": "For heroism itself is a return to movement, and emanates from an emotion—infectious like all emotions—akin to the creative act."[39] Passivity of self is a kind of action for the other, therefore.

The etymology of emotion should be taken into account here: again, Bergson is not describing the private ecstasy of some contemplative, but a type of movement rich in activity, a movement of openness.[40] It is this creative emotion that can generate a new kind of thinking: one advocating *all* in its performance as well as its content. Such an affect is opposed to neither reason nor representation, however. For instance, *The Two Sources* looks at the non-philosophical origin of ethics:

> Alongside of the emotion which is a result of the representation and which is added to it, there is the emotion which precedes the image, which virtually contains it, and is to a certain extent its cause... an emotion capable of crystallising into representations and even into an ethical doctrine.[41]

Out of such affectivity come new doctrines of ethics and politics. Yet, the affectivity in question here is not any supposedly dumb feeling, but precisely the affective thinking *in* time that precedes its spatialisation into doctrine (with an inside and an outside, insiders and outsiders):

---

[35] See Bergson, *Mind-Energy*, 153-155.
[36] See Bergson, *Two Sources*, 228.
[37] Ibid, 225.
[38] Ibid, 309.
[39] Ibid, 53.
[40] See ibid, 61-62.
[41] Ibid, 47.

> Antecedent to the new morality, and also the new metaphysics, there is the emotion… neither has its metaphysics enforced moral practice, nor the moral practice induced a disposition to its metaphysics. Metaphysics and morality express here the self-same thing.[42]

It is a new kind of thought and action. The bellicose egalitarianism of Bergson's metaphysics is also the bellicose metaphysics of Bergsonian democracy.

VI. Conclusion: The Different Logics of Consistency and Equality

We have seen how the thought of equality can undo itself in its myriad possible implementations, from Alain Badiou through Peter Singer to John Llewelyn. We can axiomatise one kind of equality, but then the thought of equality becomes unequal to itself. So the question becomes: what would it be to perform the thought of equality without principle, to unthink it as a thought? There is a materiality in one possible Bergsonian answer to this question. To begin with, we have to take a step back, however. Bergson starts with creativity in showing that equality must be creatively accommodated with freedom. Likewise, Badiou starts with equality, or a version thereof, in showing how creativity is apolitical (and thereby that Deleuzianism is politically sterile). Bergson's (and Badiou's) starting points also ensure a certain conceptual consistency, of course. Now, we could say that Bergson's axiom of creativity also involves a circle. After all, Bergson argues that creativity, or freedom, is always *creatively* accommodated with equality. This is dynamic politics or democracy, though at an even broader level that Rancière's, for it concerns not only the changing definitions of politics *qua* inclusion/exclusion or part/whole, but of what might count, at all, *as* political thought as such. For such a thought might also be a material action, a moral creativity, a new advocacy.

Which leads us back to matter. The best way to prove the possibility and reality of movement is simply to walk away, as Bergson recommended to Zeno. An action can "break the circle" of Parmenidean and sufficient reason, when we can enact a new kind of thought, of logic, and of consistency.[43] After all, there are many candidates for what counts as thought: thinking descriptively, poetically, mathematically, affectively,

---

[42] Ibid, 49.
[43] See Bergson, *Creative Evolution*, 202-3 on how "action breaks" the "circle of the given".

embodiedly, analogically, syllogistically, fuzzily, paraconsistently; thinking through a method of questions, of problems, of dialogue, of dialectic, of genealogy, of historicism, of deconstruction, and so on. And, according to Bergson's evolutionary epistemology, the thinking of bi-valent logic is moulded on solid matter, on a very specific kind of consistency. The Law of Identity in classical Aristotelian logic, moreover, the law of A=A, rests on an equality. That kind of equality, or consistency, is material. Such concepts, Bergson writes, "are outside each other, like objects in space; and they have the same stability as such objects."[44] Physical atomism and logical atomism mirror and "co-engender" each other according to *Creative Evolution*.[45] And, likewise, the consistencies and equalities that they measure. Bergson is not conflating all logical possibility with one physical possibility, however, but simply showing that each exists amongst a range of types, most of which remain to be invented or engendered. There are many consistencies to the moving, material world we are a part of: not just the one logic of solids, but also other possible logics of fluids or gases (where A is simultaneously A *and* B *and* C....). Consistency has different meanings, one of which concerns the way in which a substance, like a liquid, holds together—its thickness or viscosity. Not all logics have the hardness that a "good argument" is said to require—a thought that tries to approximate a solid object. With that, then, there might come different logics, of consistency and equality, or, together, of consistent thoughts of equality: ones that some would even find it hard to call "thoughts" at all, looking more like "actions" as they do. Yet it is these actions (involving creative emotions) that perform an openness and equality in the only consistent manner possible: by invention.

Bibliography

Badiou, Alain. *Being and Event*. Translated by Oliver Feltham. London: Continuum, 2005.

Balibar, Etienne. "Citizen Subject." In Eduardo Cadava, Peter Connor, and Jean-Luc Nancy edited, *Who Comes After the Subject?* London: Routledge, 1991.

Bergson, Henri. *Creative Evolution*. Translated by Arthur Mitchell. Basingstoke: Macmillan, 1911.

---

[44] Bergson, *Two Sources*, 169.
[45] See Mullarkey, *Bergson*, 75-8.

—. *The Creative Mind: An Introduction to Metaphysics*. Translated by Mabelle L. Andison. New York: Philosophical Library, 1946.

—. *Mind-Energy: Lectures and Essays*. Translated by H. Wildon Carr. Westport: Greenwood Press, 1975.

—. *The Two Sources of Morality and Religion*. Translated by R. Ashley Audra and Cloudesley Brereton, with the assistance of W. Horsfall Carter. Notre Dame: University of Notre Dame Press, 1977.

Critchley, Simon. *The Ethics of Deconstruction: Derrida and Levinas*. Oxford: Blackwell, 1992.

Cunningham, Conor. *The Genealogy of Nihilism: Philosophies of Nothing and the Difference of Theology*. London: Routledge, 2002.

Llewelyn, John. *The Middle Voice of Ecological Conscience*. Basingstoke: Macmillan, 1991.

May, Todd. *The Political Thought of Jacques Rancière: Creating Equality*. University Park, PA: Penn State University Press, 2008.

Mullarkey, John. *Bergson and Philosophy*. Edinburgh: Edinburgh University Press, 1999.

—. *Post-Continental Philosophy: An Outline*. London: Continuum, 2006.

—. "Performative Metaphysics." *Frankcija* 49 (2009): 143-7.

Power, Nina. "Which Equality? Badiou and Rancière in Light of Ludwig Feuerbach." *Parallax* 15.3 (2009): 63–80.

Rancière, Jacques. *Disagreement: Politics and Philosophy*. Translated by Julie Rose. Minneapolis: University of Minnesota Press, 1998.

—. *Film Fables (Talking Images)*. Translated by Emiliano Battista. Oxford and New York: Berg, 2006.

Singer, Peter. *The Expanding Circle: Ethics and Sociobiology*. Oxford: Clarendon Press 1981.

—. "All Animals are Equal." In Tom Regan and Peter Singer edited, *Animal Rights and Human Obligations*. Englewood Cliffs: Prentice-Hall, 1989.

—. *Practical Ethics*. 2nd edition. Cambridge: Cambridge University Press, 1993.

—. *Animal Liberation*. 4th edition. London: Pimlico, 1995.

Žižek, Slavoj. *Organs Without Bodies: On Deleuze and Consequences*. London: Routledge, 2003.

CHAPTER NINE

THE PROBLEM OF THE MIDDLE IN GILLIAN ROSE'S READING OF HEGEL: POLITICAL CONSEQUENCES FOR THE THEOLOGY OF JOHN MILBANK

CLARE GREER

Gillian Rose and John Milbank may seem to be an incongruent pairing of conversation partners. Rose is an allusive and ambiguous philosopher and social theorist, who emphasises civil society and the state, and is committed to modernity and statehood. Milbank, on the other hand, is a measured and systematic theologian, anti-modern and committed to the sacred *ecclesia*. For Rose, religion is in a dialectical relationship with the state, while for Milbank religion is absolutely separate from the "secular" state. However, they shared a personal friendship, and Rose engaged with Milbank at length in *The Broken Middle*; both are interested in defining the "middle" of modernity. This paper explores the critical conversation between Rose and Milbank in terms of politics.

I. Introduction: Religion and the State

Both Rose and Milbank are interested in Hegel, for philosophy and theology respectively, and central to their conversation is Hegel's reading of the relationship between religion and the state. "[Religion] and the foundation of the state", Hegel writes, "is [sic] one and the same thing; they are identical in and for themselves".[1] It is clear that Hegel's statement is only correct if his conceptions of religion and the state are so narrowly

---

[1] G.W.F. Hegel, *Lectures on the Philosophy of Religion* trans. E.B. Spiers, and J. Burdon Sanderson (London: Kegan Paul, Trench, Trübner and Co., 1895) Vol. I, 297 (translation amended by G.R). Quoted in Gillian Rose, *Hegel Contra Sociology* (London: Athlone Press, 1981), 48.

defined as to be tautological or else posed as a prescription[2]; but this raises questions concerning our actual *experiences* of religion and the state, for these appear to be the opposite of identity. If religion and the state are identical, then how is it possible that we experience them as separate in modernity? I would first like to consider how this idea of statehood as being *identical* with religion is important for our political understanding of domination, autonomy, and universality, and our religious understanding of the autonomous, even counter-political, religious life.

The question of "identity" is also the question of what, in Hegel, is called the "absolute". A key statement of the "absolute" (or "speculative statement") in Hegel is, according to Rose, his statement that religion and the foundation of state are "identical". This statement marks the point at which Rose and Milbank's readings of Hegel's "absolute" diverge. Rose understands Hegel's statement of the "identity" of religion and the state in accordance with her definition of Hegel's "absolute" as a relationship characterised by unity and tension. The "absolute" is the comprehensive thinking that transcends all dualisms,[3] and Rose attempts to articulate this comprehensive thinking in her own work. Politically, she understands the "absolute" as a relationship of unity and tension between religion and the state in what she will call "the broken middle". Whilst some commentators, including Milbank (for reasons that are outlined in section three), reject Hegel's idea of the "absolute" as rigid and totalitarian, Rose is committed to the idea that the "absolute" gives Hegel's philosophy its social import, because of its ability to mediate all dualisms *within a whole*. Thus Rose's analysis of the "absolute" sheds light on the problems of conceiving religion and the state as separate, and with the temptation to raise one to a position *over against* the other, which gets to the heart of her critique of Milbank's *ecclesia*.

We must begin, however, by clarifying the relationship between religion and state in Rose and Milbank. Rose's distinctive claim is that the "middle" between religion and the state is "broken".[4] This, Rose argues, is *the* defining feature of modernity, and also her core analytic tool in its political manifestation. Rose regards religion and the state as two halves of a "broken" unity, at odds with one another, and not adding up, and she also regards them as tending to inversion. Modern thought separated religion and the state, but postmodern theologians–and here she is thinking of Milbank in particular–often fail to take into account the ways in which

[2] Rose, *Hegel Contra Sociology*, 48.
[3] Ibid, 46, 204.
[4] Gillian Rose, *The Broken Middle: Out of Our Ancient Society* (Oxford: Blackwell, 1992), 277-278, 280.

their own forms of political or religious idealism, defined *over and against* the state, are frequently inverted into their opposite: totalitarian power and domination, bringing us once again face-to-face with the state. In Rose's view, the concept of "brokenness" allows us to hold together the two sides in a sustained tension, in order to overcome the tendency of postmodernism to "mend" and sanctify an "identical" religion and state.

To obtain a clearer account of the relationship, we need to understand what is meant by the state. Rose elucidates the idea of the state using the metaphor of "city walls". In *Mourning Becomes the Law*, she tells Plutarch's story of the wife of Phocion. Phocion was an Athenian general and a virtuous politician, but he was falsely accused of treason by political rivals. He was executed under the law, and his body left unburied outside the city walls of Athens. This captures two characteristics of the state: *boundary* and *regulation*. Poussin's famous painting, *Gathering the Ashes of Phocion*,[5] depicts Phocion's wife kneeling outside the city weeping over the body of her husband, which she buries in defiance of city laws. One reading of the wife's act of defiance is as a 'new ethics of the *unbounded* community', a rejection of Old Athens, the city or Nation State, conceived as *in itself* an unjust power to be rebelled against.[6] A similar impulse in postmodernism arose from a particularly twentieth-century suspicion of the "spurious universality" of the liberal state based on universal rights. According to this reading, by her act of perfect love Phocion's wife has symbolically founded a New Jerusalem, an anti-State without boundary or regulation. Without city walls, it delegitimates all power; characterised by the ideal of love, it is a "loveful polity", a "mended middle". Rose offers an alternative reading however, suggesting that the wife's "mourning" at the city walls necessarily *sustains* the state as regulator and boundary. The act of mourning is not *optional* but occurs whether we want it or not, because "New Jerusalem" conceals new oppressors, new boundaries, and new regulations, thereby opening up the broken middle once again. The "broken middle" is thus "modernity's ancient predicament" which Rose suggests is "always 'recently' repeated".[7]

As well as its regulative function, the state is part of a *historical narrative*, the story of the transition from the Christian Middle Ages to secular modernity. According to Milbank's account, the state has historically been shaped through time in a series of interactions with religion; however, in modernity the two have increasingly become

---

[5] Gillian Rose, *Mourning Becomes the Law: Philosophy and Representation* (Cambridge: Cambridge University Press, 1996), 23-24.

[6] Ibid, 25. Italics mine.

[7] Rose, *The Broken Middle*, xii.

separate, and the state has grown increasingly dominant. Milbank gives an account of the triumph of the modern secular state over religion, using Hegel's state as the paradigmatic example.[8] Milbank understands the state according to a pattern of "supposed-positing-reversed-into-presupposition", arguing that the idea that we are free subjects is *posited*,[9] and this imagined "community of free persons" is *presupposed* in the secular state, which conceals its illusory origin. The modern secular state is therefore *only formal*, and whilst the state may appear to be a "mysterious ideal-thing", this appearance is illusory and conceals the deeper truth that the secular state is "*nothing but* its citizens who ascribe to laws". Because it is not a true social body, it sets itself over against true religion: the Christian Church.[10] Milbank attributes the same characteristics to the state as Rose–boundary and regulation–but he argues that the state "lacks full legitimacy" because it is merely a historically specific fiction.[11] Milbank regards the state as "nihilistic" and "materialist"; by definition secular, it has "no substantive values" and exists only to uphold market systems.[12] In religion however, he wants to rediscover a truer social body in the Catholic *ecclesia*, which is neither formal nor posited, and which therefore offers grounds for opposing secular state and market domination.

What I have said so far about the relationship between religion and the state suggests that Rose and Milbank are in agreement about the political importance of religion for our understanding of the state, and, more specifically, that both are interested in exploring impulses that react *against* the state which are *religious* in character. In Rose, the anti-state is a "New Jerusalem", understood by her as religious because it disqualifies all universal notions of justice, statehood, regulation, or boundary; its "ground" is "held in transcendence" as perfect "redeeming love".[13] Milbank's Catholic *ecclesia* is a Christian version of just such a "New Jerusalem"; a rejection of the nation-state based on religious idealism, coupled with a preference for redeeming love over state power: the Christian *ecclesia* tears down the "city walls" of "Old Athens".

---

[8] John Milbank, "The Double Glory, or Paradox versus Dialectics: On not Quite Agreeing with Slavoj Žižek", in Slavoj Žižek and John Milbank, *The Monstrosity of Christ: Paradox or Dialectic?* (Massachusetts: MIT Press, 2009), 178.
[9] Ibid, 181.
[10] Ibid, 178-179.
[11] John Milbank, "Sovereignty, Empire, Capital, and Terror", in *The Future of Love: Essays in Political Theology* (Oregon: Cascade Books, 2009), 224.
[12] Ibid, 224.
[13] Rose, *Mourning Becomes the Law*, 7.

Vincent Lloyd offers the insight that the disagreement between Milbank and Rose on religion and the state may be understood in terms of the ethical and legal problem of how one should act: whether in accordance with "secular" laws and social norms, represented by Rose's "city walls" or in accordance with other authorities, such as Milbank's religious traditionalism.[14] I would suggest that a different approach is possible, one that focuses on the political, and addresses not the general legal-ethical question of how we should act, but more specifically the question of how the relationship between religion and the state should be articulated, and so how we should relate to them, as actors living in the "middle". This approach necessitates further exploration of Hegel's idea of the "absolute".

This paper will explore the concept of the "middle" in both Rose and Milbank. Then I will contextualise the "middle" with reference to its origins in the Kantian dualisms. These are politically important because it is in Kant, and in Hegel's unifying critique of Kantian dualisms, that the idea of the "middle" has its origin. I then outline Milbank's critique of Hegel, and explain how his critique is addressed in Rose's "broken middle". Rose suggests that it is the "middle" in Milbank's *ecclesia*, rather than Hegel's "absolute", which is rigidified and static. I argue that the "broken middle" offers a plausible solution to Milbank's contention that Hegel's "absolute" is totalising, because Rose is able to demonstrate the possibility of finding a Hegelian path that retains the "encompassing whole" or "absolute", *without* falling into the trap of totalising rationalism and domination. I conclude that the "broken middle" is able to secure a relationship between religion and the state that allows both for relative political autonomy, and for some form of faith. It is to an explication of the "middle" that I turn in the following section.

II. The Concept of the Middle

The Middle in Rose

Rose uses the notion of the "middle" to account for multiple areas of human experience. Perhaps because of the difficulty of her work there are differing accounts of Rose's "middle". Andrew Shanks identifies the "middle" as a mediator who renounces his or her own complicity in either

---

[14] Vincent Lloyd, *Law and Transcendence: On the Unfinished Project of Gillian Rose* (London: Palgrave MacMillan, 2009), 84.

side of a dispute and works as a "peace negotiator".[15] However, here I read the "middle" not as a "peace-negotiative ideal", but as a commitment to unity and tension between religious ideals and the state. Whilst Shanks is recommending a conversational paradigm, I will present the "middle" as a *critique*, as a *mode of thought*, and also as a *political inevitability*.

The "middle" is a critique, in the sense that the "problem of the middle" in Rose's reading of Hegel is in part an argument that postmodern theorists (particularly, though by no means exclusively, Milbank) have *misread* Hegel's "absolute" as rigidified and static–when actually it is a dynamic movement, broken in form: the "broken middle". The "middle" is, furthermore, a mode of thought, insofar as Rose argues that, in the Hegelian "absolute", thought is in a dialectical process towards the absolute in which all dualisms will be experienced as unities. Although the absolute must always be aimed towards, it is never achieved, and thus the "middle" remains broken. To be committed to the "middle" is to be committed, like Shanks, to an ideal of conversational negotiation between religion and the secular state. In order to further explicate the "middle" as a political inevitability, Rose introduces the metaphor of the "third city".[16] Located between "Old Athens" and "New Jerusalem", the "third city" is carried within human beings ourselves, when we imagine ourselves as both morally autonomous or religious and as belonging to the state: the "third city" is thus "the just city and just act, the just man and the just woman". For Rose, it is a political inevitability that in seeking the "New Jerusalem", a realm of pure ethics free from regulation, "the pilgrims, unbeknownst to themselves, carry along in their souls *the third city*–the city of capitalist private property and modern legal status".[17] Therefore they will tend to recreate old oppressions, regulations and boundaries. The political task, according to Rose, is to live in the "third city" acting out the religious and political tensions in our own lives while refusing to withdraw into either radical state dominance and a banishing of the religious, or a separatist community of love without boundary or regulation. It will be seen in the next section, however, that Milbank also lays claim to the "middle", and that in his work, the "middle" takes a very different form: an alternative Christian modernity. It is to Milbank's alternative "middle" that I now turn.

---

[15] Andrew Shanks, *After Innocence: Gillian Rose's Acceptance and Gift of Faith* (London: SCM Press, 2008), 39.

[16] Rose, *Mourning Becomes the Law*, 19-21.

[17] Ibid, 19-21.

The Middle in Milbank

In this section I outline Milbank's claim to the "middle" of modernity (his Christian anti-state or "New Jerusalem") to begin to make a critical comparison with Rose's "third city".

Milbank cites the experiences of the twentieth and twenty first centuries, during which, lacking in substantive values, the state has piled up "pure power in the name of a people", sustaining its boundaries by creating enemies, both external and internal, against which to define itself.[18] Milbank responds with an alternative vision. Whilst dialectical approaches such as that of Rose, are characterised by the implication of conflict or tension; Milbank imagines the "middle" as a "coincidence of opposites", a "belonging-together", characterised by beauty, harmony, and peace.[19] Politically, Milbank's Catholic *ecclesia* lays claim to the true "middle" of modernity. Two political observations can be made: firstly, the "opposites", for Milbank, are *not* religion and the secular state, since Milbank does not *oppose* the secular, merely denies its reality *qua* secular, regarding it instead as a heterodox mode of religion. Secondly, the "middle" is not institutional; it is an ecclesial "body of Christ" articulated in Catholic liturgical practices that disclose a divine providence irreducible to human institutions. It is non-spatial, but exists as an "enacted, serious fiction", a liturgical performance.[20] The "middle" in Milbank is the Church, understood as a "paradox"–literally *para-doxa*—"overwhelming glory"–irreducible to dialectics.[21]

What I have said here about Milbank indicates the extent of the differences between him and Rose on the "middle". According to Rose, rather than occupying the "third city" Milbank "converges on" the "third" and so destroys it.[22] She regards Milbank's "middle" as an "inflated ecclesiology". It is not, she argues, a real "middle", because it has no institutions, and so she calls it "ecstatic" and "interior", and argues that it fails to acknowledge the "intrusion" of the *polis*.[23] I will return to Rose's critique in more detail in sections three and four, but I turn now to the roots of the "broken middle" in Kant. In *Hegel Contra Sociology*, the category of the "middle"–though Rose does not use the term until *The Broken Middle*–is best described as the point of disagreement between a

---

[18] Milbank, "Sovereignty, Empire, Capital, and Terror", 225.
[19] Milbank, "The Double Glory, or Paradox versus Dialectics", 163-164.
[20] Milbank, "Enclaves, Or Where is the Church?" in *The Future of Love*, 133.
[21] Milbank, "The Double Glory, or Paradox versus Dialectics", 163.
[22] Rose, *The Broken Middle*, 284.
[23] Ibid, 284.

Kantian dualistic system, and a Hegelian system that reveals Kant's dualisms to be contradictory, and moves "through and beyond" them into the "encompassing whole" of speculative philosophy: the "absolute".[24] In the following section I place the "middle" in the context of Kant's dualisms in order to understand more precisely what is at stake in the conversation between Rose and Milbank, in particular regarding their disagreement over the efficacy of Hegelian mediation.

III. Kantian Dualisms

In this section I demonstrate that the "broken middle" can be traced back to Kant. In Kant, thought is characterised by a dualism between legality and morality, which, Rose argues, institutes a further separation between the realms of civil society and the state. Rose identifies the problems caused by this dualistic separation as follows: they reinforce an *antagonistic* relationship between religion or civil society and the state, and they banish any possible unity to an *otherworldly* realm. Whilst for Rose, the dualisms are unified, albeit in tension, in Hegel, for Milbank the dualisms are so radical that Hegel's solution, rooted in dialectical mediation, is unable to overcome them.

So what are the Kantian dualisms and why, according to Rose, does Hegel oppose them? Kant's practical reason is founded on the dualism of "legality" and "morality",[25] which Rose calls the "diremption of law".[26] According to Hegel, this dualism is *contradictory* because the will can only be moral if it is "autonomous", or free to choose to do the right thing, a principle which forms the basis of subjective morality. The will cannot be moral if it is subject to the "external sanctions of a social order" i.e. to legality.[27] Morality is inconsistent with legality, and so there is a diremption at the heart of law. Kant defines "the freedom of rational beings" "in opposition to the necessity of the spatio-temporal world".[28] He therefore presents the relationship between civil society and the state as wholly *antagonistic*.

---

[24] Peter C. Hodgson, *Hegel and Christian Theology: A Reading of the Lectures on the Philosophy of Religion* (Oxford: Oxford University Press, 2005), 7.

[25] Rose, *Hegel Contra Sociology* , 46.

[26] Rose, *The Broken Middle*, xii. Rose chooses the term "diremption" because of its overtones of sharp division, in order to indicate a commitment to thinking the absolute without any false reconciliation.

[27] Rose, *Hegel Contra Sociology*, 46.

[28] Ibid, 53.

Kant's theoretical reason is also dualistic in structure: in theoretical reason a dichotomy between finite and infinite develops out of the attempt "to prepare a *canon* of reason… a sum total of the *a priori* principles of the *correct employment* of the faculties of knowledge".[29] This dichotomy is contradictory, since in order to achieve Kant's aim, thought would have to be justified *before* it is practiced. But how can one justify something without practicing thought? If it is granted that this is a contradiction, "then thought…does not know itself [as thought] at the very point where its self-examination commences".[30] According to Rose, "[by] defining the knowable within the bounds of experience", to the exclusion of the "unconditioned" including the "transcendental unity of apperception", Kant's thought "makes even finite objects unknowable".[31] By enacting a total separation, and placing religion outside the bounds of knowledge, Kant places it in antagonism with the state.

According to Rose's understanding of Hegel's critique of Kant, the problems of the Kantian dualisms are twofold: first, Kant does not comprehend the way in which the diremption of law corresponds to a deep rift between civil society and the state, or *freedom* and *necessity*. Civil society, being the realm of freedom is in conflict with the state, being the realm of political necessity. Kant prioritises freedom over necessity, but because they both reinforce disunity between isolated individuals and the state, any unity is merely formal and so neither can conceive of substantial freedom.[32] This leads to a second problem, which is that unity or the absolute, being abstracted from social relations, is redefined as "otherworldly".[33] For Hegel a bad conception of God equals a bad state and bad laws; the unknowable God represents the experience of "lack of freedom, in social and political relations".[34] The problem according to Milbank is that to posit God as unknowable implies a complete lack of relation: it takes a sphere of pure reason ("finite human categories"), and grants it "methodological priority"–or priority to determine what it is to be, to know, and to act, predetermining how we know God, which amounts to idolatry.[35] But this, for Rose, is not Hegel's problem, Hegel's problem is that dualistic thought is unable to get beyond its own illusions,

---

[29] Ibid, 42.
[30] Ibid, 44.
[31] Ibid, 44.
[32] Ibid, 54, 56.
[33] Ibid, 93.
[34] Ibid, 92.
[35] John Milbank, Catherine Pickstock, and Graham Ward, ed., *Radical Orthodoxy* (London: Routledge, 1999), 21-22.

and therefore Hegel realizes that the absolute must be knowable *if we are to be free*. For Rose, it is impossible to use abstract principles of reason legitimately *without* making reference to possible experience, and Rose wants to show that by thinking the "absolute" (this *implied* unity) Hegel is able to make this jump. For Rose, the "absolute" is necessary for understanding reality, and therefore for enacting change.

From what I have said above it is apparent that there is a tension between Milbank and Rose. For Milbank, the problem of the Kantian state is that dualisms have made God unknowable to the extent that no mediation is possible, and there is a complete lack of relation. For Rose, on the other hand, while the problem of the Kantian dualisms is *also* that God is unknowable–compounding an antagonistic relationship between civil society and the state, and so implying a bad state and bad laws–she argues that Hegel is able to address that problem through mediation.

As I will show in the next section, the critical challenge that Milbank poses to Rose is that the "absolute" in Hegel is *false*, that it fails to achieve a genuine "whole" through mediation, and that Hegel therefore inflates political autonomy and prohibits real faith: a totalising secular radicalisation of Kant. Milbank's argument, *contra* Rose, that there can be no truly speculative "whole" in Hegel, is based on the assertion that Hegelian negation is a "myth", and leads Milbank to conclude that the Hegelian "absolute" is really a domination of the secular. It is to these matters that I turn in the following section.

IV. Milbank's Theological Critique of Hegel

In this section I will show in more detail how Milbank regards Hegelian mediation as a "myth", and why, therefore, he rejects Rose's "broken middle". Whilst Rose and Milbank agree that Kant's reinforcement of an antagonistic relationship between civil society and the state, and his definition of "God" as *otherworldly*, makes the unity of religion and state unattainable;[36] Milbank understands the Kantian dualisms as deeper and more radical than Rose imagines. Kant resolves the contradiction between "appearances" and "things-in-themselves" by arguing that knowledge can no longer depend upon the explanation of *objects* in-themselves, but only on the "appearances" of objects which "conform to our mode of

---

[36] John Milbank, *Theology and Social Theory: Beyond Secular Reason* 2nd edition (Oxford: Blackwell, 2006), 76.

representation".[37] Milbank emphasises that the consequence of Kant's delineation of unknowability is that, in Kant, knowledge can "never transcend the limits of possible experience".[38] If Kant is correct, he argues, and all that is apparent to our consciousness are mere "appearances", then it follows that Kantian consciousness, and therefore Kant's law and state, could be no more than a coalition of human laws and rules concealing a fundamental unknowability: an "abyss" or "void".[39]

In the *Phenomenology*, Hegel, like Milbank, rejects Kant's 'phenomenal restriction'. Hegel attempts to outline an alternative path by which the mind, or thought, may achieve a deeper, and *more rational*, underlying unity; a unity in which thought and reality are dialectically mediated, and in the all-encompassing unity of the "absolute". Politically, this would mean that laws could be based on a knowledge of substantive reality, leading to a reduction in antagonism between the erstwhile "formal" laws of the state, which would no longer be set *over against* civil society. Milbank's critique of Hegelian mediation, and therefore of Rose's "broken middle" on which it is based, is that Hegel's work is merely a *continuation* of the Kantian attempt to make meaning stable in an unreal domain of the "subject". Hegel fails to overcome Kant's dichotomy between the subject and substantial reality. Politically, this means that there would continue to be tension between religion and the state.

Milbank's argument is that Hegel's thought "subordinates the contingencies of human making/speaking to the supposedly 'logical' articulation of a subjectivity which is secretly in command throughout".[40] So although, Milbank argues, "negation" goes some way towards a logic of the possibility of reality, it is ultimately formal.[41] This he attributes to Hegel's pursuit of transcendental enquiry, and specifically his retention of "Cartesian-Kantian' subjectivity". In a Cartesian account of reality, the *cogito* is "the subjective [origin] of our experience",[42] but Hegel wanted to outline the path of consciousness towards "absolute knowledge" in which subject and object are revealed to be identical. In the second moment, when thought, "in the form of *pure substance*", "[passes] into otherness",

---

[37] Immanuel Kant, Preface to the Second Edition, *Critique of Pure Reason*, trans. Norman Kemp Smith (New York: Palgrave Macmillan, 2007), Bxx.

[38] Ibid, Bxix. Rose, *Hegel Contra Sociology*, 44; Milbank, *Theology and Social Theory*, 151-152.

[39] Milbank, Pickstock, and Ward, ed., *Radical Orthodoxy*, 26.

[40] Milbank, *Theology and Social Theory*, 158.

[41] Ibid, 158.

[42] Graham Bird, *The Revolutionary Kant: A Commentary on the Critique of Pure Reason* (Illinois: Open Court, 2006), 1-2.

it is as a "dissociation" that "consists in its existing in a specific or *determinate* mode":[43] Hegel writes:

> Thus the merely eternal or abstract Spirit becomes an "other" to itself, or enters into existence, and directly into *immediate* existence. Accordingly, it *creates* a world. This "creating" is picture-thinking's word for the Notion itself in its absolute movement; or to express the fact that the simple which has been asserted as absolute, or pure thought, just because it is abstract, is rather the negative, and hence the self-oppressed or "other" of itself.[44]

According to Milbank's reading of Hegel, although in Hegel "sublation" (*Aufhebung*) has the double meaning of "transcending" and "preserving", sublation fails to "preserve"–not because the self-expression is not *retained* in its "sublated" form–but because the overall mediation is merely a "return to self" from the self's "negated self-identity".[45] On this basis, Milbank contends that Hegelian negation is a "myth" and that Hegel's thought should be understood as "[pivoting] strictly around the principle of identity A=A".[46] This is an understanding of the "absolute" which casts it as a "panlogicism": a totalising identity. The "absolute" in Milbank's reading, *contra* that of Rose, is therefore in Milbank's own words, a "comprehensive, totalizing *genera*" outside which there are no others, and *within* which the only possible relation is one of opposition.[47] For Milbank, Hegel's negation is a "myth" because there are no real "others"; the "initiative" lies solely with the impulse to negation itself, which is the denial or contradiction of a single absolute identity: a dominating secular reason.[48] Hegel's work is a *radicalisation* of Kant, and of the Kantian state, rather than enacting a resolution of the dualisms.

For Milbank, if the real is not to be understood in terms of "logically necessitated" repeating laws, which would be always the same, a totalising "absolute" or sameness concealing a void, then it must be understood that

---

[43] G.W.F. Hegel, *Phenomenology of Spirit*, trans. A.V. Miller (Oxford: Oxford University Press, 1977), 464.

[44] Ibid, 467.

[45] Milbank bases his argument on passages from Hegel, *Phenomenology of Spirit*, 765-70, and G.W.F. Hegel, *Science of Logic*, trans. A.V. Miller (New York: Humanity Books, 1998), 417, 431. In these passages Hegel is describing the relationship of self to difference. In the passage to which Milbank refers in the *Science of Logic*, Hegel writes that "Difference in itself is self-related difference; as such, it is the negativity of itself, the difference not of another, but *of itself.*' Hegel, *Science of Logic*, 417. Milbank, *Theology and Social Theory*, 156.

[46] Milbank, *Theology and Social Theory*, 156.

[47] Ibid, 156.

[48] Ibid, 158.

the world is only "epistemologically" *something* if it is imbued with the "eternal permanence" of divinity.[49] Divinity makes "nothing" into "something" and communicates it to the mind. If, Milbank writes, "all knowledge occurs through the expression of reality in signs", then it is impossible to directly compare the sign (or law) to the object, and, to use the linguistic metaphor, the "fundamental function of language cannot be referential".[50] We are left with the *necessity* of having faith in our aesthetic decision, that to trust "our creative expressions" to "[fulfil] some goal which is not merely our own" will disclose "unseen depth" in the objects.[51] In Milbank, culture and history are part of the process of divine revelation,[52] the irreducibility of what he calls the "paradox". "Reason" is now to be understood as the "divine illumination" of the mind in "revealed facts" and "grace-given inner dispositions".[53] This is the theological understanding behind Milbank's argument that his *ecclesia*, or "New Jerusalem", as grace-given and divinely inspired through providence, is also *more* "rational" than the Hegelian or Kantian secular state.

This discussion of Milbank has shown that mediation between reality and knowledge is necessary if civil society (including religion) and the formal state are not to be conceived as antagonistic, although Milbank argues that it is not achieved in the work of Hegel. It shows, furthermore, that Milbank's alternative to Hegelian mediation relies on a notion of divine revelation inspiring our cultural expressions, which are conceived as participations in divine grace.

I demonstrate in the following section how Rose's work goes some way towards answering Milbank's critique of Hegel. Rose is a political philosopher and does not develop her ideas fully as theology, but her work lends a critical perspective to Milbank's understanding of the proper relationship between religion and the state. The problem that now comes to the fore is Milbank's question about whether or not Hegel's "absolute" is capable of mediating between religion and the state. I suggest that Rose's "broken middle" provides an answer to Milbank's charge that negation is a myth, and that her work thereby suggests the possibility that Milbank's criticism may be dialectically overcome within Hegel's system. It is to these matters that I turn in the following section.

---

[49] Milbank, Pickstock, and Ward, ed., *Radical Orthodoxy*, 26.

[50] Milbank, *Theology and Social Theory*, 149.

[51] Milbank, Pickstock, and Ward, ed., *Radical Orthodoxy*, 27.

[52] Milbank, *Theology and Social Theory*, 151.

[53] Milbank, Pickstock, and Ward, ed., *Radical Orthodoxy*, 23.

V. Rose's "Broken Middle" Approach

In Rose's reading of Hegel's "absolute" as developed in *Hegel Contra Sociology*, she argues that Hegel suggests that *another reality*, the "absolute", can be perceived by intuition (*Anschauung*), a reality that subsumes the Kantian dualisms into a unity. The idea of a unity, the "absolute", is a presupposition, but it is *phenomenological*.[54] Rose takes seriously Hegel's claim that a phenomenology does *not* impose a method as Kant's work does; a phenomenology perceives the movements in the absolute "according to their own methodological standards as they have occurred, or, as they appear", and "it is only at the end of this history, not at the beginning, that the 'method' of its development can be discerned".[55] Hegel's argument, suggests Rose, is that once consciousness has realised that dualistic systems create illusions and inconsistencies, it has *already* begun to transcend them. In the case of religion, Rose argues that Hegel criticises Kant for making faith in an unknowable God into a "fountain of validity of...moral action and theoretical understanding", and argues that if religion is to be rational, then God must be involved in the absolute, and not external to it: religion and the state must be united within the "absolute".

According to Rose's reading of Hegel's "absolute", Hegel attempts to give an account of how, "in a society based on...lack of identity", particularly between finite and infinite, morality and legality, "[there can] be any reference to absolute ethical life", or the political "absolute".[56] According to Rose, Hegel argues that Kant's dualisms, though illusory, are real social relations, because they are experienced in the real world, and he calls these relations "'relative ethical life' or 'the system of reality'".[57] But "absolute ethical life", or the "absolute", is in Rose's reading of Hegel, the *holding-together* in unity of religion and the state, and this, initially, is *not* a reality.

According to Rose's reading of Hegel, he argues that if religion is *only* capable of reconciling the dualisms in the imagined space of another world "beyond real social relations", then this makes our relationship to the absolute "one of impotent longing".[58] When religion (representing subjective disposition) and the state (representing legality) are separate,

---

[54] Rose, *Hegel Contra Sociology*, 46.
[55] Ibid, 47.
[56] Ibid, 73.
[57] Ibid, 56.
[58] Ibid, 77.

each becomes "fanatical", trying to "impose itself on the other".[59] The church wants to bring about "heaven on earth" and the state wants to rule without reference to people's "conscience or beliefs".[60] This, Rose argues, is a diremption at the heart of the "absolute" itself, in which "on the one hand the absolute is misconceived as the principle of political unity...and on the other hand, the absolute is misrepresented as a conception of 'God'".[61] Rose therefore, as we have already seen in the introduction, regards the major speculative statement in Hegel's work as his statement in the *Lectures on the Philosophy of Religion* that "In general religion and the foundation of the state is [*sic*] one and the same thing; they are identical in and for themselves".[62]

As we began to see in the introduction, if this is read as an ordinary statement it is false; and if it is read as a statement of what ought to be, then it posits a type of "absolute" that collapses religion into the state.[63] Rose identifies this statement as a key point at which readings of Hegel's absolute diverge. Some commentators, and Rose uses the example of Milbank, regard the absolute as a conservative, rigid, teleological unity, and try to drop it. Milbank takes the statement as evidence that Hegel's "absolute" merges religion and the state, introducing infinite *sameness* between the realm of the human and the realm of the divine, and preventing any relationship between them, which makes theology impossible. But Rose, *contra* Milbank, reads Hegel in such a way as to *retain* the absolute but precisely as an important guarantor *against* such hypostatisation, as a relational "broken middle". If her argument is sound, then Milbank has wrongly attributed to Hegel's system the kind of "false" or "holy" middle that it is actually designed to overcome.[64]

So what exactly is Rose's "broken middle", and how does it attempt to achieve the sort of mediation that Milbank regards as impossible? Rose begins to think the idea of the "broken middle" in the essay "From Speculative to Dialectical Thinking–Hegel and Adorno".[65] She quotes from a letter written by Hegel to Niethammer in which he explains that

---

[59] Ibid, 77. Rose is quoting G.W.F. Hegel, "Art, Religion and Science" from the Jena lectures (1805-6).

[60] Ibid, 77.

[61] Ibid, 92-93.

[62] Hegel, *Lectures on the Philosophy of Religion*, Vol. I, 297. Quoted in Rose, *Hegel Contra Sociology*, 48.

[63] Rose, *Hegel Contra Sociology*, 48.

[64] Ibid, 42.

[65] Gillian Rose, "From Speculative to Dialectical Thinking – Hegel and Adorno", in Gillian Rose, *Judaism and Modernity: Philosophical Essays* (Oxford: Blackwell, 1993), 60-61.

there are three forms of philosophical content – "abstract", "dialectical" and "speculative".[66] The first, abstract form is simple understanding, in which the dualisms are understood to be fixed and determinate. The second is the form of the dialectic, which is "more difficult than the first"– it "is the movement and confusion of such fixed determinateness". Hegel continues, "The [Kantian] dualisms contain deep fundamentals of the antinomical content of reason. Yet these antinomies lie concealed and are recognised in the antinomies so to speak unthinkingly and insufficiently in their truth...Nothing beyond tortuous antitheses." The third and "truly speculative form" alone is truly philosophical, and it comprises the "knowledge of what is opposed in its very oneness, more precisely the knowledge that the opposites are in truth one".[67]

Within the "oneness" of the "absolute" there is a relationality and movement of the dualisms, or the "middle". According to Rose's reading of Hegel, this movement is the essence of the "absolute". Hegel's speculative philosophy is not a method imposing itself onto the content of life, as Kant imposes form onto content. It is a *phenomenology*, in which Hegel, as the phenomenological observer "[traces] the education of self-consciousness at specific historical moments" as it moves towards the absolute, which in itself will never be known.[68] As phenomenology, Hegel argues that it is self-justifying and observable. According to Hegel, reason's movements take the form of "syllogisms". It is not unusual for philosophers to describe the form of the rational in terms of syllogisms, but Hegel's work is distinctive because he argues that the syllogism is the *content* of the rational as well as its form. "Hence", he writes, "the syllogism is the *essential ground of everything true*; and the *definition of the Absolute* from now on is the syllogism".[69] Hegel explains the syllogisms in more detail as follows:

> Expressed as a proposition this determination [that the definition of the Absolute is the syllogism] becomes: "Everything is a syllogism." Everything is a *concept*, and the way that the concept is there is the distinction of its moments, in such a way that its *universal* nature gives

---

[66] G.W.F. Hegel, *The Letters*, trans. Clark Butler and Christiane Seiler (Bloomington: Indiana University Press, 1984), 280-2. "Letter to Friedrich Immanuel Niethammer", 23 October 1812 (about how to teach philosophy to boys at the gymnasium).

[67] Rose, "From Speculative to Dialectical Thinking – Hegel and Adorno", 60-61.

[68] Rose, *Judaism and Modernity*, 185.

[69] G.W.F. Hegel. *The Encyclopaedia Logic: Part 1 of the Encyclopaedia of Philosophical Sciences with the Zusätze*, ed. and trans. T.F. Geraets, W.A. Suchting, and H.S. Harris (Indianapolis: Hackett, 1991), 257 (§181).

itself external reality through *particularity*, and in this way, i.e., as negative inward reflection, the concept makes itself into the *singular*.—Or, conversely: the actual is a *singular* that raises itself by means of *particularity* to *universality* and makes itself identical with itself.–The actual is One, but it is equally the stepping asunder of the moments of the Concept; and *the syllogism is the cycle of the mediation of its moments, the cycle through which it posits itself as One.*[70]

Rose illustrates her interpretation of the "problem of the middle" in the Hegelian syllogisms in the form of an exposition of Hegel's characterisation of truth as a Bacchanalian revel. She uses this story to develop a fuller picture of the difference between dialectical or hypostatised thought and truly speculative philosophy. Hegel writes that:

> The true is thus the Bacchanalian revel in which no member is not drunk; yet because each member collapses as soon as he drops out, the revel is just as much transparent as simple repose. Judged in the court of this movement, the single shapes of spirit do not persist any more than determinate thoughts do, but they are as much positive and necessary moments, as they are negative and evanescent. In the *whole* of the movement, seen as a state of repose, what distinguishes itself therein, and gives itself particular existence is preserved as something that *recollects* itself, whose existence is self-knowledge, and whose self-knowledge is just as immediately existence.[71]

According to Rose, the second dialectical stage, in which there is all revel and no repose (or, in Hegel's words, "nothing beyond tortuous antitheses") arrests the movement of speculative philosophy.[72] Such a party would be an endless repetition, completely self-contained and with no external point from which the revellers could see themselves as part of a *whole* movement, which disallows any real change or revolution. Religion and the state would be fixed in permanent antagonism. However, the third level, or "speculative thought", is a moment of repose in the revel, in which it is possible for the phenomenological observer to see the "*whole* of the movement". This is why the "absolute" is indispensable for the social import of Hegel's thought in terms of the relationship between religion and the state. It is the point at which theory has *realised* that oppositions are in reality "one", and this is understood by Rose as a tension or "broken middle". For Rose, Hegel is the observer at the level of truly speculative thought, the figure outside the revel who is able to see

---

[70] Ibid, 257 (§181). Last sentence, italics mine.
[71] Hegel, *Phenomenology of Spirit*, 27-28.
[72] Rose, *Judaism and Modernity*, 60-61.

and understand the *whole* of the movement. At this third level of speculative thought as Rose understands it, religion and the state are in a relationship in which although we may *experience* a lack of unity, the overall movement of *holding-together* in tension allows that overall there may be a relationship of mediation.

VI. Conclusion: Political Consequences for the Theology of John Milbank

To conclude, I have argued that the relationship between religion and the state is politically important because it concerns the way in which we live as agents in the space known as the "middle". The state, as Rose demonstrates, is characterised by *regulation* and *boundary*, and the "middle" of modernity, between religion and the state, is "broken". Rose's recommendation is that we should commit ourselves to "mourning" at the city walls, and refrain from the temptation to retreat into "New Jerusalem". Derived from Hegel's critique of Kantian dualisms, and his idea of the "absolute", the "broken middle" holds religion and the state together in a relationship of sustained tension.

My initial question for this paper, and its title, are about the political consequences of Rose's "broken middle" for the theology of Milbank. It is important to note that, as Milbank points out in his essay,[73] in Rose the middle is *perpetually* broken, and this indicates that the unity proposed in the idea of the "broken middle" is an endless deferral. However, in terms of Milbank's charge that Hegel's system collapses religion into the state, Rose offers in her reading of Hegel on the "absolute", a way to defend Hegel and an alternative way of reading his work. Rose approaches this by reading Hegel's statement about the identity of religion and the state as a "speculative" proposition. It is, argues Rose, a statement of the "absolute", and necessarily so, but the "absolute" should be understood as containing *within itself* all contradictions and dualisms. The "middle" in Gillian Rose's reading of Hegel moves in a complex and stylised manner through the hypostatised dualisms of Kant, and the false, "holy middle", towards a more dynamic "broken middle".

The most far reaching political consequence of Rose's work for Milbank is her critique of the *ecclesia*: Milbank's "New Jerusalem". Rose's "broken middle" approach suggests that attempts to trade "Old Athens" for "New Jerusalem" may find themselves dirempted back by the "broken middle" into their opposite, totalitarian power and domination, at

---

[73] Milbank, "The Double Glory, or Paradox versus Dialectics", 117.

which point we once again come face-to-face with the state. In *The Broken Middle*,[74] Rose takes issue with Milbank's attempt to overcome secular reason by *replacing* it with what Rose terms an "inflated ecclesiology" in his wish for "liberation from all structures belonging to the *saeculum*".[75] Rose warns that Milbank may replace Hegel's triune thought with a general "sociology of control", and therefore posit a new dualism and domination.[76] This is the enduring presence of the *broken middle*, as "modernity's ancient predicament".

Bibliography

Bird, Graham, *The Revolutionary Kant: A Commentary on the Critique of Pure Reason*. Illinois: Open Court, 2006.

Hegel, G.W.F. *Lectures on the Philosophy of Religion: Together with a Work on the Proofs of the Existence of God*. Translated by E.B. Spiers, and J. Burdon Sanderson. London: Kegan Paul, Trench, Trübner and Co., 1895.

—. *Phenomenology of Spirit*. Translated by A.V. Miller. Oxford: Oxford University Press, 1977.

—. *The Letters*. Translated by Clark Butler and Christiane Seiler. Bloomington: Indiana University Press, 1984.

—. *The Encyclopaedia Logic: Part I of the Encyclopaedia of Philosophical Sciences with the Zusätze*. Edited and translated by T.F. Geraets, W.A. Suchting, and H.S. Harris. Indianapolis: Hackett, 1991.

—. *Science of Logic*. Translated by A.V. Miller. New York: Humanity Books, 1998.

Hodgson, Peter C. *Hegel and Christian Theology: A Reading of the Lectures on the Philosophy of Religion*. Oxford: Oxford University Press, 2005.

Kant, Immanuel. *Critique of Pure Reason*. Translated by Norman Kemp Smith. New York: Palgrave Macmillan, 2007.

Lloyd, Vincent. *Law and Transcendence: On the Unfinished Work of Gillian Rose*. New York: Palgrave Macmillan, 2009.

Milbank, John. *Theology and Social Theory: Beyond Secular Reason*. Second Edition. Oxford: Blackwell, 2006.

—. *The Future of Love: Essays in Political Theology*. Oregon: Cascade Books, 2009.

---

[74] Rose, *The Broken Middle*, 277-296.
[75] Milbank, *Theology and Social Theory*, 391.
[76] Rose, *The Broken Middle*, xiii.

Milbank, John, Catherine Pickstock and Graham Ward edited. *Radical Orthodoxy: A new theology*. London: Routledge, 1999.

Rose, Gillian. *Hegel Contra Sociology*. London: Athlone Press, 1981.

—. *The Broken Middle: Out of Our Ancient Society*. Oxford: Blackwell, 1992.

—. "From Speculative to Dialectical Thinking–Hegel and Adorno." In *Judaism and Modernity: Philosophical Essays*. Oxford: Blackwell, 1993. 53–63.

—. *Mourning Becomes the Law: Philosophy and Representation*. Cambridge: Cambridge University Press, 1996.

Shanks, Andrew. *After Innocence: Gillian Rose's Reception and Gift of Faith*. London: SCM Press, 2008.

Žižek, Slavoj and John Milbank. *The Monstrosity of Christ: Paradox or Dialectic?* Massachusetts: MIT Press, 2009.

CHAPTER TEN

DISMANTLING THE THEO-POLITICAL MACHINE: ON AGAMBEN'S MESSIANIC NIHILISM

ADAM KOTSKO

By now the interest of European philosophers in theology has surely made the transition from being a trend to being an established fact. Even in cases such as Badiou's, where his investigation of St. Paul's account of political subjectivity was avowedly a mere illustration,[1] claims of a deeper theological basis for his thought are granted a prima facie plausibility in a way that would not have been the case, for instance, if similar claims had been made about Derrida in the early years of his English-language reception. The representatives of this "theological turn" have enjoyed a wide audience in the United States, as a variety of constituencies have laid claim to them. These constituencies of course included students of European philosophy, for whom the "theological turn" was the latest development in a debate they had long been watching unfold, but they also included various camps within academic theology and its fellow-travellers—liberal or radical theologians and biblical scholars who were energized by the attention their fields were suddenly getting from some of the world's most prestigious minds and by the fresh opportunities for dialogue this attention opened up, traditionalist theologians who took the turn to theology as evidence that the great intellectual projects of secular reason had run aground and Christianity was now the only way to turn,[2]

---

[1] Alain Badiou, *Saint Paul: The Foundation of Universalism*, trans. Ray Brassier (Stanford: Stanford University Press, 2003).

[2] Here one thinks primarily of Radical Orthodoxy, but the clearest illustration of this tendency is a lengthy book review in the right-wing Catholic publication *First Things*: Paul J. Griffiths, "Christ and Critical Theory," *First Things*, August/ September 2004,
<http://www.firstthings.com /article.php3?id_article=372> (accessed 15 September 2007).

and even intellectually curious Christians looking for either a challenge or a jolt to their faith.

These more or less instrumentalising approaches toward this broad philosophical trend have a certain plausibility in the context of the eclecticism that characterizes the most influential and normative American appropriations of Continental thought. When one is engaged in a broad discussion of "Paul and philosophy," for instance, it makes sense to mine the various authors of books on Paul (by now a kind of mini-canon: Badiou, Agamben, Žižek, Taubes) for insights and perhaps also to chide them for their inattentiveness to biblical scholarship. While such an approach has its virtues, it can also produce the temptation to project the reader's own occasionalism onto the authors under discussion, as though they just happened to have written something on a religious text they stumbled across and found interesting—or perhaps even wrote on theological topics in response to the very trend that from the American perspective they retrospectively embody.

When theologically-oriented texts are placed within the context of the entire body of work of a given author, however, a different picture emerges. On the one hand, the texts nearly always show themselves to be tightly integrated into the author's own idiosyncratic project. On the other hand, once one attains a clear view of what those texts are doing in a variety of authors' projects, a pattern begins to emerge: these European investigators of theology are looking for a way *out of* Christianity. The scholarship on this point is perhaps most advanced in connection to Derrida. In response to John D. Caputo's path-breaking *Prayers and Tears of Jacques Derrida*,[3] which portrayed Derrida as a quasi-Christian, scholars such as Michael Naas and Martin Hägglund[4] have shown that Derrida's appropriations of theology consistently aim toward a more radical and thorough-going secularism, which can only be achieved if the theological remnants that still shape our political institutions (such as the notion of sovereignty) are first recognized for what they are. I have attempted to demonstrate a similar thesis with regard to Slavoj Žižek's engagement with theology, arguing that for Žižek the "Christian experience" is fundamentally an experience of the most profound possible atheism.[5] In both cases, the impetus behind the turn to religion comes in

---

[3] John D. Caputo, *Prayers and Tears of Jacques Derrida: Religion Without Religion* (Bloomington: Indiana University Press, 1997).

[4] See Michael Naas, *Derrida From Now On* (New York: Fordham University Press, 2008) and Martin Hägglund, *Radical Atheism: Derrida and the Time of Life* (Stanford: Stanford University Press, 2008).

[5] See Adam Kotsko, *Žižek and Theology* (New York: T&T Clark, 2008).

large part from within their own intellectual projects—which could perhaps be briefly summarized as, respectively, a steadily-expanding deconstruction of the Western heritage and the quest for a "non-ideological" political form grounded in a fusion of psychoanalysis and German idealism—but the end goal of their engagement with theology remains the same: to find a way out of religion, recognizing that "the only way out is through."

This essay is in part an attempt to demonstrate that a similar pattern is at work in the philosophy of Giorgio Agamben. His role in the "theological turn" became most evident after the publication of his book on St. Paul,[6] but only with the recent publication of *Il Regno e la Gloria* and *Il sacramento del linguaggio* [*The Kingdom and the Glory* and *The Sacrament of Language*][7] did it become clear how crucial an investigation of the Christian heritage of the West was for his project in the Homo Sacer series.[8] In retrospect, however, one can see that Agamben had all along been shifting fluently between the religious and the political, a procedure he rarely thematises because the example of Walter Benjamin, perhaps his most significant intellectual influence, makes it seem like the obvious route to take. A significant portion of this essay will be taken up with a rereading of the Homo Sacer project with special attention to this continual slippage between the religious and the political. Yet for my purposes, Agamben's account of the theologico-political structure of the West is less important than the means he proposes for escaping or

---

[6] Giorgio Agamben, *The Time That Remains: A Commentary On The Letter To The Romans*, trans. Patricia Dailey (Stanford: Stanford University Press, 2005).

[7] Giorgio Agamben, *Il Regno e la Gloria: Per una genealogia teologica dell'economia e del governo* (Vicenza: Neri Pozza, 2007) and *Il sacramento del linguaggio: Archealogia del giuarmento* (Rome: Laterza, 2008). Both are forthcoming in English translation from Stanford University Press. Recognizing the fact that most readers will be using translations rather than the Italian original, references to these two texts will use chapter numbers and section numbers, respectively, rather than page numbers. For convenience, I will be referring to these volumes by the translated titles I have placed in brackets above.

[8] The remaining volumes in the series are *Homo Sacer: Sovereign Power and Bare Life*, trans. Daniel Heller-Roazen (Stanford: Stanford University Press, 1998), *State of Exception*, trans. Kevin Attell (Chicago: University of Chicago Press, 2005), and *Remnants of Auschwitz: The Witness and the Archive*, trans. Daniel Heller-Roazen (New York: Zone Books, 2005), designated as volumes I through III; *Il Regno e la Gloria* and *Il sacramento del linguaggio* are designated volumes II.2 and II.3, respectively. A fourth volume on "forms of life" is expected. When in italics, "*Homo Sacer*" refers to the first book of the series; when in normal type, "Homo Sacer" refers to the series as a whole.

suspending that structure, a means that I will characterize as "messianic nihilism." Once I have established the basic outlines of Agamben's diagnosis of what ails Western culture and his proposed way out, I will turn from the exegetical to the constructive task, considering Agamben as one of the most fruitful interlocutors among the representatives of the "theological turn" for interrogating the relationship between theology and philosophy.

I.

While the Homo Sacer project is daunting in its ambitious reach and numerous intellectual points of reference, I believe that its core insight can be stated quite simply. For Agamben, Western politics is a vast machine that attempts to capture and control life. Yet its self-appointed task is an impossible one and must, in the last analysis, always fail. Agamben's analysis in the Homo Sacer books aims to locate those points at which the machine presses its claim too far and to trace out the destructive consequences of its overreach.

Agamben's starting point in this investigation is Walter Benjamin's suggestion in his "Critique of Violence" that "it might be well worth while to track down the origin of the dogma of the sacredness of life."[9] Influenced by Martin Heidegger's use of etymologies, Agamben locates this dogma's origin in a puzzling figure from Roman law: the *homo sacer* or "sacred man," who cannot be sacrificed (or ceremonially executed) but whose killing is not considered murder. There is much that is interesting in this figure for Agamben, most notably the way that the *homo sacer* is paradoxically included in the social order by his very exclusion—that is to say, his exclusion from the protections and official punishments of the political order is the ultimate punishment, meaning that his exclusion from the political order is itself a relationship to the political order. Agamben sees a parallel insider-outsider structure at work in the figure of the sovereign authority, who is legally permitted to suspend the legal order itself, so that the sovereign's extra-legal action is paradoxically nonetheless legal.

In juxtaposing the *homo sacer* and the sovereign, Agamben traces the outer limit of the political machine's claim on life, a claim that culminates

---

[9] Walter Benjamin, "Critique of Violence" in *Reflections*, ed. Peter Demetz (New York: Schocken, 1978), 299. I have criticized Agamben's use of this text in "On Agamben's Use of Benjamin's 'Critique of Violence,'" in *Telos* 145 (Winter 2008): 119-129; I stand by these criticisms, but some of my broader concerns have been satisfied by the appearance of *The Kingdom and the Glory*.

in abandoning what it excludes to total destruction. For the political machine, what is outside of it cannot remain indifferent: the logic of its totalising claim dictates that what is outside cannot really exist. What the political machine wilfully excludes is given up to destruction and in fact is already virtually destroyed—the *homo sacer*'s survival cannot be grounded in any positive law, but is simply a reflection of the fact that no one happens to have got around to killing him yet. On the other side, if the political machine determines that the life it governs is slipping out of its grasp, as in a state of emergency where the laws no longer seem to be effective in regulating life, it can employ virtually limitless violence to subdue that life and vindicate its claim once again. These two figures are the poles between which the political machine operates: "At the extreme limits of the order, the sovereign and *homo sacer* present two symmetrical figures that have the same structure and are correlative: the sovereign is the one with respect to whom all men are potentially *homines sacri*, and *homo sacer* is the one with respect to whom all men act as sovereigns."[10]

In earlier eras, the status of *homo sacer* and the state of emergency in which the sovereign could legitimately use all necessary means to restore order were more or less clearly delineated conditions. In modernity, however, Agamben believes that the political machine is breaking down in such a way that those distinctions become increasingly hard to maintain: "If today there is no longer any one clear figure of the sacred man, it is perhaps because we are all virtually *homines sacri*."[11] In more familiar terms, this means that the political sphere of Western modernity is always virtually a concentration camp, with legal norms and citizenship serving as tenuous protections that could be removed at any time, reducing us to the "naked life" that is exposed to the limitless violence of the sovereign.

The slippage between the religious and the political is clear in both of Agamben's terms. The parallels between the sovereign and God are well-known to readers of Carl Schmitt's *Political Theology*,[12] one of the primary sources for Agamben's investigation in *Homo Sacer* and *State of Exception*. The crossing between the religious and the political is even more evident in the concept of the sacredness of life, which maintains its obvious religious overtones even though it stands as one of the guiding concepts of modern liberal politics. The dual reference is also evident in the notion of the *homo sacer*, who is withdrawn from religious rites (i.e. becoming a sacrifice) and from political protection.

---

[10] Agamben, *Homo Sacer*, 84.
[11] Ibid, 115.
[12] Carl Schmitt, *Political Theology: Four Chapters on the Concept of Sovereignty*, trans. George D. Schwab (Chicago: University of Chicago Press, 2004).

Agamben absolutely insists on the simultaneously religious and political understanding of the term, devoting an entire chapter of *Homo Sacer* to demolishing interpretations of the *homo sacer* that start from the modern theories of religion. Modern theorists tend to posit the "ambivalence of the generic religious category of the sacred"[13] or of the so-called numinous element—as in Rudolf Otto's famous *mysterium tremendum et fascinans*—and for Agamben, this is worse than question-begging, revealing a profound triviality at the heart of modern concepts of religion: "That the religious belongs entirely to the sphere of psychological emotion, that it essentially has to do with shivers and goose bumps—this is the triviality that the neologism 'numinous' had to dress up as science."[14] This restriction of the religious to the private or psychological level is the signature gesture of liberal political theory, an artificial division that has blinded the modern West to its own deep structure. Implicitly, then, only an inquiry like Agamben's, which moves freely back and forth across the border supposedly dividing the political and the religious as the analysis dictates, can truly uncover the workings of the political machine.

Thus the finding of *Homo Sacer* is that the notion of the "sacredness of life" does not, as common sense and liberal piety would have it, mean simply that human life is extremely valuable. Rather, it indicates the political machine's total claim on life. The use of the term in the abortion debate in the United States is illustrative of this point: while pro-life advocates intend to say that the unborn also deserve legal protection, the practical upshot of the pro-life position is that even what happens within the depths of a woman's body is the concern of the state. Adopting the pro-life position would be another step in a process that has long been underway, whereby positing the "sacredness of life" as a trans-political norm strengthens the claim of the political machine over life, a claim that necessarily exposes life to violence. Here as elsewhere, though, simple opposition to the pro-life position is not sufficient to get out of this general trend: the legalization of abortion also gives the state a kind of virtual claim over the womb, since what is legal can be regulated and perhaps even controlled.

Now Agamben argues that the claim of the political machine over life was not always so thorough-going. In the ancient Greek world, he claims, there was a clear division between naked or natural life (*zoē*) and the specific form of political life (*bios*)—the public life of the city was the realm of *bios*, while *zoē* fell within the non-political realm of *oikonomia* or

---

[13] Agamben, *Homo Sacer*, 80.
[14] Ibid, 78.

"home economics." The question that remains for the reader of *Homo Sacer*, *State of Exception*, and *Remnants of Auschwitz* is what caused the transition from the ancient paradigm to the modern one. One can see that the seeds of our current extreme situation are already present in the constitutive relationship between the sovereign and *homo sacer*, but what caused those two figures to propagate themselves so aggressively beyond their initially well-defined boundaries?

Agamben's answer to this question is found in *The Kingdom and the Glory*, where he maps out the introduction into political thought of concepts previously reserved for *oikonomia*.[15] This line of thinking emerged out of the demands of imperial politics. An emperor was caught between two poles. On the one hand, a single inflexible set of laws, even if supplemented by emergency powers, could not work for a large and variegated polity in the same way that it could for a small city-state. On the other hand, exercising direct authority over every dispute would be out of the question for the emperor—not only would it be impractical, but it would undermine his imperial dignity. The task of the emperor is then to set up a system that requires as few direct interventions as possible while still maintaining reliable expectations for his subjects. The solution was the establishment of a hierarchical system where those at each level were guided by broad norms, but where the skills required in dealing with the levels under their authority were more akin to those associated with the management or governance of the *oikos*. The bureaucrats at each level were concerned less with applying strict laws than with maintaining a flexible approach to keeping various constituencies happy, much as the householder had to balance the needs of his wife, his children, his slaves, and his livestock and crops.

The crucial step in Agamben's account, however, was not simply the reconception of an empire as a kind of *oikonomia*. What gave the concepts staying power was their introduction into the Christian concept of God. Not only was the Christian God (or at least the version of the Christian God that would become normative) engaged in managing the "*oikonomia* of salvation," but God's very being was an *oikonomia* among the persons of the Trinity. It was this injection of the politicised concept of *oikonomia* into theology that allowed for its development throughout the medieval period, with scholastic theologians parsing out the details and implications of God's management or governance of the world by means of divine providence. Instead of directly controlling and determining everything,

---

[15] I have compiled a detailed summary of the argument of *Il Regno et la Gloria*, available at the following web address:
http://itself.wordpress.com/category/agamben/il-regno-e-la-gloria-notes/

God set up certain broad rules (first causes), within which moral agents can act with real freedom (secondary causes)—and yet their free actions wind up moving toward the direction God is taking history. This understanding of divine providence cultivated in theology was then, in turn, transplanted back into the political realm at the dawn of modernity, as can be seen in such notions as the "invisible hand" that guides the selfish choices of individual economic actors toward the greatest general good.

The modern state is therefore explicitly conceived as an *oikonomia* from the very beginning and has as its task the management of life. The link between sovereignty and naked life was already implicit in the ancient paradigm of the polis but was kept in check by certain firm distinctions (above all *zoē*/*bios*)—in the modern paradigm, it becomes the central principle of politics. Without repudiating his thesis on sovereignty and naked life, Agamben clarifies his position: "What our research has, in fact, shown is that the true problem, the central secret of the political is not sovereignty, but governance, is not God, but the angel, is not the king, but the minister, is not the law, but the police—or the governmental machine that these form and keep in movement."[16] In this quote as in the book as a whole, it is more clear than ever that theological and political concepts are not simply identical—in the middle ages, for example, political theory was based in the reality of the feudal model while providence remained a strictly theological notion—yet they can easily migrate from one realm to the other, such that one might be justified in calling the governmental machine a theologico-political one.

What is the basis for this easy transferability? For many modern scholars, the answer is clear: religious and political concepts can change places because the religious is at the basis of the political, and indeed of all culture. In *The Sacrament of Language*,[17] Agamben utterly rejects this interpretation. Instead, by means of an analysis of the phenomenon of the oath, he claims that both religion and politics have at their basis a certain experience of language. Agamben finds that the oath confounds all our common sense divisions between religion and politics—it invokes God and at the same time produces civil obligations, for instance—and argues that this is because the oath reflects the moment in our becoming human or

---

[16] Agamben, *Il Regno e la Gloria*, appendix 1 (my translation).
[17] I have also compiled detailed notes on *The Sacrament of Language*, available online at http://itself.wordpress.com/category/agamben/il-sacramento-del-lingua ggio-notes/

"anthropogenesis" when the political and the religious were not yet separated.[18]

The experience that the oath recalls is centrally a matter of the human being *taking responsibility* for language by enforcing its claim on reality. In swearing an oath, one is attesting to the correspondence between one's words and reality—either in relation to an objective situation or a promised action over which the oath-giver has control. If one speaks in such a way as to undermine language's claim on reality, that is, if one swears falsely, then one becomes subject to a curse, to some kind of punishment or sanction. The claim of language over reality is basically identical in structure to the political's claim over life: the claim is total, and that which falls outside of it is subject to destruction.

This experience of language has provided the structure within which all of Western history has played out:

> It is in the wake of this decision, in faithfulness to this oath, that the human species, to its misfortune as much as to its good fortune, in a certain way still lives. Every naming is, in fact, double: it is a blessing or a curse. A blessing, if the word is full, if there is a correspondence between the signifier and the signified, between words and things; a curse if the word is empty, if there remains, between the semiotic and the semantic, a void and a gap. Oath and perjury, bene-diction and male-diction correspond to this double possibility inscribed in the *logos*, in the experience by means of which the living human being has been constituted as speaking being. Religion and law technicalize this anthropogenic experience of the word in the oath and in the curse as historical institutions, sorting out and opposing point by point truth and lie, true name and false name, efficacious formula and incorrect formula.[19]

Yet just as the ancient paradigm of sovereignty gradually worked out its implicit consequences to such an extreme that the concentration camp has become the paradigm of modern politics, so too have the formerly stable expectations of the oath begun to break down, which

> means that humanity finds itself today before a disjunction or, at least, a loosening of the bond that, by means of the oath, united the living human being to his language. On the one hand, there is the living human being, more and more reduced to a purely biological reality and to bare life. On the other hand, there is the speaking being, artificially divided from the former, through a multiplicity of technico-mediatic apparatuses, in an

---

[18] Agamben specifies that this moment need not refer to a historical moment—instead, it is a logical presupposition of our actual history.

[19] Agamben, *Il sacramento del linguaggio*, §29 (my translation).

experience of speech that grows ever more vain, for which it is impossible for him to be responsible and in which anything like a political experience becomes more and more precarious.[20]

This breakdown of the structure of the oath does not lead to stasis, however:

> When the ethical—and not simply cognitive—connection that unites human words, things, and actions is broken, this in fact promotes a spectacular proliferation, without precedent, of vain words on the one hand and, on the other, of legislative apparatuses that seek obstinately to legislate on every aspect of that life on which they seem no longer to have any hold.[21]

Yet as we have already seen, the machine has only one way to react to any perceived lack of control: the application of destructive violence. Ultimately, then, the Homo Sacer project traces the workings of a machine that is rotting from within and is increasingly able only to destroy that over which it lays claim.

II.

It is worth pausing for a moment to consider how radically pessimistic Agamben's diagnosis is. Normally a narrative of cultural-political breakdown will have in mind some previous era where things were working—even if one admits frankly that it is impossible to go back, one at least cherishes some sense that things could have gone differently. In Agamben's account, however, the corruption seems to be essentially inevitable. However long the Western theologico-political machine managed to maintain a steady state, it was always, eventually and ineluctably, going to wind up where we are now. The reader of *State of Exception* could have been forgiven for assuming that the solution to the problem of sovereignty run amok was a return to some kind of "normal" liberal democracy. In the wake of *The Kingdom and the Glory*, however, it becomes clear that it is precisely the advent of the liberal democratic state that allowed for the exaggerated forms of confrontation between sovereignty and naked life that we now see. More than that, in *The Sacrament of Language*, it is even claimed that our very relationship to language is the foundation for the machine. There is still a sense in which

---

[20] Ibid.
[21] Ibid.

things could have turned out differently—we became human in a specific, contingent way—and yet everything we know, everything that gives us meaning, delivers us over to death.

Agamben's proposed solution to this problem is not to set the theologico-political machine back to a previous, less destructive stage, nor is it to let it run its course and attempt to build something new amongst the ruins. Rather, he contends that we need to find a way to stop the machine, to suspend its operation. In attempting to think what stopping the machine might mean, he draws upon a mode of thought that is itself at once theological and political: messianism. Here as elsewhere, Agamben is heavily influenced by Walter Benjamin, inheriting from him what one might call a "negative messianism." In contrast to a more common sense concept of messianism where a saviour arrives and establishes a utopia, Benjamin, drawing on his study of messianic texts guided by Gershom Scholem, regards the messianic revolution as a kind of brake on history.

What Agamben adds to Benjamin's account is his particular take on the relationship between potentiality and actuality in Aristotle. To put it very schematically, Agamben sees potentiality not as a deficient form of actuality (i.e., one that has not become actual yet), but as more primordial than actuality. Thus the messianic is that which restores actuality to its full potentiality. This is most vividly illustrated in Agamben's retelling of the rabbinic idea that the primordial heavenly law is nothing but the sequence of letters which have all possible meanings (and, Agamben extrapolates, therefore no meaning)—this is what becomes of the law in the messianic era. By being restored to its proper potentiality, the law is severed of its relationship with force. The following passage, drawn from a discussion of Kafka in *State of Exception*, is particularly evocative in this regard:

> One day humanity will play with law just as children play with disused objects, not in order to restore them to their canonical use but to free them from it for good.... This liberation is the task of study, or of play. And this studious play is the passage that allows us to arrive at that justice that one of Benjamin's posthumous fragments defines as a state of the world in which the world appears as a good that absolutely cannot be appropriated or made juridical.[22]

In light of his reflections in *The Sacrament of Language*, one can take a further step here: in the messianic age, the world also appears as a good that absolutely cannot be made *meaningful*. Indeed, in that book Agamben enters a plea—apparently paradoxical in light of his diagnosis of the

---

[22] Agamben, *State of Exception*, 64.

destructive effects of the breakdown of the experience of the oath—that we radically rethink the prestige in which language is held in Western culture.

It is this radical evacuation of everything that we know as meaning that informs my claim that Agamben's particular form of messianism is best termed messianic nihilism. Yet the method of messianic nihilism is not an attempt at simple negation, because the machine is much too all-encompassing for us to easily leap to a place where we can straightforwardly oppose it. Instead, the approach is one of critique in something like the Kantian sense: an operation that resolutely faces the fact that we are within the machine and attempts to trace out its limits from the inside. This method underwrites Agamben's fascination with contradictions within the theologico-political machine, such as the insider-outsider status of the sovereign and the *homo sacer*—those contradictions are the moments when the machine begins to undermine itself, signalling its limits. Often, Agamben presents the task as one of doing the machine one better, overloading it with one contradiction beyond what it can handle. For instance, he characterizes the status of the law in the messianic era as a kind of suspension of the state of exception—a double suspension that, far from abrogating the law, actually fulfils it by suspending its force along with its already-suspended content or meaning, effectively bringing it to a state of pure potentiality.

As *The Sacrament of Language* makes clear, however, the goal of the messianic operation is not simply to bring us to a halt for its own sake. Rather, the complete suspension achieved in the messianic gesture is the only way to open up a space for fresh thought in the face of the totalising sway of the theologico-political machine. Using the term "philosophy" rather than his more customary "messianism" to refer to the kind of critical discourse he practices, Agamben concludes the book with an urgent exhortation:

> Philosophy is... constitutively critical of the oath: that is, it calls into question the sacramental bond that links the human being to language, without for that reason simply speaking haphazardly, falling into the vanity of speech. In a moment in which all the European languages seem condemned to swear in vain and in which politics can only assume the form of an *oikonomia*, that is, of a governance of empty speech over bare life, it is once more from philosophy that there can come, in the clear awareness of the extreme situation at which the living human being that has language has arrived in its history, the indication of a line of resistance and of change.[23]

---

[23] Agamben, *Il sacramento del linguaggio*, §29 (my translation).

The understated phrase "a line of resistance and of change" gets at one of the apparent paradoxes at the heart of Agamben's project: for all its sweeping ambition, its attempt to provide a unified account of the structure and necessary failure of the enterprise of Western civilization, his proposed solution is not the violent overthrow of the theologico-political machine. The messianic world is the same world in which we now live— as Walter Benjamin says, "Everything will be as it is now, just a little different." [24] We will still be human, but we will have found a way to become human—and keep continually becoming human—just a little differently.

III.

At this point, it should be clear that Agamben's use of theology is motivated by a desire to find a way out of theology, to suspend the theologico-political machine. What is particularly fruitful about Agamben's particular variation on this by now very common theme is his use of an explicitly theologico-political notion to name the operation of suspension. Messianism is not the only name he gives to this operation; as we have seen, he can also refer to it simply as philosophy. Yet the messianic is the guiding motif, the simultaneously theological and political name for the way back behind the machine, for the way to return to the moment of our "anthropogenesis" so as to effect the minimal displacement that will represent the most truly radical change of all.

There is a sense in which Agamben is actually opposing the messianic to theology. In *The Kingdom and the Glory*, for instance, the theology that is in question is mostly one that is geared toward understanding God and the divine ordering of the world. One could characterize Agamben's messianic nihilism in such a way as to make it indistinguishable from Christian theology: after all, what is the task of the Christian theologian if not to keep finding fresh ways back to the messianic event? Agamben acknowledges the messianic origins of Christianity when he calls the letters of St. Paul "the fundamental messianic text for the Western tradition."[25] At the same time, it is clear that for Agamben, Christianity set aside its messianic task, putting itself forward as an institution and downplaying the Jewish context within which Paul's messianism arose and always remained.[26]

---

[24] Quoted in Giorgio Agamben, *The Coming Community*, trans. Michael Hardt (Minneapolis: Minnesota University Press, 1993), 53.

[25] Agamben, *The Time That Remains*, 1.

[26] Ibid, 2.

Yet he is careful to note that the messianic element never entirely disappeared from Christian theology, because the divine governance of the world would eventually reach an end in the last judgment. The messianic and the theological are not in perfect harmony: Agamben points out that the Christian identification of God with the *oikonomia* of salvation leaves open the embarrassing question of what God is to do after salvation has been achieved. Indeed, for Agamben, it is only the messianic endpoint that makes the machinery of divine providence bearable. In one of the most satisfying moments in his analysis, he implies that Christian theologians perhaps had some inkling of the radical hopelessness of our present global *oikonomia*, insofar as there is only one area where the machine of divine governance never rests: hell. Without the hope of a messianic suspension, eternal governance can only be hellish.[27]

The indefinitely deferred messianic moment is small consolation, however, when one considers that the abandonment of its authentic messianic task meant that the "displacement" effected by the Christian assumption and development of the logic of the *oikonomia* effectively displaced nothing at all, in the long run serving only to exacerbate the destructive contradictions at the heart of the theologico-political machine. Yet we might ask whether this kind of danger is present also in Agamben's messianic nihilism. In many ways, Agamben's own method is parallel to how he presents Paul's, whose messianism necessarily entailed diagnosing the contradictions in the political machine and proposing alternative ways of building human community. For later generations of theologians, however, Paul's diagnoses came to seem like prescriptions, and his alternatives were incorporated into the machine the messianic community was attempting to suspend, in the end increasing its destructiveness.

Could someone do the same with Agamben's work? Such a redeployment would go against Agamben's intentions, but there seems to be no sure way to prevent it.[28] Messianism can always collapse back into theology, and theology in turn can keep at least traces of messianism alive. Yet insofar as Agamben's messianic nihilism attempts to avoid such a collapse and to reawaken the messianic potentiality that lays dormant in the tradition, it begins to sound uncannily like Christian theology—though not just any kind of Christian theology. Agamben's analysis, when taken seriously, deprives theologians of the comfortable apologetic stance of criticizing

---

[27] Agamben, *Il Regno e la Gloria*, ch. 6.

[28] Indeed, I would be very surprised if there failed to be some member of the Radical Orthodoxy school who would take it upon himself or herself to selectively appropriate Agamben's work, particularly *The Kingdom and the Glory*, in exactly this way.

liberalism and calling for a return to Christianity, making it clear that liberal modernity is the practical outworking of the traditional Christian concept of God, and in so doing it also renders redundant the well-intentioned attempt to develop a Christianity that would be compatible with the best of liberalism. The theology that corresponds to Agamben's project is instead a radical theology that critiques the tradition from within so as to suspend its authority and free it for a new use—or for play. If this move seems to assimilate theology to philosophy, perhaps that is an indication that these two disciplines, which have always been uncomfortably intertwined, share the same dangers and the same promise. At their worst, they can both reinforce the claim of the theologico-political machine over life and can indeed offer it fresh resources to expand its grasp. Yet at their most radical, both set themselves the task of clearing a space in thought that can allow us to become human—again, differently—and to hope against hope that we may after all be delivered from this body of death.

Bibliography

Agamben, Giorgio. *The Coming Community*. Translated by Michael Hardt. Minneapolis: Minnesota University Press, 1993.

—. *Homo Sacer: Sovereign Power and Bare Life*. Translated by Daniel Heller-Roazen. Stanford: Stanford University Press, 1998.

—. *Remnants of Auschwitz: The Witness and the Archive*. Translated by Daniel Heller-Roazen. New York: Zone Books, 2005.

—. *State of Exception*. Translated by Kevin Attell. Chicago: University of Chicago Press, 2005.

—. *The Time That Remains: A Commentary On The Letter To The Romans*, Translated by Patricia Dailey. Stanford: Stanford University Press, 2005.

—. *Il Regno e la Gloria: Per una genealogia teologica dell'economia e del governo*. Vicenza: Neri Pozza, 2007.

—. *Il sacramento del linguaggio: Archealogia del giuarmento*. Rome: Laterza, 2008.

Badiou, Alain. *Saint Paul: The Foundation of Universalism*. Translated by Ray Brassier. Stanford: Stanford University Press, 2003.

Benjamin, Walter. "Critique of Violence." In *Reflections*, edited by Peter Demetz. New York: Schocken, 1978. 277-300.

Caputo, John D. *Prayers and Tears of Jacques Derrida: Religion Without Religion*. Bloomington: Indiana University Press, 1997.

Griffiths, Paul J. "Christ and Critical Theory." *First Things* (August/September 2004). <http://www.firstthings.com/article.php3 ?id_article=372>. Accessed 15 September 2007.

Hägglund, Martin. *Radical Atheism: Derrida and the Time of Life.* Stanford: Stanford University Press, 2008.

Kotsko, Adam. "On Agamben's Use of Benjamin's 'Critique of Violence,'" *Telos* 145 (Winter 2008): 119-129.

Kotsko, Adam. *Žižek and Theology.* New York: T&T Clark, 2008.

Naas, Michael. *Derrida From Now On.* New York: Fordham University Press, 2008.

Schmitt, Carl. *Political Theology: Four Chapters on the Concept of Sovereignty.* Translated by George D. Schwab. Chicago: University of Chicago Press, 2004.

CHAPTER ELEVEN

FANATICISM, REVOLT AND THE
SPIRITUALISATION OF POLITICS[*]

ALBERTO TOSCANO

I. Fanaticism and the Politics of Truth

Wherever we look, the effort to bind political action and truth, subjectivity and intransigent conviction, is confronted with the accusation of fanaticism. Any attempt to evaluate the theoretical and organisational manifestations of a politics of truth, or even its most basic preconditions, cannot afford to evade the ambient idea of egalitarian politics as a properly fanatical pursuit, a denial of mediation and representation—in short, the view of radical emancipation as a practice that would simply secularise (in some acceptation of this conflicted notion) certain theological, cultic or even archaically ritual motifs. Though the refrain and reproach of fanaticism (and related concepts of millenarianism, chiliasm, and political messianism) is manifestly entangled with the "classical" critique of totalitarianism and Terror, it is of special and urgent interest because of its concern with political subjectivity and what anti-fanatical discourse sees as the *religious matrix* of uncompromising or "true" political action. Rather than merely engaging in historico-political categorisation and condemnation, the notion of fanaticism targets the transcendental and epistemological errors that underlie any attempt at a robust linkage of emancipatory politics and truth, and dramatises the pathological product of any such fusion of transcendence and transformation: the fanatic. Unlike totalitarianism and Terror, its cousins in a lexicon of demonisation, fanaticism is unique in binding theology and politics, religion and subjectivity, in a particularly unstable amalgam, one that has proved very

---

[*] A version of this paper was first delivered at the conference "Is the Politics of Truth Still Thinkable?", Birkbeck College, 25-26th November 2005. Many of the arguments sketched herein are dealt with at greater length in my *Fanaticism: On the Uses of an Idea* (London: Verso, 2010).

attractive to pundits and paladins in sundry culture wars, clashes of civilisations, wars on terror, and skirmishes of lesser moment.

With its circulation across the terrains of theology, philosophy, psychology and polemic, fanaticism is to my mind a privileged conceptual object, at once over-determined and under-determined, for any contemporary attempt to consider what is at stake in ascribing religious substance to political action, or political valences to religious convictions. Any philosophy of religion which wishes to confront the ontology of the present cannot afford to ignore the idea of fanaticism, and the contexts of conflict, both practical and theoretical, it is embedded in. Fanaticism is an abiding object of horrified fascination, but also, more generally, its invocation is often a symptom of a poverty of analysis and imagination, bound to the wish to remain within a closed horizon defined by the mastery of differences and finite possibilities afforded by our political common sense. The domain of history, and of the theses proffered to account for certain key conjunctions of politics and truth, most often in a religious or spiritual vein, is crucial in this respect. Fanaticism, when ascribed to singular subjects or movements, is a political and historical judgment, a judgment that incorporates the idea that an egalitarian politics of truth is in some sense a-historical and therefore anti-political. The point of intersection between theology and social protest thus remains one through which any politics of truth or principle must pass, if only because its adversaries and detractors have set up their tribunals there long ago.

The subsumption of egalitarian politics under the rubric of fanaticism is hardly a recent fact. Writing of the French Revolution, Edmund Burke castigated an "epidemical fanaticism", which, in continuity with the plebeian depredations of the Anabaptists of Munster, afflicted an anti-clerical revolutionary France. He asked: "To what country in Europe did not the progress of their fury furnish cause for alarm?"[1] In this respect, we might observe that the demonising discourse on fanaticism is the reactionary obverse of what Alain Badiou and François Balmès termed "communist invariants" in their 1976 tract *De l'idéologie*. The Cold War saw a rich, if monotonous, seam of tracts and analyses focussing on fanaticism as the subjective determinant, affect, cognitive position or ethical stance which uncovered a supposed continuity between mediaeval millenarian uprisings and communism. Norman Cohn's seminal *The Pursuit of the Millennium* used as a resource even in anti-systemic works such as Raoul Vainegem's *The Movement of the Free Spirit*, is canonical in this respect and remains a widely quoted reference—by the likes of

---

[1] Edmund Burke, *Reflections on the Revolution in France*, ed. Frank M. Turner (New Haven: Yale University Press, 2003), 129.

John Gray in *Black Mass* or Anatol Lieven in *America Right or Wrong*, as they seek to unearth the millenarian roots of contemporary American nationalist fanaticism. In an erudite, albeit *nouveax-philosophical* vein, we could cite Dominique Colas sometimes shrill but instructive *Civil Society and Fanaticism: Conjoined Histories*. In such treatments, fanaticism designates a form of anti-representational, apocalyptic politics. Or rather, inasmuch as politics is prejudicially identified with liberal civil society, and with the maintenance of certain "natural" levels of inequality and distinctions of culture, ethnicity and identity, fanaticism—and its supposed search for an absolute and incarnate truth—is designated as violent anti-politics *par excellence*. Of course, many other texts could be considered, for instance J.L. Talmon's influential *The Origins of Totalitarian Democracy*, with its thesis of a continuum between the French revolution and twentieth-century "totalitarian movements" in terms of a concept of political (or totalitarian) messianism.

More to the point perhaps is the indication of the fundamental continuity between the anti-communist denunciation of political fanaticism—also present within the philosophical field in Merleau-Ponty's attack on Sartre's "ultra-bolshevist" decisionism—and the proponents of a post-Marxist "radical democracy". Ernesto Laclau's endorsement of Cohn's work on the millenarian character of communism in the concluding passages of *New Reflections on the Revolution of Our Time* is more than symptomatic in this respect, inasmuch as he considers the millenarian tendency to betoken a "limitless representability", that famous transparency of the social which Marxist and revolutionaries have allegedly sought, ravaging the world with their impossible, hysterical demands. Laclau's use of Cohn is also revealing inasmuch as it shows the reversibility or coincidence within the notion of fanaticism between anti-representation—in what Kant in the *Critique of Judgment* regarded as the delusion to see the infinite in a positive presentation—and total representation, such that perfect (i.e. unmediated) representability is indistinguishable from the death of representation.[2] As Colas notes, of course, the reproach of fanaticism, and its oppositional pairing with civil society, runs throughout modernity—featuring in such works as Leibniz's *Theodicy*, Voltaire's *Fanaticism, or Mahomet the Prophet* and more recently, John Paul II's *Centesimus annus*. However, following Colas' lead, I shall focus on the uses of the idea of fanaticism with regard to two key manifestations of a religious politics of conviction: the German Peasants' War of 1525 and the Iranian Revolution of 1979.

---

[2] Ernesto Laclau, *New Reflections on the Revolution of Our Time*, (London: Verso, 1990), 3–85.

II. Millenarianism and the Theology of Revolution

"Anno domini 1525, at the beginning of the year, there was a great, unprecedented upheaval of the Common Man throughout the German lands", thus we read in *Stumpfs Reformationschronik*, bearing witness to what Marx too would call "the most radical fact of German history". Since the reaction to the supposedly delusional politics of messianic truth at the heart of this upheaval is the *locus classicus* of the discourse on fanaticism, I'd like to dwell here on some of the theoretical responses to it. These orbit, for the most part, around the character of the German Peasants' War as a manifestation of what Alain Badiou, in *D'un désastre obscur*, has dubbed "the eternity of communism" – of a politics of truth based on a hypothesis of non-domination, i.e. on axiomatic equality (as encapsulated in the statement "people think", *les gens pensent*) and the systematic dismantling of any mastery over truth. In this respect, the conservative or reactionary tradition that has reiterated its attacks on a supposed political fanaticism for the past 500 years is perhaps to be grasped first and foremost as an attack on the possibility of a thought that would refuse a mastery or authority over truth and its partition, as a putting of truth in its proper place and a termination of any socially efficacious "raving with reason" (to use Kant's term)—an attack on a politics of truth which, as Badiou himself put it in *Peut-on penser la politique?*, might seek to make inegalitarian statements *impossible*.

Reading the proclamations, drafts and constitutions collected in compendiums such as the recent *The German Peasants' War*,[3] we can say that the drastic repudiation of mastery in the 1525 revolt, despite the customary references to the Pauline and Lutheran requirement to respect worldly authorities, is patent and that this—rather than the unruly, deep-seated and brooding passion of *Schwärmerei* as Kant would have it—is the key to these political movements. Of course, Thomas Müntzer, whose statement *Omnia sunt communia* (let everything be in common) is perhaps the emblem of Badiou's communist invariance, did take this repudiation of authority into passionate theological terrain, proposing, in his theology of crucifixion, that the ascetic assumption of suffering – and the desire, as he put it in his reading of the Book of Daniel, to make oneself insane in what is most intimate – was akin to a *becoming God*. This utter repudiation of mastery went to the extent of bridging the gap between scatology and eschatology. Melanchthon thus transcribes what was allegedly one of his enemy's favourite formulae: "I shit on God, if he does not put himself at

---

[3] Tom Scott and Bob Scribner eds, *The German Peasants' War: A History in Documents* (London: Humanities Press, 1991).

my service like he did with Abraham and the Prophets." Yet, when the likes of Michael Gaismair, revolutionary leader in Tyrol and the author of an astoundingly lucid programme for the constitution and economic structure of a non-capitalist republic in Switzerland, write of creating a union of "masterless men"—in terms of a *rupture* with the order of authority and privilege, rather than an ascetic and fanatical *rapture*—we can begin to see that the theme of fanaticism might be cloaking the reality of a communist politics in the state of mind of a communist apocalypse.

The figure of Müntzer, recently resurrected in the historical novel *Q.*, also features in *History and Class Consciousness*, where Lukács articulates an unsparing critique of Ernst Bloch's utopianism—as manifest in the latter's 1919 book, *Thomas Müntzer: Theologian of the Revolution*. Whilst Bloch was unequivocal about his Marxist allegiance, Lukács, adamant about the irreplaceable role of the proletariat in a *historical* materialism, attacked the former's positing of an *Ubique*—a trans-historical, mystical kernel of revolt that Marxism actualised despite itself, and which was only being unearthed by what Bloch regarded as the "religious element" in the Russian revolution. For Lukács—who inserts his critique of Bloch's *Müntzer* within a broader assault on the shortcomings of any revolutionary humanism—the impasse of the peasants' revolt lies in the principle, inherited from Christianity and the gospels, of starting from man. This entails either the conservative ontology underlying a moral defence of the status quo, i.e. the Pauline-Lutheran political theology of authority mentioned above; or a utopian response which is in turn split into *apocalypse* as the global annihilation of empirical reality, on the one hand, and the ascetic psychology of the *saint*, on the other. In this Christian speculative Leftism, as it were, relaxation of utopia equals the capitulation to conservatism, a capitulation which Lukács contends is written into the very undialectical fabric of the utopian instinct. Revolutionary utopianism is thus mired in an undialectical humanism, as well as what Lukács dismisses as a "consumption communism". Such a millenarian communism depends on the idea that an unblemished internal life could be awakened independently of man's concrete historical life, that we could simply organise the exodus from the apparatuses of production and reproduction impinging on the realisation of a non-dominated human essence. What is more, Lukács reaffirms the Weberian thesis whereby it is no accident that such a revolutionary messianism developed in the heartlands of capitalism, and was thus but the preparation for a subjection to the imperatives of capital. As he puts it:

> For the union of an inwardness, purified to the point of total abstraction and stripped of all traces of flesh and blood, with a transcendental

philosophy of history does indeed correspond to the basic ideological structure of capitalism.[4]

The target of Lukács' polemic is thus the "irreducible quality and unsynthesised amalgam of the empirical and the utopian" that he finds obscured by the elemental subjective vigour of Müntzer. Bloch-Müntzer is guilty of the wishful, fanatical sin of trying to *see* the truth of revolution without wielding the tools of change in the scientifically propitious moment. As he says: "It is trapped in the same 'dark and empty chasm', the same 'hiatus irrationalis' between theory and practice that is everywhere apparent where a subjective and hence undialectical utopia directly assaults historical reality with the intention of changing it". Providing a Marxist twist to the critique of fanatical immediacy proper to the post-Kantian tradition, Lukács argues that, contrary to Bloch's hopes for a vivifying fusion of the religious with the socio-economic, Müntzer's proclamations merely show that social actions are "wholly independent of the religious utopia". In making this argument, Lukács, who also contends that Bloch *underestimates* the depth of the restructuring of life called for by historical materialism, nevertheless remains faithful to the Engelsian orthodoxy: the revolt is an anachronism; for it, a definition of the problem of emancipation was "objectively impossible".[5] Crucially, Lukács holds that it is strictly impossible for the individual to exit the situation of reification, especially through an affirmation of inner freedom which is merely the utopian counterpart of a frozen empirical realm. The species, or even *Gattungswesen, qua* mythologized individual, is also incapable of such a feat. "And the class, too, can only manage it when it can see through the reified objectivity of the given world to the process that is also its own fate".[6]

---

[4] Georg Lukács, *History and Class Consciousness*, trans. R. Livingstone (Cambridge, MA: MIT Press, 1971), 192.

[5] Similarly, Mannheim argues in *Ideology and Utopia* that the revolts of 1525, inasmuch as they are motivated by the apocalyptic sermons of the likes of Müntzer, were anarchistic (or "leftist" in the parlance of Bolshevism), not socialist: "Chiliasm considers the revolution as a value in itself; it is not at all a means to attain a rational purpose, but rather is conceived as the only creative principle in the present."

[6] Lukács, *History and Class Consciousness*, 193. Lukács thus converges to some extent with Badiou's early criticism of a speculative Leftism of revolt, of the kind that would resurface in the *nouveaux philosophes*—though Badiou, in order not to hold what he thinks is the unacceptable thesis of the complete unconsciousness of revolt to itself—that is in order to affirm a pre-proletarian or pre-revolutionary political space not entirely under the thrall of ideological dissimulation (not a mere

The figure of Müntzer and his peasant hordes also haunts Karl Mannheim's *Ideology and Utopia*, where millenarian fanaticism or chiliasm is presented as the paradigm, or zero-degree, of utopia, defined as: "A state of mind... incongruous with the state of reality within which it occurs", and, significantly, as a state of mind, or situationally transcendent idea, which strives towards some kind of realization. For Mannheim there are four types of utopia: chiliastic, liberal, conservative, and socialist-communist, with the first two characterised by a kind of indeterminism or a notion of *contingency* (fanatical and decisionist in the first case, regulative and deliberating in the second) and the latter two by a determinateness or a notion of *necessity* (inert in the first case, transformative in the second).

Chiliasm is the zero-degree of utopia inasmuch as it is pitted against the old order in a total and uncompromising manner (to the point of pushing for a veritable exodus from the world). Its conjunction with the "social question" amounts to a historical explosion:

> The decisive turning-point in modern history was... the moment in which 'Chiliasm' joined forces with the active demands of the oppressed strata of society. The very idea of the dawn of a millennial kingdom on earth always contained a revolutionizing tendency, and the church made every effort to paralyse this situationally transcendent idea with all the means at its command.[7]

What is more, this moment, in which "chiliasm and the social revolution were structurally integrated" is the birth of modern politics, "if we understand by politics a more or less conscious participation of all strata of society in the achievement of some mundane purpose, as contrasted with

---

symptom)—puts forward his theory of communist invariants. Badiou's early assessment of these events in his 1976 *De l'idéologie*, co-authored with François Balmès, whilst providing the occasion for formulating his theory of communist invariants, and tending toward the most positive characterization possible of the part played by non-ideological subjectivity in such a revolt, nevertheless seems to follow the Marxist vulgate in declaring the material and historical necessity of its failure. Indeed, the theory of the communist invariants proposed by Badiou functions as a kind of antidote against the kind of anti-dialectical celebration of an eternal and eternally defeated plebeian resistance which were later to be found in some of the less compromised texts of the *nouveaux philosophes*. Thus, the standoff between Badiou's early dialectical materialism and the angelic philosophy of plebeian resistance put forward by his friends Christian Jambet and Guy Lardreau in their *L'Ange*, seems in a sense to recapitulate this debate.

[7] Karl Mannheim, *Ideology and Utopia* (London: Routledge, 1936), 190.

the fatalistic acceptance of events as they are".[8] In other words, the chiliasm of Müntzer, John of Leyden and their epigones is for Mannheim *the first anti-systemic movement*, and modernity is not born of a secularisation of politics but, as he puts it, of its *spiritualisation*.

> One of the features of modern revolution... is that it is no ordinary uprising against a certain oppressor but a striving for an upheaval against the whole existing social order in a thorough-going and systematic way.[9]

Mannheim's distinction between utopia and ideology is also a possible antidote against the pervasive trope of fanaticism—which depicts "religious" revolts as delusions, anti-political explosions of the social or failures of mediation. Utopias such as that of the peasants', according to Mannheim, "are not ideologies, i.e. they are not ideologies in the measure and in so far as they succeed through counteractivity in transforming the existing historical reality into one more in accord with their own conceptions".[10] Far from being reducible to a kind anti-representational frenzy, the chiliastic utopia is best seen as a creation of a new temporality by determinate social strata in a process which is formative of political consciousness. Contrary to what he condemns as the "liberal-humanitarian prejudice" that politics is a matter of ideas and representations, such a transformation mobilises a political affect which is pre-representational without necessarily being anti-representational. What is more problematic in Mannheim is the unwillingness to think through the specifically political forms and political demands of this religious politics (among which are the Christian Unions and the peasant assemblies). This disavowal of organisational thought—dominant in most analyses of millenarian political movements—once again manifests itself in the fatal attraction to Müntzer, the apocalyptic preacher, over any other leader in the wars against the German lords.

The limitations of Mannheim's sociology are especially evident in terms of the question of time:

> It is the utopian element... which determines the sequence, order, and evaluation of single experiences. This wish is the organising principle which even moulds the way in which we experience time. The form in which events are ordered and the unconsciously emphatic rhythm, which the individual in his spontaneous observation of events imposes upon the

---

[8] Ibid, 190, 191.
[9] Ibid, 195 (note 2).
[10] Ibid, 176.

flux of time, appears in the utopia as an immediately perceptible picture, or at least a directly intelligible set of meanings.[11]

In other words, the time of revolution is wholly subordinated to the static and visible time of utopia, a time of synchronic apperception of the future. Political time is stifled by the supposedly primary role of subjective time, of a mindset or worldview. This inattention to the specific organisations, prescriptions and constituent processes undertaken by these putatively religious movements—and the documentary record is a rich and surprising one—means that the link between ideas, religion and social protest is ultimately read internally in terms of a *suspension of time* and externally or methodologically in terms of a variant of the philosophy of history. On the first count, Mannheim plausibly argues that not ideas but "ecstatic-orgiastic energies" were at stake in the revolt's spiritualisation of politics, and that chiliasm is marked by a "tendency always to dissociate itself from its own images and symbols".[12] But in so doing he reduces his own image of the peasant revolts to the cognitive state of "absolute presentness", where there is "no inner articulation of time", and in which revolution is "the only creative principle of the immediate present".[13] On the second count, though not replicating the ideas of an "anachronism" of the Peasants' War which features in much of the literature, Mannheim still argues that "every age allows to arise (in differently located social groups) those ideas and values in which are contained in condensed form the unrealised and the unfulfilled tendencies which represent the needs of each age".[14]

But do such stances really do justice to the relation between politics and theology in the Peasants' War and similar events? Do they not simply reaffirm one of the constants in the diagnosis of fanaticism—the depoliticising idea of a historical anachronism, an epistemological misfit between religious form and political or social content? Much of the recent historical work on the "radical fact" of 1525 argues against such an appraisal and what can be seen as a fallacious *overestimation* of the theological or spiritual element in so-called chiliastic politics. In this respect it goes against the grain of some Marxist readings, from Engels on the "early bourgeois revolution" to Badiou's "communist invariants", via Lukács, which in order to bolster the logical singularity of the proletariat as class subject must overplay the importance of the mask of theology in

---

[11] Ibid, 188.
[12] Ibid, 193.
[13] Ibid, 193, 196.
[14] Ibid, 179.

historical events such as 1525—thereby skating over the invention of modalities of political thought and subjectivity which are not merely immature social forces whose impossibility of translating themselves into political action bursts into history through the visionary violence of a fanatical project.

This is what emerges from the work of Peter Blickle, who counters Engels' idea of an "early bourgeois revolution" with the thesis of the "revolution of the common man". According to this thesis the Peasants' War was a transversal alliance, across class groupings, to maintain urban independence and peasant autonomy in the face of the concentration of princely power and the devastations wrought by the rise of money capital, personified by the figure of the banker Jacob Fugger—an explicit nemesis both of Luther and of peasant leaders like Gaismair. Here the subjective figure of the common man is neither an invariant doomed to failure, nor a mere unwitting vehicle for the irruption of a bourgeois revolution, nor even a theologically over-determined figure that substitutes for the proletariat as the only subject conscious of its own revolt and that revolt's conditions—it is instead a political configuration in its own right, in which the religious element does not play the overweening ideological role elsewhere ascribed to it.

In his essay "Social Protest and Reformation Theology", Blickle investigates the war in terms of "the mutual dependence of Reformation theology and social protest", asking the following questions: "(1) where and how is social protest articulated; (2) how does it stand in relationship to Reformation theology, and (3) what consequences arise from the possible combination of these two movements"? Contrary to the single-minded focus on the fanatical form taken by the politics of those groups and movements which triggered the Peasants' War of 1525, Blickle is attentive to the manner in which seemingly pragmatic and specific demands are combined with religious themes and citations from Biblical authority—which are accorded the function of *minimal*, if perennial, criteria of justice. As he puts it: "Concrete economic and social demands are arranged within a vindicatory nexus with 'the Word of God' and 'the Gospel'—via the use of certain 'logograms' (4) proper to religious discourse".[15] This articulation is divided by Blickle into *positive protest*, via the Gospel and towards a more just socio-economic order; and *negative protest*, via the Gospel and away from the socio-economic order altogether (what he calls "the exodus from history"). It is the *vindicatory*

---

[15] Peter Blickle, "Social Protest and Reformation Theology" in *Religion, Politics, and Social Protest: Three Studies on Early Modern Germany*, ed. K. von Greyerz (Boston: Allen and Unwin, 1984), 4.

nexus which here not only has legitimising force but manages to make the urban protests of guilds converge with the demands of peasant communities and assemblies:

> It provides the basis for urban and rural anticlericalism, with its cutting-edge against the monasteries and orthodox clergy; it legitimises the demand for communal autonomy, exemplified in the call for the right to decide issues of correct religious doctrine, to elect the minister and to allocate tithes; and it is ultimately made the yardstick of social and political order.[16]

Urban demands in the German context primarily centre on representation and religious freedom, peasant demands around economic equality and autonomy. According to Blickle, reference to the Gospel allowed the putting forth of demands which would have been impossible with the prior form of legitimation (reference to the "old order"), such as the abolition of serfdom.[17] There is thus a definite sequence, both causal and chronological, from urban to rural to chiliastic (or Anabaptist)—inasmuch as "the very experience of transforming Reformation theology into political practice was a necessary pre-condition of Anabaptist, negative protest".[18] Negative, "fanatical" protest—which takes the form of *separation* of the community of the faithful and Müntzer's proclamation of a "total reversal of the secular order" is thus seen to follow from a failed reformation in the city and military defeat in the countryside.

Interestingly, it is scripture which here, contrary to some of its later fundamentalist transformations, results in a *negation* of dogma and doctrinal authority.[19] Most significantly, behind this oppositional and revolutionary use of Biblical "logograms", which opened the way for a traversal of the town and city distinction in the figure of the common man, there lay the development of new political and organisational, as well as

---

[16] Ibid, 8.

[17] Ibid, 9.

[18] Ibid, 11.

[19] Against the idea that the "common man" misunderstood the reformation, Blickle states: "One must be permitted to ask whether social protest could not be better characterised as congeniality, finality and consistency: congenial to Reformation theology in the sense that the Gospel was adopted as the normative principle; final in the sense that the Gospel was made the imperative for the entire worldly sphere; and consistent in the sense that all forms of social protest sought to establish the same principles—autonomy of the individual, community as the principle of socio-political organisation, and the common weal as the ethical legitimation of human existence." Ibid, 16.

military forms (such as the Christian Union), institutional inventions that force us to move beyond the purely ideational and historico-philosophical interpretation of these phenomena crystallised in notion of fanaticism and related concepts of millenarianism and chiliasm. If the German Peasants' War, or revolution of the common man, is really the founding moment of modern politics, what is the role of the trope or accusation of fanaticism and of the theorization of political millenarianism in the estimation of contemporary political events?

III. The Spiritualisation of Politics

Here I want to turn to Foucault's notorious chronicles of the Iranian revolution, written for the Italian newspaper *Il Corriere della sera*. The articles cover many of the themes we have already discussed: the spiritualisation of politics (a term Foucault uses repeatedly), the figure of Müntzer (who Foucault mentions together with Savonarola and Cromwell in writing about Khomenei), the matter of the temporality proper to religious politics (he speaks of the "continuous impatience" which drives political Shi'ism) and, of course, the accusation of abetting fanaticism (forcefully put to Foucault in the pages of *Le Monde* by an Iranian woman dissident). Throughout these texts—which are not devoid of the kind of two-dimensional "plebeian" anti-Marxism of the *nouveaux philosophes* (with whom he sympathised at the time)—Foucault tries to resist and provoke what he sees as a typically Occidental supercilious dismissal of religious politics. He highlights the importance, within the mounting social turmoil in Iran, of a religious resistance to what he calls the "modernisation-corruption-despotism" series, explicitly trying to resist the capture of the situation in Iran by the "millenarian concept" of fanaticism.[20] Foucault also counters some of the more naïve or platitudinous responses to the spiritualisation of politics and its relation to the social. In a typically acerbic remark, he says:

> Do you know the phrase that makes the Iranian sneer the most, the one that seems to them the stupidest, the shallowest, the most Western? 'Religion is the opium of the people.' Up to the time of the current dynasty, the mullahs preached with a rifle by their side in the mosques.[21]

---

[20] Michel Foucault, *Dits et Écrits, tome 2: 1976-1988* (Paris: Gallimard, 2001), 708.

[21] Ibid, 701.

Shi'ism is thus seen by Foucault not as inertial form, as the ideology that true revolutionaries need to cloak their discourse in, or even as a simple common vocabulary for popular aspirations. Religion is viewed not as a mask or vehicle but, somewhat in the terms used by Blickle to deal with the 1525 revolt—and indeed, in another passage on the subject, Foucault makes the analogy entirely explicit, in reference to the Anabaptists—as a veritable *crystallising force*, inasmuch as it represents "a mode of social relations, a supple, and widely accepted, elementary organisation, a way of being together, a manner of speaking and listening, something which allows people to comprehend one another and will together".

In his 1977 preface to the English translation of Deleuze and Guattari's *Anti-Oedipus*, Foucault had uttered the following directive for what he famously called a non-fascist ethics of thought: "Do not use thought to ground a political practice in Truth; nor political action to discredit, as mere speculation, a line of thought. Use political practice as an intensifier of thought, and analysis as a multiplier of the forms and domains for the intervention of political action."[22] It is thus striking to see how, at certain moments in his reports, and for all the micro-political methodology elsewhere employed, with its techniques, technologies, discourses and *dispositifs*, Foucault turns to one of the most classical forms of the grounding of political truth, the collective will. Explicitly sidelining the occidental prism of power struggles and political intrigues – not to mention the unabashedly "representational" discourse of legal religious authority which was Khomenei's crucial innovation—Foucault depicts in the Iranian revolution one of those insurgencies of the "plebs" so dear to the anti-party, anti-Marxist, renegade Maoist rhetoric of the *nouveaux philosophes*. Whence the constant theme of a religious mass *against the State*. At the very time that he was lecturing in the Collège de France on the molecular administrative practises of governmental biopolitics, he encounters mass religious politics—and not political Islamism *per se*—as a peculiar realisation of something like an unmediated Rousseauian scene.

Faced with the advance of the revolution, Foucault asks himself whether the idea of Islamic government is to be seen as a reconciliation, contradiction or the threshold of a novelty?[23] His intuition was that the supposed absence of a classical political programme driving the revolutionary uprising was matched by the strength of will, "the collective will of a people"—"an abstraction in political philosophy encountered for

---

[22] Michel Foucault, "Preface" in Gilles Deleuze and Félix Guattari, *Anti-Oedipus* (London: Athlone, 1977), xiv.
[23] Foucault, *Dits et Écrits*, 694.

the first time in the flesh".[24] Tellingly, Foucault seems to elide the idea
that Iran manifested a finally embodied Rousseauianism with the
provocative notion that this appearance of the popular will in a religiously
articulated uprising was a *general strike against politics*. Or, more
precisely, that it demonstrated a political will not to allow any grip within
the uprising for politics as it is classically understood. The question for
Foucault then, who remains rather pessimistic on this count, is that of
knowing *when* this popular or general will, this spiritual plebeian
irruption, was to be replaced by the instrumental exercise of politics.

It is undeniable, rereading the *Corriere* articles, that the supposedly
non-representational will of this "spiritual politics" exerted a massive
fascination on Foucault. So that, despite himself, and in order to flee from
the specific rationality of the historical materialist explanations he was
opposing at the time, Foucault too fell prey to the lure of fanaticism,
witness the following statement:

> It is the same protest, the same will which is expressed by a doctor from
> Tehran and a mullah from the provinces, by a petrol worker, by an
> employee of the post office and by a student under her chador.[25]

In what would prove to be a misunderstanding of his "art of governing",
Khomenei is dramatised as attacking the very scene of politics, in "the first
great insurrection against planetary systems, the most modern form of
revolt and the maddest".[26] In this short-circuit between an immovable
spiritual leader and a convergent mass, the limit-concept of a totally anti-
systemic politics, born with the German Peasants' War and its intimations
of negative protest, scuppers the attempt to think, in a determinate and
organised form, the nature of a politics of truth. The anti-Marxist stance—
which leads Foucault to argue that there is no classical social or political
revolution at stake in Iran, no evident class struggle, social contradictions
or political vanguard—together with the methodological focus on an
eventality indifferent to consequences crystallises in a return, via a
reference to François Furet, to the dichotomy and disjunction of revolt and
revolution; a temporal and subjective asymmetry between the domain of
social contradiction and change, on the one hand, and the specific
(spiritual) intensity of the political act. Religion, no longer an ideology or
a space of conciliation, is here "the vocabulary, the ritual, the atemporal
drama wherein one could lodge the historical drama of a people which

---

[24] Ibid, 746.
[25] Ibid, 715.
[26] Ibid, 716.

puts its existence on a balance with that of its sovereign".[27] It is this that allows Foucault to endorse the mythic figure of a revolt of *the people against the power*, in a "bond between collective actions, religious ritual and act of public right or law"[28] which *suspends* history:

> Because it is thus 'outside history' and in history, because everyone puts his or her life on the line, we can understand why uprisings have easily found in religious forms their expression and dramaturgy. Promises of the beyond, return of bygone periods, wait for the saviour or empire of the last days, undivided reign of the good, all of this has constituted for centuries, where the form of religion allowed it, not an ideological costume, but the very way of living uprisings.[29]

Iran thus dramatises for Foucault a definitive refusal of the analytical schemas of either liberal or Marxist thought, or of "Western" thought *tout court*, the irruption of a different "regime of truth".[30] Reconnecting with a tradition whose roots lie in Stirner, revolt is seen by Foucault as the point of insertion of subjectivity within history, a protest against any notion of political "evolution" or progress, such that a spiritualisation of politics is read, via a projection onto Shi'ism, as a total, internal revolution (an inner exodus of the kind promoted in Müntzer).[31] As Christian Jambet notes, for Foucault:

> It is a matter not of the politics of a future State, but of the essence of an uprising, of the 'spiritual' politics that makes it possible, and this is, consequently, a 'transcendental' interrogation: under what conditions can a

---

[27] Ibid, 746.

[28] Ibid, 748.

[29] Ibid, 791.

[30] Ibid, 753.

[31] Foucault's thesis, which fully assumes the later sedimentation of the revolutionary moment in the grim machinations of political struggles and instrumentalities (ibid, 750), is that the collective will manifested in the revolutionary moment or event is autonomous from its capture by sociological determinants and political struggles. As he says, "Uprisings belong to history, but in a certain sense, they escape it." (Ibid, 790) Hence his attention, in his dialogues with participants in the revolution, to the manifestations of a new intensity of experience and the overcoming of danger and fear. Foucault's thesis is ultimately then a variation on the theme (which can be found in sundry thinkers, among them Sorel and the early Blanchot) of the irreducibility of revolt.

culture determine a revolt, on the basis of an experience and a hope marked by 'events in the sky'?[32]

Foucault's customary method of "microanalysis" is thus inflected in an explicitly non-teleological and indeed (contrary to the usual image of his thought) anti-strategic sense, witness Foucault's motto: "Be respectful when a singularity rises up, intransigent when power violates the universal."[33] It is perhaps here, in the fantasy of a mass anti-systemic singularity, of a primal capacity for resistance against which revolution is a mere rationalist domestication, that lies Foucault's subjection, in the final analysis, to the trope of fanaticism.

IV. Conclusion

In philosophy's enlightened battle with the delusions of a speculative theology, and its attempt to circumscribe the domain of religious faith from the cognitive and political transgressions of an intellectual intuition beyond the bounds of finitude, the idea of fanaticism (*Schwärmerei*) played a signal role.[34] The development of philosophy of religion after Kant is inextricable from the prolongations of, or reactions to, the gesture of limitation and demarcation that saw fanaticism—that swarming admixture of theological adventurism, philosophical hubris and political unruliness—as the principal nemesis of an ordered relationship between the philosophical, the religious and the political. Contemporary attempts to affirm a philosophy and politics of finitude have inherited this aspect of the discourse on and against fanaticism.[35] Though not unrelated to the philosophical genealogy of fanaticism, its inscription within contexts of revolt (such as the two considered in this article, Germany in 1525, Iran in 1979) throws up rather different questions for a philosophical reflection on the relation between religion and politics. Forestalling any quick recourse to the notion of a political theology, or to the tendency of viewing religious revolts as the pernicious effects of a theology of revelation that breaks with finite social mediations, attention to such cases suggest that

---

[32] Christian Jambet, "The Constitution of the Subject and Spiritual Practice" in Timothy J. Armstrong ed, *Michel Foucault Philosopher* (London: Routledge, 1991), 234.

[33] Foucault, *Dits et Écrits*, 794.

[34] See Toscano, *Fanaticism*, Chapter 3: "Raving with Reason: Fanaticism and Enlightenment".

[35] See Alberto Toscano, "A Plea for Prometheus" in *Critical Horizons*, 10.2 (2009), 241-56.

the equation between religious politics and theological politics should not be asserted too hastily. The role of religious conceptions of justice and collectivity in the vindicatory nexus of the German Peasants' War or in the spiritualised collective will of the Iranian Revolution, as presented respectively by Peter Blickle and Michel Foucault, put an emphasis on religion as a resource for political crystallisation rather than on theology as an ideological framework for politics. Though both are very much open to historical and political criticism, they do open up the possibility of thinking a political philosophy of religion that would take its distance from a widespread schema that sees theological notions as more or less surreptitiously secularised in political programmes. In other words, to a political philosophy of religion that would not be hostage to a philosophy of history that posits either the consummate incarnation of religious drives into a secular dispensation, or, in what is simply the inversion of this linear tale, the termination of political theology by liberal politics. Forging the tools to investigate the contingent insertion of religious principles into political struggles, in terms of the kinds of subjectivity they elicit or the notions of temporality they require, could contribute to breaking the spell of those perspectives for which the fanatical confusion of the religious and the political is the one and only obstacle to emancipation. Mannheim suggests that the most extreme variant of religious activism, chiliasm, was the occasioning cause of a modern politics whose historicity also involves the possibility of a refusal or interruption of history. If so, the heated philosophical debates around the religious revolts like the German Peasants' War or the Iranian Revolution may yet have something to teach us.

Bibliography

Badiou, Alain. *D'un désastre obscur*. Paris: Editions de l'Aube, 1998.

Badiou, Alain and François Balmès. *De l'idéologie*. Paris: Maspero, 1976.

Blickle, Peter. "Social Protest and Reformation Theology." In *Religion, Politics, and Social Protest: Three Studies on Early Modern Germany*, edited by K. von Greyerz. Boston: Allen and Unwin, 1984. 1-23.

Burke, Edmund. *Reflections on the Revolution in France*. Edited by Frank M. Turner. New Haven: Yale University Press, 2003.

Foucault, Michel. "Preface." In Gilles Deleuze and Félix Guattari, *Anti-Oedipus* London: Athlone, 1977. xi-xiv.

—. *Dits et Écrits, tome 2: 1976-1988*. Paris: Gallimard, 2001.

Jambet, Christian. "The Constitution of the Subject and Spiritual Practice."
    In Timothy J. Armstrong edited, *Michel Foucault Philosopher*.
    London: Routledge, 1991. 225-32.
Jambet, Christian and Guy Lardreau. *L'Ange: Ontologie de la revolution I*.
    Paris: Grasset, 1976.
Laclau, Ernesto. *New Reflections on the Revolution of Our Time*. London:
    Verso, 1990.
Lukács, Georg. *History and Class Consciousness*. Translated by R.
    Livingstone. Cambridge, MA: MIT Press, 1971.
Mannheim, Karl. *Ideology and Utopia*. London: Routledge, 1936.
Scott, Tom and Bob Scribner edited. *The German Peasants' War: A
    History in Documents*. London: Humanities Press, 1991.
Toscano, Alberto. "A Plea for Prometheus." *Critical Horizons* 10.2
    (2009): 241-56.
—. *Fanaticism: On the Uses of an Idea*. London: Verso, 2010.

CHAPTER TWELVE

HISTORICAL NATURALISM AND POLITICAL HUMANISM: LUDWIG FEUERBACH AND PAOLO VIRNO

NINA POWER

I have sketched... the historical solution of Christianity, and have shown that Christianity has in fact vanished, not only from the reason but from the life of mankind, that it is nothing more than a fixed idea, in flagrant contradiction with our fire and life assurance companies, our railroads and steam-carriages, our picture and sculpture galleries, our military and industrial schools, our theatres and scientific museums.[1]

For Feuerbach, Christianity—in the wake of both the secularising effects of German Philosophy and the industrialisation of human life—is outdated, outmoded and irrelevant. Its insights regarding love, universality and the relation between the finite and the infinite (particularly in the figure of Christ) are, for Feuerbach, more relevant than ever. Feuerbach's critique of Christianity, although devastating, is of a quite different order than Marx's far more thoroughgoing attack a few years later. Nevertheless, Feuerbach achieves one of the first concrete analyses of religion as a natural fact, as part and parcel of what it means to be human, and of what it means to reclaim the capacity to think in the light of alienation. Feuerbach's tools, the way he deploys his historical naturalism against Christianity has many parallels with contemporary projects to try and unpick the structures and character of today's affective capitalism. The method Feuerbach uses to critique the Christianity of his day in the name of a new philosophy of the future, a kind of realistic humanism, has significant parallels with certain kinds of contemporary post-Marxist political thought: the method of the critique of religion has become the unwitting and unacknowledged template for the critique of capitalism.

---

[1] Ludwig Feuerbach, *The Essence of Christianity*, trans. George Eliot (Amherst, New York: Prometheus Books, 1989), xliv.

In this paper, then, I will argue that Feuerbach's influence, however underplayed in the literature, remains central in some contemporary political theorists. In particular, the work of Paolo Virno, and indeed much of what gets called post-*Operaismo*, cannot but return to certain Feuerbachian themes, given the post-Marxist repositioning of the centrality of the subjectivity of labour rather than capital. Given the shifts and transformations in Feuerbach's own position (from a kind of concretised Hegelian theory of consciousness in which universality and infinity are the immediate qualities of thought to a kind of sensualist materialism in which the categories of love and happiness are central), it is important not to imagine that there is one Feuerbach—the early inverted Hegelian, the middle-period critic of religion, the late humanist empiricist and so on. Nevertheless, by reading Feuerbach's positions diagnostically we can start to map out the repetitions of his positions (and the problems with them) onto today's political thinkers. By suggesting that Feuerbach deserves to be remembered a hundred and fifty years after his work briefly lit up Europe before being mostly forgotten, I am by no means straightforwardly suggesting that we should return uncritically to his ideas; on the contrary, I wish to present Feuerbach and the shifts within his position as precisely something to be wary of, as a constellation of temptations to understand in order to avoid repeating them in the same way. There is, at the same time, however, something important that persists in Feuerbach's idiosyncratic combination of rationalism and empiricism, his emphasis on the universality and infinity of human consciousness and his proposal for a philosophy of the future that would at the same time be a non-philosophy. I have written elsewhere about the links between Feuerbach's rationalist universalism, his claims about the generic nature of human thought, and similar claims in the work of Alain Badiou, for whom the human is an animal possessed of the "singular human capacity" to think the infinite.[2] In this article, I want to focus on another aspect of Feuerbach's work—his naturalism or, more specifically, his *historical* naturalism.

---

[2] Alain Badiou, *Ethics*, trans. Peter Hallward (London: Verso, 2001), 132. For my earlier work on the relationship between Badiou and Feuerbach see: "Badiou and Feuerbach: What is Generic Humanity?" in *Subject Matters: A Journal of Communication and the Self* 2.1 (2005) and "Towards an Anthropology of Infinitude: Badiou and the Political Subject" in *Cosmos and History* 2 "The Praxis of Alain Badiou" (2006).

I.

Before I turn to the importance of Feuerbach's naturalism, I want to briefly run through a few of the common reasons why Feuerbach is, if he is discussed at all, so blithely dismissed, in reverse order of importance. Firstly, there is the meta-philosophical suggestion that Feuerbach is just not a "proper" philosopher, because his work is not original enough, and the concomitant meta-historical suggestion that Feuerbach is retroactively a transitional figure between the far more important thinkers, Hegel and Marx. Secondly, there is the Heideggerian edict against philosophical anthropology and humanism (in other words, against neo-Kantianism as much as Sartre) that has had a profound effect on Continental philosophy's use of such terminology, injecting an anxiety that an original thinking of man's essence is pre-emptively hidden or covered-over by metaphysical determinations, even at the same time as Heidegger reintroduces heavily politicised terms such as "community". We can trace Heidegger's continued influence on this point (and others) in the work of Foucault (in part) and Agamben, who in *The Open* states that "faced with [the] extreme figure of the human and the inhuman, it is not so much a matter of asking which of the two machines (or of the two variants of the same machine) is better or more effective—or rather, less lethal and bloody—as it is of understanding how they work so that we might, eventually, be able to stop them".[3] Counter to what we might call a phenomenological antihumanism, we have the work of Etienne Balibar (as fragmentary as it is) on the recasting of a notion of philosophical anthropology which explicitly takes issue with Heidegger: "We should remark, following Heidegger, that this fundamental equation [namely that metaphysics equates the essence of man with the subject] can also be read *the other way round*: as an equation that provides the clue to *all questions of essence*, to the 'metaphysical questions' in general."[4] For Balibar it is not Descartes but Kant who "invents" the subject in the modern sense, by identifying that universal aspect of human consciousness which provides philosophy with its foundation and measure. This leads directly to questions of cosmopolitanism, of the idea of the human subject being at the same time a political subject, a global citizen subject, as in Kant's obscured fourth question "What Is Man?" Thus the historical emergence of certain forms of subjectivation—man, citizen, and so on—are legitimately the questions

---

[3] Giorgio Agamben, *The Open,* trans. Kevin Attell (Stanford: Stanford University Press, 2004), 38.
[4] Etienne Balibar, "Subjection and Subjectivation" in Joan Copjec ed, *Supposing the Subject* (London: Verso, 1994), 4.

of philosophy and politics at the same time, contra Heidegger. I will return
to this question of the nature of the emergence of philosophical-political
terms in a moment. Before that, it is important to identify another couple
of anti-Feuerbachian strands in European thought.

Firstly, the "true" materialist critique of Feuerbach which objects to the
centralising of man in his otherwise pantheistic and scientific (or at least
scientistic) account of nature. This can be neatly captured in Lange's
summary in 1865 in the important *History of Materialism*, which as we
know was a key text for Nietzsche:

> In this undue prominence given to man lies a trait which is due to the
> Hegelian philosophy, and which separates Feuerbach from strict
> Materialists. That is to say, it is only the philosophy of spirit over again
> that meets us here in the shape of a philosophy of sensibility.[5]

Thus Feuerbach is antithetical to the theoretical antihumanism of Spinoza
and his French followers, who conveniently forget that Feuerbach had
identified atheism as "reversed pantheism" and Spinoza as the flip-side of
Hegel. As he writes in the "Preliminary Theses on the reform of
Philosophy": "The philosophy of identity [i.e. Hegel] distinguished itself
from that of Spinoza only by the fact that it infused into Spinoza's
substance—this dead and phlegmatic thing—the Spirit of idealism."[6] A
kind of diffuse suspicion of talking about the human, which owes more to
Heidegger than it wants to admit, stems from a line of French Spinozism.
We could add that the loathing that psychoanalysis has for Feuerbach, as
evidenced in the brief but splenetic (and therefore revealing) references to
him in the works of Joan Copjec and Slavoj Žižek stems partly from what
is perceived to be Feuerbach's emphasis on consciousness at the expense
of darker elements of the mind, as if he took an image of the light,
optimistic Hegel without the concomitant theory of lack and desire that we
find in the *Phenomenology*. Ernst Bloch, in his *prima facie* Feuerbachian
project, *Atheism in Christianity*, similarly accuses Feuerbach of a kind of
naivety, of not realising the tricks that institutional religion could play.
Bloch talks of Feuerbach's "divided-self and alienation theories of
religion, according to which religion's roots lie not in trickery but in

---

[5] Friedrich Lange, *The History of Materialism,* trans. Ernest Chester Thomas (New York: Harcourt, Brace, & Co., 1925) 248.
[6] Ludwig Feuerbach, "Preliminary Theses on the Reform of Philosophy" in *The Fiery Brook: Selected Writings of Ludwig Feuerbach*, trans. Zawar Hanfi (New York: Anchor Books, 1972), 154.

impenetrable illusion."[7] Feuerbach is a little too trusting of the positive dimension of Christianity's rhetoric: Christian love is merely human love made mystical.

Most significantly, and most seriously, of course, we have Marx's own damning indictment of him in the "Theses on Feuerbach" and elsewhere, partly characterised by the irritation that comes from having taken a position on board too quickly and being unable as yet to fully shake off its form. Marx's displacement of Feuerbach's contemplative theory of religious alienation in favour of the analysis of the "ensemble of the social relations" is well-known, and retains much of its force, even if Marx's definition of "sensuous human activity" is itself still theoretical at this point in 1845. Marx's realisation that what Feuerbach deletes in his critique or inversion of Hegel is history no doubt galvanises him to create a new approach that would overcome the contemplative-practical divide, or what we might call the theory-practice opposition, in the name of a new synthesis – historical materialism. Consciousness is determined by practice and philosophy, according to this position, must give up on its belief that it is capable of talking about real labour when it is in truth only dealing with a kind of abstract work.

In the current context, however, with a turn to theories of immaterial labour, cognitive capital, affectivity and so on, we could begin to consider a return to pre-Marxist concerns *in the name of Marx*. This is a complicated question, shot through with all kinds of ideological pitfalls and potential missteps, but it seems to me clear that at least in some quarters, it is the turn to abstraction that characterises the return of a supposedly Marxist continuity. Peter Osborne has spoken of the "reproach of abstraction", of a kind of allergic reaction to the universalisms and purported one-sidedness of philosophy's drive to totalise.[8] But we could speak equally too of a "revenge of abstraction", a return in contemporary thought to questions of universality and human cognitive capacity but, crucially, in the name of a new present. We can see the negative image of this "revenge of abstraction" in reflections on the recent economic crisis, in which the practice of traders was deemed so complicated that not even those involved were able to understand it. There is a generalised sense in which we know that things are increasingly and profoundly abstract— work, the economy, social relations—but at the same time, somehow "responsible" for the concrete devastations, inequalities of the "real world". As an aside, the environmental movement can in some sense be

---

[7] Ernst Bloch, *Atheism in Christianity*, trans. J. T. Swann (London: Verso, 2009), 48.
[8] Peter Osborne, "The Reproach of Abstraction" in *Radical Philosophy* 127 (September/October, 2004): 21-28.

seen as an attempt to short-circuit the gap between felt abstraction and the spectre of the concrete, but is too often predicated on oppositions between the individual and the corporation or the individual and nature, as if the solution to global catastrophe was merely atomised changes in lifestyle (the political corollary of this position is a kind of prevalent anarchist neo-primitivism in which all serious discussion about state planning and infrastructure is blocked off, as if, come the revolution, as people used to say, or come the end of the world, as they now say, the planet would magically "return" to green fields and syndicates, with nary a skyscraper or motorway to be seen). As Peter Osborne puts it: "Are certain experiences of abstraction not the necessary condition of *any* global social interconnectedness in such a way that it makes no sense to criticise them for their abstraction per se... What new possibilities of the human are produced by the mediating force of actual abstraction?"[9]

II.

In the 1844 Manuscripts, Marx wrote that: "Communism as completed naturalism is humanism and as completed humanism is naturalism".[10] In the Preface to the Second Edition of *The Essence of Christianity*, written a year before, Feuerbach claims that in his analysis of religion he is "nothing but a natural philosopher in the domain of mind."[11] For Feuerbach, this means analysing ideas and ideologies as natural facts: so religious belief is as amenable to study as plants and animals. Feuerbach has often been criticised for his naive praise of science, for his idea that "Philosophy must again unite itself with natural science, and natural science with philosophy".[12] In Marx's formulation of naturalism as humanism and vice versa, which he would later criticise in the name of both history and the critique of political economy, we see too a kind of rhetorical hyper-Feuerbachianism. What, frankly, would a "completed naturalism" look like? We know full well that science, if anything, displaces the human— no longer the centre of the cosmos, or the most important material being, or anything other than a series of evolutionary adaptations—so why would naturalism in principle have a necessarily positive relationship to humanism, completed or otherwise? Surely it is grand abstractions like

---

[9] Ibid, 27.
[10] Karl Marx, "Economic and Philosophical Manuscripts" in *Early Texts*, trans David McLellan (Oxford: Blackwell, 1971), 148.
[11] Feuerbach, *The Essence of Christianity*, xxiv.
[12] Ibid, 172.

"nature", "being" and "humanity" that mislead any non-ideological attempt to analyse the concrete transformations in modes of work and resistance.

Yet naturalism has not gone away. Nor have many other Feuerbachian elements, however undermined by the Heideggerian, psychoanalytic, anti-humanist critique they might appear to be: a turn to universalism, questions of the generic, a kind of political anthropology and so on. Feuerbach's very transitional status, as the mediator between Hegel and Marx, is his perverse strength, as it is in between questions of empiricism and rationalism, abstraction and the concrete that we find the ground of many of today's political questions. Contemporary political discussions of the anthropological dimensions of work and struggle owe more to Feuerbach's immanently dialectical anthropological critique of philosophy and other ideologies than we might think. Nowhere is this debt more apparent than in the work of Paolo Virno, who has, perhaps more than any other recent thinker, turned once again to questions of naturalism and the emergence of the possibility of thinking once again about that most thorny and supposedly outdated thing, human nature. Before I turn to Virno, though, I would like to present a brief discussion of Feuerbach's own claims about the same question.

In an early section of *The Essence of Christianity* entitled "The Essential Nature of Man", Feuerbach lays out his theory of human capacities as a way of understanding how these same capacities can be turned towards religious feeling. Feuerbach, common to many philosophers of his age and others, begins by opposing man to "brute". Animals are possessed of an immediate egoistical relation to the world; men and women, on the other hand, possess consciousness "in the strict sense": "Consciousness in the strictest sense is present only in a being to whom his species, his essential nature, is an object of thought."[13]

Feuerbach's theory of thought, the idea that all thinking is immediately human in its structure, is his crucial starting-point. If thought is, as Feuerbach thinks, in its very nature, anti-individualist, it is because it is thought itself that reveals to us the generic, that is shared, nature of consciousness—the fact that it is something that all humans, by virtue of being human, can perform, regardless of whatever content it contains. As Feuerbach puts it, "Where there is this higher consciousness there is a capability of science. Science is the cognisance of species."[14] Science here is to be understood in the broadest possible sense, as the sum of all human knowledge and capacities. Whatever knowledge human beings acquire

---

[13] Ibid, 1.
[14] Ibid, 2.

belongs in principle to all of them because every new thought or discovery is an immediate reflection of generic human abilities. Feelings of individuality in the face of the anonymous mass of other people or worthlessness in the face of God are basically misunderstandings—or, in Feuerbach's crucial term, forms of alienation (*Entfremdung*). To experience solipsism or imperfection is an indication not of the fundamental truth of human being, but precisely the opposite: the things that are *most* human—our ability to think, to create, to collectively organise—are, for reasons peculiar to human psychology, handed over to higher authorities, whether they be secular ones or religious ones. Thus in the case of the latter phenomenon, God becomes all-powerful, the Creator and infinite, whereas, as Feuerbach will never cease arguing throughout his work, it is in fact human beings that possess the power to create, to invent and to "think the infinite". Feuerbach's humanism is thus a universalism, a kid of pan-intellectualism in which every human being, living or dead, is the bearer of human knowledge as a whole, or at least has the potential to understand the insights of others. A useful example of Feuerbach's argument can be shown in the idea that once a scientific or mathematical formula has been constructed, however difficult, it becomes possible to explain the achievement to others such that they too can understand it, even if they as individuals would never have come up with the hypothesis themselves. Furthermore, for Feuerbach, humanity is a cumulative project: "Each new man is a new predicate, a new phasis [sic] of humanity."[15]

Feuerbach's claim about the openness of human knowledge and learning is not merely an epistemological claim but also an ethical one: "Man is at once I and thou; he can put himself in the place of another."[16] Feuerbach's project in *The Essence of Christianity* is keen to stress this ethical dimension. Christianity is not wrong in stressing forgiveness, charity, faith and love—merely, for Feuerbach, that these should be understood as *human* emotions that are useless if pointed in the direction of heaven, but incredibly powerful if directed towards other humans. Thus both the relationality of Hegelian dialectics as well as the emphasis on forgiveness and love in the Bible indicate for Feuerbach that a formal illusion (that structures are somehow "out there", that human emotions are directed towards the fulfilment of a religious life) has been perpetrated. The species-being of humanity (*Gattungwesen*)—a term Marx will later use in his early writings—is the real being of humanity, not the systems of

---

[15] Ibid, 23.

[16] Ibid, 2. We are reminded here of the importance of these categories for later thinkers, particularly Martin Buber and Erich Fromm.

idealism or Christianity which try to place this real being outside of humanity itself.

It is his critique of these "systems of idealism" combined with his claims about the infinite, universal yet concrete nature of human nature that lend Feuerbach his continued relevance: Feuerbach may not have adequately described or critiqued capitalism, as Marx was to go on to do, but he describes very well the problem of how to relate human capacities to systems that both depend upon them yet are parasitic and destructive of them. But we are immediately confronted with questions of essentialism, of the dubiousness of positing theories of human nature or consciousness that do not pay attention to material changes in the very production of these things. The problem of history, of shifts in the mode of production and changes in human organisation seems to make a mockery of essential claims about what human nature "really is".

III.

It is this question of the contingent emergence of general features of the species at a particular point in human development that will form the basis of Virno's own work, for instance in his recent essay "Natural-Historical Diagrams: The 'New Global' Movement and the Biological Invariant".[17] It is also a question of, as one of the section headings has it, the "always already just now". This is Virno's wager—that it is only now, when the differential traits of the species (i.e. that which separates us from other animals, namely verbal thought, the transindividual character of the mind, the lack of specialised instincts) are the "raw material" of capitalist organisation, that we can return again to the question of a politics of human nature. Thus the problem of the "natural" emerges *contingently*, that is, at a certain historical moment, yet as if for the first time. We are reminded here of Althusser's perceptive reading of Feuerbach in which the latter features as a theorist of "transcendental biology". Virno reminds us of Marx's claim again from the *1844 Manuscripts* that:

---

[17] Paolo Virno, "Natural-Historical Diagrams: The 'New Global' Movement and the Biological Invariant", trans. Alberto Toscano, in Lorenzo Chiesa and Alberto Toscano eds, *The Italian Difference: Between Nihilism and Biopolitics* (Melbourne: re:press, 2009).

It can be seen how the history of *industry* and the *objective* existence of industry as it has developed is the *open* book of the essential powers of man, man's psychology is present in tangible form.[18]

Virno's claim that it is only now that we can turn to the question, or really the problem, of human nature is double-edged. He argues that it is, on the one hand, the content of the "global movement" since Seattle that reveals that "the public sphere is nothing less than human nature": yet at the same time, the movement is rooted

> in the epoch in which the capitalist organization of work takes on as its raw material the differential traits of the species (verbal thought, the transindividual character of the mind, neoteny, the lack of specialized instincts, etc.). That is, it is rooted in the epoch in which human praxis is applied in the most direct and systematic way to the ensemble of requirements that make praxis human. The stake: those who struggle against the mantraps placed on the paths of migrants or against copyright on scientific research raise the question of the different socio-political expression that could be given, here and now, to certain biological prerogatives of *Homo sapiens*.[19]

He goes on:

> We are therefore dealing with a historically determinate subversive movement, which has emerged in quite peculiar, or rather unrepeatable, circumstances, but which is intimately concerned with that which has remained unaltered from the Cro-Magnons onwards. Its distinguishing trait is the extremely tight entanglement between 'always already' (human nature) and 'just now' (the bio-linguistic capitalism which has followed Fordism and Taylorism).[20]

It is not simply a question of swapping Feuerbach's Christianity for Virno's bio-linguistic capitalism, however: the image of humanity in each case has important differences, even if the attempt to make the link between the "always already" and the "just now" shares important parallels in each case. In *Multitude Between Innovation and Negation*, in particular, Virno's is no happy account of humanity. On the contrary, *Homo sapiens* is, if anything, constituted entirely negatively as "the animal whose life is characterised by negation, by the modality of the possible, by

---

[18] Karl Marx, *Early Writings*, trans. Rodney Livingstone & Gregor Benton (London: Penguin, 1992), 354.
[19] Virno, "Natural-Historical Diagrams", 131.
[20] Ibid, 131.

regression to the infinite".[21] Against the phenomenological idea of the world as a kind of background and source for all our other possibilities, Virno understands the world as a space of natural conflict, a source of perpetual confusion and a constitutive disorientation. If we are to return to a kind of natural political theory, Virno would want us to understand that this is, above all, an *unhappy* naturalism. We are far removed from Feuerbach's conciliatory vision of love as the essence of humanity ("Love is the true *ontological* demonstration of the existence of objects apart from our head"[22]).

To return to the question of naturalism for a moment: Virno turns to recent biological research into two main areas relating to human development: neoteny (the retention of formerly juvenile characteristics produced by the retardation of somatic development) and mirror neurons (the neurophysiological phenomenon whereby when we see someone performing an action, the same neurons are activated in the frontal lobe of the observer, demonstrating a kind of original intersubjectivity that precedes the constitution of the individual mind). But rather than take the relative openness of our species and our apparent inability *not* to empathise with others as the basis of political optimism, Virno reminds us that "every naturalist thinker must acknowledge one given fact: the human animal is capable of *not* recognizing another human animal as being one of its own kind".[23] Virno's Hobbesian edge separates him both from Feuerbach's rather more optimistic account of underlying communicativity but also from contemporary thinkers such as Chomsky for whom co-operation and communication are in a sense the bedrock of human praxis.

IV.

The final problem I want to raise, if briefly, is this question of non-recognition or of exclusion. If *Operaismo*, and that which came after, emphasises the subjectivity of "labour" instead of that of capital (as Massimo de Angelis puts it), then we are perhaps tempted to overplay the generalised nature of this subjectivity. This is certainly what Hardt and Negri seem to be engaging in when they argue that there is "one figure of labour" that slowly causes the others to adopt its main qualities. When they talk about immaterial labour, much of their position resonates with

---

[21] Paolo Virno, *Multitudes: Between Innovation and Negation*, trans. Isabella Bertoletti, James Cascaito, Andrea Casson (New York: Semiotext(e), 2008), 18.
[22] Ludwig Feuerbach, "Principles of the Philosophy of the Future" in *The Fiery Brook*, 226.
[23] Virno, *Multitudes*, 181.

Virno's insights, but they are unwilling to follow his naturalist line, understanding themselves as the heirs to Deleuze and Foucault's anti-essentialist anti-humanism, which would precisely prevent this affiliation. Whilst Virno stresses the possibility of a lack of recognition or inclusion in his conception of the other universal species traits, Hardt and Negri opt for a much looser but more inclusive notion of the multitude—which is precisely not the working class because this category excludes the unwaged. Moreover, for Virno, following Feuerbach, the generic is a matter of potential and capacity, meaning that his multitude, unlike Hardt and Negri's, is not a historical subject. At the same time, Hardt and Negri are strangely more clumsily Feuerbachian than Virno precisely because they are unwilling to acknowledge serious splits and antagonisms between different workers or non-workers and different kinds of employment, as well as the new pathologies and ambivalences of the multitude (cynicism, opportunism, servility, etc.). As David Camfield puts it, "As immaterial labour defines social production, even the unemployed poor become participants in biopolitical production. Empire needs the biopolitical production of the entire population of the world: 'no group is "disposable".''[24] But this inclusive definition of the Multitude is a tautology: every living human being is a participant and all labour tends towards a single model, that of the immaterial laborer. But, apart from being overly simplistic, this conception of humanity neglects the fundamental opposition between a political anthropology that would incorporate alienation, antagonism, negativity and opposition and one that simply states that there is a living body of human being. For Hardt and Negri, it is through "the becoming common of singular forms of labor, the singularity of local human contexts in a common global anthropology, and the common condition of poverty and productivity" that "the conditions of possibility for the formation of the multitude" are established.[25] This common global anthropology is too non-specific to really grasp the differences between, say, a freelance graphic designer and a crop farmer. The problem here is that Hardt and Negri's global anthropology is predicated on the blunt (and historically reactionary) category of life, rather than on the contingent emergence of certain forms of alienated consciousness or language, as Feuerbach and Virno would have it.

As Massimo De Angelis puts it in a review of Virno's *A Grammar of the Multitude*, we should not overlook the fact that "different constituents

---

[24] David Camfield, "The Multitude and the Kangaroo: A Critique of Hardt and Negri's Theory of Immaterial Labour" in *Historical Materialism* 15.2 (2007), 28.
[25] Michael Hardt and Antonio Negri, *Multitude: War and Democracy in the Age of Empire* (New York: Penguin, 2004), 211-12.

('singularities') of the global multitude produce and reproduce their livelihoods by threatening the *livelihoods of others*, of distant others, of 'strangers'. In the global work machine of contemporary capital, the 'stranger' is not simply a condition of being, it is a result of a mode of doing, of a mode of articulation among the global plurality of singularities."[26]

A notion of generic humanity that can conceive of the structural difficulties generated by various forms of exclusion is the question raised by Feuerbach's description of the historical emergence of certain kinds of alienated consciousness. Paolo Virno's updated version of Feuerbach's historical naturalism shifts the object from Christianity to capitalism: our question today thus becomes what do we do when our natural capacities – to speak, to think, to communicate – are alienated from us?

Bibliography

Agamben, Giorgio. *The Open*. Translated by Kevin Attell. Stanford: Stanford University Press, 2004.

Badiou, Alain. *Ethics*. Translated by Peter Hallward. London: Verso, 2001.

Balibar, Etienne. "Subjection and Subjectivation." In Joan Copjec edited, *Supposing the Subject*. London: Verso, 1994.

Bloch, Ernst. *Atheism in Christianity*. Translated by J. T. Swann. London: Verso, 2009.

Camfield, David. "The Multitude and the Kangaroo: A Critique of Hardt and Negri's Theory of Immaterial Labour." *Historical Materialism* 15.2 (2007): 21-52.

De Angelis, Massimo. "Strange Common Places." *Mute* 28 (Summer/Autumn 2004). Available on-line <http://www.metamute.org/en/Strange-Common-Places>. Accessed 01/02/2010.

Feuerbach, Ludwig. "Principles of the Philosophy of the Future." In *The Fiery Brook: Selected Writings of Ludwig Feuerbach*, translated by Zawar Hanfi. New York: Anchor Books, 1972.

—. "Preliminary Theses on the Reform of Philosophy." In *The Fiery Brook: Selected Writings of Ludwig Feuerbach*, translated by Zawar Hanfi. New York: Anchor Books, 1972.

---

[26] Massimo De Angelis, "Strange Common Places", *Mute* 28 (Summer/Autumn 2004). Available on-line: <http://www.metamute.org/en/Strange-Common-Places>. Accessed 01/02/2010.

—. *The Essence of Christianity.* Translated by George Eliot. Amherst, NY: Prometheus Books, 1989.

Hardt, Michael and Antonio Negri. *Multitude: War and Democracy in the Age of Empire.* New York: Penguin, 2004.

Lange, Friedrich. *The History of Materialism.* Translated by Ernest Chester Thomas. New York: Harcourt, Brace, & Co., 1925.

Marx, Karl. "Economic and Philosophical Manuscripts." In *Early Texts,* translated by David McLellan. Oxford: Blackwell, 1971. 75-112.

—. *Early Writings.* Translated by Rodney Livingstone and Gregor Benton. London: Penguin, 1992.

Osborne, Peter. "The Reproach of Abstraction." *Radical Philosophy* 127 (September/October, 2004): 21–28.

Power, Nina. "Badiou and Feuerbach: What is Generic Humanity?" *Subject Matters: A Journal of Communication and the Self* 2.1 (2005): 35-46.

—. "Towards an Anthropology of Infinitude: Badiou and the Political Subject." *Cosmos and History* 2 "The Praxis of Alain Badiou" (2006): 186-209.

Virno, Paolo. *Multitudes: Between Innovation and Negation.* Translated by Isabella Bertoletti, James Cascaito, Andrea Casson. New York: Semiotext(e), 2008.

—. "Natural-Historical Diagrams: The 'New Global' Movement and the Biological Invariant." Translated by Alberto Toscano. In Lorenzo Chiesa and Alberto Toscano edited, *The Italian Difference: Between Nihilism and Biopolitics.* Melbourne: re:press, 2009. 131-49.

CHAPTER THIRTEEN

SOVEREIGN AUTOIMMUNITY: HÄGGLUND, BATAILLE AND THE SECULAR

ALEX ANDREWS

I. Introduction

The following essay attempts to draw together the work of George Bataille and Martin Hägglund on the question of the religious and the relation of this question to those of the secular and the political. This is partially a work of construction, highlighting a link between the theo-political question of the exercise of sovereignty and the problem of time that is not yet explicit in Hägglund's oeuvre. In the first section, I summarise Martin Hägglund's fresh reading of Derrida and give an overview of his critical project with regard to religion. In the second section, Hägglund's understanding of finitude and religion is compared with Bataille's own comprehension of these themes, in an attempt to mutually reinforce their respective theories. As we shall see, the point of similarity is that for Hägglund and Bataille religion is only possible when atheism is in fact true: the sacred only operates if the secular (or immanence in Bataille's terms) is primary. Put differently, for Bataille and Hägglund, God must not exist in order for religion to function. As Adrian Johnston has noted in his excellent summary and critique of Hägglund's project, what is radical in Hägglund's radical atheism is that "Freud claims that humanity eventually will become atheist. Hägglund claims that humanity always has been atheist."[1] The same will be argued with regard to Bataille. Other theories of religion presuppose finitude and suggest that religion is an attempt to avoid the consequences of mortality and time through the construction of various illusions. In contrast, Bataille suggests

---

[1] Adrian Johnston, "Life Terminable and Interminable: The Undead and the Afterlife of the Afterlife—a Friendly Disagreement with Martin Hägglund," *CR: The New Centennial Review* 9.1 (2009), 150.

that religion is an attempt to fully embrace rather than reject finitude. In the final section, this controversial contention leads into a discussion of the notion of power and the political. This discussion furthers Hägglund's project of pursuing the logic of radical atheism he builds from Derrida, and the co-terminus notions of autoimmunity, desire, time and survival, into the realms of politics. For one, any wielding of any power is potentially destructive of that power, and opens an opportunity for resistance to it. Power requires the exercise of power in order to maintain itself, so its maintenance is its destruction. In a conclusion orientated towards further research, this reflection on power will be turned onto the political constitution of the secular in modernity – the constitution of power that is secularism. It will be argued that secular sovereignty is autoimmune in Hägglund's terminology Finally, it will be suggested that the Hägglund/Bataille combination is superior to currently popular accounts of religion and that it is attractive to both religious traditions as well as political, yet sometimes areligious, traditions such as Marxism.

II. Martin Hägglund: Derrida and Radical Atheism

Martin Hägglund is an interesting figure when placed against the wider background of development and change in Continental philosophy. In the first instance, his reading of Derrida emphatically rejects the "postmodern" reading of his work, and the influence of this reading on the "turn to religion" that has been so significant for Derrida influenced Continental philosophy of religion. For the likes of John Caputo, Jean-Luc Marion and Hent de Vries, there is a definite religious core to Derrida's work (say a move toward negative theology or a critique of ontotheology or idolatry), or, more commonly, that Derrida's later work "turns" from questions of language to those of religion, justice and ethics beginning roughly with the publication of *Spectres of Marx*. This is perhaps why Hägglund polemically associates the label "radical atheism" with Derrida's thought. In the second instance, this new reading allies Derrida with those in the "speculative turn" who attempt to distance themselves from the intellectual trend for (what can be broadly designated as) "postmodernism". The image of Derrida from partisans of speculation, at its most polemical, is of someone concerned with close textual analysis and exhibiting an indifference to metaphysics bordering on a form of near-nihilist textual idealism.[2] Derrida's work is seen as irreducibly postmodern and paradigmatic

---

[2] Aaron F. Hodges gives an excellent summary of the "old" Derrida that Hägglund rejects: "There is a familiar view of deconstruction according to which the latter is supposed to be concerned, first and foremost, with structures of language...

of everything negative about the postmodern and rejected by the "speculative turn". However, in Hägglund's reading of Derrida, it turns out that ultimately Derrida is a metaphysician, though one who is attempting to overturn certain traditions of metaphysics. Derrida as "anti-philosopher" is relegated to the dustbin of history and we have a Derrida far closer to speculation than postmodernism.

Hägglund's reading of Derrida hinges on demonstrating the consistency of Derrida's thought and avoiding a decisive break in his writing that forms the "turn to religion". Hägglund claims that despite the seeming breadth of Derrida's work, and the numerous fields that Derrida interrupted, there is a consistent logic at work across his forty years of writing. Hägglund's reading of Derrida begins with Derrida's concept of autoimmunity, first visited in his later works on democracy and so, necessarily, begins at the same point as those many commentators who see an ethical-religious "break" in Derrida's thought. Starting an account of Derrida's work here allows Hägglund to demonstrate the central logics of deconstruction; in his view:

> The link between time and autoimmunity is at the centre of my exposition... Autoimmunity brings out the most provocative implications of deconstructive logic and the problem of time opens the most consistent way to defend the rigour of that logic.[3]

Two aspects therefore define Hägglund's reading on Derrida and deconstruction: autoimmunity and time. Autoimmunity is a biological concept that refers to when an organism fails to recognise parts of itself as self, causing the immune response of an organism to work against these falsely recognised elements and ultimately itself. For Derrida, the very

---

Deconstruction represents some variety or other of linguistic idealism, revealed by the privilege it confers to the order of words over the order of things... Deconstruction's essential endeavour is modelled on the impossibility of linguistic, hence conceptual, access to the world or to reality-in-itself... This endeavour, we are told, culminates in the reverent surrender to the unspeakable, the nonconceptual, the untranslatable, the ineffable, the absolutely other, or the impossible, to which language or thought aspires but can never reach... Deconstruction turns out to be a kind of silent fideism, a faithful and paradoxical affirmation of impossible transcendence." Aaron F. Hodges, "Martin Hägglund's Speculative Materialism," *CR: The New Centennial Review* 9.1 (2009), 87-88. The co-implication of the postmodern "textual" Derrida and the "religious" Derrida is clear from this short extract.

[3] Hägglund, *Radical Atheism: Derrida and the Time of Life* (Stanford: Stanford University Press, 2008), 11-12.

nature of democracy is autoimmune, since democracy is threatened not only by what is external to it, but also by its own internal dynamics, including the aspects of democracy that attempt to maintain and uphold democracy. In short, democracy is threatened by its own immune system. Derrida gives the example of the Nazi rise to power. Here the will of the people voted democratically to erase democracy, as is always possible (from Plato to Badiou, the ability of a people to vote for their own dictatorship is considered one of democracy's constitutive flaws). A more sophisticated example can be given regarding recent debates over resurgent fascist parties in the United Kingdom. Nationalist parties like the British National Party (BNP) seek to impose inegalitarian policies regarding the treatment of those they consider to be "non-ethically" British. These policies would be opposed to the very nature of democracy itself, its essence of equality and egalitarianism, yet would be brought about in part by the processes of democracy. However, at the same time, some argue that preventing the BNP from publicly demonstrating their view is opposed to one of the central principles of democracy, that is, free speech. Indeed, the BNP themselves often say that censoring them would only prove their point that the United Kingdom's democracy was in fact a "liberal dictatorship" that is wilfully ignoring the problems of "indigenous British" it seeks supposedly to defend. Democracy is then turned against itself. In the case of the BNP, the immune system of democracy that calls for free speech results in an attack on the very foundations (egalitarianism, equality of all races and creeds) of that democracy. Democracy is autoimmune; the BNP are using the immune system of democracy that is intended to prevent dictatorship (free speech) in order to bring about their goals of erasing the openness of democracy.

Yet this autoimmunity is not a wholly destructive process restricted to debates regarding the extreme right. Much the same arguments are made in order to "save the name" of democracy. For example, the alter-globalisation movement have rightly questioned if democracy as currently practiced is in fact democratic at all. Rather than the undemocratic combination of parliamentary representation in collaboration with extra-governmental corporations and unelected international bodies such as the World Bank, such activists seek to include some manner of control over the market, calling for an "economic democracy", a move that is opposed to what is currently considered democratic. At the same time though, these activists may be seen as a threat to democracy by elected democratic powers, "domestic extremists" who should be attacked, even if they are in fact the saviours of democracy from slavery to capital. Hence the immune system of democracy may kill those who would ensure that democracy is properly healthy. The openness of democracy therefore—the definition of citizenry and its methodology of voting, its tradition of critique—the very openness that constitutes democracy and its internal defence, at the same time constitutes the possibility of its demise, regardless of external threats. They are the possibility of the modification of not merely democracy in its current form into a potentially better form, but of its change into a form that renders democracy its other, dictatorship. However, if it were not the case that democracy contained the seeds of its own end, democracy would both be non-democratic and nothing new could emerge. Democracy without the potential for change, questioning, or production (that is, democracy in stasis) would be dictatorship, the death of democracy. What Derrida is concerned with in the concept of the "democracy to come" is autoimmunity. We are never aware of the risks both external to democracy and internal to its own dynamics. Democracy may be open to its becoming dictatorship, but equally this same risk to openness is the possibility that every actually existing democracy may outstrip its negative shackles—that a corrupt parliamentary democracy may change into a participatory democracy based upon the principle of the common. Democracy faces the future at risk, the risk that it may itself be erased by virtue of its very openness, but this risk constitutes what is positive about it as a form of government in the first place. Hägglund writes:

> To be sure, the essential corruptibility of democracy can have the most devastating effects. But for Derrida corruptibility is also the possibility for anything to happen. A form of government that would be able to guarantee its own legitimacy—exempted from the risk of powers being misused or principles corrupted—would short-circuit the possibility of politics and of life in general. The only way to secure an absolute peace would be to extinguish everything that could possibly break the peace and thereby extinguish the undecidable time to come that is the condition for anything to happen.[4]

Put differently "to be democratic, democracy must be open to critique… But for the same reason democracy is open to what may alter or destroy it. It must both protect itself against its own threat and be threatened by its own protection".[5] What attacks the immune system of a body may be an outside element threatening to it, but may also be an important constitutive element of that body causing its destruction. Worse, what the immune system misses and what is welcomed may be destructive to that body. Yet,

---

[4] Martin Hägglund, "The Necessity of Discrimination: Disjointing Derrida and Levinas," *diacritics* 34.1 (2004), 69. Repeated in Chapter Four of *Radical Atheism*.
[5] Hägglund, *Radical Atheism*, 14.

the immune system remains entirely necessary, despite the risk.

Beginning with this example, Hägglund goes on to stress that autoimmunity is the core logic of deconstruction—and that autoimmunity can be best defended by an analysis of time. For Hägglund, life is autoimmune; life, like democracy, opens to the possibility of its demise. This is due to time, which Hägglund believes is encapsulated in the Derridean term *différance*. *Différance* is an ultra-transcendental, the possibility of anything. Due to time, no object is truly self-present to itself, but always slipping away from its centre. The Derridean trace names what survives, but may be erased in the passage from one moment to the next. All other aspects of deconstruction are recast under these two rubrics. For example, the resistance to metaphysical dualism and its binary suppositions that deconstruction is famous for is recast with regard to time. As one end of the constitutive dyad is implicated with the other, there can never be a complete clarity of one or the other, and so slipping between the two is a result of the presence of a trace of the one in the other and the shifting between the two is the result of time. The trace is the meeting of time and space and the transcendental condition of everything temporal (which is to say, everything). Every dyad is therefore corrupted by the presence of its other, in precisely the same manner that is ascribed in auto-immunity. While linguistic interpretations of Derrida maintained that what is emphatically signified will ultimately slip its current signification, Hägglund draws our attention to the fact that the reason for this is the structure of time itself and, relatedly, finitude, since all finitude is characterised by what Hägglund calls Derrida's "spacing of time"—the centre of all deconstruction. Linguistic interpretations were right that all signification slips, but did not apply this slipping to the whole of reality, restricting it to solely textual artefacts. Hence, Life is subject to autoimmunity, life contains its own destruction; this is what it is to be a finite creature, because time is structured as such[6]: "The threat of loss is not extrinsic... It is intrinsic to its being as such."[7]

Since everything that is will eventually slip away in the flow of time,

---

[6] For an intriguing discussion of the relation between this thought on time and physics, see Vicki Kirby, "Tracing Life: 'La Vie La Mort'," *CR: The New Centennial Review* 9.1 (2009). See also Arkady Plotnitsky, *Complementarity: Anti-Epistemology after Bohr and Derrida* (Durham: Duke University Press, 1994). For a discussion of Derrida in relation to contemporary naturalism see Henry Staten, "Derrida, Dennett, and the Ethico-Political Project of Naturalism," *Derrida Today* 1.1 (2008), 19-41. What is now required is a placing of Hägglund's work within the tradition of philosophy of time.

[7] Hägglund, *Radical Atheism*, 34.

since all things are impermanent, should we seek a state where autoimmunity would be removed all together, a time and place, where as some religions suggest, there is a time without time? Hägglund's radical atheism stresses that not only is such a state undesirable, but that desire itself, even the desire for this state of "absolute immunity", presupposes a condition of impermanence. For Hägglund's Derrida "the common denominator for all religions is that they promote an ideal of absolute immunity beyond the condition of survival, namely, the ideal of something that would be unscathed by time and loss".[8] This absolute immunity might be represented by a timeless and undying deity, eternal and beyond time, or a state beyond life in immortality, or the state of Nirvana. Atheism is in general a resistance to such notions of absolute autoimmunity, recognising them as fictions, but Hägglund's problem is that most atheisms still believe absolute immunity to be desirable, even if it is impossible.

In a response to his critics, Hägglund outlines a taxonomy of various kinds of atheism against which radical atheism is set. There is the melancholic form of atheism which laments the impossibility of absolute immunity (Hägglund gives the example of Simon Critchley), pragmatic atheism which sees the desire for absolute immunity as an illusion, though one necessary for investment in ethical or political projects (Laclau and Mouffe are his examples) and therapeutic atheism (represented by psychoanalysis, in particular Freud and Lacan) which attempts to resolve this desire for a passage beyond autoimmunity as it is a source of damage.[9] In contrast, Hägglund's radical atheism does not celebrate the desire for fullness, non-time or absolute immunity contained within these various forms of atheisms. Rather, radical atheism claims that this fullness is not desirable because it would erase the very progression of time and autoimmunity that is part of the very definition of life itself. Just as removing autoimmunity from democracy would remove democracy from democracy (making it dictatorship), to remove autoimmunity from life would be to be dead. To be alive is to be mortal, hence to be non-mortal is to be dead. Put otherwise, to quote the Talking Heads song "Heaven", this immortality and fullness is for Hägglund a place where "nothing ever happens", where there can be no possibility of the new—it is static, immovable, indistinguishable from objecthood, dead.[10] While atheism for Hägglund claims God is Dead, radical atheism claims that "God is

---

[8] Martin Hägglund, "The Challenge of Radical Atheism—a Response," *CR: The New Centennial Review* 9.1 (2009), 228.

[9] Ibid, 229.

[10] I am grateful to David Bell for continued philosophical reflection on this Talking Heads song.

Death".[11] God, immortality, and the other-worldly erase what is truly life.

What motivates the desire for fullness as expressed in religion? The desire for immortality is seen by Hägglund as, in actual fact, the desire for more temporal life rather than the incorruptible. This can be seen in all religions in Hägglund view; indeed in Christianity, Islam and some versions of Judaism, it is clear that life after death is a matter of the resurrection of the body (and often the completion of the currently existing material world), not the ascent of some immaterial soul, and hence, in some completed sense, the after-life is a continued temporal life. But such an incorruptible life—for Hägglund a life without life—would erase the possibility of life, which is openness to risk. Radical atheism for Hägglund questions not simply the incorruptible, the immortal, but, in contrast to rival atheisms, the desirability of this state. As Adrian Johnston remarks,

> 'Everlasting life' is a contradiction-in-terms—and this insofar as the essential temporality of life renders the insatiable thirst for more life, often (mis)represented as a craving for an eternal life transcending time, a yearning for remaining open to the perpetually renewed alterity of time *à venir*, with the incalculable numbers of dangers and risks this openness to futurity necessarily and unavoidable entails.[12]

This can be illustrated in mainstream debates concerning theodicy. Consider Philip Goodchild's discussion of an argument made by Christian philosopher Richard Swinburne regarding death, a discussion that we may extend to autoimmunity:

> [For Swinburne] the existence of death gives our actions moral significance; it enables us to perform acts of self-sacrifice; it makes the consequences of our actions irreversible; it allows the young to grow to maturity uninhibited by their elders; and it gives a limit to the duration of suffering... In spite of this, the obvious corollary, that an after-life free from death and suffering would lack all moral significance, is not emphasized by Swinburne.[13]

Suffering, the theodicist claims, has some purpose: it is necessary for humans to lead a full and moral life, even if it seems apparently destructive and purposeless, since it teaches human beings (by punishing their wrongs, for example) and enables direction and even love by

---

[11] Hägglund, *Radical Atheism*, 8.

[12] Johnston, "Life Terminable and Interminable", 149.

[13] Philip Goodchild, "Death and Enlightenment in Twelve Brief Episodes," *Angelaki* 7.2 (2002), 43.

providing some resistance and permitting persons to grow. In a simple version, some suffering is required for the health of a person. Hence the autoimmunity in life is a condition of moral significance. Suffering has a value and it may even enable greater goods; it is thus permitted by God. Yet the goal of life, eternal life without suffering, is then the erasure of moral significance, greater goods and even love. If one is arguing that human life requires some suffering in order for health (either moral, physical or spiritual), then the afterlife could not be a healthy life—the existence of eternal life undercuts the argument made for the necessity of autoimmunity in this life. Goodchild, then, anticipates Hägglund's move. For Hägglund, life is autoimmunity. If for Swinburne moral significance is a result of the autoimmune possibility of death, then to be immortal would have no peculiar moral significance—eternal life is worse, morally, than mortal life. Life contains its other, without it it would not be life. Hence eternal life is not morally significant.

If the desire for immortality is rather the desire for more mortal life that is intrinsically desirable to us, then what of other desires? This can be seen as Hägglund's opening to ethics, centred around the concept of survival: "I argue that the attachment to mortal life precipitates every positive and every negative affective response. If one were not attached to mortal life, one would not care either about oneself or any other. Only a mortal being requires care, since only a mortal being can be lost, injured, or violated."[14] Or alternatively, "The finitude of survival opens the chance for everything that is desired and the threat of everything that is feared."[15] Autoimmunity exists, it is a truth of time and it is the reason why we try and grasp onto things, in order to protect them: "Whatever is desired is finite in its essence."[16] Indeed, "the radically atheist argument is that one cannot want absolute immunity and that it has never been the aim of desire".[17] Immortality as removal from autoimmunity is a desire for survival beyond which depends upon the prior value of survival in this life. The desire for survival is not only limited to human subjects, but extends to the relations of all life subject to time—that is to say, all life.

At the very least, the remembering of a particular event, or the inscription of this event in writing, is an attempt to make something survive, the trace of one moment to the other, open to the possibility (just like writing) of erasure. Evolution itself resists the flow of the second law

---

[14] Hägglund, *Radical Atheism*, 34.
[15] Ibid, 2.
[16] Ibid, 34.
[17] Ibid, 119.

of thermodynamics towards more dissolution and chaos.[18] Moreover, all supplementary responses ascribed to religion (for example, those of ethics and care), for Hägglund, derive from this desire for survival:

> The desire for survival—namely, the desire for a mortal being to live on— is thus presupposed in all our engagements with the world. For example, all the virtues that traditionally are assumed to be based on religious faith—compassion, love, responsibility for the other, and so on—in fact presuppose the radically atheist desire for survival. To feel compassion or take responsibility for the other, I have to be invested in a being who is susceptible to suffering and who consequently is mortal. The same goes for the experience of love. To love someone or something is to distinguish it from everything else as singularly precious. If the beloved could not die, however, it would not be possible to distinguish it as precious in the first place, since the beloved would not be irreplaceable. It is because the beloved can be lost that we seek to keep it. Or more generally: it is because things can be lost, because they have not always been here and will not always be here, that we value them.[19]

It is not so much that death is an aberration for Hägglund, but death is a fact of reality, without which there would be no life. Desire for survival stems from this fact, but at the same time contains the seeds of its own destruction since to attempt to survive, or more specifically, to attempt to make another object survive is implicated with risk, the risk that comes with autoimmunity, the possibility of its erasure, that caused us to care for it in the first place, since "temporal finitude—far from being a privation— is the reason why anything is desirable in the first place"[20]. For example, I feel compassion for the other because I recognise that it like me is weak, voluble and mortal—that it risks absolute erasure. Survival, which is the result of an immanent, temporal, finite life, is then the condition of every act for Hägglund:

> Far from leaving the category of immortality intact, the logic of survival allows us to see that what has been called a desire for immortality is in fact a desire for survival, so the opposition between mortality and immortality is deconstructed from within.[21]

---

[18] Martin Hägglund, "Radical Atheist Materialism: A Critique of Meillassoux," in Levi Bryant, Nick Srnicek and Graham Harman eds, *The Speculative Turn: Continental Materialism and Realism* (Melbourne: re.press, 2011), 114-29.

[19] Hägglund, "The Challenge of Radical Atheism", 229.

[20] Johnston, "Life Terminable and Interminable", 155.

[21] Martin Hägglund, "Time, Desire, Politics: A Reply to Ernesto Laclau," *diacritics* 38.1-2 (2008), 192.

III. Bataille's Theory of Religion

I will now compare Bataille's theory of religion[22] with the understanding of religion that I have drawn from Hägglund's reading of Derrida. What is key to this comparison is that both locate the reason for phenomena, even religion, in finitude—for Hägglund desire for the immortal emerges, like all desires, from the desire for continued survival, for Bataille religion springs from the half-realised need to return to the intimacy of immanence. For both immanence/finitude are the key to understanding religion, rather than the standard account whereby religion is an escape from finitude.

Bataille's account of religion begins with an account of immanence. Immanence is the heart of the religious impulse: just as for Hägglund, mortality (temporality) is the very heart of the desire for immortality. To imagine immanence, Bataille says, is also to imagine immediacy in nature. He begins by considering the situation of an animal eating another animal. When this occurs, an animal is eating another animal – there is no hierarchy here, no "subordination", since no object has been posited that a subject has control of. The lion is not genuinely king of nature, but one wave overturning lesser waves—the lion never is sovereign over the animals in a formal sense, such formalities belong only to the human world that posits objects like "sovereign" that make master and slave. This brings Bataille to his point: "That one animal eats another scarcely alters a fundamental situation, every animal is in the world like water in water."[23] Every animal is, for Bataille, fully immanent in the world. Man however is not (for the most part), and this form of immanence is closed to us. This closure is a source of anguish, since we cannot easily close off the elements of humanity that prevent us from being in the world like water in water. Indeed, the whole process of becoming human was a process of leaving this kind of intimacy behind, one that we still yearn for, in part because it is so foreign to our form. Unlike other animals, though in fact remaining animals, humans are the only creatures where "the transcendence of things in relation to consciousness (or of consciousness in relation to things) is manifested."[24] The creation of tools establishes something extracted from this "water", and then subordinates it to human use, and enables conceptual positing of an object (a thing) and this creates differentiation, the possibility of a not-I. In particular with tools, we know

---

[22] Bataille, *Theory of Religion*, trans. Robert Huxley (New York: Zone Books, 1989).
[23] Ibid, 19.
[24] Ibid, 24.

the object clearly since we have made it, fashioned it and formed it out of previously undifferentiated nature, and this ability to make "stuff" into an object enables the realisation that all other stuff could well have the status of objects. Hence, the fact that "men situated on the same plane where the things appeared (as if they were comparable to the digging stick of the chipped stone) elements that nonetheless remained continuous with the world, such as animals, plants"[25] leads to human beings placing themselves on this plane too. Humans have discovered the ability to make objects, separate objects have been individuated and then placed on the same level as human beings that are also seen as objects (all becoming objects or as Bataille calls them *things*) and hence establishing some equivalence between acting subjects and truly inactive objects (like rocks), a sensation increased when a tool had shown that objects could have the powers of subjects when moved by human beings: "The transcendence of the tool and the creative faculty connected with its use are confusingly attributed to the animal, the plant, the meteor; they are also attributed to the entire world".[26] The process is four-fold: the creation of tools that renders an object and makes it useful, the division of the world into objects as a result, the realisation that this tool is a weird subject-object, then the extension of subject-objects to the whole world of objects. This levelling of all things, both subjects (humanity) and what would normally be considered objects (rocks), creates god and spirits, since it allows things to also be subjects. We are living subject-objects, so we believe in this potential for others. The creation of gods renders them into a hierarchy, where the highest spirits are not associated with a body, just as the largest things in the natural world produce the largest spirits. This leads man, insomuch as he is both spirit (tool-maker) and non-spirit, to diminish his bodily life. As the domain of objects is considered profane, this leads also to the further diminishing of the "real" world and a further transcendence from it. Bataille writes:

> Insofar as it is spirit, the human reality is holy, but it is profane insofar as it is real. Animals, plants, tools, and other controllable things form a real world with the bodies that control them, a world subject to and traversed by divine forces, but fallen.[27]

Yet, this creation of tools is problematic for humankind. Making tools has allowed men to create conceptual objects and in addition it has subjugated

---

[25] Ibid, 31.
[26] Ibid, 32.
[27] Ibid, 34.

nature to man, "Nature becomes man's property but it ceases to be immanent to him".[28] This making nature into an object of manipulation permits humankind to forget that he is in fact part of nature, that:

> Everything in my power declares that I have compelled that which is equal to me no longer to exist for its own purpose but rather for a purpose that is alien to it.[29]

This continual making of things, creates external spirits that testify to the inferiority of the material to the spiritual, and so concludes in a situation where man himself, on self-reflection, becomes a thing.

We now have god as a result of tools and humans alienated from their essence by the construction of objects that makes man also an object, a thing. What then of religion? How does this fit in here? Religion is an attempt to un-thing an object and in the process to un-thing a human. Bataille begins with the phenomenon of sacrifice. The intention of sacrifice is to liberate the thing, the object we have created, from the realm of things. Therefore, sacrifice never sacrifices that which is not useful, but something that we have made useful, something "subjugated, domesticated, and reduced to being a thing"[30], "objects that could have been spirits"[31]. Hence slaves are sacrificed because they are *useful* not because they are other to citizens. Though sacrifice is apparently concerned with the destruction of something, it is only concerned with destroying the status of that object as a thing. Sacrifice removes the victim from the "world of utility", the world in which the sacrificed becomes object, and returns it to one where it no longer has this function, that is to immanence. Sacrifice is an apology to the sacrificed for reducing it to a thing, when (as previously stated) it is could have been a spirit. Sacrifice "restores it to that of unintelligible caprice"[32], it restores the thing to immanence. But simultaneously, this return to intimacy of the object affects the sacrificer, as it requires the sacrificer to also return to intimacy: "The sacrificer needs to sacrifice in order to separate himself from the world of things and the victim could not be separated from it in turn if the sacrificer was not already separated in advance."[33] This could not occur any other way, since the only real reason for the objects' transcendence from intimacy is the

---

[28] Ibid, 41.
[29] Ibid.
[30] Ibid, 50.
[31] Ibid.
[32] Ibid, 43.
[33] Ibid, 44.

sacrificer's separation, his objectification of the object. Wielding the sacrificial knife the sacrificer says: "I call you back to the intimacy of the divine world, the profound immanence of all that is."[34] In consequence, "The individual identifies with the victim in the sudden moment that restores it to immanence"[35].

In short then, sacrifice enables human kind to glimpse the possibility of a life of immanence and intimacy. Bataille suggests, "Life's disappearance in death [cannot be prevented] from revealing the invisible brilliance of life that is not a thing".[36] Hence the secret of religion, festival and war, is that religion "is the search for lost intimacy".[37] Or put in the register of Hägglund, while religion may claim to be about immortality, it is in fact about mortality, immanence. In both cases, religion only "works" if immanence is true: in Hägglund's case because only immanence requires survival, in Bataille's because a return to immanence is what is sought. In both cases, the secular is key to the religious in such a way that religious desire is in fact desire for the secular. Bataille's atheism avoids Hägglund's categorisations of rival atheisms in that Bataille's religion undermines the suggestion that objects like immortality are desirable.

It is insufficient to simply point out this similarity. Instead, we must ask: how do these two conceptions of religion complement and deepen one another? Moreover, what are the elements that divide them? Let us deal with the latter first. It is the case that there are elements that are here plainly problematic and that there is a rebuttal here that is obvious. For Bataille, religion is an attempt to be more, not less immanent to the natural – it is not an attempt for transcendence but immanence, just as for Hägglund the desire for eternal life is in fact the desire for more mortal life. So far so good. But could it not be the case that the desire for intimacy that Bataille considers the core of religions is itself a desire for a state of absolute immunity? It seems that Bataille's talk of a return to immanence is an attempt to do away with what makes humans human, indeed he admits that there is an implicit tension in that humans, as signifying animals, cannot finally return to intimacy. The fact that humans signify things as things is the reason why human beings are alienated from intimacy in the first place and attempt to return to it. But it is precisely the erasure of this signification, and the intrinsic difficulty of being human, that in Hägglund's schema is criticised. The desire for intimacy seems to erase the conditions for life (risk, temporality, etc.) and the struggle for

---

[34] Ibid, 44.
[35] Ibid, 51.
[36] Ibid, 47.
[37] Ibid, 57.

survival, just as much as the contradictory desire for the afterlife does. Rather than becoming like angels, for Bataille, we become like animals—is this not merely an escape from life in the opposite direction? To lack the representation of objects and recognition of the symbolic difference between life and death, which is for Bataille present in animals, would be the same as being immortal, it would equally remove the conditions of life. There is a response that Bataille is capable of giving here that seems minimally satisfying. Complete intimacy is, as I have mentioned, impossible for humanity, precisely because man wishes to survive as man. Over-coded with Hägglund's terminology, man's desire for survival is what resists absolute intimacy with nature. Indeed, man's ability to survive significantly longer than animals is perhaps grounded in man's ability to make differentiations, to make "critical discernments".

What then does such a combination yield that the two uncombined lack? First, Hägglund frees Bataille from an overreliance upon a form of idealism (in that man conjures forth objects through social relations) and provides for him, via the structure of the trace, a metaphysical basis on which immanence can be rendered. Hägglund offers the possibility that Bataille's account can be rendered metaphysically, reinforcing his account of religion against those who would view it as irretrievably correlationist. Second, as we shall see, Hägglund provides Bataille with a clear theory of temporality and enables a more profound reading of the concept of sovereignty. For Hägglund, Bataille provides an account of religion that is fuller of the types of things religious people actually do—sacrifice, live communally, etc—rather than focusing on specific beliefs they have regarding the need for the incorruptible. But this theory begins with Hägglund's logic that what is desired in all cases is what is mortal. It thus avoids the pitfalls of the analyses of religion offered by his other taxonomical forms of atheism by beginning with immanence as what religions are genuinely after. Indeed, Bataille's religion is an attempt by humans to become more mortal—more sensitive to the movement of time. Moreover, by providing an account of religion that draws on the material facts and seems to have some basis in the manner in which human beings evolved (in that we evolved from tool-using apes for one, the semi-ecological notion of Bataille's "general economy" as the movement of matter and energy) it may provide help for Hägglund in accounting for the sheer range of religious phenomena under his slim rubric.

IV. Sovereignty and Time

At the time of writing, the application of Hägglund's thought to political questions is relatively limited, encompassing a brief encounter with Ernesto Laclau in the final chapter of Radical Atheism and a discussion between the two of them in the pages of *diacritics*.[38] Bataille's writing on politics are more complete, his reactions to political events of his time fuller. Let us briefly turn to Bataille's late essay, "The Obelisk"[39], to see how the mutual complement of Hägglund and Bataille might deepen our understanding of power (what Bataille calls "established sovereignty") as temporal.

Bataille begins his meditation with a discussion of the death of God, repeating the speech of the madman who announces this death. Of course, announcing "God is Dead" rather than "God does not exist" has two distinct functions. First, more banally, it makes the statement necessarily existential, as it was for the fictional crowd who denied the truth of the madman. Second, and with regard to the issue at hand, the statement does not mean that God ever existed and then died, but rather for Nietzsche that the concept of God has become subject to the logic of time. What seemed to be an enduringly certain concept is subject to the same temporality as everything else. To place this in Hägglund's terminology, religious concepts, though apparently eternal, are subject to the ultra-transcendental condition of time. With this is mind, Bataille states: "The Place de La Concorde is the space where the death of God must be announced and shouted precisely because the obelisk is its calmest negation"[40]. The Luxor Obelisk in the *Place de la Concorde* stands still in the busy flux of life, when the madman announces something so distressing, the obelisk counters with an atemporal certainty. The Obelisk is not merely present, it anchors things against change and in particular it anchors sovereign power against change. This is certainly how Bataille believes the Egyptians viewed it. Bataille writes:

The obelisk is without a doubt the purest image of the head and of the

---

[38] Ernesto Laclau, "Is Radical Atheism a Good Name for Deconstruction?," *diacritics* 38.1-2 (2008) and Hägglund, "Time, Desire, Politics."

[39] Georges Bataille, "The Obelisk," in *Visions of Excess: Selected Writings, 1927-1939*, ed. Allan Stoekl (Minneapolis: University of Minnesota Press, 1985). I was drawn to this essay by Benjamin Noys' excellent introduction to Bataille. Benjamin Noys, *Georges Bataille: A Critical Introduction* (London: Pluto Press, 2000), 73. As Noys notes, Derrida calls Bataille a "Hegelianism without reserve"—what could be a better statement for the ultra-transcendental of time? On this see Jacques Derrida, "From Restricted to General Economy: A Hegelianism without reserve," in *Writing and Difference*, trans. Alan Bass (London, Routledge 2002), 317-349.

[40] Bataille, "The Obelisk", 215.

heavens. The Egyptians saw it as a sign of military power and glory, and just as they saw the rays of the setting sun in their funeral pyramids, so too they recognized the brilliance of the morning sun in the angles of their splendid monoliths: the obelisk was to the armed sovereignty of the Pharaoh what the pyramid was to his dried-out corpse. *It was the surest and most durable obstacle to the drifting away of all things.*[41]

The Obelisk represents the eternal military might of the sovereign pharaoh; the pyramid perpetuates this might beyond his death. When death, the sheer logic of mortal time, catches the Pharaoh, doubt at the existence of such consistent truths is raised. The huge size and enduring construction of the pyramids are an attempt to "halt the flow of time"[42], to "reestablish the order of things"[43] in the wake of this. They allow the Pharaoh to enter the place of the gods and somehow remain alive, while their physical presence "assures the presence of the unlimited sky on earth."[44] The Obelisk was but one attempt of "man to set the most stable limits on the deleterious movement of time".[45] It was a representation of "the combat of "established sovereignty"[46] against the destructive and creative madness of things", the "immutable stone's response to the Heraclitean world of rivers and flames".[47] It was an attempt to make the mortal, immortal, but more specifically to make temporal sovereignty eternal.

The effect of time of sovereignty that Bataille describes is memorably illustrated in the poem *Ozymandias* by Percy Bysshe Shelley that describes another monument to a sovereign. Yet this is a ruined monument. Discovering the remains of a statue in the desert, a traveller finds that:

On the pedestal these words appear:
'My name is Ozymandias, King of Kings:
Look on my works, ye mighty, and despair!'
Nothing beside remains. Round the decay
Of that colossal wreck, boundless and bare,
The lone and level sands stretch far away.[48]

---

[41] Ibid. Italics mine.
[42] Ibid.
[43] Ibid, 216.
[44] Ibid.
[45] Ibid.
[46] Ibid.
[47] Ibid.
[48] See http://www.online-literature.com/shelley_percy/672/ for one of many online sources of this poem.

The political message of the poem is clear. All sovereignty, even the kind of power that can build great monuments and statues, is still subject to the endless onslaught of time that will ultimately bring it to ruin, and turns them to the desert. Monuments attempt to capture sovereignty, to crystallise it, to remove it from the ultra-transcendental (that is, time) but these too will be reduced. Yet due to time, the continuation of sovereign power is a matter, in Hägglund terms, of survival, an attempt at resisting the forces of political entropy. Since sovereign power is a matter of survival in time the co-implication is that time is autoimmune (recall for Hägglund's Derrida autoimmunity is best argued for *via* time—the existence of the future, the movement of *différance*). The Pharaoh must build a pyramid to convince people that his power remains intact despite his mortality, and in doing so he is only gaining a condition of absolute immunity. Such a condition violates the possibility of his power itself, which must be used, must be dispensed with. Just like life, power contains within it the seeds of its own destruction. This is a message for tyrants and for the activists who seek to defeat them—all use of power, like all movements of life, permit the possibility of dissolution. It is not surprising that Bataille says, "Sovereignty is NOTHING, a nothing that is slipping away from the subject."[49] Or as Derrida puts it time or *différance* "is not far from announcing the death of the tyrant".[50]

What of turning this analysis to the concept of the secular itself? Surely the secular is also a form of sovereignty, that is, the attempt of authorities (in particular, state authorities) to not "take sides" and adopt positions on religious debates, yet remain in power; surely it is autoimmune? The term postsecular bears witness to the possibility of secularity itself being subject to time, as much as the discovery of its fashioning in time.[51] Realising secularity is temporal is the realisation that secularism is autoimmune; it has an immune system, that sometimes risks its own constitution. Let me give some body to this political conjecture. On the one hand, in theory, secularity is an attempt to provide a neutral place that is above the divisions between religious traditions and even between believers and non-believers. Secularism provides freedom of religion in the sense that a myriad of religious positions are permitted yet none are particularly endorsed. Yet, on the other hand, all too often this results practically in secularism being formally opposed to religious traditions, in that it

---

[49] Bataille, "The Obelisk", 65.
[50] Derrida, "Différance" in *Margins of Philosophy*, trans. Alan Bass (Chicago: University of Chicago Press, 1982), 3.
[51] For one detailed account of the process of the creation of the secular, see Charles Taylor, *A Secular Age* (Cambridge, MA: Harvard University Press, 2007).

requires the removal of their public symbols or codes of dress from the supposedly neutral public sphere. Religious people are right to object that secularity applies equally to atheism as it does to religion—indifference towards metaphysical claims of different traditions cannot simultaneously be the affirmation of one particular metaphysical claim, atheism. What secularism attempts to prevent, the imposition of one metaphysical tradition over all others and the potential for violence engendered in this, opens the possibility of this very thing. Just as any act of justice risks the possibility of injustice, any act of attempting to remain neutral to religious questions is the potential for the neutrality to become its opposite, metaphysical dogmatism. Secularity is a concept that is always constitutively open to the possibility (or indeed the inevitability) of its dissolution, even though we might argue that it is necessary. For those who endorse secularism, people must be attentive to its internal structure in order to do "the lesser violence" and be consistently secular. Yet on the opposite side, there are religious people and some public intellectual atheists (those who claim that atheism is the only possibility and wish to dissolve the metaphysical indifference of secularism) who attempt to resist secularity by attacking its political constitution. Rather than resist secularity by resisting secularity, they should in fact endorse secularism since it will necessarily undo itself. Just as the perverse Marxist spends much time at the hypermarket buying shoes made in sweatshops because capitalism will only be destroyed once it has become sufficiently violent and oppressive to provoke revolution, anti-secularists should endorse secularism because its form of political constitution can only ever lead to its dissolution.

The hybrid combination of Bataille-Hägglund presents an attractive combination for both the religious and the non-religious. For believers, it presents a far more attractive option, a far more interesting, not to mention friendly "opposite number" than the current banner bearers of secularism (like Dawkins). For Marxists, as for Bataille-Hägglund, religion is not an irrational reaction to reality, but a reaction to reality. For non-believers, or those within the Marxist tradition, which at the very least Bataille admits he is heir to, it allows an account of religion that is non-reductive, and permits or perhaps requires collaboration between religious and non-religious political projects aimed at emancipation. Hägglund writes:

> A radical atheist perspective allows for not only a critique of religion but also a critique of traditional critiques of religion. Rather than a priori dismissing political struggles that are fought in the name of religious ideals as deluded, the logic of radical atheism allows us to see that these

struggles, too, proceed from an investment in survival.[52]

For Hägglund, it does not follow from the logic of radical atheism that we should oppose political struggles that are fought in the name of religious ideals. It is not a matter of renouncing struggles for health or of denouncing hopes for salvation, since for him "the struggle for health and the hope for salvation have never been driven by a desire to be immortal but by a desire to live on as mortal".[53] In politically pressing times such as these, with the combination of financial and ecological crises, where the survival of every thing is threatened, this ability of one perspective to see another in sympathy could not be more important.

Bibliography

Bataille, Georges. "The Obelisk." In *Visions of Excess: Selected Writings, 1927-1939*. Edited by Allan Stoekl. Minneapolis: University of Minnesota Press, 1985. 213-22.
—. *Theory of Religion*. Translated by Robert Huxley. New York: Zone Books, 1989.
Derrida, Jacques. "Différance." In *Margins of Philosophy*. Translated by Alan Bass. Chicago: University of Chicago Press, 1982. 3-27.
—. "From Restricted To General Economy: Hegelianism without reserve." In *Writing and Difference*. Translated by Alan Bass. London: Routledge, 2001. 317-349.
Goodchild, Philip. "Death and Enlightenment in Twelve Brief Episodes." *Angelaki* 7.2 (2002): 39-50.
Hägglund, Martin. "The Necessity of Discrimination: Disjointing Derrida and Levinas." *diacritics* 34.1 (2004): 40-71.
—. *Radical Atheism: Derrida and the Time of Life*. Stanford: Stanford University Press, 2008.
—. "Time, Desire, Politics: A Reply to Ernesto Laclau." *diacritics* 38.1-2 (2008): 190-99.
—. "The Challenge of Radical Atheism—a Response." *CR: The New Centennial Review* 9.1 (2009): 227-52.
—. "Radical Atheist Materialism: A Critique of Meillassoux." In *The Speculative Turn: Continental Materialism and Realism*. Edited by Levi Bryant, Nick Srnicek and Graham Harman. Melbourne: re.press, 2011. 114-29.

---

[52] Hägglund, "Time, Desire, Politics", 197.
[53] Hägglund, "The Challenge of Radical Atheism", 249.

Hodges, Aaron F. "Martin Hägglund's Speculative Materialism." *CR: The New Centennial Review* 9.1 (2009): 87-106.

Johnston, Adrian. "Life Terminable and Interminable: The Undead and the Afterlife of the Afterlife—a Friendly Disagreement with Martin Hägglund." *CR: The New Centennial Review* 9.1 (2009): 147–90.

Kirby, Vicki. "Tracing Life: 'La Vie La Mort'." *CR: The New Centennial Review* 9.1 (2009): 107-26.

Laclau, Ernesto. "Is Radical Atheism a Good Name for Deconstruction?" *diacritics* 38.1-2 (2008): 180-89.

Meillassoux, Quentin. *After Finitude: An Essay on the Necessity of Contingency*. Translated by Ray Brassier. London: Continuum, 2008.

Noys, Benjamin. *Georges Bataille: A Critical Introduction*. London: Pluto Press, 2000.

Plotnitsky, Arkady. *Complementarity: Anti-Epistemology after Bohr and Derrida*. Durham: Duke University Press, 1994.

Staten, Henry. "Derrida, Dennett, and the Ethico-Political Project of Naturalism." *Derrida Today* 1.1 (2008): 19-41

Taylor, Charles. *A Secular Age*. Cambridge, MA: Harvard University Press, 2007.

PART III

CONTEMPORARY SPECULATIVE PHILOSOPHY AND RELIGION

CHAPTER FOURTEEN

WHAT CAN BE DONE WITH RELIGION?: NON-PHILOSOPHY AND THE FUTURE OF PHILOSOPHY OF RELIGION

ANTHONY PAUL SMITH

I. "I Cry Out, 'Violence!'"

Standing before the murdered dead, before all the murderous disasters of history, one must give attention to and acknowledge the relationship of violence to religion. To be sure, this relationship is not one-sided, for there are numerous instances of religious resistance in the history of human violence. There are instances of struggle, from the liberationists in South America to the Buddhists in Vietnam, where that struggle appears to be inextricably religious in thought and practice. Yet, for all of these moments of human beauty, where religion is the strong and beautiful human protest against suffering, where it is the sigh of the oppressed, and even when it is the site of a human being standing before God himself and crying out violence, one cannot help but see that religion is also a privileged site for Authorities, that it shelters the murderers who perpetuate violence, that it dresses up oppression and stirs up violence under the sign of the holy of holies. Before this fundamental duality of religion it seems that one can only stand and ask resignedly, "What can be done with religion?"

One can see this question throughout the history of philosophy and the answers range, on the extremes, from the pious ("It can be defended!") to the aggressive ("It can be eliminated!"). In each case, though, philosophy itself is not in question. That religion is, like everything, philosophisable is never doubted, and this faith is what François Laruelle calls the "principle of sufficient philosophy". The question can be asked in a different posture where all the Gods and idols of human history and thought, be they philosophical or religious, are stripped of their divine authority and taken for the simple material they are. With this material one may begin to construct the future and construct it otherwise than it currently is. One may construct a truly humane future. The goal here is not to change the World, for the World is always the specular golem of Man, but to struggle immanently within the World using it to construct a future that is no longer worldly.[1] This is a task beyond any one philosopher or any one faith, and it would be foolish to propose yet another political philosophy that is supposed to begin the liberation of humanity. Instead, the task of this essay is more modest, asking how the methodology of Continental philosophy of religion can be changed, mutated even, along the lines of a non-philosophy in order to see religion as simple material for the construction of such a future. No longer satisfying ourselves with being the handmaiden of theology, as some analytic philosophers and phenomenologists have done, nor with simply eliminating religion from the philosophical realm in the hopes of eliminating it from the wider World as well, instead we can only be satisfied with locating what is most human in religion and leaving behind every sense of religious authority, becoming heretics to both philosophers and theologians.

The question "What can be done with religion?" is no longer posed dejectedly, as if we were hostage to religious others, but instead becomes a practical question of how to fashion the future using simple material put to theoretical use in a struggle against and for the World. What the essay proposes, following the work of François Laruelle, is a science of philosophy of religion that allows us to separate out the identities of religion and philosophy in order to develop a unified theory of philosophy and religion from the position of a practice focused around the minority identity of humanity. Such an identity is neither philosophical nor theological—it is non-philosophical. This is not, however, an essay about Laruelle's non-philosophy as such.[2] Though I discuss Laruelle's own work

---

[1] The World is, in non-philosophy, a name for the confusion of some form of thought with the Real. During the first phases of his career, Laruelle is concerned primarily with philosophy and thus World often refers to the confusion of philosophy with the Real. Worldly thought means auto-sufficient thought, thought taking itself as distinct from the Real, and thus thought that has fallen into error. In terms that will become important in the coda to this piece, Mullarkey writes that "all philosophical thought is really about itself, it is auto-sufficient. Its so-called world – *x* – is actually a mirror of itself" (John Mullarkey, *Post-Continental Philosophy: An Outline* (London: Continuum, 2006), 140).

[2] For a more traditional study of Laruelle's thought in relation to themes in philosophy of religion, specifically the concept of the Absolute, see Anthony Paul Smith, "A Stumbling Block to the Jews and Folly to the Greeks: Non-Philosophy and Philosophy's Absolutes", *Analecta Hermeneutica* 3 (2011).

with religion, I am not concerned primarily with explicating what can already be found in his writings, but instead with tracing the method he deploys so as to provide a model for a non-philosophical future of philosophy of religion. As Laruelle's work draws and shares some commonalities with philosophies of immanence I have found it necessary to attend to two such philosophies at some length in order to contextualise Laruelle's own thinking, which he characterizes as thinking from radical immanence, and to differentiate this radical immanence from phenomenological immanence and absolute immanence. I then trace a non-philosophical identity of religion via the methodology of non-philosophy. Finally I end by discussing the possibility of non-theology as a name both for a mutated form of philosophy of religion as non-philosophy and as a science of non-philosophy.

II. Immanence and Religion as a Universal Category

As we strive to discover the solution to our problem of religion, it is necessary to consider the relationship between philosophy and religion, this intertwining of the two discursive fields in what we call Continental philosophy of religion. Continental philosophy of religion has always had a complicated relationship with religion and the various theologies found therein. Continental philosophy of religion, split between the phenomenology of religion and those working out of the modern tradition (Spinoza, Kant, Hegel, etc.), has always been, in varying degrees, compromised with theological material. It isn't necessary to repeat the various forms this compromise of philosophy has taken, as many have already done so at great length. Rather, it is more illuminating, from our perspective, to show the weaknesses of those philosophies that have tried to resist this compromise, as it will then allow us to construct a non-philosophical identity of religion. For, at the heart of the immanent critiques of religion, safeguarding themselves from religious material, is the universal status of religion constructed via a transcendental philosophical judgement.

Perhaps the most famous or nefarious form of this mutation (depending on one's perspective) is the so-called "theological turn" in Francophone, and subsequently Anglophone, phenomenology. Taking on the role of philosophical diagnostician, Dominique Janicaud locates the origin of the turn in Emmanuel Levinas' phenomenology of alterity, which has its roots in Jewish religious thought.[3] This turn is extended in the more explicitly Christian theological phenomenologies of Jean-Luc Marion, Jean-Louis Chrétien, Jean-Yves Lacoste, Michel Henry, Jean-François Courtine, and, in a less radical manner, Paul Ricœur, all figures that dominate contemporary discussions of phenomenology.[4] Clearly, Janicaud's criticisms in both his short essays on the theological turn were not concerned with forbidding phenomenological investigations of religious phenomena, but with what he calls "the overburdening of immanence with a transcendence that is none other than that of subjectivity in its various guises and at its various levels", which is located at the very foundations of phenomenology itself.[5] Janicaud wants to restore phenomenology to immanence—but what is his immanence? It already claims an atheistic posture—though this doesn't mean a doctrine denying the existence of God, but instead a doctrine that is "without a god or God".[6] In the practice of bracketing, which is at the heart of the phenomenological method, both dogmatic theism and atheism must be suspended, but in this moment it is methodologically atheistic.[7] In the theological turn it is not so much the turn to religious material that Janicaud sees as a threat to the methodological immanence of phenomenology, but the way that theological ways of thinking are taken up in phenomenology that infects it with a certain "maximalism". This maximalism goes beyond the immanence of a given object to establish some single aspect of reality as the pivot point of all reality, as seen in the Arch-Ipseity of Henry or the

---

[3] Throughout his writings, Laruelle is very explicit in crediting Jewish thought with forming a real challenge to the Greek character of philosophy. In one interview he remarks that, "Judaism has become the principal interlocutor for philosophy... And it is true that, without Judaism, contemporary thought would probably be boring, dogmatic and very inhumane (setting Deleuze aside, anyway)." (François Laruelle, *En tant qu'Un. La « non-philosophie » expliquée aux philosophes* (Paris: Aubier, 1991), 235). All translations mine unless noted.

[4] Others sometimes include Jacques Derrida, though the claim is not uncontroversial. I tend to follow those readings of Derrida that see in his thought a certain creative antagonism to the theological turn, meaning he engages with religious thought in order to challenge it. See Martin Hägglund, *Radical Atheism: Derrida and the Time of Life* (Stanford: Stanford University Press, 2008) and Michael Naas, "Derrida's *Laïcité*" in *Derrida From Now On* (New York: Fordham University Press, 2008).

[5] Dominique Janicaud, *Phenomenology "Wide Open": After the French Debate*, trans. Charles N. Cabral (New York: Fordham University Press, 2005), 80.

[6] Ibid, 16.

[7] Ibid, 18.

givenness of Marion—these being the two philosophers with the most advanced cases of said theological infection.[8]

Thus, Janicaud locates within a certain strand of Continental philosophy of religion a theological mutation of philosophy that is maximalist, rather than a phenomenological description of religion that would be one instance of a philosophical operation on religious and theological material. In other words, Janicaud appears to object to the *totalising* characteristic of this theologically mutated phenomenology where the whole of reality is explained by recourse to some single feature, or phenomenology's temptation to become a kind of "crypto-theism".[9] Yet, implicit in Janicaud's own critique of the theological turn is the very same Principle of Sufficient Philosophy, what Laruelle describes as the essence of the philosophical act invariantly determining an act as philosophical. In this case, Janicaud objects to the very notion that philosophy's practice, here made minimal, can be changed by its object. Philosophy's autonomy, at least in principle, is unconditional while the object may be transformed by philosophy. Thus Janicaud elides the difference between Levinas' theological turn, which is Jewish in particularity, and the Christian character, predominately Roman Catholic, of the majority involved in the theological turn in France.[10]

Janicaud's immanence is an immanence of things, or the local immanence of the thing-in-itself which is given in its appearing to us. It is from this notion of immanence that we can see the weakness of his criticism of the theological turn. For this is a merely relative immanence that remains philosophical mute in the face of theological transcendence, relying on it to provide meaning for its relativity. In other words, immanence is relativised in Janicaud's phenomenology by splitting it. This is seen in its claim that there is a reciprocal noema-noematic structure to all phenomena. Thus the phenomenology of this phenomena = X itself is not a thinking from immanence, but a mixture of the immanence of the thing-in-itself and the transcendental conditions for its being thought

---

[8] Ibid, 6-7. Here Janicaud appears most frustrated with Henry appearing to think of him as a hopeless case, since "the Arch is presented [as] 'take it or leave it'." (7) While he takes quite seriously Marion's theological maximalism, devoting a whole chapter to its critique. See ibid, 27-45.

[9] Ibid, 21.

[10] This is to say nothing of the Protestant character it takes in some Anglophone appropriations.

which co-appear with the thing-in-itself; a perfect instance of the essence of philosophy's amphibology between transcendence and immanence.[11]

There is another conception of immanence, one that establishes it as absolute, arising out of the modern tradition, that finds its most articulate anti-religious voice in the philosophy of Gilles Deleuze and Félix Guattari. Deleuze and Guattari take their vision of immanence from the pre-critical philosophy of the Greeks who first instituted a "plane of immanence like a sieve stretched over the chaos" and Spinoza who "showed, drew up and thought the 'best' plane of immanence".[12] For them immanence is what holds together bodies in the midst of prephilosophical chaos, making the very possibility of relations between bodies possible. Immanence does not organize chaos itself, but filters it for us so that a relationship between thought and life can form.[13] This is in contrast to those religious forms of thinking that posit a transcendent order from some outside, one that saves us from chaos by ordering us via the same outside order. This leads them to sharply distinguish between philosophy and religion:

> Whenever there is transcendence, vertical Being, imperial State in the sky or on earth, there is religion; and there is Philosophy whenever there is immanence, even if it functions as arena for the agon and rivalry.[14]

It is instructive to consider these two defensive techniques of rival philosophies of immanence extracted from their local discursive field and refracted through a debate within the anthropology of religion. Anthropology has taken part in the postsecular turn common to the global "return of the religious" where religious beliefs and practices are again understood as a major components of human society and politics. For anthropology this has meant turning away from the idea of religion as a universal category towards an understanding of religious practice arising out of historically situated power structures. Clifford Geertz's descriptive definition of religion has been influential in the social-scientific study of religion and it describes religion, in sum, as:

> 1) a set of symbols which acts to 2) establish powerful, pervasive and long-lasting moods and motivations in men by 3) formulating conceptions of a general order of existence and 4) clothing these conceptions with such an

---

[11] See Smith, "A Stumbling Block to the Jews and Folly to the Greeks," for a more detailed discussion of the structure of the philosophical decision.

[12] Gilles Deleuze and Félix Guattari, *What is Philosophy?*, trans. Hugh Tomlinson and Graham Burchell (New York: Columbia University Press, 1994), 43, 60.

[13] Ibid, 38, 44.

[14] Ibid, 43.

aura of factuality that 5) the moods and motivations seem uniquely realistic.[15]

This "thick description" of religion, despite its attempts to move beyond reductive definitions, is ultimately a form of thinking of religion as a universal category. Talal Asad, in his essay on Geertz, shows how Geertz's universal description relies on the image of religion that Western religions provide, ultimately focusing on the notion of belief and the way religions provide a kind of optic through which its believers perceive the world. Asad does not go on to offer a better universal definition (descriptive or otherwise), instead he suggests that we need only return to the particularity of religions in their particular constitution as "products of historically distinct disciplines and forces."[16] The anthropologist should not be concerned with subsuming religion under a universal category, but only with treating religion as a particular site of forces. In summary, for Geertz religion determines the perspective of a particular believer and thus the way that particular believer will act in a certain situation. Belief determines act, which in turn determines the structures that make up human society. For Asad, religion has no universal definition, but is the product of different local disciplines and forces that exist as relative within the same discursive field as politics and economics.

This debate in anthropology maps on to the two instances of philosophical self-defence, giving credence to Laruelle's repeated claim that the scientific character of the human sciences is compromised in its philosophical filiations.[17] This is further supported by Asad's own research where he shows the roots of the anthropological definition of religion in that strand of philosophy of religion culminating in Locke and Kant.[18] Ultimately neither philosophers nor anthropologists are concerned, as Laruelle is, with the *radical* immanence of Man, but rather with the formation, potential transformation, and thus degradation of that radical immanence. The individuation of Man is seen via Authorities and not from the Minority solitude of Man from his World. Stated otherwise, there is,

---

[15] Clifford Geertz, "Religion as a Cultural System" in *The Interpretation of Cultures* (New York: Basic Books, 1973), 90.

[16] Talal Asad, *Genealogies of Religion: Discipline and Reasons of Power in Christianity and Islam* (Baltimore: The Johns Hopkins University Press, 1993), 54.

[17] See François Laruelle, *Une Biographie de l'homme ordinaire. Des Autorités et des Minorités* (Paris: Aubier, 1985), 7-38. There he remarks that, "Man has never been the object of the human Sciences" (8). Rather Man is subsumed into some other aspect of the World (which he calls Authorities) in the search for a logic of man (the anthropo-logical is the amphibology of logic and Man).

[18] Asad, *Genealogies of Religion*, 40-43.

for both philosophers and anthropologists, a confusion of Man with the World. Thus Janicaud's minimalist phenomenology seeks to protect itself from religion by ascribing to religion the same status as the natural attitude; it is an unscientific and therefore unphenomenological perspective. But Janicaud's phenomenology is left defenceless in the face of the real threat to the absolute autonomy of philosophical practice. It is not religious beliefs, but the shared radical immanence of the Real which determines-in-the-last-instance the production of religion just as it determines the production of philosophy, while granting relative autonomy to both. In short, Janicaud's immanence is not a real immanence, but only an immanence as irreal.

Asad's position roughly maps on to that of Deleuze and Guattari. It differs, of course, as Asad is closer to Foucault than to the particular character of Deleuze and Guattari's minoritarian philosophy, but both posit an immanent field of forces from which religion is produced. Immanence here is absolute as the site of both conflict and construction; there is not outside to immanence but only an immanent outside; immanence is both prephilosophical and unthought while still within philosophy and thought. When religion is plunged into the plane of immanence, does it tell us anything about Man in his radical immanence, let alone about religion's minority identity? In regard to this local question and following their own pronouncements about religion, Deleuze and Guattari's plane of immanence becomes, within the regional discursive field of religion, a figure of transcendence that subsumes the real identity of religion within figures of authority, casting it, at its core, as merely an instance of the authorities alone.[19] Even those few instances of religious philosophy they celebrate, where belief in God is separated from concern for God's existence, exist only to serve the plane of immanence by opening it up and recharging our ability to once again attempt to think it in the face of the chaos which remains (immanently) outside of it.[20] Yet this very conception of immanence, which excludes religion for philosophy,

---

[19] See Philip Goodchild, *Gilles Deleuze and the Problem of Philosophy* (London: Associated University Presses, 1996), 154-162. Goodchild's critical appraisal of the absolute character of Deleuze and Guattari's plane of immanence shares much in common with Laruelle's. See François Laruelle, "Response to Deleuze", trans. Taylor Adkins *Pli* 20 (2009): 138-164. My own reading of Deleuze and Guattari is more sympathetic than Laruelle's, though I agree in this instance they fail to think immanently about religion. For my own reading where I try to locate when Deleuze and Guattari's philosophy succeeds in thinking from immanence, see Anthony Paul Smith, "Believing in this World for the Making of Gods: On the Ecology of the Actual and the Virtual", *SubStance* 38.3 (April 2010): 101-112.

[20] See Deleuze and Guattari, *What is Philosophy?*, 74, 92.

threatens Deleuze and Guattari's philosophy with the loss of immanence, for they would then fall foul of their own critique of religion. For them, Spinoza becomes Christ *for the philosophers*, rather than Christ becoming a name for any Future Man, and in this way they set up one Imperial Christic-philosophical State over the others, one philosophical faith upon the plane of immanence. If Spinoza is the Christ for one people (the philosophers), then this philosophy of absolute immanence becomes a kind of "over-Church", the organon for the Principle of Sufficient Church, which plagues these majoritarian forms of religion.[21] One must become as if Sons of Spinoza in order to be free. One must become a Greek-Jew, bringing together the Greek forms of philosophy where immanence is agon, with the Jewish figure of Spinoza and his absolute immanence. Insofar as all of Western philosophy shares this amphibology between Greek and Jewish thought, the difference that Deleuze and Guattari try to construct by subsuming religion into the plane of immanence only serves to elide the fact that this form of philosophy is already, at its core, compromised with the theological imperative to repeat anew the words of the faith.

III. The Radical Immanence of Non-Philosophy

Laruelle's non-philosophy is situated within immanence, though it aims to short-circuit the rivalry between phenomenology and the modern tradition by making them equivalent in their identity as philosophy.[22] This making equivalent of all philosophy is extended in Laruelle's later work to a making equivalent of all forms of Authority, and this requires thinking within and from immanence. He differentiates the radical immanence of non-philosophy from the "misadventures" of philosophical immanence stating, "In philosophy, Marxism included, immanence is an objective, a proclamation, an object; never a manner or style of thinking."[23] Immanence loses its radial character in philosophy because it becomes confused with philosophy's ultimate object, Being, which takes on a transcendent aspect. According to Laruelle, even for Spinoza, the real causality of immanence "remains inscribed... in the transcendence of a quasi-thing above consciousness or man", just as, for Henry, material phenomenology's immanence slips into an Absolute immanence of auto-affective Life that

---

[21] See François Laruelle, *Le Christ futur. Une leçon d'hérésie* (Paris: Exils Éditeur, 2002), 81-84.

[22] "My problem: how to be neither Greek nor Jew? Only science can render all philosophies equivalent." (Laruelle, *En tant qu'Un*, 253)

[23] François Laruelle, *Introduction au non-marxisme* (Paris: PUF, 2000), 40.

elides and excludes real causality.[24] In distinction to these two forms of immanence, which map roughly to the two forms of immanence we've discussed above (Spinoza: Deleuze/Guattari, obviously, and Janicaud: Henry, less obviously—though the difference here lies in the scope of what a "thing" is), Laruelle's radical immanence creates a unified theory of these two errant forms of immanence describing itself as radical immanence (like Henry, contrary to Spinoza) but real and not transcendental (like Spinoza, contrary to Henry).[25]

The posture or style of thought that Laruelle's non-philosophy engages in is thinking *from* or *according to* immanence, rather than *of* immanence. Thus it is radical immanence because it begins from the only actual experience—this one. This postural immanence is given the name of Man-in-person, which locates thought within the radical immanence (of) self. This postural immanence is derived from the axioms of non-philosophy that mark it off from philosophy as such. If, as Laruelle claims, "Philosophy is defined and delimited by two 'confusions' which form a system: of the real-One with Being and of thought with logic"[26], then non-philosophy is marked by a rejection of the philosophical forgetting of the real-One and of locating thought in-the-Real as the power of theory.[27] Ultimately, non-philosophy's appeal to radical immanence "is no longer about philosophically changing metaphysics but rather changing our gaze [*regard*] or our 'vision' of it."[28] The axiom that radically orients non-philosophy is that the One in its radical immanence is prior to both thought and Being and they in turn are determined-in-the-last-instance by the One. This style of thinking is given the name unilateralization and dualysis, a dual method of thinking via a "vision-in-One" performed on the various dualities that are found in philosophy and religion. In every duality, each term must be given equivalent relative autonomy that in-the-last-instance is determined by the radical immanence of the One as either non(-One) or (non-)One. The first term refers to those aspects that are philosophically named "transcendence", for they too are equivalent as real but only in-immanence, while the second term refers to the term that names radical immanence but is still not the One in its radical immanence. This dual non(-One)/(non-)One character does not structure any phenomenon whatsoever=X, but is the (non-)One structure of every dualism in-the-last-

[24] Ibid, 41.
[25] Ibid, 42.
[26] François Laruelle, *Principes de la non-philosophie* (Paris: PUF, 1996), 173.
[27] Ibid, 174.
[28] Ibid, 225.

instance. It is the condition for the *individual* character of every actual thing (and everything is actual and real in-the-last-instance).[29]

IV. The Non-Philosophical Identity of Religion

Laruelle's "science of philosophy" is often misunderstood by philosophers, even those friendly to Laruelle's vision, to be an outright assault on philosophy; non-philosophy is confused with anti-philosophy. Alain Badiou, upon being asked about Laruelle's work in an interview, remarked that:

> I have difficulty in understanding Laruelle [laughs] especially regarding the Question of the Real. The strength of philosophy is its decisions in regards to the Real… Beyond this, and not to judge a thinker by his earliest work, his recent work has a religious dimension. When you say something is purely in the historical existence of philosophy the proposition is a failure. It becomes religious. There is a logical constraint when you say we must go beyond philosophy. This why, in the end, Heidegger said only a God can save us.[30]

Let us set aside both the incoherence of some of Badiou's remarks considering his own interactions with religion and the usually frustrating (for philosophers) response of non-philosophers that of course Badiou, as a philosopher, has difficulty understanding Laruelle's non-philosophy. Taken outside of its polemical context this remark remains instructive insofar as it identifies a religious dimension at work in non-philosophy. Badiou isn't merely addressing Laruelle's work on religion, but making a claim that there is a religious aspect underlying the practice of non-philosophy itself. I think he is right, though I have difficulty understanding Badiou's critique, and so think he is right by accident and that the consequences of this religious character (really a theological character) are radically different than what Badiou suggests.

---

[29] It is difficult to express in a single word the meaning of *individual* in English as Laruelle differentiates *individual* from *individuel*. The first is a neologism of his own construction playing on the sense of "dual" in order to express the fundamental duality of individuals and the second is the term that is usually translated into English as individual, but he plays with the "duel", which means the same in English as it does in French, to signify that it is a fundamentally antagonistic concept. See Laruelle, *Biographie*, 17.

[30] Alain Badiou, interview with Ben Woodward, "Badiou on Speculative Realism". Available online: <http://speculativeheresy.wordpress.com/2009/08/21/badiou-on-speculative-realism/>. Accessed 01/02/2010.

Laruelle does not run scared from religion nor does he build a wall of absolute demarcation between philosophy and religious thought. While he does not hold back when critiquing philosophers, even those like Deleuze and Levinas for whom he nevertheless expresses a great deal of respect, Laruelle equally does not let religion go by without an equal amount of vitriol. For if philosophy operates with a kind of theoreticism that denigrates Man, religions are the site of terror, for they provide all sorts of hallucinatory justifications for the murder of Man from an imagined transcendent source. Laruelle thus shares much with Asad and Deleuze and Guattari in terms of his understanding of religion. Religion is a construction of forces, yes, and these forces ultimately point to a real *human* cause of religious practices, but religion cannot be understood via a universal category captured by a description, thick or otherwise. For the operation of non-philosophy upon religion does not aim to merely describe religion anymore than it aims to eliminate or protect it in the name of either a liberated philosophy or an enslaved philosophy. Instead, non-philosophy aims at appropriating religion: "Axioms and theorems, these are our methods, us men-without-philosophy, so that we can appropriate religion and adapt the divine mysteries to our humanity rather than to our understanding."[31]

Importantly, this method does not involve blending philosophy and religion together, but treats them as relatively autonomous within a unilateral duality. Laruelle must deal with religion, for religion is actual and thus Real, but also because religion has been the *occasion* and *material* of struggle against Worldly Authorities: "The paradox is that it is above all from the side of the religious reality, in its dualysis, that the *occasion* finds itself for an emergence of subjects as Futures."[32] In the construction, not of *the* future, but of human Futures (like Moderns or Ancients), religion appears in world history as an instance where human beings, not gods, struggle in-immanence with and for the World. In his *Le Christ futur*, Laruelle aims to make use of the specificity of Christian religious material to first alter the practice of philosophy by introducing the experience of heresy into philosophy, and then to perform a non-philosophical operation on religion to put it to human use. He locates what is different between philosophy and religion via the same non-philosophical dualysis—that is, in terms of the relationship between their Authorities and Minorities:

---

[31] Laruelle, *Le Christ futur,* 31.

[32] François Laruelle, *Mystique non-philosophique à l'usage des contemporains* (Paris: L'Harmattan, 2007), 33.

There is a difference here from philosophical systems that are partitioned according to the dominant (but not unique) axes of truth and appearance (or illusion from the point of view which has as an object the theory of that partition), for a religion has as its principle or dominant difference that of orthodoxy's division, from the rigour of orthology (as the policing of opinions or dogmas) and heresy, which it sometimes mixes with the philosophical that it anyhow cuts again.[33]

For, in the duality between Authority and Minority, heresy becomes the organon of radical immanence determining in-the-last-instance the human identity of religion.

Thus, religions are not only sites of Authority, though this is their non(-One) aspect, but they are also, in their particularity, *occasional causes* for human struggle, struggles as Minorities. This aspect of religion is obscured insofar as philosophers of religion tend to focus on the orthodox aspects of any particular religion. Even when a philosopher aims for a radical critique of religion or a radical appropriation (as in Badiou's own work on St. Paul), they do not look to the victims of religion, to the *religious* victims of religion decried as heretics by the orthodox. Instead, they play with the orthodox material, ignoring the heretical material, even if they are unconcerned themselves with falling into heresy. This is why Laruelle, in his own non-philosophical working with religious material, gives a great deal of attention to the various strains of thought called Gnosticism. For, though Christian philosophers and theologians may identify all aspects of modern Western society with Gnosticism, there are no actual Gnostics left in the World. The "Gnostic question" prefigures the "Jewish question" and shares with it the fact that, for both questions, the answer from the side of orthodoxy was found in fire. Thus, in the unilateral duality of religion, where the dualism is one between Authorities and Minorities, orthodoxy and heresy, it is always the heretic, as subject-in-struggle and not merely a passive victim, that determines-in-the-last-instance the identity of the particular religion that non-philosophy may then work with. In short, non-philosophy demands a unilateral thinking from the subject-in-struggle, rather than the victim or the orthodox.

Rather than philosophically working out problems inherent to certain religious thoughts, Laruelle gives "first names" to identify these occasions of the Real (that is, their identity as Minority) within a particular religion. This, then, is the meaning of that strange appellation "Future Christ": from the material of religion non-philosophy removes "the future" from its inscription in a Time-World, inscribed as it is within a philosophically

---

[33] Laruelle, *Le Christ futur*, 44.

determined understanding of the future. Instead Laruelle inscribes the future in the radical immanence of Man. The future is given its identity only as it is "lived without purpose", a future radically immanent (to) anyone and thus without telos as a subject formed in that radical immanence.[34] This appellation is derived from three sources that are blended within "the-Christianity", or Christianity as formed by the Authorities or orthodox, which are separated via a non-philosophical naming of them:

> The first is the properly Gnostic experience of the definition of man by the primacy of knowledge over faith, an untaught or unlearned knowledge that we must radicalise as Man-in-person, Lived-without-life or even as the Real. The second is the more general heretical aspect, of the separation with the World, here extended and universalized beyond its Christian and even Gnostic aspects. The third is the specifically Christian aspect of universal salvation, for the World and for every man, that works through the person of Christ, which we must also radicalize in a Christ-subject.[35]

In this sketch of Laruelle's working with religion and philosophy the particular power of non-philosophy is revealed. For there is certainly a wild, heretical freedom at work that offends the scholarly tone of philosophy of religion and the piety of theologians patiently working out the Truth through faith and/over reason, and this heretical freedom comes from non-philosophy's beginning from axioms derived from the real-One, rather than from the philosophical history of Being or Alterity. But, non-philosophy's declaration of the One also restrains non-philosophical naming and provides it with a certain amount of theoretical rigour as that naming must, by the very same axioms, work through the material as *actually* given.

In his incredibly clear introduction to non-philosophy, Jean-Luc Rannou remarks that non-philosophy has the singular ability to respond not only to transcendental questions like "What is religion?" but also to those singular questions like "What is the Qur'an?"[36] Non-philosophy has this generic ability because it aims to think equivalently as both science and philosophy, theology and philosophy, art and philosophy, erotics and philosophy and it calls these equivalencies "unified theories" that perform

---

[34] See Ibid, 47.
[35] Ibid.
[36] Jean-Luc Rannou, *La non-philosophie, simplement. Une introduction synthétique* (Paris: L'Harmattan, 2005), 114.

a real democracy (of) thought.[37] This is the task before any philosophy of religion separated from its authoritarian form, a philosophy of religion that is non-philosophical, to consider both generic religion (rather than religion subsumed into a universal category) and occasional particulars (like Christ and the Qur'an) from within the radical immanence of Man determined-in-the-last-instance by the Real.

To conclude this essay I want to step back from expositing Laruelle's method and consider the possibility of a non-theology as both the name of a non-philosophical philosophy of religion and as a science of non-philosophy. The first is obvious enough and follows Laruelle's own limited remarks on the possibility of a non-theology. He calls non-philosophy "a human mathematics", a formulation he opposes to "Leibniz's conception of philosophy as a 'divine mathematics'."[38] From non-philosophy springs a number of new possibilities for thought, one of which he calls "non-theological". This non-theological thought appears to be essentially what I've described above: a thinking of religious material under the aspect of Man in his radical immanence as minority, an "inversion of the philosophies of transcendence and of the divine call", the construction of a future against and for the World, etc.[39] The point here is to use religious material to challenge philosophical practice and to transform the material of religion so that it is not longer a golem, but once again any material whatsoever.

V. A Non-Theological Coda: Or, Non-Theology as the Science of Non-Philosophy

By naming a non-philosophical philosophy of religion non-theology I am indicating that non-theology should begin with the same axioms as non-philosophy. However, it has to deal with the theological material that infects philosophy of religion *as* theological material and in turn create axioms in response to them. It is here where non-theology becomes a name for the science of non-philosophy. Laruelle began the work of non-

---

[37] It goes without saying that his democracy is real and transcendental to any kind of form of representational democracy which remains subsumed in politics rather than enacting any kind of real democracy. See Rannou, *La non-philosophie*, 76.

[38] François Laruelle, "A New Presentation of Non-Philosophy", working paper, L'Organisation Non-Philosophique Internationale, February 11th, 2004. Available online: <http://www.onphi.net/texte-a-new-presentation-of-non-philosophy-32.html>. Accessed 01/02/2010.

[39] Ibid.

philosophy by first locating, and then taking a heretical stance towards, the principle of sufficient philosophy. This principle, Laruelle tells us, lies at the core of philosophy more so than any other philosophical principle (such as the principle of sufficient reason) and is, in itself, not a philosophical principle at all insofar as philosophy is unable to see it. The principle of sufficient philosophy lies outside of philosophy's vision much in the same way that Narcissus does not see the pool that reflects his image back to him. It is thus only non-philosophy's refusal of this principle that brings it into vision. As already discussed in the Introduction, the principle of sufficient philosophy can be summed up in the belief that everything is philosophisable. In this way philosophy gives itself a fundamental or necessary status in the discourses in which it shares (philosophy of art, political philosophy, philosophy of science, philosophy of religion, etc.). Laruelle has said time and time again that non-philosophy does not aim to overcome or destroy philosophy. The principle of sufficient philosophy is merely identified as a fact about philosophy which may explain its many failures and that, once identified and turned into material, may be used in other ways as well. It is, as such, simple material for future human use.

Laruelle, we have seen, attempts to use this material while thinking according to the Real, seeing through the vision-in-One according to and not about the Real. In this way, the Real appears to take on a quasi-divine character in so far as the Real can only be described via axioms. The nature of an axiom, however, is that it is fundamental for some system but cannot itself be proven directly. One must simply work out the system from the consequences of the axiom upon the material presented and its validity will be given if the system works.[40] Yet this axiomatic approach is the only way to actually refuse the philosophical decision as it makes the decision relative to the Real. This method decides nothing, rendering everything equivalent before the Real, finally escaping from the principle of sufficient philosophy as it throws itself prostrate before the Real—non-philosophy has and recognizes its limits.[41]

There nevertheless remains a temptation to philosophise, for who can think according to the Real and not ask about the nature of the Real itself?

---

[40] Janicaud's criticism of the theological turn as beginning from a method of "take it or leave it" suggests an axiomatic character to the theological turn as well and so suggests that Laruelle is infected by the same philosophical illness as Henry and Marion.

[41] This is one of the most refreshing aspects of Laruelle's passage from Philosophy I to IV, the up-front recognition of his own works' failures and inadequacies as non-philosophy is continually performed anew in the light of new material. See Laruelle, *Principes*, 19-42.

Such is a temptation to heresy, but also to orthodox codification; that is, it is *a temptation to theology*. Laruelle's axioms become, as is suggested in his *Le Christ futur,* a form of unlearned knowledge [*savoir indocte*], differentiated from the learned ignorance of Nicholas of Cusa. Unlearned knowledge is not mystical obfuscation, but the unlearned knowledge of the Real that is radically immanent in Man-in-person and from which one necessarily proceeds. There is then a similarity one may draw between non-philosophy's method and theology. Theology has its own self-sufficient problem analogous to philosophy's—the principle of sufficient theology. This is different from philosophy's narcissism and may find some elucidation by a comparison with the other figure in the myth of Narcissus, the nymph Echo.

The history of all theology hitherto has been that of the interplay between echo and control (the figure of Hera). Theology, it is often said, has no object proper. It is simultaneously simply in the service of the central event of faith (for Christianity the death and resurrection of Jesus Christ), claiming to merely echo that event, while also its complex task has been to codify the truth of that event into some sort of universal doctrine. The Creeds perform this function of theological determination brilliantly as a perfect instance of learned ignorance.[42] The Creeds respond to the historical heresies, and one may generalize about heresy by claiming that, in contradistinction to orthodoxy, they always say too much, either making a claim to learned knowing or to radical gnosis (Laruelle himself discerns this very difference between his unlearned knowledge and the principle of sufficient heresy).[43] At the same time, the Creeds go on to say quite a bit, all of it very learned, which is to say, with Laruelle, all very Greek and sometimes, though very rarely, Jewish, but all of it quite ignorant of the radical immanence of Man. Echo and control is learned ignorance.

Non-philosophy appears to mimic theology in its thinking from the Real and not of it. Simply replace the Real with the name of God. Theology thinks from God and not of God (in the same way that philosophy would think of God). Theology cannot think of God without first thinking from God and in this way theology is an axiomatic practice like non-philosophy. Yet it is this very axiomatic aspect of theology's practice that underlies its principle of sufficient theology where everything is theologisable because theology's non-object, God, is related or even

---

[42] See Philip Goodchild, *Capitalism and Religion: The Price of Piety* (London: Routledge, 2002), 51-57. Here Goodchild traces the ways that the Christian Creeds were codified into a "metaphysical, universal, eternal spiritual and written" truth that could then be exchanged across cultures (53).
[43] See Laruelle, *Le Christ futur*, 173-176.

meta-related to everything that is. In non-philosophy's methodological cloning of theology, how does it avoid its own self-sufficiency? The principle of sufficient theology is clearly in a different register than philosophy's self-sufficiency principle in that it does not claim to have a privileged place in the thinking of everything *self*-sufficiently, but as auto-donation of Divine sufficiency from its own notion of the Real. Laruelle suggests in *Le Christ futur* that it is the figure of the heretic that must be taken up and that the Gnostic Christ is a model of heresy. Yet, the historical Christ reportedly wanted to draw all things unto himself, and, as we have seen, Laruelle locates this universal salvation as one of the sources of his appellation "Future Christ". Can one still have this sort of theological universal, even as cloned in non-religion (whatever that may come to really look like), and avoid theology's principle of sufficient theology? Does not, then, non-philosophy need to be unified with non-theology in order, then, to overcome the temptation to this principle?

Non-theology thus follows Gnosticism in rejecting the so-called paradoxical dialectic of faith and knowledge, which always obscures the real dialectic of echo and control. It posits a radical gnosis in Man-in-person, but in so doing it subjects this gnosis of the real-One to the non-theological ultimatum that non-philosophy remain generic (with the making equivalent of non-philosophy and theology the organon of this ultimatum). This remaining generic means that a unified non-theology and non-philosophy constitutes a real secularity (of) thought open to further mutations of non-philosophy's axioms. In short, for non-philosophy to transform the practice of philosophy of religion, Laruelle must become as if a Church Father, but within a discursive field where there are only Church Fathers and where anyone may be a Future Christ.

Bibliography

Asad, Talal. *Genealogies of Religion: Discipline and Reasons of Power in Christianity and Islam.* Baltimore and London: The Johns Hopkins University Press, 1993.

Badiou, Alain. Interview with Ben Woodward. "Badiou on Speculative Realism". Available online: <http://speculativeheresy.wordpress.com/2009/08/21/badiou-on-speculative-realism/>. Accessed 01/02/2010.

Deleuze, Gilles and Félix Guattari, *What is Philosophy?* Translated by Hugh Tomlinson and Graham Burchell. New York: Columbia University Press, 1994.

Geertz, Clifford. "Religion as a Cultural System." In *The Interpretation of Cultures*. New York: Basic Books, 1973.

Goodchild, Philip. *Gilles Deleuze and the Problem of Philosophy*. London: Associated University Presses, 1996.

—. *Capitalism and Religion: The Price of Piety*. London: Routledge, 2002.

Hägglund, Martin. *Radical Atheism: Derrida and the Time of Life*. Stanford: Stanford University Press, 2008.

Janicaud, Dominique. *Phenomenology "Wide Open": After the French Debate*. Translated by Charles N. Cabral. New York: Fordham University Press, 2005.

Laruelle, François. *Une Biographie de l'homme ordinaire. Des Autorités et des Minorités*. Paris: Aubier, 1985.

—. *En tant qu'Un. La « non-philosophie » expliquée aux philosophes*. Paris: Aubier, 1991.

—. *Principes de la non-philosophie*. Paris: PUF, 1996.

—. *Introduction au non-marxisme*. Paris: PUF, 2000.

—. *Le Christ futur. Une leçon d'hérésie*. Paris: Exils Éditeur, 2002.

—. "A New Presentation of Non-Philosophy". Working paper. L'Organisation Non-Philosophique Internationale, February 11th, 2004. Available online: <http://www.onphi.net/texte-a-new-presentation-of-non-philosophy-32.html>. Accessed 01/02/2010.

—. *Mystique non-philosophique à l'usage des contemporains*. Paris: L'Harmattan, 2007.

Mullarkey, John. *Post-Continental Philosophy: An Outline*. London: Continuum, 2006.

Naas, Michael. "Derrida's *Laïcité*." In *Derrida From Now On*. New York: Fordham University Press, 2008.

Rannou, Jean-Luc. *La non-philosophie, simplement. Une introduction synthétique*. Paris: L'Harmattan, 2005.

Smith, Anthony Paul. "Believing in this World for the Making of Gods: On the Ecology of the Actual and the Virtual." *SubStance* 38.3 (April 2010): 101-112.

—. "A Stumbling Block to the Jews and Folly to the Greeks: Non-Philosophy and Philosophy's Absolutes." *Analecta Hermeneutica* 3 (Forthcoming 2011).

CHAPTER FIFTEEN

THE PLASTICITY OF CONTINENTAL PHILOSOPHY OF RELIGION

CLAYTON CROCKETT

This chapter offers a constructive reading of the contemporary French philosopher Catherine Malabou and her notion of plasticity. Plasticity is understood as the ability to give and to receive form, as well as the annihilation of form itself. Malabou derives her understanding of plasticity from Hegel, and she applies it to contemporary neurology and the ideas of neuroplasticity. I suggest that thinking about religion in terms of plasticity is a fruitful and potentially productive pursuit, and it counters the broadly messianic understandings of religion in earlier forms of Continental philosophy of religion. Before turning directly to Malabou's work, then, I want to contextualise the history of Continental philosophy of religion, and then show where I think Malabou's philosophy is significantly relevant. I will show how Continental philosophy of religion emerges in relation to Derrida's so-called religious turn, which is also a political turn, and how it then shifts from predominantly focusing on Derrida and Levinas to engaging with the philosophy of Slavoj Žižek, Alain Badiou and to some extent Antonio Negri. In some ways, these newer forms of Continental philosophy argue for a Christian and/or Jewish exceptionalism, despite their evident atheism, which plasticity allows us to get beyond. I will draw out some implications of Malabou's philosophy, partly in relation to Jean-Luc Nancy, and conclude with a consideration of how plasticity helps us better think about religion.

I.

A Continental philosophy of religion emerged in the 1990s, following Derrida's so-called religious 'turn,' although this shift in emphasis was also a political turn in many respects. In 1989, Derrida published his

influential essay, "Force of Law: The Mystical Foundation of Authority."
This essay, presented in English at a conference on "Deconstruction and
the Possibility of Justice" at Cardozo Law School in New York, directly
addresses the criticisms that deconstruction has nothing to do with ethics,
morality, law and justice. Derrida distinguishes between law and justice in
this essay, by appealing to the complexity of the term right, in French
droit. Right here refers both to the justice or rightness of a law, as well as
the status of positive law, including the ability to enforce a law. Strikingly,
Derrida aligns deconstruction with justice, where justice is the ungrounded
promise or horizon of any determinate law. Justice is ungrounded, it rests
upon no stable foundation, and the institution of law itself is a kind of
mystical event.

Derrida affirms that "deconstruction is justice," insofar as justice is
undeconstructible, whereas law is always and necessarily deconstructible.[1]
Deconstruction works between law and justice, but it is on the side of
justice, or works in the name of a justice that can never be fully
encapsulated or expressed in law, but rather makes law itself possible. The
fact that justice is in some respects "infinite" leads it directly to issues of
religion, and here Derrida's later philosophy resonates with Levinas: "I
would be tempted, up to a certain point, to bring the concept of justice—
which I am here trying to distinguish from law—closer to Levinas'. I
would do so just because of this infinity and because of the heteronomic
relation to the other [*autrui*], to the face of the other that commands me,
whose infinity I cannot thematise and whose hostage I am."[2] Religion,
then, or even God, would indicate the desire for justice which is itself
undeconstructible, even if every particular religious tradition is
deconstructible.

In the second half of "Force of Law," which was not presented at the
Cardozo conference, Derrida gives a reading of Walter Benjamin's essay
"Critique of Violence." The German word for violence is *Gewalt*, which
means force, but it is not immediately clear whether this force is legitimate
or illegitimate force, and Benjamin plays with this in-distinction. A few
years later, in *Specters of Marx*, published in French in 1993 and translated
into English in 1994, Derrida develops a reading of Marx that makes use
of Benjamin's idea of a weak messianic power, taken from his important
essay, "Theses on the Philosophy of History." Derrida argues that a
spectre haunts the triumph of Western-style democratic capitalism in the
wake of the collapse of the USSR. Derrida develops a "hauntology" in

---

[1] Jacques Derrida, "Force of Law: The Mystical Foundation of Authority," in *Acts
of Religion*, ed. Gil Anidjar (London: Routledge, 2002), 243.
[2] Ibid, 250.

which the ghosts of Marx and others continue to haunt philosophical and political discourse, just as Marx was haunted by his own ghosts (as Marx reveals in his critique of Max Stirner in *The German Ideology*). We can never exorcise the messianic eschatology of the formal structure of the promise that exceeds all content. Deconstruction is this weak messianic power, because it attends to the survival of these ghostly promises. "What remains irreducible to any deconstruction," Derrida claims,

> what remains as undeconstructible as the possibility itself of deconstruction is, perhaps, a certain experience of the emancipatory promise; it is perhaps even the formality of a structural messianism, a messianism without religion, even a messianic without messianism, an idea of justice—which we distinguish from law or right and even from human rights—and an idea of democracy—which we distinguish from its current concept and from its determined predicates today.[3]

The spirit of emancipatory Marxism is religious, or messianic, in some respects, even if it is not religious or messianic in a positive or determinate sense. And this spirit is also the spirit of deconstruction.

Derrida's later work is marked by this shift of emphasis, but it is not really a turn away from or towards something in the sense that his whole philosophy changes. For many reasons, Derrida emphasizes these political and religious aspects of deconstruction in the 1990s, but there were traces already in his earlier work. In any case, however one reads the trajectory of Derrida's philosophy, my claim is that the political and religious aspects of this shift are inseparable, and it is this shift itself that opens up what we can recognize as a distinct Continental philosophy of religion, most notably in the work of John D. Caputo. In the mid-1990s, as philosophers moved away from more conventional analytic approaches to religion (and sometimes what we could call post-analytic, inspired by broadly Wittgensteinian themes), and theologians backed away from some of the more radical aspects of postmodern theology, Derrida's opening to religion, as thematised in Caputo's magisterial book *The Prayers and Tears of Jacques Derrida*, became the predominant force for thinking about religion in postmodern terms. Derrida was not the only locus of this conversation, but he was probably the most prominent, with Levinas a close second.

Caputo brought Derrida to Villanova University a number of times for what became celebrated conferences on "Religion and Postmodernism."

---

[3] Jacques Derrida, *Specters of Marx: The State of the Debt, The Work of Mourning, & the New International*, trans. Peggy Kamuf (New York: Routledge, 1994), 59.

Derrida and Caputo engaged with religious and theological interpretations of Levinas, and representatives of what became known as the New Phenomenology of religion, including Jean-Luc Marion, Michel Henry, Jean-Louis Chretien, Jean-Yves Lacoste, and others. Important English-speaking philosophers of religion included Merold Westphal, Richard Kearney, William Desmond and Kevin Hart. These conferences and debates gave rise to a Society of Continental Philosophy and Theology, which has held four conferences since 2003. While these discussions have been important, what was lost was the political urgency that informed Derrida's engagement with religion.

Around the turn of the century, however, Continental philosophy's political turn became more apparent in the English-speaking world, as the theoretical coma induced by the victory over communism and the explosive growth of the US stock market wore off. New Continental philosophers emerged who were more difficult to fit into the label of postmodernism such as Slavoj Žižek, Alain Badiou, and Antonio Negri. In some ways, these thinkers distinguished themselves by their criticisms of postmodernism, especially Badiou and Žižek, while in others they still seemed symptomatic of postmodernism more generally. These philosophers also wrote about religion in provocative and interesting ways, even if they claimed to be atheists.

Many scholars and students of religion, religious studies and radical theology interested in Continental thought turned towards these figures in the early 2000s, especially Žižek. Žižek has consistently engaged with religious themes throughout his career, but this aspect of his work became most explicit with the publication of *The Fragile Absolute* in 2000 and *The Puppet and the Dwarf* in 2003. The subtitles, "Why the Christian Legacy is Worth Fighting For," and "The Perverse Core of Christianity," respectively, show the relevance of these books for religion and theology. In these works, Žižek argues for a Christian atheism that best captures the radically subversive nature of what Christianity really represents: the gap or separation between God and humanity is not what is essential, but rather the gap within the divine, which is the same gap that resides within humanity. "We are one with God only when God is no longer one with Himself, but abandons Himself, 'internalizes' the radical distance that separates us from Him. Our radical experience of separation from God is the very feature that unites us with Him."[4] Žižek claims not that God exists, but that the experience of a separation internal to God equates to a radical separation within human beings, and when understood and

---

[4] Slavoj Žižek, *The Puppet and the Dwarf: The Perverse Core of Christianity* (Cambridge: MIT Press, 2003), 91.

deployed this becomes a potent political force. Žižek applies results of Lacanian psychoanalysis to Christianity and Judaism, as well as popular culture, German idealism from Kant to Hegel, and an idiosyncratic Marxist-Leninist reading of politics and capital. The result produces dizzying but highly insightful and entertaining readings, and Žižek's rock star popularity in academic terms brought a great deal of attention to his work, which then also rewarded careful philosophical interpretation. Žižek criticized the excesses and blindspots of postmodernism and its celebration of diversity and multiculturalism, although in many respects his work can be read in continuity with other so-called postmodern thinkers.

At the same time, Žižek discussed, advocated, and helped introduce the philosophy of Alain Badiou to a wider English-speaking audience, and this process was accelerated with the translation of Badiou's provocative book *Saint Paul: The Foundation of Universalism* in 2003. Badiou, like Žižek, does not believe in the existence of God or the literal truth of Christianity, but he also suggests that there is a conceptual core that is revolutionary and powerful, and Badiou locates this core in the teaching of Paul. Paul shows us what it means to have fidelity to an event, and this fidelity brings a new universal subject into being by overcoming death configured as sin. Sin is revealed by the law, but to overcome sin and death one must overthrow the law. This is what resurrection means: to bring a subject to life in a mode of faith beyond the confines of the law and the gap that the law introduces between desire and its object. According to Badiou, "the word *pistis* (faith, or conviction) designates precisely this point: the absence of any gap between subject and subjectivation. In this absence of a gap, which constantly activates the subject in the service of truth, forbidding him rest, the One-truth proceeds in the direction of all."[5]

Badiou, like Žižek, develops an understanding of the revolutionary force of Christianity, by reading it in Lacanian psychoanalytic terms, and attending to both its theoretical and political significance. Both dismiss the truth of Christianity on its own dogmatic terms as irrelevant to the formal truth of Christian universalism, understood as atheism. To put it in terms of Lacan, the big Other (God) does not exist, but that does not mean that it still does not exert effects upon human life and culture. Christianity precisely reveals that this Other/God doesn't exist, despite the fact that most Christians claim otherwise, but belief in God has important theoretical and political implications. The Christian atheism of Žižek and Badiou provides a more materialist and political understanding of human

---

[5] Alain Badiou, *Saint Paul: The Foundation of Universalism*, trans. Ray Brassier (Stanford: Stanford University Press, 2003), 81.

existence, but one that still argues for the significance of religion and religious discourse.[6]

Antonio Negri does not explicitly argue for a Christian atheism, but in his philosophical and political works, including the books he has co-authored with Michael Hardt, *Empire* (2000) and *Multitude* (2004), Negri adopts religious or quasi-religious language and terms in his efforts to elaborate a revitalized language for communism. Negri's thought is influenced by Gilles Deleuze, but whereas Deleuze became less obviously engaged with political issues and ideas towards the end of his life, Negri has intensively developed and applied his communism to urgent political issues. Communism means being in common, which is a created or constructed condition, and it is the result not of a sovereign one, but of a multitude. Negri is inspired by Spinoza as well as Marx, and in his book *The Savage Anomaly*, Negri argues that Spinoza's metaphysics *is* his politics. At the beginning of the modern world, Spinoza opens up a vision of democratic power based upon the *potentia* (potential constitutive power, rather than active force) multitude rather than the one, even the sovereignty of one people, or a general will, as later European political philosophers like Locke and Rousseau will call it. The clue to Spinoza's political thought can be found in his unfinished *Political Treatise*, and this is read back into his *Ethics*. The freedom of the people can be found in the expression and regulation of antagonisms, which composes a multitude, or *multitudo*. "It is the *multitudo* that constitutes itself in society with all its needs. Neither is peace simply security. It is the situation in which the

---

[6] Badiou is admittedly very critical of the so-called return to religion as well as religious appropriations of his thought. According to Badiou, the interest of Continental philosophy in religion is ironically a symptom of the postmodern obsession with finitude. He claims that "as long as finitude remains the ultimate determination of existence, God abides….as that whose disappearance continues to hold sway over us" (Alain Badiou, "Philosophy and Mathematics," in *Theoretical Writings*, ed. and trans. Ray Brassier and Alberto Toscano (London: Continuum, 2006), 28). Understanding the infinite in properly mathematical terms, on the other hand, frees us from the pathos of finitude and from this disappeared God. At the same time, his description of the universal formal structure of subjectivity in Pauline terms indicates an affinity with the Christian atheism championed by Žižek. Žižek, despite his appreciation of Badiou's politics, his insistence upon truth, and his stress on universalism over against the relativism and scepticism of conventional postmodernism, does not understand ontology solely in mathematical terms.

consensus organizes itself in the form of a republic."[7] The understanding of Spinoza in *The Savage Anomaly*, combined with Negri's reading of Marx in *Marx Beyond Marx*, and finally his two essays published under the title *Time For Revolution*, underlie the extraordinary efforts *Empire* and *Multitude*, co-authored with Michael Hardt.

In *Empire*, Negri and Hardt sketch an understanding of the political conditions of late capitalism, which is marked by the dissolution of the sovereign nation state. Capital forms an empire, which like the state feeds off of and exploits the living labour of its subjects. Along with the new political form of empire comes a new political subject, which is called multitude. According to Hardt and Negri, "the multitude is the real productive force of our social world, whereas Empire is a mere apparatus of capture that lives only off the vitality of the multitude."[8] The multitude is seen in quasi-salvific if entirely secular terms, as the new protagonist in the struggle against empire. In the sequel, *Multitude*, Hardt and Negri sketch out a vision of radical democracy based upon their conception of multitude, and this understanding of democracy is based upon a secularised notion of Christian love. War is a total condition of empire, and since war has become ubiquitous not simply between but within what used to be sovereign nation states, it can be characterized as a general state of civil war. The constituent power of the multitude that overcomes war is love, and this love is related directly to Christian and Jewish forms of love that resonate with the discussions of Žižek and Badiou. Hardt and Negri declare that "people today seem unable to understand love as a political concept, but a concept of love is just what we need to grasp the constituent power of the multitude." In order to do this, "we need to recuperate the public and political conception of love common to premodern traditions. Christianity and Judaism, for example, both conceive love as a political act that constructs the multitude."[9] This political understanding of love is materialist rather than transcendent or idealist, and it is directly forceful in its effects and its workings against the violence of empire and its wars.

So Continental philosophy of religion after 2000 has moved somewhat away from an explicit engagement with Derrida and Levinas, and more in the direction of a political reading of Christian and Jewish monotheism,

---

[7] Antonio Negri, *The Savage Anomaly: The Power of Spinoza's Metaphysics and Politics*, trans. Michael Hardt (Minneapolis: University of Minnesota Press, 1991), 201.

[8] Michael Hardt and Antonio Negri, *Empire* (Cambridge: Harvard University Press, 2000), 62.

[9] Michael Hardt and Antonio Negri, *Multitude: War and Democracy in the Age of Empire* (New York: Penguin, 2004), 353.

following Žižek, Badiou, and Negri. I would suggest that Derrida's work on religion has continued to be marked by political concerns up until his death in 2004, and this is true of his essay "Faith and Knowledge: The Two Sources of Religion Within the Limits of Reason Alone," as well as his book *Rogues*, even if Continental philosophy of religion has not always fully attended to the political contexts and implications of Derrida's thought.

In taking up the work of Žižek, Badiou, and Negri, one danger lies in the privileged and exceptionalist perspectives offered on Christianity and sometimes Judaism in terms of their significance for theoretical and political understanding. One of the main claims of postmodernism, and one of the reasons that postmodernism is directly related to the return of religion, is the awareness of the continuity between premodern, usually Christian, religious traditions and European modernity. Although this is largely true in historical terms, in political terms it tends to reinforce a hegemonic Western identity that is then defended over against a non-Western Asian other, whether explicitly identified as Muslim or not.

The academic study of religion has demonstrated the complicity of the study of religion and world religions with imperialism and colonialism, but many philosophers of religion remain somewhat naïve to these insights. In her book *The Invention of World Religions*, for example, Tomoko Masuzawa demonstrates how the establishment of world religions as a categorical framework was established in the late nineteenth century, and part of its agenda was a "strong drive to hellenize and aryanize Christianity" at the same time as it aspired "to semitize Islam."[10] Although the world religions curriculum has largely replaced the seminary model in American universities, it has inaugurated a micro-specialized study of particular religions that makes it extremely difficult to effectively philosophise across religious traditions without appearing at best as an outsider, and at worst as an amateur. On the other hand, one strategy that has been employed to overcome the hegemony of Protestant Christianity in terms of the study of religion has been to excommunicate theology as intrinsically biased and non-objective in order to constitute religion or religious studies as a responsible academic subject. Beyond the question whether it is possible to completely divorce theology from religious studies, which I doubt, one of the effects of this strategy, at least in the American academy, has been to eliminate philosophy as a method of academic religious studies along with theology, and to explicitly favour

---

[10] Tomoko Masuzawa, *The Invention of World Religions: Or, How European Universalism was Preserved in the Language of Pluralism* (Chicago: University of Chicago Press, 2005), xii.

social scientific methods. To repudiate philosophical approaches to the study of religion is to invite stupidity, even if philosophers of religion, including Continental philosophers of religion, have been and remain relatively ignorant about non-Christian and non-Western religious traditions.

II.

In the more constructive part of my essay, I would like to consider the philosophy of Catherine Malabou, in particular her notion of plasticity. In her book *What Should We Do With Our Brain?*, Malabou posits a link between the neuroplasticity of the brain and what has been traditionally called history, and this link is a political link, to which I will return. I suggest that plasticity is a better concept with which to think about religion than the messianism that pervades discussions of Levinas and Derrida, and it avoids the temporal prejudice that privileges Christian (and sometimes Jewish) exceptionalism in terms of the West, which some of the work of Žižek, Badiou and Negri implies.

Malabou, a student of Jacques Derrida, wrote her dissertation on Hegel in which she developed the concept of the plasticity of the subject that she discovered in the *Phenomenology of Spirit*.[11] This positive reading of Hegel, in which plasticity characterizes the nature of the dialectic, counters the stereotypical postmodern critique of Hegel as a totalising philosopher. In fact, Derrida wrote a Foreword in which he was compelled to retract many of his criticisms of Hegel in light of Malabou's reading.[12] Malabou's reinterpretation of Hegel accords with other reassessments of the significance of Hegel's work for thinkers working in Continental and broadly postmodern traditions, including Slavoj Žižek.[13]

Following her constructive reading of plasticity in Hegel, Malabou has turned towards the neurosciences, and engaged with cutting-edge research on neuroplasticity. This culminates in her book *What Should We Do With Our Brain?*, which directly engages with neuroscientific research and provides a philosophical framework to comprehend and assess this research. According to Malabou, plasticity comes from the Greek *plassein*, which means to mould, and she understands it in three distinct ways. On

---

[11] See Catherine Malabou, *The Future of Hegel: Plasticity, Temporality and Dialectic*, trans. Lisabeth During (London: Routledge, 2005), 26.

[12] See Jacques Derrida, Preface in Malabou, *The Future of Hegel*, vii-xlvii.

[13] On the significance of this new reading of Hegel, see Clayton Crockett, Creston Davis, and Slavoj Žižek eds, *Hegel and the Infinite: Religion, Politics and the Dialectic* (New York: Columbia University Press, 2010).

the one hand, plasticity means to receive form in a passive way, and on the other hand, plasticity means to give form, to shape something in a more active manner. Thirdly, however, "plasticity is also the capacity to annihilate the very form it is able to receive or create."[14] So plasticity has active, passive, and destructive aspects, but what is crucial is that it pertains to form.

Part of the significance of the reading of Derrida and Levinas that strongly influences early Continental philosophy of religion is the emphasis upon trace over form, a valorisation of absence over presence. The spectral messianicity that characterizes the spirit of deconstruction is based upon the absence of any self-presence, the deferral of formal self-constitution, which is always hovering but remains "to-come." This messianic "to-come" that marks the religious nature of the promise— something is promised that never arrives, and we remain haunted by its absence and the anticipation of its arrival—means that every event is not fully and completely an event, but constitutes an event by means of the fact that it instantiates only a trace. This trace is the fundamental sign of alterity, and it indicates that the quasi-messianic promise is not yet—not ever—fulfilled. Malabou's insistence upon form opposes the trace as it is usually understood in Derridean and Levinasian terms. Over against Levinas, she affirms "the mutual convertibility of trace and form," which means that trace cannot be taken in any absolute sense.[15] The insistence upon form as opposed to trace is an opposition to messianism, and a kind of return to Hegel.

This return to Hegel, however, is marked by deconstruction, which Malabou does not simply oppose, and in her book *Plasticity at the Dusk of Writing* she situates plasticity in relation to Hegel, Heidegger and Derrida. Plasticity is Hegelian, but it is not the accumulative, triumphal march of Absolute Spirit, or the totalising swallowing of differences. Plasticity is auto-plasticity, a relationship of form of and on form, and this positivity works against the negative implications of the trace and its messianic provenance. The dialectic is plastic; it develops but it does not simply progress. Like Žižek, Malabou emphasizes the wounded and broken character of the dialectic, how it reveals the impotence of spirit by means of a complex operation of form folding upon form. If dialectic is auto-

---

[14] Catherine Malabou, *What Should We Do With Our Brain?*, trans. Sebastian Rand (New York: Fordham University Press, 2008), 5.

[15] Catherine Malabou, *La plasticité au soir de l'écriture: Dialectic, destruction, déconstruction* (Paris: Éditions Léo Scheer, 2005), 87. English translation: *Plasticity at the Dusk of Writing*, trans. Carolyn Shread (New York: Columbia University Press, 2009).

development of form, it does not possess a simple telos, and more importantly, it is non-messianic.

What is wrong with messianicity? Well, despite Derrida's insistence upon an absolute deferral, messianicity continually allows the recouping and thereby salvaging of time, specifically Western and Christian time. Jean-Luc Nancy's recent work allows this point to be seen more clearly. In his book *Dis-Enclosure: The Deconstruction of Christianity*, Nancy identifies deconstruction with the self-overcoming of Christianity because he asserts that the essence of what we call the West is Christian. "Christianity is inseparable from the West," Nancy writes, and here he is following the work of Marcel Gauchet in *The Disenchantment of the World*.[16] Insofar as Christianity is identified with the West, and deconstruction with the process of self-overcoming of Christianity, we can read Nancy in terms of a certain messianism that understands Western history and culture as the distribution of a religious truth that never comes to an end, because it continually perpetuates itself in its ending, or overcoming. According to Nancy, "the structure of origin of Christianity is the proclamation of its end."[17] Christianity and the West continue to live off of this infinite deferral, this ability to extend themselves back into their tradition, and their ability to transcend themselves into an indefinite future that is always to-come. We can of course distinguish between a more Christian and a more Jewish messianism, and this would be an important difference, but in another sense, what we call the West is constituted by a Judeo-Christian promise grafted onto a Greco-Roman structure that is then perpetuated over against all the other cultures, peoples and religions by means of this dynamic messianism.

The promotion of messianism reflects at least in part a strategy to defend Eurocentrism and Western culture by linking it essentially with its temporal history, and cutting off spatial diffusion into contamination by separate cultures. As Nancy affirms, the spirit of Christianity is identified with the spirit of the West, and even if some of its forms are criticized as dangerous, superstitious, fundamentalist or malevolent, this spirit remains accessible to "us" in the form of messianic time. While the European Enlightenment came to represent a secular break with a religious past, it also served as a cloak for Protestant Christianity to set itself apart from other religious forms such as Judaism and Roman Catholicism. In a postsecularist context, the primary separation shifts from a temporal break

---

[16] Jean-Luc Nancy, *Dis-Enclosure: The Deconstruction of Christianity*, trans. Bettina Bergo, Gabriel Malenfant, and Michael B. Smith (Fordham: Fordham University Press, 2008), 142.

[17] Ibid, 149.

between religious and secular to a more essential differentiation between traditions or cultures. A messianic or quasi-messianic temporality, which in a post-Heideggerian sense is the essence of being, composes the identity of cultures in a historical sense, with Western culture privileged as always, but now the boundary between its religious and its non-religious identity is blurred. The hard, brutal form that religious identity takes today is fundamentalism; the soft, liberal form is messianism.

So to save Christianity/the West is to lose it, but to lose it is also to save it, to recoup its essence at a higher level, a very subtle and sometimes not so subtle quasi-Hegelian sublation. Strikingly, Derrida warns Nancy that this call for self-overcoming or "Dechristianization" will be "a Christian victory."[18] On the other hand, plasticity does not have this messianic temporal structure. It avoids the self-overcoming and the possibility of recouping because it is more fundamentally related to space than to time, and here is where Malabou subjects the Hegelian dialectic to deconstructive spacing in a way that challenges Hegel's overwhelming emphasis upon temporal development. Plasticity is about creating, opening up a new space to think and live, even if that process also involves destruction. Plasticity brings nothing to an end, neither Christianity nor the West; it is not concerned with ending but rather with beginning, with natality.

Although Nancy's deconstruction of Christianity is marked by this messianism, in the last chapter of his book, *Dis-Enclosure*, Nancy offers an understanding of deconstruction that is closer to Malabou's idea of plasticity. Dis-enclosure is related to enclosure, an enclosing or fencing off of the territory of the earth, which is part and parcel of globalization. What Columbus established in 1492 was "a world in the process of eclosing in the world, and even more in the process, if I may say so, of eclosing the world within it and around it."[19] Eclosing is not a familiar word, and it translates the French *éclosion*, which means to hatch or to give birth. This hatching of the modern world is at the same time a birthing that occurred by means of setting up boundaries, such that eclosing is also enclosing. Today, Nancy claims that "another life, another respiration, another weight, and another humanity is in the process of emerging. And consequently, what distinguishes itself today, what is in the process of spatializing itself, presents itself as spatialization itself."[20]

---

[18] Jacques Derrida, *On Touching—Jean-Luc Nancy*, trans. Christine Irizarry (Stanford: Stanford University Press, 2005), 54

[19] Nancy, *Dis-Enclosure*, 160.

[20] Ibid, 160.

This process of spatialization means that the birthing or hatching of the modern world is itself giving birth to something else, but Nancy here describes it in spatial rather than temporal (i.e. messianic) terms. The eclosure of the world in modernity took place against a given background, it was a hatching but also a fencing in, or enclosing, of what was not emerging in the modern world. Now, today, dis-enclosing (French, *déclosion*) "is the eclosure of eclosure itself and the spacing of space itself."[21] According to Nancy,

> Neither places, nor heavens, nor gods: for the moment it is a general dis-enclosing, more so than a burgeoning. Dis-enclosure: dismantling and disassembling of enclosed bowers, enclosures, fences. Deconstruction of property—that of man and that of world.[22]

The eclosure itself bursts wide open, which means that it is not a question of perpetuating the essence of Christianity or Judaism or the West, but rather an "explosion." This explosion is very similar to what Malabou means by the third, explosive aspect of plasticity, which is the auto-annihilation of form itself.

The plasticity of our world and the plasticity of our brain is inter-linked. One does not precede and cause the other in a simple manner. Malabou posits this link in *What Should We Do With Our Brain?*. Although her focus on neuroplasticity would seem to represent a narrowing of focus, and an application of her philosophy to a specialized field of scientific research, Malabou in fact opens up the plasticity of the brain and connects it with Hegelian plasticity, although in the case of this book more explicitly with Marx. Malabou emphasizes the structural "bond between brain and history" that makes neuroplasticity a social and political concept as well as a neurological one.[23] The open-ended nature of history has become stifled and claustrophobic at the turning of the twenty first century. We do not feel the possibilities of history, of our ability to make and create history and society anew. Malabou identifies our creative possibilities with the plasticity of our brains, and asserts that it is this opening that replaces the more conventional modern conception of history in a post-Hegelian and post-Marxist context. This interpretation of brain plasticity constitutes "a new freedom, which is to say: a new meaning of history."[24]

---

[21] Ibid, 160.
[22] Ibid, 161.
[23] Malabou, *What Should We Do With Our Brain?*, 1.
[24] Ibid, 13.

At the same time, a common understanding of neurological function coincides with the contemporary capitalist form of social organization. Malabou asks, "What should we do so that the consciousness of the brain does not purely and simply coincide with the spirit of capitalism?"[25] She warns that we must be careful to distinguish plasticity from flexibility, which resonates with the passive adaptability that characterizes employability in late capitalist society, with its emphasis upon a retail service economy and cheap, temporary and disposable labour. "If I insist on how close certain managerial discourses are to neuroscientific discourses," she writes, "this is because it seems to me that the phenomenon called 'brain plasticity' is in reality more often described in terms of an economy of flexibility."[26] Plasticity, including fundamentally brain plasticity, should be understood more along the lines of reliance than in terms of flexibility. Plasticity is also a rigidity (although not a hyper-rigidity), a persistence in form, not simply a passive acceptance of form.

Malabou concludes *What Should We Do With Our Brian?* with an appeal to what she calls "a biological alter-globalism," an alternative to the contemporary forces and forms of global capitalism and an alliance with scientific and biological models, understood in a complex and sophisticated rather than a simple, deterministic or positivistic manner.[27] Such a biological alter-globalism is also dialectical, informed by the spirit of Hegel, "who developed a theory of the relations between nature and mind that is conflictual and contradictory in its essence."[28] A dialectical thinking about the brain escapes the tired debates about reductionism and anti-reductionism that often distort discourses about the relationship between humanity and nature, including discussions about religion.

My constructive suggestion in this essay is to think religion in terms of plasticity along the lines that Malabou defines and describes it. A plastic understanding of religion helps sidestep useless arguments about reductionism, and it avoids the messianism that pervades earlier forms of Continental philosophy of religion. Religion is constructive and creative, it is passive and active, as well as destructive; it is plastic. Plasticity, including brain plasticity, offers a way to think about religion in materialist terms, but again, this is not a crude reductive materialism. If religion is understood solely in transcendent terms, as the revelation of divinity, then philosophy of religion would be an attempt to re-describe this revelation in rational and comprehensible terms. On the other hand, if

---

[25] Ibid, 12.
[26] Ibid, 46.
[27] Ibid, 80.
[28] Ibid, 80-81.

philosophy of religion follows the trajectory of Continental philosophy in the twentieth century, religious belief becomes questionable, but it's hard to escape the Heideggerian conclusion: we cannot grasp being/god/the real; only a god can save us, or a new manifestation of being.

Plasticity is dialectically related to earlier forms of Continental philosophy, including deconstruction, but it is also a different way of configuring thought and nature, including religion. Religion is universal in human terms; we cannot escape or eradicate it, for better and for worse. Plasticity allows us to put religion to work, to work and rework religion in plastic terms, as we shape our history and our future. Plasticity is material form rather than messianic force, and force cannot be thought apart from form. Material plasticity concerns the basis of (human and natural, biological) existence, including the threat of its extinction due to the over-exploitation of physical resources.

According to Alain Badiou, the twentieth century is characterized by a "passion for the real."[29] The passion for the real means that we are suspicious of symbolic representation, linguistic and perceptual distortion of reality, the ruses of the unconscious and the traps of ideology. The more we strive for the real, the more it appears to recede. At the same time, in this century, we are witnessing a reappearance of nature, a new or neo-realism, sometimes expressed as a "speculative realism," and this is both encouraging because it avoids the extremes of solipsism and subjectivism, and dangerous because it risks naïveté in regard to contemporary scientific results. As Deleuze remarks in his still remarkable essay "Postscript on the Societies of Control," "There is no need to fear or hope, but only to look for new weapons."[30] My hope is that plasticity might prove to be a useful weapon with which to think and rethink Continental philosophy of religion, as well as philosophy and religion themselves.

Bibliography

Badiou, Alain. *Saint Paul: The Foundation of Universalism*. Translated by Ray Brassier. Stanford: Stanford University Press, 2003.
—. "Philosophy and Mathematics." In *Theoretical Writings*, edited and translated by Ray Brassier and Alberto Toscano. London: Continuum, 2006, 22-40.

---

[29] See Alain Badiou, *The Century*, trans. Alberto Toscano (London: Continuum, 2007).
[30] Gilles Deleuze, "Postscript on the Societies of Control," *OCTOBER* 59 (Winter 1992), 3-7 (accessed online at http://www.n5m.org/n5m2/media/texts/deleuze.htm, 08/09/2009).

—. *The Century*. Translated by Alberto Toscano. London: Continuum, 2007.

Caputo, John D. *The Prayers and Tears of Jacques Derrida: Religion Without Religion*. Bloomington: Indiana University Press, 1997.

Crockett, Clayton, Creston Davis and Slavoj Žižek edited. *Hegel and the Infinite: Religion, Politics and the Dialectic*. New York: Columbia University Press, 2010.

Deleuze, Gilles. "Postscript on the Societies of Control." *OCTOBER* 59 (Winter 1992): 3-7.

Derrida, Jacques. *Specters of Marx: The State of the Debt, The Work of Mourning, & the New International*. Translated by Peggy Kamuf. New York: Routledge, 1994.

—. "Force of Law: The Mystical Foundation of Authority." In *Acts of Religion*, edited by Gil Anidjar. London: Routledge, 2002. 230-98.

—. *On Touching—Jean-Luc Nancy*. Translated by Christine Irizarry. Stanford: Stanford University Press, 2005.

Hardt, Michael and Antonio Negri. *Empire*. Cambridge: Harvard University Press, 2000.

—. *Multitude: War and Democracy in the Age of Empire*. New York: Penguin, 2004.

Malabou, Catherine. *The Future of Hegel: Plasticity, Temporality and Dialectic*. Translated by Lisabeth During. London: Routledge, 2005.

—. *La plasticité au soir de l'écriture: Dialectic, destruction, deconstruction*. Paris: Éditions Léo Scheer, 2005.

—. *What Should We Do With Our Brain?* Translated by Sebastian Rand. New York: Fordham University Press, 2008.

—. *Plasticity at the Dusk of Writing*. Translated by Carolyn Shread. New York: Columbia University Press, 2009.

Masuzawa, Tomoko. *The Invention of World Religions: Or, How European Universalism was Preserved in the Language of Pluralism*. Chicago: University of Chicago Press, 2005.

Nancy, Jean-Luc. *Dis-Enclosure: The Deconstruction of Christianity*. Translated by Bettina Bergo, Gabriel Malenfant, and Michael B. Smith. Fordham: Fordham University Press, 2008.

Negri, Antonio. *Marx Beyond Marx: Lessons on the Grundrisse*. Translated by Harry Cleaver, Michael Ryan and Maurizio Viano. New York: Autonomedia, 1991.

—. *The Savage Anomaly: The Power of Spinoza's Metaphysics and Politics*. Translated by Michael Hardt. Minneapolis: University of Minnesota Press, 1991.

—. *Time for Revolution*. Translated by Matteo Mandarini. London: Continuum, 2003.

Žižek, Slavoj. *The Fragile Absolute: Or, why is the Christian Legacy Worth Fighting For?* London: Verso, 2000.

—. *The Puppet and the Dwarf: The Perverse Core of Christianity*. Cambridge: MIT Press, 2003.

CHAPTER SIXTEEN

THE HOPE OF SPECULATIVE MATERIALISM

MICHAEL O'NEILL BURNS

I. Introduction

In the past two years, the philosophical sensibility generally referred to as "Speculative Realism" has garnered a considerable amount of attention as well as leading to a surprising amount of debate and controversy. While this moniker refers to little more than the title of an initial conference and the common philosophical motives shared between those involved (Ray Brassier, Iain Hamilton Grant, Graham Harman, Quentin Meillassoux), it has gone on to represent a leap away from the anthropocentric positions affiliated with Kantian correlationism, and towards a speculative philosophy which claims to be able to "get at" the absolute. Unsurprisingly, this reaction against the years of Continental domination by traditional phenomenological approaches (which fail the test of correlationism) has carried with it an absolute rejection, or at least disregard, of the theological and religious questions that gained such prominence during the religious turn of French phenomenology. Surprisingly, however, is that amongst those considered to be the original members of "speculative realism", Quentin Meillassoux (the lone Continental member) has once again opened the way for the question of the religious, or at least the divine, into speculative philosophy.

In light of this, the current chapter will attempt a critical and constructive evaluation of Meillassoux's engagement with philosophy of religion, or in his terms, *divinology*. We will begin with an explication of the core of his basic philosophical project as set forth in *After Finitude*, focusing in particular on the importance of his principle of the necessity of contingency. From there we will go on to introduce Meillassoux's divinology as it is outlined in the short piece, "Spectral Dilemma". We will then consider the recent critique of Meillassoux's divinology from Martin Hägglund. Before ultimately contending Hägglund's critique, we will provide our own constructive critique of Meillassoux's divinology which will involve a subtle, but crucial, re-positioning of the notion of possibility in relation to the divine. We will conclude by using the debate between Hägglund and Meillassoux to identify some of the stakes of contemporary materialist thought, and in particular the role of the religious (if any) in this debate.

Ultimately, we will argue that any materialist project which hopes to provide an account of socio-political change and transformation must necessarily provide an account of hope, and further, that this account must be grounded in a thought that recognizes the primacy of justice over the crassly bio-political conception of survival. This will be argued in relation to the thought of a triad of thinkers: Søren Kierkegaard, Alain Badiou, and Slavoj Žižek. We will also make the claim that unless it holds onto its potential to offer a radical ideological critique grounded in the potential to think the possibility of "another world", religious thought will have little to offer twenty-first century materialist philosophy.

II. Meillassoux's *After Finitude*

Of primary concern in Quentin Meillassoux's concise work *After Finitude* is a rigorous over-turning of what he sees as the problematic correlation of thought and being (or, subject and object) associated with post-Kantian philosophy. Along with this overturning of the anthropocentrism at the heart of post-Kantian philosophy, Meillassoux also develops what he calls the necessity of contingency, primarily in response to Hume's theory of causation. While his work is concise and accessible enough to make a lengthy summary unwarranted, we will however recount some of the key elements of his project that serve the purpose of the present work. Of major importance to us at this point will be the notions of ancestrality and contingency in *After Finitude*, and how these concepts lay the groundwork for his divinology.

Meillassoux begins his assault on correlationism with a chapter that develops his notion of ancestrality. One of the goals of this concept is to discover a way to get at qualities of objects which they possess in-themselves. So rather than describe an object based on subjective sense perception, Meillassoux contends that only "those aspects of the object that can be formulated in mathematical terms can be meaningfully conceived as properties of the object in itself."[1] Thus, the entire notion of

---

[1] Quentin Meillassoux, *After Finitude*, trans. Ray Brassier (London: Continuum, 2008), 3.

sensibility only exists in regards to a subjective relation to the world, but mathematizable properties of objects are left unconstrained by this subject-world relation, and pure number allows us to access qualities of the in-itself.

The question thus arises, what can we know about objects independent of a subject-based relation to these objects? The correlationist response would simply be that we cannot know anything about the object in-itself, but only through this subject-object relationship. As Meillassoux puts it, "Correlationism consists in disqualifying the claim that is it possible to consider the realms of subjectivity and objectivity independently of one another."[2] Meillassoux wants to respond to the correlationist dogma by strongly asserting that we can know things about objects considered independent from subjective apprehension. Through a utilization of mathematics, he argues that we can ostensibly "get at" qualities of objects which existed before the emergence of human life, and which are thus clearly outside the bounds of any subject-object correlation. He thus calls *ancestral* "any reality anterior to the emergence of the human species—or even anterior to every recognized form of life on earth."[3] Meillassoux refers to ancestral objects as "arche-fossils", which are "material[s] indicating the existence of an ancestral reality or event; one that is anterior to terrestrial life."[4] It is crucial to briefly note the difference between the use of the term "ancestral", which indicates matter that pre-dates the emergence of life, and "ancient", which merely signifies objects outside the realm of our contemporary subjective experience. While the correlationist can provide a theory of "ancient" objects, the notion of "ancestral" objects forces them outside the safety of the correlationist circle.

An example of an "arche-fossil" would be an ancestral isotope, whose rate of radioactive decay (which we can access through mathematics) tells us that this material has existed before the emergence of human life. Meillassoux's primary challenge to the correlationists is simply, how are they able to interpret such ancestral statements? Though a complete summary is out the scope of this essay, Meillassoux eventually reaches the conclusion that the correlationist has no way of dealing with such statements. Whereas the correlationist can only "know" what is given to the subject in reality, these ancestral examples are instead anterior to givenness, and thus outside of the subject-object relationship predicated on

---

[2] Ibid, 5.
[3] Ibid, 10.
[4] Ibid.

givenness.[5] As Meillassoux bluntly states, "There is no possible compromise between the correlation and the arche-fossil: once one has acknowledged one, one has thereby disqualified the other."[6] These are the stakes with which Meillassoux paints the contemporary philosophical situation, and through the ancestral argument Meillassoux challenges the correlationist with the possibility of thinking a "world without thought."[7]

Meillassoux subsequently argues, however, that "we cannot go back to being metaphysicians".[8] This is because he finds in dogmatic metaphysics the persistence of the thesis of real necessity. This thesis states that within a metaphysical system, there is always at least one entity that is absolutely necessary. Meillassoux has no interest in continuing a metaphysical tradition which claims to be able to access an absolute entity through the principle of sufficient reason, but rather in developing a speculative approach to questions of the absolute which moves beyond dogmatic notions of necessary entities. To develop this speculative thought that avoids the absolutist traps of dogmatic metaphysics, Meillassoux attempts to "uncover an absolute necessity that does not reinstate any form of absolutely necessary entity."[9] To do this Meillassoux posits the ideas that "everything is equally possible"[10] as an absolute, and this absolute is a contingency that posits nothing as necessary but rather designates a pure possibility.[11] He goes on to note that "our absolute, in effect, is nothing other than an extreme form of chaos, a hyper-chaos".[12] To put it simply, all of this means for Meillassoux that anything is possible, except something that is necessary.

Before moving on to an explicit discussion of Meillassoux's *divinology*, it is necessary that we provide an account of Meillassoux's response to Hume's problem, the resolution of which paves the way for the introduction of his divinology. Meillassoux states Hume's problem as follows: "Is it possible to demonstrate that the same effects will always follow from the same cause *ceteris paribus*, i.e. all other things being equal?"[13] Put simply, Hume's theory of causation states that while there is no way to prove through reason that a certain effect will always be

---

[5] Ibid, 14.
[6] Ibid, 17.
[7] Ibid, 28.
[8] Ibid, 29.
[9] Ibid, 34.
[10] Ibid, 58.
[11] Ibid, 62.
[12] Ibid, 64.
[13] Ibid, 85.

produced by a certain cause, through habit and custom one can eventually learn to expect the laws of nature to remain stable. In this sense, the Humean will see no problem in continually presupposing the existence of stable physical laws. In opposition to this, Meillassoux argues not only that we can show that there is a stability to natural laws, but also, in fact, this stability is little more than the necessity of an absolute instability and contingency. Rather than developing habits which inform our understanding about the laws of physical reality, Meillassoux instead posits that there is no underlying necessity to natural laws, and in fact, things could always be otherwise. In this sense, Meillassoux does not so much provide a solution to "Hume's problem" as much as he turns this problem into a possibility for thought.

While one can then pose the question of "why don't the laws governing physical reality change for no reason in contingent patterns?" Meillassoux attempts to cut this argument off by showing the "precise condition for the manifest stability of chaos"[14]—the transfinite. Following in the footsteps of his teacher Alain Badiou in utilizing the set theoretical work of Cantor, Meillassoux shows how the detotalisation of number seen in set-theory (the transfinite) provides us with a way to think (mathematically) the detotalisation of being-qua-being. While it would be an unnecessary detour to describe in length Cantor's set-theory, and in particular ZF (Zermelo-Fraenkel), we can briefly allude to why this is so crucial for Meillassoux's thought on the necessity of contingency.

To argue against the probabilistic reasoning that says if something *can* happen, then at some point it *should* happen, Meillassoux notes that this position is only valid on the condition that what is thought to be a priori possible be thinkable in terms of numerical totality.[15] In this sense, one needs to first acknowledge the existence of a totality of conceivable possibilities, if one is to subsequently affirm the calculable frequency of these possibilities' emergence. This argument, however, does not hold for Meillassoux, as following Cantor he affirms, "We can no longer guarantee the totalisation of the thinkable."[16] The Cantorian concept that leads Meillassoux to this strong conclusion is the notion of the *transfinite*, which is the detotalisation of number, and the mathematically formal way by which one can distinguish between contingency and chance. Meillassoux exemplifies this through an example of "Cantor's Theorem". In this example, he posits the existence of a set, A, which consist of a given number of elements. One can then develop another set, B, which consists

---

[14] Ibid, 101.
[15] Ibid.
[16] Ibid, 103.

of the possible groupings of elements from set A. According to Cantor's theorem, we will always end at the same result, set B (the possible groupings of the elements from set A) will always be larger than set A, even if A is infinite. If one was to continue this process by making a set C that consisted of all the possible groups of the elements of set B, and another set D which consisted of all the possible groupings of set C, and so on, one would simply get the series of transfinite cardinals, which is a series that cannot be totalised into some ultimate quantity. The point of all of this is that no matter how many times one makes a new set which contains the possible grouping of elements from a previous set, one can never arrive a set of all sets which would contain all possible grouping of elements from every set. It is important to note as well that this "set of all sets" is not just too big for us to conceive of, it simply does not exist.[17]

For Meillassoux, "At the very least, this axiomatic demonstrates a fundamental uncertainty regarding the totalisability of the possible"[18], and once again it helps him argue that it is impossible to put forth an argument which holds that the laws of nature are necessary and consistent, since when the possible is detotalised, we can no longer consider any set of possibilities as either wholly necessary or unnecessary. Translated into ontological terms, this means that we can no longer conceive of reality as a consistent whole, and rather than being a One (or, necessary entity) at the heart of being, there is rather a no-thing. From this Meillassoux can assert, "There is no longer a mystery, not because there is no longer a problem, but because there is no longer a reason."[19] When the in-itself is nothing but a chaos-without-reason, we can no longer make claim to some total and absolute necessity or reason that orders the laws of reality. Because of this debatable conflation of the ontological with the mathematical, the inexistence of a set of all sets allows Meillassoux to firmly claim that there is also no set of necessary laws or possibilities.

III. The Inexistence of the Divine

While his large-scale work *L'inexistence divine* has yet to be completed, Meillassoux has provided a small dose of his thought on the religious in a short piece entitled "Spectral Dilemma". Meillassoux brings his speculative materialism to bear on the question of the divine through the introduction of what he refers to as the *spectral dilemma*, which is the problem created by the existence of unmournable deaths. For Meillassoux,

---

[17] Ibid.
[18] Ibid, 105.
[19] Ibid, 110.

these unmournable deaths are of a horrific nature and are exemplified in cases of rape, genocide, and the murder of innocent children. These deaths leave behind spectres, which Meillassoux defines as a dead person who has not been properly mourned. These spectres are thus the memories of those taken in ways that seem undeniably and inherently unjust, and in recent times it seems clear that we have been increasingly faced with such spectres, whether they be innocent children killed by a failed military bombing, families swept away in violent floods, or the thousands of people in the third world who die each year due to a simple lack of food. If ever there has been a generation haunted by a multitude of spectres, it surely seems it must be ours.

The question thus remains: can the problem of mourning created by horrific and unjust death ever be solved? Meillassoux thinks so, and calls this completion of the mourning of essential spectres "essential mourning". This essential mourning entails "the accomplishment of a living, rather than morbid, relation to the survivors to these terrible deaths."[20] For essential mourning to be accomplished, Meillassoux argues that we must be able to "to live with essential spectres, thereby to no longer die with them."[21] While the notion of a mourning that would entail that we are once again able to live *with* the dead may sound absurd, Meillassoux provides a rigorous conception of how this situation could at least be possible, and one which builds on the necessity of contingency which he outlines in *After Finitude*.

Before elucidating his response to the problem created by essential mourning, Meillassoux first outlines the contemporary responses to this question, a position that can be simplified down to two options, "either god exists, or he doesn't."[22] The positions affiliated with either side of this dichotomy are obviously the religious position and the atheist position. Not surprisingly, Meillassoux sees both as unfit to provide a solution to the problem of essential mourning.

The first position, which is that of the religious person, posits that there is some merciful spirit which transcends all humanity and brings justice to the departed after their horrific earthly deaths. The religious person cannot cope with the horrific nature of tragic death, and cannot see any hope of an earthly justice that would somehow make these lives mournable. Instead, they hold a belief in a deity outside of our reality, which will somehow provide a justice for the dead. This faith is grounded in a despair which

---

[20] Quentin Meillassoux, "Spectral Dilemma", trans. Robin Mackay, *Collapse* IV (2008), 262.
[21] Ibid.
[22] Ibid, 263.

would not allow the individual to live unless there was some hope of justice for the essential spectre. One of the obvious contradictions of this position is that the same person who holds a faith in a divine being who will provide justice for the dead after their passing, also believes that this divine being himself allowed this atrocious acts to be committed in the first place. This is the point at which the atheist stakes their position. Whereas the religious person posits faith in a God to hope for some justice in the next world, the atheist wants nothing to do with a future justice initiated by the same God who allowed horrific suffering to happen in the present world. What the religious person sees as heaven, the Atheist sees as hell, as it entails an eternity controlled by the entity which allowed the rape, murder, genocide, and horror that created the problem of essential mourning in the first place. As opposed to this idea of an eternal hell (or heaven), the atheist instead claims that they would prefer for themselves a nothingness that would at least conserve the dignity of the essential spectre, rather than leaving them in the hands of an angry God.

Meillassoux finds both positions problematic, and notes that each position is only supported by the weakness of the other: "The atheist is atheist because religion promises a fearful God; the believer anchors his faith in the refusal of a life devastated by the despair of terrible deaths."[23] The point on which each position is grounded is despair—"either to despair of another life for the dead, or to despair of a God who has let such deaths take place."[24] The spectral dilemma is thus the problematic dichotomy existing between atheism and religion when it comes to the possibility of mourning essential spectres. This issue comes down to the dichotomy with which the religious question is usually posed, namely, either God exists or he does not exist. Rather than grant autonomy to the terms of this debate, Meillassoux instead wants to resolve the problem with a third position which rest on the notion of the inexistence of God, a position plainly stated as "God no longer exists."[25] From this statement Meillassoux formulates a thesis that he will call the "divine inexistence."[26] This thesis rests on the assertion that while we can clearly argue that god does not currently exist, we have no reason to believe that he could not one day exist, and thus the notion of a God-to-come is philosophically tenable.

We can now see how the problem of essential mourning and the notion of a God-to-come is predicated on the necessity of contingency as argued

---

[23] Ibid, 265.
[24] Ibid.
[25] Ibid, 268.
[26] Ibid

for in *After Finitude*. Meillassoux's problem with both the religious and atheist position are that they each posit that it is absolutely necessary that god either exist or not exist. The religious person is not willing to concede that while God may exist now, he may soon perish; and the atheist will not concede that while God currently doesn't exist, he may one day soon come into existence. In each case the position leads to a dogmatic metaphysics predicated on a necessary existence or non-existence. As we have already seen, this is the sort of metaphysics Meillassoux is out to annihilate.

One issue that emerges in Meillassoux's theorization of the God-to-come is the question of just what sort of God this would be. Following the theory of the necessity of contingency, which he developed in *After Finitude* in response to Hume, Meillassoux first asserts that this God must currently be inexistent and possible. Along with this, if this God ever did come into existence, it must be contingent and unmasterable. The question then remains, what would need to happen for this emergence of an inexistent God to solve the problem of essential spectres? Clearly, the solution to this problem must involve the ability of the living to live-with the dead, and it is clear that this community of the living and dead seems to fly in the face of what we consider to be the laws of nature. But following his previous arguments for absolute contingency, Meillassoux reminds us that this dilemma is insoluble only insofar we admit "the necessity of the laws of nature."[27] For Meillassoux, it is thus this belief in the necessity of natural laws that leads to both the atheistic belief in the impossibility of the existence of God, as well as belief in the impossibility of the resolution of the problem of essential mourning.

Now, we have already seen Meillassoux's solution to Hume's problem and subsequent argument for the necessity of contingency and abandonment of any notion of stable laws of nature in favour of a notion of absolute chaos. In relation to this divinology, he now argues that "from this point on, God must be thought as the contingent, but eternally possible, effect of a chaos unsubordinated to any law."[28] He goes on to state that "the existential resolution of the spectral dilemma passes by way of the speculative, but non-metaphysical, resolution of Hume's problem".[29] Meillassoux closes this short essay not with a set of strong assertions for what his divinology will look like, but rather asserts that responses to these traditionally religious questions (what can I hope for? what will this God be like?) will determine an original regime of thought which will exist in rupture with both theology and atheism: divinology.

---

[27] Ibid, 272.
[28] Ibid, 274.
[29] Ibid, 275.

At this point, it may be useful to consult another of Meillassoux's short essays, "Potentiality and Virtuality". While this piece does not discuss divinology as such, or the religious in general, it provides a discussion on contingency and potentiality that seems to mesh well with the ontological implications of his divinology. This similarity likely stems from the fact that this essay, like much of his available work, is primarily structured as a response to Hume. In this work he links the concept of contingency with that of virtuality, distinguishing the later from potentiality. He states:

> I will call contingency the property of an indexed set of cases of not itself being a case of a set of sets of cases; and virtuality the property of every set of cases of emerging within a becoming which is not dominated by any pre-constituted totality of possibles.[30]

This distinction is crucial as the notion of potentiality signifies entities or situations which already exist as potentials for being. He goes on:

> I posit that time can bring forth any non-contradictory set of possibilities. As a result, I accord to time the capacity to bring forth new laws which were not 'potentially' contained in some fixed set of possibilities; I accord to time the capacity to bring forth situations which were not at all contained in precedent situations.[31]

Using terms once again reminiscent of his former teacher Badiou, Meillassoux here emphasizes the potential for new situations to emerge that were not prefigured in an existing situation. Bringing in a new element, he connects virtuality with temporality, and argues that novelty and creation are both inherently linked to this notion of temporality.

Meillassoux's notion of virtuality serves as a useful supplement to his project of divinology, since it allows one to hold a belief in the idea that "another world is possible", an idea shared by a long tradition of religious thinkers, most notably those associated with the civil rights movement and liberation theology. In this sense, it does not require much to read a concept of liberatory potential out of Meillassoux's insistence on the emergence of situations not predicated on presently existing possibilities.

---

[30] Quentin Meillassoux, "Potentiality and Virtuality", trans. Robin Mackay, *Collapse* II (2007), 72.
[31] Ibid.

IV. Hägglund's Radical Atheist Response to Divinology

While Meillassoux's published work on divinology is no longer than a short essay, it has already elicited at least one serious response (with many more surely to come) from Martin Hägglund in an essay entitled, "Radical Atheist Materialism: A Critique of Meillassoux". In this essay, Hägglund reads Meillassoux's divinology against his own theory of religion, "radical atheism". While much of this work is concerned with a critique of Meillassoux's notion of the arche-fossil and the implications this theory has for Meillassoux's notion of temporality, our concern here is to simply recount Hägglund's critique of Meillassoux's divinology and the implications it provides for both materialist and socio-political thought. Of primary importance here are the socio-political implications of Hägglund's radical atheist materialism, and likewise Meillassoux's divinology. While in each case there seems to be a somewhat problematic jump from the ontological to the socio-political, our concern here will be with the *possibility* for radical socio-political transformation enabled by each thinker's ontology. Rather that a materialism which provides room for little more than raw human survival, we hope to instead argue for a radically contingent materiality in which anything is possible, and thus one could at least hope for justice.[32]

Focusing on temporality, Hägglund notes from the outset of this piece that for Meillassoux, the absolute is nothing more than the absolute power of time.[33] Following this, God is only possible as a potential production of the chaos and contingency of temporality itself. It is our contention that the primary issue arising between Hägglund's "radical atheism" and Meillassoux's "divinology" is a debate between the primacy of either survival or justice. For Hägglund, "Care for survival is inextricable from even the most elementary organization of life."[34] Whereas religious virtues like care and compassion are traditionally attributed to the religious imperative for peace and justice, Hägglund instead argues that, rather than

---

[32] It is worth noting here that one of the most crucial implications for the socio-political emerging from Meillassoux's ontology is the way in which he radically separates the two. Because no metaphysical system is ever necessary, there can be no political system that necessarily follows from any given ontology. Subsequently, Meillassoux leaves the socio-political field completely open to radical contingency and possibility.

[33] Martin Hägglund, "Radical Atheist Materialism: A Critique of Meillassoux" in Levi Bryant, Graham Harman, Nick Srnicek eds, *The Speculative Turn* (Melbourne: re:press: 2011), 114-29. My thanks to Martin Hägglund for providing a draft version of his paper.

[34] Ibid, 124.

being grounded in some call for justice, they are simply products of the imperative for human survival and the maintenance of life.

In his work, *Radical Atheism: Derrida and the Time of Life*, Hägglund begins by arguing that the notion of survival he develops is incompatible with any form of immortality, and notes that "to survive is never to be absolutely present; it is to remain after a past that is no longer and to keep the memory of this past for a future that is not yet." [35] For Hägglund, every moment of life is a matter of survival, and everyone is engaged in this survival, without exception. [36] In regards to the relationship between survival and justice, Hägglund equates to the two, and argues that the struggle for justice is in reality a struggle for survival. [37] He goes on to connect justice to exclusion, remarking, "Justice can only be brought about by 'living mortals' who will exclude and annihilate by maintaining the memory and life of certain others at the expense of other others." [38] He later reiterates this connection between justice and exclusion, stating, "The power of the people can only constitute itself by drawing a border that defines who does and who does not belong to 'the people.'" [39] Thus for Hägglund, it seems as if survival is equal to justice, and that justice is always a process of one group working towards the exclusion of another.

Because for Hägglund and his theory of "radical atheism" there is only this one world and the set of possibilities contained within it, "there is no line of flight from the exigencies of the actual world and its particular demands." [40] Thus there is no room for a thought of a new situation not contained within the possibilities of the present, as all human struggle is a struggle for raw survival and not an attempt at transforming an existing situation. So while Meillassoux's theory of necessary contingency allows for one to always affirm that "another world is possible" and that no socio-political situation is necessary, Hägglund's radical atheist materialism instead claims that there is no God or justice to come which will rectify our contemporary situation. Instead, the logic of radical atheist materialism "seeks to articulate *why* everything remains to be done, by refuting the untenable hope of redemption." [41] Rather than following Meillassoux's utilization of Cantor in arguing for the non-totalisable nature of reality,

---

[35] Martin Hägglund, *Radical Atheism: Derrida and the Time of Life* (Stanford: Stanford University Press, 2008), 1.
[36] Ibid, 2.
[37] Ibid, 140.
[38] Ibid.
[39] Ibid, 175
[40] Hägglund, "Radical Atheist Materialism", 129.
[41] Ibid.

and subsequently using this to affirm a notion of absolute possibility, Hägglund seems to promote the brand of materialism which claims that there is what there is, nothing more, nothing less.

It seems as if the materialism of Hägglund and that of Meillassoux differ on the following issue: Meillassoux's account offers room for such terms as hope and justice (as absolute equality), while Hägglund simply provides an account of survival. We will return to this distinction between survival and justice at the end of the essay.

V. God as Possibility

We will now put forth the argument that one of the major shortcomings of Meillassoux's divinology is the notion of God as possible. While interesting in a purely speculative register, this conception of a "possible God" (or, of a God who May be) offers little more than a possible philosophy of religion that is able to critically co-exist with contemporary materialist philosophy. It will, instead, be our contention that rather than conceiving of God as possible, it is a more constructive move to think about God as the very name of possibility itself. In this sense, philosophy of religion is more than a discipline in waiting, ready for the possible advent of the divine, but rather a branch of philosophy concerned with possibility itself. It names the critique of ideology inherent to ontology and allows one to posit that things could always be other than they currently are, and that no situation carries with it a sense of absolute necessity.

To briefly outline this subtle (but crucial) modification of Meillassoux's divinology, we will follow Slavoj Žižek's recent materialist appropriation of Søren Kierkegaard. This reading shows us that once any necessarily existing and totalising transcendent entity is removed, Kierkegaard provides materialist philosophy with a way to conceive of the divine as the absolute possibility existing once thought moves beyond the constraints of finitude.

In his 2007 work, *The Parallax View*, Žižek dedicates almost an entire chapter to a materialist reading of Kierkegaard. According to Žižek, "Only a thin, almost imperceptible line separates Kierkegaard from dialectical materialism proper", largely because, for Kierkegaard, "in the last resort, there is no theory, just a fundamental practico-ethical decision about what kind of life one wants to commit oneself to."[42] In this sense, we can already see that for Kierkegaard, because there is no necessary metaphysical order underlying reality, one is always forced to decide what

---

[42] Slavoj Žižek, *The Parallax View* (Cambridge: MIT Press, 2006), 75.

commitments will order one's life. Žižek reads Kierkegaard as a thinker of absolute becoming who wants to "reintroduce the openness of the future into the past", and for whom totalised metaphysical systems do little more than point out the comic figure of the philosophy professor who has managed to step outside of existence and view objective reality as a totalised and logical whole.

Žižek acknowledges that Kierkegaard "admits the radical openness and contingency of the entire field of reality" and goes on to note:

> Kierkegaard's God is strictly correlative to the ontological openness of reality, to our relating to reality as unfinished, "in becoming". God is the name of the absolute other against which we can measure the thorough contingency of reality. [God] is nothing but the mode of how we relate to him; that is to say, we do not relate to him, he is this relating.[43]

As Žižek rightly notes, for Kierkegaard God is possibility itself, because "God is this—that all things are possible."[44] Whereas for Meillassoux, because anything is possible, God can be conceived of as possible, for Kierkegaard, God *is* that anything is possible. Rather than signifying a potential "what", Kierkegaard's God is an actual "how". God is that we relate to reality as open and contingent. Clearly this breaks with Meillassoux on another level, since for Kierkegaard God signifies a mode of relation between subject and reality, but as some commentators (most notably, Peter Hallward[45]) have noted, this absolute lack of relationality is one of the more problematic aspects of Meillassoux's thought, and one in need of supplementation if his work is to have any serious efficacy in philosophy of religion (as religion, if anything, signifies the way in which one relates to the world and others). But it must also be noted, as Žižek rightly does[46], that Kierkegaard shares with Meillassoux a critique of the philosophies of finitude. But whereas Meillassoux responds to the totalised metaphysical constructs of the philosophies of finitude with ancestrality, Kierkegaard responds with humour. Žižek notes that this humour is always founded in the inevitable remainder, or gap, left by the philosophers of finitude. Once again, it seems clear that this remainder left by totalised metaphysical systems is the very space (or lack thereof) in which religious thought can (and should) operate.

---

[43] Ibid, 79.
[44] Søren Kierkegaard, *The Sickness Unto Death*, translated by Howard V. Hong and Edna H. Hong (Princeton: Princeton University Press, 1980), 40.
[45] Peter Hallward, "Anything is Possible: Review of Quentin Meillassoux's *After Finitude*" in *Radical Philosophy* 152, 51-56.
[46] Žižek, *Parallax View*, 110.

One of the important aspects of this reading of Kierkegaard, and one which he shares with Meillassoux, is the use of absolute contingency and possibility as a tool for the critique of dominant ideologies. In *After Finitude* Meillassoux claims:

> The critique of ideologies, which ultimately always consists in demonstrating that a social situation which is presented as inevitable is actually contingent, is essentially indissociable from the critique of metaphysics... For the kind of dogmatism which claims that this God, this world, this history, and ultimately this actually existing political regime necessarily exists, and must be the way it is—this kind of absolutism does indeed seem to pertain to an era of thinking which is neither possible nor desirable to return.[47]

In one of the only moments in *After Finitude* that discusses the political, and connects political and ontological possibility, Meillassoux once again reiterates that, just as natural laws and ontological entities can in no way be necessary, no reigning political, social, or religious ideology can ever claim to be absolutely necessary. In this respect, Meillassoux's necessity of contingency allows one to always be able to critique dominant powers on the grounds that they are in no way necessary, and that things could always be otherwise. In a similar vein, Kierkegaard's conception of God as absolute possibility provides him with the tools to critique not only the totalising metaphysical ideology espoused by the Danish Hegelians, but more importantly, allows him to launch an ethico-religious critique of the present age, in which the "Triumphant Church" has claimed to be the consummation of truth and religion, and there is no longer room for militant and creative praxis. This theorization of the critical potential of God has led Mark Dooley to comment that this critical and liberatory potential places Kierkegaard's God in close proximity with the God of liberation theology.[48]

So, while he was writing long before the developments of Cantor, it could be said that Kierkegaard would likely be in fundamental agreement with Meillassoux's (and Badiou's) ontological utilization of set theory to emphasize the contingent and open nature of reality. However, unlike Meillassoux and Badiou, but like Cantor himself, Kierkegaard would likely have called this infinite openness God.

---

[47] Meillassoux, *After Finitude*, 34.
[48] Mark Dooley, *The Politics of Exodus* (New York: Fordham University Press, 2001), 19.

VI. Justice or Survival?

We will now return to the earlier distinction between survival and justice that was discussed in relation to Hägglund's response to Meillassoux's divinology. To make more sense of this distinction, we will follow Alain Badiou in locating two dominant strands in contemporary philosophical thought, and argue that while one of these positions contains within it a notion of possibility which allows one to hope for that which is presently impossible, the other position leaves one with little more than an emphasis on the raw survival of biological life.

In his most recent work, *Logics of Worlds*, Alain Badiou opens with a dichotomous cartography of the two dominant strands of materialist philosophy. The first, which Badiou equates with "natural belief", is *democratic materialism*, which can be summed up in the statement *"there are only bodies and languages."*[49] This line of thought equates existence with the individual body, and Badiou argues that the humanist protection of all living bodies functions under the scientific name of "bioethics."[50] This materialism is a "materialism of life", or "bio-materialism", as it is structured around the preservation of raw biological life. While Badiou equates this type of thought, to varying extents, with both Antonio Negri and Gilles Deleuze, it seems as if Hägglund's radical atheist materialism fits equally well within this demarcation of thought. For Hägglund, because there are only bodies and languages and no divinity or source of eternal truths, all human activity must be focused on the activity of survival and the preservation of the material conditions of life. Hägglund's materialism is no doubt a bio-materialism.

In opposition to this position Badiou presents his own, that of the *materialist dialectic*, which can be summed up by the statement *"There are only bodies and languages, except that there are truths."*[51] For Badiou, these truths only exist as exceptions to what there is, and can equally be thought of as the "except that" of a given situation. Badiou, much like Meillassoux, rests this ontology on the work of Cantor and its implications for thinking through the question of totality. Because we know that reality is transfinite, one can never say something like "this is all that there is." Instead, when we rule out the existence of a set of all sets, one must acknowledge that things could always be otherwise, and that anything is possible. Because of this, we find it reasonable to say that if forced to

---

[49] Alain Badiou, *Logics of Worlds*, trans. Alberto Toscano (London: Continuum, 2009), 1.
[50] Ibid, 2.
[51] Ibid, 4.

designate himself with one of these labels, Meillassoux would likely follow his teacher Badiou and join the materialist dialecticians.

To reiterate our purposes for introducing this distinction, it can clearly be seen that if all that exist are bodies and languages, and that if our materialism is a bio-materialism, we have no room to hope for novel situations which are not contained in the present. Instead, the best we can do is to organize our efforts to democratically fight for and distribute the basic means for biological life to survive. To think of justice would be to step outside the possibilities of the situation. On the other hand, for the materialist dialectician, truth provides the possibility of an "except that", a possibility capable of inaugurating a completely new situation which shows the logic of the previous ideology to be non-necessary and contingent. This is why the materialist dialectician always has room to hope that things could be otherwise, and this hope creates a space of creative dialogue with the sort of religious position that would also hold to the possibility of justice and hope of the creation of another world. To further explicate this subtle difference, it will be useful to briefly look at Žižek's recent discussion of the survival-justice distinction.

In his most recent work, *First as Tragedy then as Farce*, Žižek points out four antagonisms contained within global capitalism that are capable of preventing its indefinite reproduction. These antagonisms are: the looming threat of ecological catastrophe; the inappropriateness of the notion of private property in relation to intellectual property; the socio-ethical implications of new techno-scientific developments, especially in the field of biogenetics; and finally the creation of new forms of apartheid, new walls and slums dividing society. He identifies a gap between this last antagonism and the first three, and that is the gap it creates between the included and excluded. Even more importantly for our concerns, Žižek goes on to note that there is another crucial difference between the first three antagonisms and the fourth, "The first three effectively concern questions of the survival of humanity, but the forth is ultimately a question of justice."[52]

Unintentionally, but helpful for our purposes, Žižek highlights the socio-political implications of the debate we have highlighted between Meillassoux's use of *justice*, and Hägglund's emphasis on *survival*. While the first three antagonisms are solely concerned with the biological survival of the human species as such, the fourth is the one that posits the necessity of an emancipatory process in which there could be such a thing as justice for those in situations of stark oppression with seemingly no way

---

[52] Slavoj Žižek, *First as Tragedy Then As Farce*, (London: Verso, 2009), 91.

out.[53] Ironically, we have already seen that for Hägglund justice itself is always a matter of inclusion and exclusion, so it is clear that for him the justice of which Žižek speaks is not even possible. It seems as if, at least loosely, this debate can once again be one which follows Badiou's distinction between the democratic materialist and the materialist dialectician. Just as Žižek associates the collection of the first three antagonisms with the work of Michael Hardt and Antonio Negri[54], Badiou uses Negri as an explicit example of the democratic materialist. In this example, a process of radical inclusion would serve as the ultimate political "expect that" in an otherwise bio-political situation. Following this, only the materialist dialectician could conceive of the new order in which the included-excluded distinction could be eliminated.

VII. The *Matter* of Hope

For Hägglund, the possibility of change is tied to a (democratic) materialism in which there are only bodies and languages, with no possibility of any "expect that" that could emerge to provide the opening for a new situation. Because of this, he has no need to think about philosophy of religion, or even to consider the possibility of any future divine existence. The materialism of Hägglund, and of democratic materialism in general, is thus a hope-less materialism, with little to offer contemporary debates in philosophy of religion and political theology.

On the other hand, following Badiou, Meillassoux provides a thought of infinite possibility, and one in which, while no necessary divinity currently exists, there is always hope of a God (or situation) to-come. For this line of thought, which we can loosely associate with materialist dialectics, we are free to hope for a justice which will move beyond a distinction of included-excluded and provide us with political possibilities which move beyond the bio-material struggle for survival. In opposition to Hägglund's submission of life to the death which is surely coming through the absolute power of time, Badiou holds onto a notion of the infinite, arguing for the need to "to think existence without finitude—that is the libratory imperative, which extricates existence from the ultimate signifier of its submission, death."[55]

Such is what this line of thought offers philosophy of religion, a way to critique ideologies which claim "this is all there is", and instead affirm the possibility of an "except that" which leave room for hope in another

---

[53] Ibid, 98.
[54] Ibid, 95-96.
[55] Badiou, *Logics of Worlds*, 268

world. And this seems to be the stake of materialist philosophy in the twenty-first century: either this one world is all that we have, or, on the other hand, that the transfinite and non-totalised nature of reality means that we can work towards a new world, as *anything is possible*.

Bibliography

Badiou, Alain. *Logics of Worlds*. Translated by Alberto Toscano. London: Continuum, 2009.

Dooley, Mark. *The Politics of Exodus*. New York: Fordham University Press, 2001.

Hägglund, Martin. "Radical Atheist Materialism: A Critique of Meillassoux." In Levi Bryant, Graham Harman, Nick Srnicek edited, *'The Speculative Turn: Continental Realism and Materialism*. Melbourne: re:press, 2011. 114-29.

—. *Radical Atheism: Derrida and the Time of Life*. Stanford: Stanford University Press, 2008.

Kierkegaard, Søren. *The Sickness Unto Death*. Translated by Howard and Edna Hong. Princeton: Princeton University Press, 1980.

Meillassoux, Quentin. *After Finitude*. Translated by Ray Brassier. London: Continuum, 2008.

—. "Potentiality and Virtuality." Translated by Robin Mackay. *Collapse* II (2007): 55-81.

—. "Spectral Dilemma." Translated by Robin Mackay. *Collapse* IV (2008): 261-275.

Žižek, Slavoj. *First as Tragedy Then as Farce*. London: Verso, 2009.

—. *The Parallax View*. Cambridge: MIT Press, 2006.

CHAPTER SEVENTEEN

LANGUAGE AFTER PHILOSOPHY OF NATURE: SCHELLING'S GEOLOGY OF DIVINE NAMES

DANIEL WHISTLER

Each mineral is a real philological problem.[1]

Future commentary on Dante belongs to the natural sciences... No one has yet approached Dante with a geologist's hammer, in order to ascertain the crystalline structure of his rock, in order to study the particles of other minerals in it, to study its smoky colour, its garish patterning, to judge it as a mineral crystal which has been subjected to the most varied series of accidents.[2]

What happens to language after the post-linguistic turn?
In what does a speculative approach to religion consist?
Such are the two questions around which this essay is structured. It is not my purpose to give a comprehensive answer to either question; rather, I am concerned with one very specific approach that could be taken, and this is the approach of F.W.J. Schelling. Schelling has never been so relevant, and this is in no small part thanks to Iain Hamilton Grant's *Philosophies of Nature after Schelling*. Grant's work—part of the recent resurgence in speculative philosophies—has been instrumental in presenting Schelling's *Naturphilosophie* as a viable pursuit for philosophy in the wake of Deleuze. This chapter is intended as a "regional application" of Grant's presentation of Schelling onto philosophy of language and religion. It is important to stress straight-off that, while language and the numinous may well be two of the deconstructionist's

---

[1] F.W.J. Schelling, *Werke* vol. 5, ed. K.F.A. Schelling (Stuttgart: Cotta, 1856-61), 247; F.W.J. Schelling, *On University Studies*, trans. E.S. Morgan and ed. Norbert Guterman (Athens: Ohio University Press, 1966), 40.
[2] Osip Mandelstam, "Conversation about Dante" in *Selected Poems*, trans. Clarence Brown and W.S. Merwin (New York: New York Review, 1973), 119, 128.

favourite tools for undermining theoretical discourse, this chapter has no such aim. This chapter is and remains an exercise in filling in the gaps.

Much could be written about religion in Schelling's corpus, and even about its role in Grant's interpretation of it. I am interested, however, in providing an account which answers both of the above questions simultaneously. In order to do so, I will begin by pursuing the question of language, and only towards the end of the paper link it up with considerations of religion. The dual answer, I will conclude, is to be found in Schelling's *The Deities of Samothrace* which identifies etymological enquiry into divine names with geological excavation.

I. Testing the Extensity of Speculative Philosophy

The past few years have witnessed a marked speculative turn in Continental philosophy, not only through the gradual appropriation of Deleuze and Badiou by the philosophical mainstream, but also through a number of post-Deleuze/Badiou philosophical experiments which have labelled themselves "speculative". While to call these common experiments in speculative philosophy a "movement" may well be both premature and reductive, it seems undeniable that they exemplify a new impetus in Continental thought. Iain Hamilton Grant has been one of the foremost pioneers of this new-found speculative bent. His reading of Schelling has become a key reference point for thinking through what a re-injection of the speculative into philosophy would look like. It is Grant's Schelling, of course, with whom this chapter is primarily concerned; however, before turning to Grant's project in detail, it is worth considering the collective "speculative vision"—especially with respect to language and religion.

Like all new philosophical movements, recent speculative thought has constructed its own genealogy. Kant is here the central figure, and his centrality is ensured by means of a double gesture. On the one hand, all philosophy since 1780 is dependent upon and determined by Kant's (dis)solution of the problems of the philosophical tradition, but, on the other hand, this (dis)solution is seen as "more or less exhausted" and urgently in need of surpassing.[3] The task of speculation is to overcome the questions of access and representation which Kant bequeathed to

---

[3] See Harman in Brassier *et al*, "Speculative Realism," *Collapse* III (2007), 368. Grant, it must be said, has a more ambivalent relation to Kant than Harman. See Grant in Brassier *et al*, "Speculative Realism", 348-50 (in answer to a question concerning Schelling's relation to Kant).

philosophy, to rediscover, in Meillassoux's words, "the *great outdoors*, the *absolute* outside of pre-critical thinkers."[4]

Recent speculative experiments have also gained identity by defining themselves against many of the trends of twentieth-century philosophy (which, it is claimed, were still in thrall to the post-Kantian settlement). In no respect is this more evident than in their negative attitude to "the linguistic turn" and "the theological turn". This critical attitude is most virulent with respect to language. The linguistic turn at the beginning of the twentieth century is the most extreme manifestation of the Kantian (dis)solution of the problems of the philosophical tradition. Language is another form the problem of our access to the world assumes. Meillassoux in this regard quotes Francis Wolff, "We are locked up in language… without being able to get out… We are in consciousness or language as in a transparent cage. Everything is outside, yet it is impossible to get out."[5] In a similar way, Harman speaks of "this ghetto of human discourse and language and power" to which philosophy has confined itself "for the past two hundred and twenty years."[6] Analytic philosophy of language and post-structuralism both fall afoul of speculation's criticisms. They turned their attention away from "the great outdoors", to obsess over how language gets (or, more accurately, fails to get) us there.[7]

---

[4] Quentin Meillassoux, *After Finitude: An Essay on the Necessity of Contingency*, trans. Ray Brassier (London: Continuum, 2008), 7. Similar diagnoses can be found in Harman's attack on the dominance of the subject-object relation in post-Kantian thought and Grant's critique of representation. Graham Harman, "On Vicarious Causation", *Collapse* II (2007), 172-3 and Iain Hamilton Grant, "Schellingianism and Postmodernity: Towards a Materialist *Naturphilosophie*", paper presented to the Twentieth World Congress of Philosophy in Boston, MA, 10th August 1998. Available at: www.bu.edu/wcp/papers/cult/cultgran.htm. Accessed 01/11/2009.

[5] Meillassoux, *After Finitude*, 6.

[6] Harman in Brassier *et al*, "Speculative Realism", 381. Thus, Harman writes elsewhere (with Bryant and Srnicek) that in the twentieth century "the mediation of language becomes all-encompassing, as the phenomenal realm of subjectivity becomes infested with linguistic marks. Throughout this process, any possibility of a world independent of the human-world correlate is increasingly rejected." It is for this reason they respond, "We propose [the term] 'speculative turn' as a counterpoint to the now tiresome 'linguistic turn'." (Levi Bryant, Graham Harman and Nick Srnicek, "Towards a Speculative Philosophy" in Bryant, Srnicek and Harman eds, *The Speculative Turn: Continental Realism and Materialism* (Melbourne: re:press, 2011), 1, 4.)

[7] Badiou's "Philosophy and Mathematics" is, in this regard, the foundational text for subsequent speculative philosophy. Badiou decries "the sophistical tyranny of language" that has ruled over Western philosophy since Hegel. Alain Badiou,

In *Philosophies of Nature after Schelling*, Grant makes similar criticisms of the linguistic turn. For example, Heidegger is upbraided because, in his thought, "language... supplants nature as the substrate in which beings adhere."[8] And, more generally, Grant attacks "the linguistic idealism that represents 'nature' as determined solely in and for language."[9] The turn to language in twentieth-century philosophy has been, according to Grant, largely a forgetting of nature and the possibilities of *Naturphilosophie*—and it is such possibilities that he wishes to resuscitate (as we shall soon see). It is for reasons such as these that recent speculative philosophy has situated itself on the other side of a post- or anti-linguistic turn, a turn away from the obsessions with language that dominated so much twentieth century philosophy.

Similar things can be said about speculation and religion. There is widespread suspicion about the "theological turn in Continental philosophy".[10] Such tendencies are extensively critiqued by Meillassoux in *After Finitude* under the label of "fideism": "The end of metaphysics," he claims, "has taken the form of an exacerbated return of the religious."[11] Post-Kantian philosophy of religion is condemned to a fideism which renounces philosophy's rights, in order to open the field to theology.

Such, therefore, is a brief survey of speculative positions on religion and language. Much could, of course, be criticised in these somewhat simplistic and rather sweeping comments and, if one were so inclined, one could simply point out that speculation may well be subject to the same vicissitudes of signification as any other philosophy. However, this is not my intention here. Rather, I will assume in what follows the cogency of the speculative position (which, after all, has its attractive elements). My method of proceeding will be as follows: given these positions, I will explore how far they are compatible with one of Grant's own criteria for philosophy—"the extensity test".

"Every philosophical construction," Grant states, "undergoes the test of the *extensity* of its concepts."[12] Elsewhere he elaborates as follows,

---

Theoretical Writings, ed. and trans. Ray Brassier and Alberto Toscano (London: Continuum, 2004), 38.

[8] Iain Hamilton Grant, *Philosophies of Nature after Schelling* (London: Continuum, 2006), 6.

[9] Ibid, 16.

[10] Again, Badiou's "Philosophy and Mathematics" provides a crucial precedent.

[11] Meillassoux, *After Finitude*, 45.

[12] Grant, *Philosophies of Nature*, 194.

[Philosophy] is 'the infinite science', and cannot therefore be 'conditioned' by eliminating anything a priori from its remit... The infinite science must test itself against the All, which lacks neither nature nor Idea. It is the *extensity* therefore, the *range* and *capacity* of philosophical systems that is being tested... [Schelling] challenges systems to reveal what they eliminate. Insofar as philosophy still leaves nature to the sciences, it continues to fail Schelling's test, and becomes a conditioned, that is, a compromised antiphysics.[13]

My contention is that speculation's negative attitude toward language and religion raises this very question which Grant himself poses to the rest of post-Kantian philosophy. This test of the "extensity of philosophical systems" needs to be turned back on Grant himself. We must challenge Grant (and speculative thought in general) as to whether his philosophical enterprise eliminates language and religion, and so here displays its blind spot. An attempt to construct Grant's answer to such testing will form the basis of the rest of this essay. *Do speculative philosophies in general and Grant's philosophy of nature in particular have the range and capacity to provide an adequate account of language and religion?*

Let us pause a moment over what this means—taking language as our example. The problem is that language has been seen during the twentieth century as a barrier to speculation, as something which stands between thought and being. The play of signifiers bars us from the signified. My question, however, is the following: can language (and also religion) become *an object of speculation*? What happens when we treat language as one object among others? This, of course, requires bracketing off "the play of signifiers", the disruptive elements of language generally and even the very fact that philosophy is propagated in a linguistic medium. However, such bracketing may well be worth the effort if it were possible, through this act, to conceive of a speculative linguistics in parallel to a speculative physics. In other words, the question is: can language be transformed from the universal medium in which philosophy takes place into a regional object on which philosophy speculates?

II. The Resurrection of *Naturphilosophie*

In order to answer these questions, it is first necessary to give an initial sketch of Grant's project and his reading of Schelling, so as to be able to sound out its "extensive value".

---

[13] Ibid, 19-21. Grant is here quoting from Schelling, *Werke*, 2:56.

The project is best summed up by the opening of Grant's contribution to the first "speculative realist" workshop: "The basic thing I want to talk about is the philosophical problem of nature, and I think this is a springboard for speculation—not opportunistically, but necessarily"[14]; moreover, according to Grant, by far the most significant speculative resolution of the problem of nature was provided by F.W.J. Schelling. Schelling's insistence on "the eternal and necessary bond between philosophy and physics"[15], Grant maintains, is a timeless alternative for philosophy, one that puts it back in touch with its speculative roots. "Schellingianism is resurgent every time *philosophy reaches beyond the Kant-inspired critique of metaphysics, its subjectivist-epistemological transcendentalism, and its isolation of physics from metaphysics.*"[16]

Schelling's *Naturphilosophie*, therefore, is to be opposed to much of the philosophical tradition. In fact, even Badiou (darling of much speculative thought) and Deleuze (Grant's preferred contemporary philosopher) fall short of it.[17] They—along with the rest of post-Cartesian philosophy—manifest the tendency to *philosophical antiphysics*, Schelling's *bête-noire*. "The whole of modern philosophy since its inception (through Descartes)," Schelling famously writes, "has this common deficiency— that nature does not exist for it."[18]

This forgetting of nature is exemplified most clearly in Schelling's immediate forebear, Fichte. Time and again, Schelling attacks Fichte for eliminating nature from philosophy, or, what is the same thing, for treating nature from a merely ethical perspective. To take merely one example of Schelling's criticism,

---

[14] Grant in Brassier *et al*, "Speculative Realism", 334.

[15] Schelling, *Werke*, 7:101; Iain Hamilton Grant, "The 'Eternal and Necessary Bond Between Philosophy and Physics': A Repetition of the Difference Between the Fichtean and Schellingian Systems of Philosophy", *Angelaki* 10.1 (2005), 54. As my concern in this section is with Grant's Schelling: as well as citing the German, I will cite Grant's translation of it (where available) as opposed to other English translations. Where no English citation is given, translations are my own.

[16] Grant, *Philosophies of Nature*, 5.

[17] On Badiou, see Grant, *Philosophies of Nature*, 8-9 and Iain Hamilton Grant, "'Philosophy Become Genetic': The Physics of the World Soul" in Judith Norman and Alistair Welchman eds, *The New Schelling* (London: Continuum, 2004), 129. On Deleuze, see especially Grant, *Philosophies of Nature*, 190-7.

[18] Schelling *Werke* 7:356; F.W.J. Schelling, *Philosophical Inquiries into the Nature of Human Freedom*, trans. James Gutmann (La Salle: Open Court, 1936), 30.

[Fichtean philosophy] consists of nothing but a moralizing of the entire world that undermines life and hollows it out; a true disgust towards all nature and vitality except that in the subject, and a crude extolling of morality and the doctrine of morals as *the one reality in life and science*.[19]

In such condemnations, Schelling depicts Fichtean "nature-cide"[20] to be a result of the "ethical process" in which philosophy is entrapped. This ethical process is that by which philosophy instantiates the primacy of practical reason at the expense of a speculative approach to nature: "the substitution of ethics for ontology".[21] For both Grant and Schelling, this ethicisation of nature is "as untenable as it is ubiquitous".[22] And it is precisely against it that both their philosophical enterprises are directed.

There are two specific symptoms of nature's elimination and the triumph of the ethical that Grant observes in modern philosophy. The first is the sharp distinction therein between organic and inorganic nature. When in the third *Critique* Kant makes organisms the key to reflective judgment, he in effect draws a boundary between the organic as philosophically significant and the inorganic as philosophically insignificant. Nature is limited to life—and that which subsists below this threshold of animation is ignored.[23] Biology is of interest to philosophy, but geology is not.

The second symptom of the post-Cartesian forgetting of nature is its phenomenalism, and consequently its somatism (i.e. its reduction of the natural world to a series of bodies). That is, modern philosophy limits nature to what can be experienced, and thus to a theory of bodies.[24] This is

---

[19] Schelling, *Werke*, 7:19; Grant, *Philosophies of Nature*, 61.

[20] Grant, "The Eternal and Necessary Bond", 45.

[21] Iain Hamilton Grant, "Being and Slime: The Mathematics of Protoplasm in Lorenz Oken's 'Physio-Philosophy'", *Collapse* IV (2008), 288-9. Kant's third *Critique* is the paradigm instance of this. It manifests "the fatal decay of modern European *Wissenschaft* from *physis* to the ethico-teleological." (Grant, *Philosophies of Nature*, 104)

[22] Grant, "Being and Slime", 289.

[23] "Postkantian philosophy has repeatedly reverted to organism, to the phenomena of *life*, precisely to head off naturephilosophical incursions. In other words, inherent in the problem of organism… is a *two-worlds physics*. Life acts as an Orphic guardian for philosophy's descent into the physical." (Grant, *Philosophies of Nature*, 10)

[24] In fact, Grant traces this view all the way back to Aristotle, who, he claims, perverts Platonic physics by transforming it into a science of bodies. Grant reads Schelling's Platonism precisely as an attempt to overthrow this Aristotelian perversion (Grant, *Philosophies of Nature*, 54).

a product of philosophy's indolence with respect to nature, its disinclination to go beyond the given and uncover its conditions. Indeed, when it comes to nature, Kant and Fichte (for example) were *not transcendental enough*—accepting phenomenal experience without considering its physical conditions. Philosophy has only been interested in natural phenomena (not productive nature) and, in consequence, cannot get at what exceeds such phenomena (either the infinitesimally small or the "arche-fossil"[25] or cosmological temporality).

What, then, does a speculative *Naturphilosophie* freed from "the ethical process" look like? The basis of Schelling's *Naturphilosophie*, Grant claims, is his rejection of somatism in favour of dynamics: "Forces before bodies."[26] Central to this change in perspective is a tireless concern with *how the phenomenal is generated*; it is this which is of interest, *not* phenomenal bodies themselves.

This change in focus from somatics to dynamics requires the philosopher to go beyond what is phenomenally apparent and discover that which exists below the threshold of the given. In passing beyond the phenomenal, *Naturphilosophie* is therefore able to treat everything which cannot be contained within our human powers of representing. Significantly for our purposes, Schelling's non-phenomenological physics is thus able to examine geological and cosmological time-spans, that is, the durations which give birth to fossils and to new species. Such periods are inaccessible to the individual human's capacity of imagination; they are, in Kantian language, sublime. Yet, in moving beyond the phenomenal, Schelling is able to begin to think about "the timescales involved in natural becomings [which] exceed the phenomenological capacity not only of individuals, but also of any and all species."[27] Such is Schelling's point when he notes,

> The alterations to which organic as well as inorganic nature are subjected may have happened in *far greater periods of time than our lesser time periods can provide a measure for*, and that are so great that until now no such experience has been lived through.[28]

---

[25] The "arche-fossil" is Meillassoux' label for that which precedes all possible experience. See Meillassoux, *After Finitude*, 9-10.

[26] Grant, "Physics of the World Soul", 137.

[27] Grant, *Philosophies of Nature*, 127.

[28] Schelling, *Werke*, 2:349; Grant, *Philosophies of Nature*, 139.

At the heart of Schelling's new dynamics of nature lies the concept of "non-linear recapitulation". It is Carl Friedrich Kielmeyer's initial exposition of this notion in his 1793 *On the Proportions of Organic Forces throughout the Series of Organisations* that leads Schelling to exclaim that "a new epoch in natural history" has begun.[29] Basically put, non-linear recapitulation denotes the process by which the productive forces which constitute nature repeat themselves in ever higher potencies *ad infinitum* (i.e. without a teleological endpoint).[30] The same forces recur incessantly and it is the job of the philosopher of nature "to plot their recursion and mutation throughout each and every branch of the system of nature."[31] Such a theory of the self-recapitulation of forces is *non-linear*, because, unlike linear recapitulation, it does not posit one body (namely, the human) as the end-point of the mutation, as the point where the forces perfect themselves.[32] Instead, non-linear recapitulation is in principle *endless*: the same proportion of forces can recur in ever higher potencies *ad infinitum*.

Because it is exactly the same forces that recapitulate in producing different bodies, there is *no gulf* between the organic and inorganic for Schelling and Kielmeyer. What is more, nature does not just extend into the geological and inorganic, but also into the mental realm. Grant insists that *Naturphilosophie* should be able to explain ideas as well. It is for this reason he comes up with the extensity test considered in the previous section: *Naturphilosophie* to really count as the "physics of the All" must be able to give an account of ideogenesis (otherwise it would be conditioned by something it excluded). It needs to provide "a dynamics… of the concept".[33]

It is non-linear recapitulation which achieves just such a one-world physics. The proportion of forces that produce real phenomena repeats itself in all that exists, and so recurs in ideal phenomena too. Schelling's is

---

[29] Schelling *Werke*, 2:565; Grant, *Philosophies of Nature*, 110.

[30] Grant quotes extensively from Kielmeyer to this effect in *Philosophies of Nature*, 129.

[31] Grant, *Philosophies of Nature*, 119.

[32] *Linear* recapitulation is a theory of the analogous relation between different *bodies* (a microcosm/macrocosm relation). It establishes a "hierarchy" of beings with man at the top. Grant thus speaks of "the ethico-teleological project of the linear recapitulationists" (Grant, *Philosophies of Nature*, 131) and its "somatic-phenomenal" basis (ibid, 131).

[33] Grant, *Philosophies of Nature*, 21.

"an uninterrupted physicalism leading from 'the real to the ideal'".[34] In Schelling's words, the task for a *Naturphilosophie* that intends to become "absolute" is to trace "a natural history of our mind"[35]—"to pursue the dynamic process from nature to ideation."[36]

Such "a non-somatic and non-phenomenal dynamic *physis* of ideation"[37] is possible, according to Schelling, on the premise that the transcendental conditions of experience are located in the dynamic interaction of forces, rather than the play of faculties. *Naturphilosophie*, in Schelling's words, "materialises the laws of intelligence into laws of nature."[38] It follows the self-recapitulation of nature into thought, and realises that intelligence "is a simple consequence of nature's incessant potentiation".[39] Consciousness, therefore, becomes, *pace Kant*, a regional phenomenon, one more object among other objects (to use Harman's language).

Such, therefore, is Grant's Schelling: a Schelling who rejects the somatism and phenomenalism of more dominant strands of philosophy by looking to the empirically inaccessible forces which generate the phenomenal world; a Schelling who—through the concept of non-linear recapitulation—provides a dynamics which includes both the idea and the geological. Schelling's philosophy is, Grant claims, a speculative physics which, as absolute, excludes nothing from its purview—from the oldest rock to the newest idea.

Does it, however, include language and religion? Such is the question to which I now turn. I am interested in discovering the way in which Grant's Schelling could make room for a speculative account of these two fields in his absolute philosophy. In order to anticipate an answer, it is worth reconsidering the manner in which Grant absorbs ideas and ethics into this absolute philosophy. This will provide a preliminary clue to how we should expect language and religion to be so incorporated. Grant (following Schelling) attacks the "idealist" and "practicist" orientations which dominate philosophy and eliminate nature; however, his attitude towards them is not merely critical, since—having reinstated a speculative

---

[34] Ibid, 11 (quoting Schelling, *Werke*, 3:272-3). Grant puts it elsewhere as follows, "Nature thinks just as nature 'mountains' or nature 'rivers' or nature 'planetises', or what have you. These things are the same to all intents and purposes." (Grant in Brassier *et al*, "Speculative Realism", 344)

[35] Schelling, *Werke*, 2:39; Grant, *Philosophies of Nature*, 45.

[36] Grant, *Philosophies of Nature*, 172.

[37] Ibid, 113.

[38] Schelling *Werke*, 3:352; Grant, *Philosophies of Nature*, 29.

[39] Schelling, *Werke*, 4:76; Grant, "The Eternal and Necessary Bond", 48.

viewpoint on nature—Grant returns to the *topoi* of ideas and ethics to show how they, in fact, are regional manifestations of nature itself. For Fichte, theory of consciousness is the whole of philosophy and "it is only…in [one] small region of consciousness that there lies a world of the senses: nature"[40]; for Schelling, the exact reverse is true.[41] The ideal realm is *downgraded* from its position as determining the whole of a philosophy of consciousness (through its privileged relation to the subject) to a mere *regional object of philosophy of nature*. Schelling, that is, inverts Kant and Fichte's "idea of nature" into a "physics of the idea". Nature, not consciousness, becomes the subject of philosophy. This *regionalisation* is, what I will dub, *the speculative process*: whereas "the ethical process" is that by which ethics supplants nature, "the speculative process" reverses this, supplanting ethics with a speculative philosophy of nature (one regional object of which is ethics). It is such a process that I will attempt to locate in *Naturphilosophie*'s attitudes to language and religion.

III. Fichte's Ethical Dissolution of Language

I will begin with language, for—as we shall discover—it is by pursuing the speculative attitude to language that we will end up discovering the appropriate speculative attitude to religion. My procedure will be to return to Schelling himself to uncover any answer (or intimations of an answer) which he may have given as to the role of language (and religion) in *Naturphilosophie* and, in consequence, which can be incorporated into Grant's account. However, as Hennigfeld points out, language is not a particularly popular topic for Schelling: "There is no elaborate philosophy of language in Schelling's corpus; there are, however, a few significant indications of isolated beginnings of a philosophy of language."[42] It is two such "isolated beginnings" on which I

---

[40] J.G. Fichte, "Letter to Schelling, 31/05/1801" in F.W.J. Schelling, *Briefe und Dokumente* vol. 2, ed. Horst Fuhrmans (Bonn: Grundmann, 1973), 343; translated in "Selections from Fichte-Schelling Correspondence (1800-1801)" in Jochen Schulte-Sasse *et al* ed, *Theory as Practice: A Critical Anthology of Early German Romantic Writings* (Minneapolis: University of Minnesotta Press, 1997), 83.

[41] Hence, he replies to Fichte, "I know sufficiently well in what small region of consciousness you have to situate nature, due to the concept you have of it. It has for you absolutely no speculative significance, but only a teleological significance." "Letter to Fichte, 03/10/1801" in Schelling, *Briefe* 2:354.

[42] Jochem Hennigfeld, "Schellings Philosophie der Sprache", *Philosophisches Jahrbuch* 91.1 (1984), 16. My translation.

will concentrate in what follows and, through them, I hope to reconstruct Schelling's speculative linguistics.

However, before turning to the first of these "isolated beginnings", it is worth pausing for a moment over Fichte's theory of language. This is because, *in exact parallel to the reduction of nature to ethics that Grant and Schelling attack in Fichte's writings, a reduction of language to the ethical can also be discerned therein.* Language too is subject to the ethical process and, through it, becomes a tool of intersubjective interaction.

Fichte's essay on the subject ("On the Linguistic Capacity and the Origin of Language") is an attempt to chart "the 'genesis' of language transcendentally considered."[43] As with all Fichte's forays into transcendental philosophy, the task is therefore to exhibit *the primacy of the practical* in this field of philosophy enquiry. Language, Fichte claims, enables a relationship between subject and subject that can acknowledge the pre-existing spontaneity of each party. Through language, "an interchange between freedom and purposiveness is revealed."[44] Language is the means by which we recognise the purpose spontaneously formed by the other—we realise the other is already ethical too:

> I wish that the other might know my intention so that he would not act against me and, for the same reason, I wish to know the intentions of the other. Thus arises the task of inventing fixed signs by which we can communicate our thoughts to others.[45]

Fichte writes elsewhere even more explicitly, "The character of the sign is [an] eliciting of freedom by freedom... a summons to free activity through the influence of a rational being."[46] Language is a product of intersubjective, ethical relations.

The Fichtean account of language is, then, a *pragmatic* account—a reduction of language to the ethical. Language is subjected to the "ethical process" just as nature is elsewhere in Fichte's corpus.

The question therefore becomes even more insistent: does Schelling respond to the Fichtean ethicisation of language as he responds to his

---

[43] Jere Paul Surber, *Language and German Idealism: Fichte's Linguistic Philosophy* (New Jersey: Humanities, 1996), 28.

[44] J.G. Fichte, "On the Linguistic Capacity and the Origin of Language", trans. J.P. Surber in Surber, *Language and German Idealism*, 123.

[45] Ibid, 124.

[46] J.G. Fichte, "Lecture Notes on Platner's *Aphorisms*", trans. J.P. Surber, in Surber, *Language and German Idealism*, 156-8.

ethicisation of nature? Is there a speculative rebuttal of such an elimination of language which parallels his *Naturphilosophie*'s rejection of Fichtean "nature-cide"?

IV. Schelling's Speculative Linguistics

One intimation of a response is to be found in Schelling's 1811 speech to the Munich Academy, *Bericht über den pasigraphischen Versuch des Professor Schmid in Dilligen*. In the *Bericht*, Schelling is intent on incorporating philosophy of language into *Naturphilosophie*. The first suggestion that this is specifically what he intends can be discerned from the following,

> One may ask whether there are not... homologous language formations like there are mountain formations that can recur in quite different places in the world independently of each other.[47]

Can words, Schelling asks, be thought of as physical phenomena, produced by dynamic forces analogous to those which generate other natural phenomena (like mountains)? That is, is a physics of language possible?

Later in the *Bericht*, Schelling goes even further,

> When one cognises the physical in language, and pursues and arranges the facts of the history of peoples and language in connection or at least in analogy to the geological, what wondrous and (at present) unbelievable regularity and lawfulness will then appear before our eyes![48]

This quotation is crucial, and I will return to it repeatedly in what follows. First, Schelling insists on the need to "cognise the physical in language." This is a remarkable recommendation and one that can be flatly opposed to Fichte's reduction of the linguistic to intersubjective communication. Language, Schelling implies, is a natural object like any other: it is constituted from natural forces and can be absorbed into a naturephilosophical account of reality. Just as Schelling conceived of a dynamics inclusive of the idea, so too here he suggests the need for a dynamics that takes account of the word. By "cognising the physical in language", words become objects of a speculative physics, the appropriate subject-matter of *Naturphilosophie*.

---

[47] Schelling, *Werke*, 8:453.
[48] Ibid.

Second, Schelling advocates understanding the history of language "in connection or at least in analogy to the geological". This is key to my present purposes. Here, Schelling goes beyond his own initial comparison with mountain formations: language should not be merely thought of *"in analogy"* to geological phenomena, but—more than that—*"in connection"* with them. This connection goes beyond a merely regulative metaphorical relation to a determinative, ontological one. Schelling transcends his initial cautious separation of the linguistic from the geological, so as to discover their common ground. *The geo-logical supersedes the ana-logical.*

Schelling's comments here are consistent with Grant's insistence on the "more than analogical" relation between disparate realms in Schelling's work. Deleuze writes, for example, in imitation of Schelling, "Depth is like the famous geological line from NE to SW, the line which comes diagonally from the heart of things and distributes volcanoes."[49] Grant dubs such mimicry a failure, however: Schelling is "as different from the Deleuzian as from the Kantian."[50] This is all down to the "like" which appears—this is not Schellingian, but rather Kantian. Deleuze follows Kant in building a merely *analogical* bridge between nature and thought, physics and metaphysics (and by extension, geology and linguistics). Schelling's bridge, on the contrary, is built of stone! Deleuze remains in thrall here to a logic of representation, whereas Schelling is more Deleuzian than Deleuze. For Schelling, "the likeness involved in such correspondences is not ideal or analogical, but physical."[51] *Linguistics and geology are to be welded together.*

---

[49] Deleuze, *Difference and Repetition*, trans. Paul Patton (London: Athlone, 1994), 230; Grant, *Philosophies of Nature*, 200.

[50] Grant, *Philosophies of Nature*, 201.

[51] Ibid, 200. Indeed, in the corresponding passage from Schelling the "like" is conspicuously absent (Schelling, *Werke*, 4:504-5; Grant, *Philosophies of Nature*, 201). Grant makes the same point in his article, "The Chemistry of Darkness", picking on a passage in which Deleuze asks, "What, after all, are ideas, if not these ants which enter and leave through the fracture of the I?", and asking in return, "What sort of ideas are ants? Actual ones (do thoughts *ant*?), virtual ones, or... are ants *like* ideas?" (Iain Hamilton Grant, "The Chemistry of Darkness", *Pli* 9 (2000), 39) Indeed, later in the article, Grant returns to this question. After having quoted Deleuze's imitation of Schelling's "geological line", Grant asks, "What sort of earth does depth give us? a *quasi* earth, an *'als ob'*, regulative rather than constitutive earth, a *merely subjective*, or Kantian earth. Ants are like Ideas, and depth is *like* the heated profiles of tectonic plates." (Ibid, 42) The geo-logical/ana-logical opposition is again discussed in Iain Hamilton Grant, "Kant after Geophilosophy: The Physics of Analogy and the Metaphysics of Nature" in

V. Linguistics and Geology: The Weak Claim

However, we are still not in a position to understand how this is the case. There is a weak and a strong claim here: first, *words are analogous to rocks* and, second, *words are rocks*. To get an idea of how the strong claim is possible, it is worth beginning with the weaker claim concerning the similarity of linguistics and geology. In order to do so, let us turn to the second "isolated beginning" of a Schellingian philosophy of language. This is located at the end of Schelling's third 1803 lecture, *On University Studies*.

Once again, we find language and geology juxtaposed. Schelling compares the hermeneutic faculty needed to study dead languages with the method required for studying the hidden strata of nature. In both, one needs to "recognise the living spirit" in a seemingly dead product, to discover, that is, the abyss of productivity underlying it. Schelling continues,

> Even those who investigate nature only empirically need to know her language in order to understand utterances which have become unintelligible to us. The same is true of philology in the highest sense of the term. The earth is a book made up of miscellaneous fragments dating from very different ages. Each mineral is a real philological problem. In geology we still await the genius who will analyse the earth and show its composition as Wolf [the 18th century German philologist] analysed Homer.[52]

We have here a claim very similar to one made a few years earlier by Novalis: "Similarity of historical geology and mineralogy to philology".[53] Schelling and Novalis both insist on the methodological parallels between the two disciplines.

Why? Let us recall Schelling's rejection of phenomenalism in his *Naturphilosophie*: by undercutting somatic physics with a dynamics of the productive forces which generate bodies, Schelling goes beyond what is phenomenally given to ground his *Naturphilosophie* in a non-phenomenological realm. To quote Grant,

> The fact that the Earth's creatures are merely the 'outward phenomenon' of the proportions of forces, poses the challenge: *if the ground cannot be*

Andrea Rehberg and Rachel Jones eds, *The Matter of Critique: Readings in Kant's Philosophy* (Manchester: Clinamen, 2000), 37.

[52] Schelling, *Werke*, 5:246-7; Schelling, *On University Studies*, 39-40.

[53] Novalis, "On Goethe" in *Philosophical Writings*, ed. and trans. Margaret Mahony Stoljar (Albany: SUNY, 1997), 125 (§21).

sought in bodies, and if all bodies are accessible to sense, then the forces themselves are unintuitable.[54]

A "physical abyss"[55] thus opens up before the philosopher of nature—an unintuitable realm of immeasurable productivity.

The attraction of geology given such considerations is obvious.[56] Geology excavates beneath the surface of nature to its grounds; it makes possible a thinking of the non-phenomenal forces which ground reality. Schelling insists on this in a remark made contemporaneously with the lectures *On University Studies*: apart from geological research, "we have no analogue amongst the known processes for the process of... eruption."[57] Only geology can deal with the unruly eruptions which emerge out of extra-phenomenal realms. The first draft of the *Weltalter* insists on this point,

> The oldest formations of the earth bear such a foreign aspect that we are hardly in a position to form a concept of their time of origin or of the forces that were then at work. Everything that surrounds us refers back to an incredibly deep past... A mass of strata [is] laid one upon the other; the labour of centuries must be stripped away, in order to finally reach the ground.[58]

The philological enterprise is, in essence, the same: a hermeneutical exercise at uncovering the hidden grounds beneath surface meaning. For example, etymology (the focus of *The Deities of Samothrace*) traces the language given to us in the present back to its hidden origins. Just like geology, therefore, philology strips away the sediment to uncover what is primordial. Both sciences proceed beyond the phenomenally given to the forces which generate them, and, as such, both venture into empirically inaccessible depths.

---

[54] Grant, "Physics of the World Soul", 135.

[55] Ibid.

[56] Although it should be borne in mind in what follows that Schelling seems to have a very specific type of geology in mind: geognosis. Geognosis was a late eighteenth and early nineteenth branch of geology, focused specifically on *knowledge of the earth's crust*. Schelling sees such knowledge as paradigmatic of geology as a whole, hence the use of "excavation" models throughout.

[57] Schelling, *Werke*, 4:504-5; Grant, *Philosophies of Nature*, 201. For the historical context out of which Schelling's engagement with geology emerged, see Grant, "Kant After Geophilosophy", 44-53.

[58] F.W.J. Schelling, *Die Weltalter: Fragmente in den Urfassungen von 1811 und 1813*, ed. Manfred Schröter (Munich: Beck, 1946), 11-2; Grant, *Philosophies of Nature*, 204.

This, therefore, is the similarity between geology and philology. What, however, of their identity? To understand this, a further excursus into Schellingian geology is required.

VI. 1809 *Inquiries*: From Dynamics to Geology

At the end of Schelling's 1811 *Bericht*, having flagged up the "connection" between language and geology, Schelling continues: the study of language is one of those "subjects which push us back into the abyss of human nature".[59] To study language, therefore, is to peer into an abyss, and such abysses form the subject matter of Schelling's *Philosophical Inquiries into the Nature of Human Freedom*. Moreover, it is with the *Philosophical Inquiries* that we also return to the question of religion in Grant's Schellingianism.

The role of religion in the *Inquiries* provides us with the answer to the second question with which this essay began: in what does a speculative approach to religion consist? In line with the "speculative process" outlined above, religion is conceived in the *Inquiries* as no longer determinative of philosophy in general, but rather relegated to *a regional object of Naturphilosophie*. Schelling task here is to present a "dynamics of religion". Once more, non-linear recapitulation is the key. God and freedom are the self-recapitulation at a higher potency of the forces which constitute the natural world, just as the mental realm is. Freedom is "the final potentiating act... through which the whole of nature found its transfiguration... All philosophy strives only to find this highest expression."[60] Similar things are said of God:

Nothing can be achieved at all by such attenuated conceptions of God [which] separate God as far as possible from all of nature. God is more of a reality than he is a mere moral world-order, and he has in him quite other and more vital activating powers than the barren subtlety abstract idealists ascribe to him. The abhorrence of all reality, which might sully the spiritual through any contact with it, must naturally blind the eye to the origin of evil too. Idealism, if it is not grounded in a vital realism, will become [an] empty and attenuated system.[61]

---

[59] Schelling, *Werke*, 8:454.

[60] Schelling, *Werke*, 7:550; Schelling, *Inquiries*, 24-5. Translation modified. (Although, if Grant is right and Schelling's notion of recapitulation is genuinely non-linear, no product is ever "final".)

[61] Ibid, 7:356; 30.

God is an assemblage of natural forces too—and it is only philosophy's disdain for nature (its "abhorrence of all reality") which has blinded it to the fact that *nature recapitulates in God*. A doctrine of God, Schelling continues, "could only be developed from the fundamental principles of a genuine philosophy of nature" which "sought out the vital basis of nature".[62]

Nature self-recapitulates in God—such is Schelling's overarching polemic in the *Inquiries* against those philosophers whose disdain for nature have blinded them to the physical connection of all things. Thus, the *Inquiries* ends by insisting that there is no need to rely on the Bible or historical faith in order to understand religion. Nature is a sufficient key to any theory of the divine: "We have an earlier revelation than any written one—nature. If the understanding of that unwritten revelation were inaugurated, the only true system of religion and science would appear."[63] Just as the original Schellingian project insisted that there is no gulf between the real and the mental, so too here Schellingian dynamics is *extended* even further, and consequently becomes even more "unconditioned".

However, this is not the whole story. Schelling is no longer interested in providing a *purely dynamic* account of religion, but instead offers a *geology of religion*. This is not so much a substantial change as a shift in attitude. From the beginning, Schelling was aware of the non-phenomenality of the productivity out of which nature was generated. It is only, however, in 1809 that Schelling faces this issue head-on.

Schelling here focuses even more extensively on the philology of geological excavation he had so briefly invoked in *On University Studies*. He writes in the *Inquiries*,

> The world as we now behold it is all rule, order and form; but the unruly lies ever in the depths as though it might again break through... This is the incomprehensible basis of reality in all things, the irreducible remainder which cannot be resolved into reason by the greatest exertion but always remains in the depths.[64]

---

[62] Ibid, 7:377-8; 54-5. Thus, Schelling concludes later in the *Inquiries*, "We have explained God as the living unity of forces" (ibid, 7:394; 74). Indeed, his famous distinction between ground and existence in God is a distinction between different potentiations of nature (ibid, 7:357-8; 32).

[63] Ibid, 7:415-6; 98.

[64] Ibid, 359-60; 34.

Schellingian dynamics has to deal with the "the unruly". It is for this reason geology becomes Schelling's new model for *Naturphilosophie—a model* (as we saw in regard to *On University Studies*) *that can cope with the unruly abyss with which the philosopher is confronted.* In the *Inquiries, Naturphilosophie* finally becomes "transcendental geology".[65]

The *Inquiries* follows *On University Studies* in re-appropriating for philosophy geology's struggle with what is unruly, excessive and threatening. It is only geology which can cope with "a phenomenal catastrophism"[66]. It is this sustained conjunction of geological thought with a naturephilosophical account of God which has turned the stomach of so many readers of the *Inquiries* from the first (Eschenmayer and Jacobi) through to Manfred Frank. As Eschenmayer acutely observed on the work's publication,

> Your essay on human freedom seems to me a complete transformation of ethics into physics, a consumption of the free by the necessary... of the moral by the natural, and above all a complete depotentiation of the higher into the lower order of things.[67]

To which Grant adds, "We can image Eschenmayer's shock: why does this work on the subject of freedom contain so much geology?"[68]

The geological foundations of the *Inquiries* are fully manifest in the history of religion Schelling sketches. As one might expect, this historical sketch follows the unruly depths of nature as it self-recapitulates in increasingly higher potencies. Nature generates itself into fuller, more actualised forms. As time goes on, the basis self-recapitulates in increasingly more *ideal* forms, transforming itself into light, spirit and finally love.[69] *However*, (and it is here Schelling decisively moves beyond a "dynamics of religion" to a "geology of religion") interspersed between these successive potentiations of nature into the divine are a series of *catastrophes*. For example, "Because the principle of the depths can never give birth for itself to true and complete unity, the time comes in which all this glory decays as through horrible disease, and finally chaos again ensues"[70], or again,

---

[65] Grant, *Philosophies of Nature*, 192.

[66] Ibid, 142.

[67] Schelling, *Werke*, 8:150; Grant, *Philosophies of Nature*, 202.

[68] Grant, *Philosophies of Nature*, 202.

[69] Schelling, *Werke*, 7:378-80; *Inquiries* 56-8.

[70] Ibid, 379; 56.

At last there results the crisis in the *turba gentium* which overflow the foundations of the ancient world as once the waters of the beginning again covered the creations of primeval time.[71]

History in the *Inquiries* incorporates a catastrophic flooding, or, in Grant's words, "a geological eruption in the midst of the philosophy of freedom."[72] *Naturphilosophie* must not only chart the series of bodies *generated* through nature's self-recapitulation, but also the "series of bodies *repeatedly swept away* by this periodic recapitulation of primal forces".[73] This is why a geological model is necessary.

We are now in a position to understand the identity—and not just the similarity—of philology and geology which Schelling intimated in *On University Studies*. Moreover, we are now able to do as the 1811 *Bericht* advises: think words in connection with the geological. As we have seen, religion is nature recapitulated: there is no separation between the two; rather, an identity. In the same way, following the Schellingian notion of non-linear recapitulation, rocks and words *are* nature in different potencies. Both philology and geology attempt to uncover *exactly the same ground*. The unruly itself is the ultimate goal of both endeavours. What is more, religion should now be added to the mix. Nature self-recapitulates its unruly basis in forming God just as much as in forming minerals and syllables. They all have the same ground (the unruly) and are generated by the same subject (productive nature). As such, religious studies, philology and geology are identical pursuits. *This is no mere analogous relation, but a physical one.* Just as we saw Schelling speak of the need to "cognise the physical in language", so too the *Inquiries* insists upon "cognising the physical in God". By so doing, language and religion are subjected to the speculative process: they are incorporated as regional subjects of an overarching, unconditioned *Naturphilosophie*.

VII. *The Deities of Samothrace*: Excavating Nature's Experiments in Divinity

To chart the unruly is to record nature's experiments in religions and languages, and crucial to Schelling are nature's past experiments, and especially the experimental catastrophes which seem to obey no laws. It is

---

[71] Ibid, 380; 57-8.
[72] Grant, *Philosophies of Nature*, 17.
[73] Grant, "Physics of the World Soul", 135. My emphasis.

only by measuring such ancient test-runs that Schelling hopes to unlock the secrets by which future experiments will succeed. He geologically, philologically and theologically excavates the manner in which the abyss of forces potentiated itself and disrupted its own potentiations over millions of years.

The Deities of Samothrace is one such geological excavation of nature's experimentation, and, as always, *this language must be taken literally*. If there is anything that we have learnt from the foregoing, it is the need to take Schelling at his word, to interpret his language literally, not metaphorically. Schelling's ultimate concern in the *Deities*—the etymology of the names of the gods of the ancient Samothracian mystery-cult (the Cabiri)—is achieved *by means of a very concrete and literal geological survey of the island itself*. The work opens,

> The island of Samothrace rises from the northern part of the Aegean Sea... Ancient geographers surmised that great convulsions of nature afflicted these regions even up to human times. It may be that the waters of the Black Sea, raised simply by flooding, first broke through the Thracian Strait, and then through the Hellespont. Or that the force of a subterranean volcano altered the level of the waters. The oldest Samothrace stories, transmuted into monuments exhibited in commemoration, preserved an account of this event, and from that time on they fostered the reverence and patronage of the native gods.[74]

Geology is the starting point of the inquiry and, in particular, the geological irruption (commemorated in "the oldest Samothrace stories") which triggered a new reverence for the divine among the people of Samothrace. The Samothracian mystery-cult, Schelling implies, was born from a "great convulsion of nature" (the "*turba gentium*" of the *Inquiries*). Schelling lingers over this circumstance further in a note to the paragraph,

> At that time when large tracts of Asia would have been covered continuously, others for a time, the lowlands of Samothrace also were inundated, as the inhabitants reported; on the highest mountain peaks they had sought aid with persistent vows to the native gods. Diodorus Siculus adds that around the circumference of the whole island still stand altars which identify the limits of the peril and the deliverance.[75]

---

[74] Schelling, *Werke*, 8:347; F.W.J. Schelling, *The Deities of Samothrace*, ed. and trans. Robert F. Brown (Missoula: Scholars Press, 1977), 15.
[75] Ibid, 8:372; 31.

Schelling's point could be mistaken for a Humean one: an ignorant humanity fabricated superstitions to cope with nature's irregularity. However, nothing could be further from the case and Schelling never tired of heaping scorn on Enlightenment explanations of religion.[76] Instead, Schelling's point is that the names of the Cabiri *commemorate and bear witness to this ancient natural catastrophe*. As Schelling himself writes, the flooding was "transmuted into monuments exhibited in commemoration." By "cognising the physical in language" and recognising "the connection" between the linguistic and the geological, an excavation of the names of the Cabiri can reveal how nature operates in its more catastrophic moments. For example, the name *Axiokersus* contains the Hebrew root *hrs* which, in turn, is connected to fire, and, in this way, it manifests the ancient wisdom that (according to Heraclitus): "The world is an eternal living fire, which at intervals… flares up and is extinguished."[77] The catastrophic unruliness of nature is implicitly contained in these names, and *to etymologically analyse the names is also simultaneously to reveal the workings of nature itself.* Recalling his evocation of nature in the *Inquiries* as "an earlier revelation than anything written" and "the only true system of religion and science", Schelling here speaks of the "scientific system" preserved in the names of the Cabiri as "a primordial system older than all written documents, which is the common source of all religious doctrines and representations."[78] Schelling's etymological analysis reveals nature as it operates over a time-span too great for human representation to bear.

However, once again, to maintain that the names "bear witness" to natural catastrophe *is to reduce a geological to a representational relation*, and so to dilute Schelling's intent. The names, in fact, *are* the unruly ground of this natural catastrophe recapitulated. Etymological excavation *is* (and does not merely "aid") geological excavation. "The secret history of the gods"[79] is that they are generated from the same forces as the *turba gentium*, and so "the hazardous path of philology"[80] is the same path taken by geology. The names of the Cabiri are not just analogous to the system of potencies in nature; *they are its recapitulation. They do not reflect nature, but repeat nature.*

---

[76] For example, see ibid, 8:400-1; 37.
[77] Ibid, 8:391; 34 (Diels-Kranz reference for the Heraclitean fragment: B30).
[78] Ibid, 8:401; 37.
[79] Ibid, 8:348; 15.
[80] Ibid, 8:351; 18.

This view is summed up in Schelling's idiosyncratic translation of a Heraclitean fragment; a fragment in which, Schelling notes, "all of antiquity and the finer humanity... is reflected fully":

> Das Eine weise Wesen will nicht das alleinige genannt seyn, den Namen Zeus will es!
> The One wise nature does not wish to be called that exclusively; it wishes the name 'Zeus'.[81]

Nature, that is, self-recapitulates in the divine names.

VIII. Conclusion

Such, then, is one possible answer to the two questions with which I began: what happens to language after the post-linguistic turn? and in what does a speculative approach to religion consist? According to Schelling, language and religion must undergo "the speculative process", relegating them from philosophical media impeding our access to the world to regional objects of a speculative *Naturphilosophie*. A physics of language and a physics of religion are the preliminary result of such a philosophical operation, and they are thus the means by which Schelling himself passes the extensity test we posed of him. *Naturphilosophie* is unconditioned because it *absorbs* linguistics and theology. Moreover, according to Schelling, these two distinct fields of physical enquiry can be further united in a "geology of divine names", an attempt to think together the abyss of forces recapitulated in both language and religion. Nature recurs and mutates into Zeus, Christ and Krishna, as well as into the names, "Zeus", "Christ" and "Krishna". What is more, the Schellingian philosopher of nature—if she truly wishes to practice an absolute, unconditioned form of philosophy—must follow nature even there. To pass Grant's test of extensity, speculative philosophy must be willing *to chart all of nature's experiments.*

And this, in consequence, is precisely what is required of twenty-first century speculative philosophies. They must dare to pursue nature into its most esoteric phenomena, leaving behind their comfort zones of Lovecraftian monsters and Okenian slime, so as to go after those products of nature that sit less easily with their ethos; those products, that is, which contemporary speculative philosophies still need to incorporate so as to become genuinely unconditioned. We still await speculative accounts of the names of Allah and the words of the Nicene Creed.

---

[81] Ibid, 8:362; 25 (Diels-Kranz reference: B32).

Bibliography

Badiou, Alain. *Theoretical Writings*. Edited and translated by Ray Brassier and Alberto Toscano. London: Continuum, 2004.

Brassier, Ray, Iain Hamilton Grant, Graham Harman and Quentin Meillassoux. "Speculative Realism." *Collapse* III (2007): 307-450.

Bryant, Levi, Graham Harman and Nick Srnicek. "Towards a Speculative Philosophy." In Bryant, Srnicek and Harman edited, *The Speculative Turn: Continental Realism and Materialism* (Melbourne: re:press, 2011). 1-18.

Deleuze, Gilles. *Difference and Repetition*. Translated by Paul Patton. London: Athlone, 1994.

Fichte, J.G. "On the Linguistic Capacity and the Origin of Language." Translated by J.P. Surber. In Surber, *Language and German Idealism*. 119-44.

—. "Lecture Notes on Platner's *Aphorisms*." Translated by J.P. Surber. In Surber, *Language and German Idealism*. 155-65.

Fichte, J.G. and F.W.J. Schelling. "Selections from Fichte-Schelling Correspondence (1800-1801)." In Jochen Schulte-Sasse *et al* edited, *Theory as Practice: A Critical Anthology of Early German Romantic Writings*. Minneapolis: University of Minnesotta Press, 1997. 73-90.

Grant, Iain Hamilton. "Schellingianism and Postmodernity: Towards a Materialist *Naturphilosophie*." Paper presented to the Twentieth World Congress of Philosophy in Boston, MA. August 10th 1998. Available at: www.bu.edu/wcp/papers/cult/cultgran.htm. Accessed 01/11/2009.

—. "The Chemistry of Darkness." *Pli* 9 (2000): 36-52.

—. "Kant after Geophilosophy: The Physics of Analogy and the Metaphysics of Nature." In Andrea Rehberg and Rachel Jones edited, *The Matter of Critique: Readings in Kant's Philosophy*. Manchester: Clinamen, 2000. 37-60.

—. "'Philosophy Become Genetic': The Physics of the World Soul." In Judith Norman and Alistair Welchman edited, *The New Schelling*. London: Continuum, 2004. 128-50.

—. "The 'Eternal and Necessary Bond Between Philosophy and Physics': A Repetition of the Difference Between the Fichtean and Schellingian Systems of Philosophy." *Angelaki* 10.1 (2005): 43-59.

—. *Philosophies of Nature after Schelling*. London: Continuum, 2006.

—. "Being and Slime: The Mathematics of Protoplasm in Lorenz Oken's 'Physio-Philosophy'." *Collapse* IV (2008): 286-322.

Harman, Graham. "On Vicarious Causation." *Collapse* II (2007): 171-206.

Hennigfeld, Jochem. "Schellings Philosophie der Sprache." *Philosophisches Jahrbuch* 91.1 (1984): 16-29.

Mandelstam, Osip. "Conversation about Dante." In *Selected Poems*, translated by Clarence Brown and W.S. Merwin. New York: New York Review, 1973. 101-53.

Meillassoux, Quentin. *After Finitude: An Essay on the Necessity of Contingency*. Translated by Ray Brassier. London: Continuum, 2008.

Novalis. "On Goethe." In *Philosophical Writings*, edited and translated by Margaret Mahony Stoljar. Albany: SUNY, 1997. 111-9.

Schelling, F.W.J. *Werke*. 14 vols. Edited by K.F.A. Schelling. Stuttgart: Cotta, 1856-61.

—. *Philosophical Inquiries into the Nature of Human Freedom*. Translated by James Gutmann. La Salle: Open Court, 1936.

—. *Die Weltalter: Fragmente in den Urfassungen von 1811 und 1813*. Edited by Manfred Schröter. Munich: Beck, 1946.

—. *Briefe und Dokumente*. 3 vols. Edited by Horst Fuhrmans. Bonn: Grundmann, 1962-73.

—. *On University Studies*. Translated by E.S. Morgan and edited by Norbert Guterman. Athens: Ohio University Press, 1966.

—. *The Deities of Samothrace*. Edited and translated by Robert F. Brown. Missoula: Scholars Press, 1977.

Surber, Jere Paul. *Language and German Idealism: Fichte's Linguistic Philosophy*. New Jersey: Humanities, 1996.

CHAPTER EIGHTEEN

MAKING ALL THINGS NEW:
KANT AND RANCIÈRE
ON THE UNINTENTIONAL INTENTIONAL
PRACTICE OF AESTHETICS

BRADLEY A. JOHNSON

In recent years there has been an increased interest in the intersection
of aesthetics and theology. Broadly speaking, this interest has come in
three forms. The first form has focussed on the arts as potential source
material for confessional practice. A representative example of this
approach in the Anglo-world is Jeremy Begbie, who in his growing corpus
has attempted to show how a variety of musical forms have exemplified
fundamental Christian doctrines like election, ecclesiology and Christology.[1]
While this has been an exciting and productive development in
contemporary theology, for reasons that will become abundantly clear as
we progress deeper into our argument, we will not explicitly engage it in
this essay. Suffice it to say at the onset, though, ours is a conception of
theology deeply at odds with the ambitions and tasks of traditional
theology. For some, this may be called an example of secular or aesthetic
theology, while, for many others, it may simply be heresy. In any event,
we will insist, perhaps to the point of readerly frustration, on appealing to
the term "theology." In doing so, we are seeking neither to resuscitate an
ailing theology nor revalorise its place vis-à-vis aesthetics .While we are
opposed to the "theologisation" of aesthetics (and philosophy of religion in

---

[1] Jeremy Begbie, *Voicing Creation's Praise: Towards a Theology of the Arts*
(Edinburgh: T&T Clark, 1991) and *Theology, Music and Time* (Cambridge:
Cambridge University Press, 2000). For a broad view of others who share this
interest, also see Begbie's edited volumes, *Beholding the Glory: Incarnation
Through the Arts* (Grand Rapids: Baker, 2000) and *Sounding the Depths: Theology
Through the Arts* (London: SCM, 2002).

general), which in many respects is the theoretical foundation for the ecclesiological programme of someone like Begbie, we do not necessarily reject the possibility that our conclusions here may in fact have a kind of, shall we say, "impractical relevance" to the specificities of confessional practice and doctrine. For the sake of economy and rhetorical precision, though, we leave it both to the reader and/or a future time to explore this more fully.

The other two most prevalent forms that the recent interest in aesthetics and theology has taken are indebted, respectively, to Hans Urs von Balthasar and Paul Tillich. Where both theologians emphasize the importance of an aesthetic approach to theology, they diverge fundamentally in what this approach ultimately means. For our part here, we will attempt to negotiate a way between both, in order that we might present the contours of a viable alternative. Of this alternative, however, we will not claim to have identified a middle or neutral path between our two representative theologians. The decisive point of departure this alternative will take, via the contemporary political philosophy of Jacques Rancière, probably says enough already about the secularity of our theological predisposition. In this privileging of a non-confessional discourse we betray our alternative as being closer to Tillich than Balthasar; and yet, nevertheless, we will show the differences herein remain crucial and decisive. Indeed, the alternative we will present in what follows cannot be characterized so much as a novel approach, completely divorced from what has come before it, asserted triumphantly in some grand gesture of ingenuity. Rather, we shall argue it is one which, in spite of its always already being there, has been denied a proper place, and thus denied being acknowledged at all—one which now does not assert its role as an alternative so much as it redefines the horizon of alternatives on offer. In the course of doing so, we will substantiate a place of privilege for what we call an "unintentional intentional practice" of aesthetics that intervenes in the traditional enclosure of theological determination.

I.

Though his significant contributions to theology are many, for our purposes here Balthasar is most noteworthy for his resistance to the notion, perhaps most pronounced in Kierkegaard, that revelation and aesthetics are separate (and to some extent even contradictory).[2] Balthasar's position is

---

[2] Søren Kierkegaard, *Concluding Unscientific Postscript to* Philosophical Fragments, Vol. 1, ed. and trans. Howard V. Hong and Edna H. Hong (Princeton: Princeton UP, 1992), 434-47, 524-25, 560-61.

precisely the opposite. For him, theological aesthetics is primarily concerned with thinking about the concept and nature of beauty, for indeed beauty is ultimately indistinguishable from divinity. It is, he writes, "nothing else but the immediate appearance of the groundlessness of Ground out of everything that is grounded. It is the transparency of the mysterious background of being through all appearance."[3] In other words, there is a (divine) truth to sensible reality that is immanent to but ungraspable by reality. As such, this truth, that is, this revelation or expression of God, is a real, continuous occurrence, but one in which there is never a complete identification of divinity with its appearance in the world.[4] Consequently, Balthasar continues, when the faithful are guided by grace, they may then identify the truth of images in aesthetic judgment as the analogous beauty of divine mystery.[5] Inasmuch as the revelation of the beautiful form is based on this inseparability of its inadequate *reference* to divinity and the profound *presence* of the divine,[6] Balthasar argues that we can go even further and conclude then that beauty is the fundamental structure of being itself, "the third transcendental, to complement the vision of the true and the good."[7]

Paul Tillich, in contrast, is decidedly uneasy about ascribing theological significance to the concept of beauty. This uneasiness speaks to his sense of religion as both the subject and object of "ultimate concern," which he defines as "unconditional, independent of any conditions of character, desire, or circumstance."[8] Theology, as such, is set apart by its two "formal criterion":

---

[3] Hans Urs Von Balthasar, *Truth of the World*, Vol. 1 of *Theo-logic: Theological Logical Theory*, trans. Adrian Walker (San Francisco: Ignatius Press, 2000), 223.

[4] Ibid, 251-54.

[5] Hans Urs von Balthasar, *Seeing the Form*, Vol. 1 of *The Glory of the Lord: A Theological Aesthetics,* trans. Erasmo Leiva-Merikakis (San Francisco: Ignatius Press, 1982), 20-21, 36.

[6] Ibid, 119.

[7] Ibid, 9. This discussion of Balthasar's theological aesthetics is especially indebted to Stephan Van Erp's *The Art of Theology: Hans Urs von Balthasar's Theological Aesthetics and the Foundations of Faith* (Leuven: Peeters, 2004). Also see Aidan Nichols, *The Word Has Been Abroad: A Guide Through Balthasar's Aesthetics* (Edinburgh: T&T Clark, 1998).

[8] Paul Tillich, *Systematic Theology*, Vol. 1 (Chicago: University of Chicago Press, 1951), 12.

[1st] The object of theology is what concerns us ultimately. Only propositions are theological which deal with their object insofar as it can become a matter of ultimate concern for us.[9]

[2nd] Our ultimate concern is that which determines our being and non-being. Only those statements are theological which deal with their object insofar as it can be become a matter of being or not-being for us.[10]

Not unlike Balthasar, Tillich warns against the idolatry of assuming that knowledge, or the basic level of appearance, encapsulates the totality of ultimate reality. Knowledge, for Tillich, is directed primarily towards a more or less detached *reception* of truth: that is, it occurs through a "cognitive union" of subject and object that assumes a distance between the one who 'looks' and that which is looked upon 'at a distance'.[11] The aesthetic, on the other hand, aspires to express ultimate reality *immediately* by means of the creation of "images," which is Tillichean shorthand for aesthetic creation in general.[12] Instead of ascribing beauty to these creations, however, he prefers the term "expressive power" or "expressiveness," by which he means their capacity to disclose sensually infinite meaning and ultimate significance.[13] The result, Tillich concludes, is that a truly religious art is consumed by its infinite possibilities for expressing the unconditional.

The important differences between Tillich and Balthasar begin to emerge at this point. For where Balthasar identifies in beauty an analogy between the divine and presentations of the divine, Tillich instead stresses the infinite fullness of the divine (that is, its "being-itself") *in its very presentations*, whether they be beautiful or not. Indeed, it is on this basis that he distinguishes between 'authentic' and 'inauthentic' art. On the one hand, inauthentic art is so "either because it copies the surface instead of expressing the depth or because it expresses the subjectivity of the creating artist instead of his [sic] artistic encounter with reality." On the other hand, authentic art occurs when "an otherwise hidden quality of a piece of the universe (and implicitly of the universe itself) is united with an otherwise hidden receptive power of the mind (and implicitly of the person as a whole)."[14] Consequently, the style in which a religious/authentic idea is

---

[9] Ibid, 12.
[10] Ibid, 15.
[11] Ibid, 94-107.
[12] Paul Tillich, *Systematic Theology*, Vol. 3 (Chicago: University of Chicago Press, 1963), 65-66.
[13] Ibid, 64. Also see Tillich, *Systematic Theology* Vol. 1, 91-92.
[14] Tillich, *Systematic Theology* Vol. 3, 64.

formed is far more important than the particular subject matter this style might depict. (As a matter of fact, Tillich points out, many overtly religious works of art actually fail *because* they get lost in focussing on the specificity of explicit religious imagery, and thus fail to point toward ultimate reality.)

It is with this duality in mind that Tillich's stylistic typology—the "numinous," "the abstract" (or "mystical"), the "naturalistic," the "idealistic," and "the expressionistic"—makes sense.[15] The numinous is a kind of realism in which everyday reality is depicted in such a way that it becomes frightening and/or mysterious. (The danger here, Tillich says, is that this style has a tendency to lead to idolatry.) If the religious imagination expresses ultimate reality without the mediation of or reference to a specific reality, then it fits the abstract (or mystical) style. (According to Tillich this style too commonly results in a "mere emptiness," the expression of nothing at all.[16]) In naturalism, the artwork's subject matter is emphasized *as an object*, to the point that, at its most extreme it ends up being a simple imitation of nature. Authentic forms of this style, though, reveal the latency of ultimate truth within the very minutiae of our daily lives.[17] Idealism moves beyond the stuff of naturalistic, everyday life to things in their essence, showing "the potentialities in the depths of a being or event, and bring[ing] them into existence as artistic images."[18] The problem with the idealistic style, however, is that it can easily generate into sentiment or kitsch, as often happens in explicitly religious or political art, if elements are added that dishonestly beautify the object. Although Tillich does not think it impossible for these styles to express ultimate reality, he is far more positive about the potential for the expressionistic style. Here

> the expressive element in a style implies a radical transformation of ordinarily encountered reality by using elements of it in a way which does not exist in the ordinarily encountered reality. Expressionism disrupts the naturally given appearance of things... That which is expressed is the 'dimension of depth' in the encountered reality, the ground and abyss in which everything is rooted.[19]

---

[15] Paul Tillich, *On Art and Architecture* (New York: Crossroads, 1987), 143-53.
[16] Ibid, 146.
[17] Ibid, 147-48.
[18] Ibid, 149.
[19] Paul Tillich, *Theology of Culture*, ed. Robert C. Kimball (New York: Oxford University Press, 1964), 74.

For Tillich, the danger of this style—namely, that when done poorly it simply showcases the individuality of the artist—is far outweighed by its theological power to reflect on ultimate reality. It is, he writes, "essentially adequate to express religious meaning directly, both through the medium of the secular and through the medium of traditional religious subject matter."[20]

Importantly, then, according to Tillich what sets apart a religious experience from a non-religious one is the emphasis (in the former) on the form an experience of ultimate reality takes, rather than this experience's actual content. Clayton Crockett has argued convincingly that here Tillich is informed by his understanding of Kant's transcendental philosophy.[21] For both the theologian and philosopher, where form is necessary (that is, as a formal condition for the possibility of knowing in general), content (that is, the stuff of knowledge) is arbitrary and contingent upon the finite bounds of time and space.[22] Crockett appeals to this transcendental formality in order to revivify theology. He writes:

> Theology cannot save itself by reconstituting its object in a reactionary and traditional manner, in defiance of all scholarly norms, if it desires to remain relevant for modern life. If theology becomes formal, then it retains a method of asking questions of ultimate concern, and theology is then able to read other texts…under the pressure of existential or soteriological figurations of intensity and importance.[23]

A revived theology, that is to say, one whose attention is that of ultimate concern, must be willing to "interrogate the adequacy and applicability of ideas of reason."[24] Such a theology, Crockett continues, is ultimately concerned with that which fundamentally resists the conditions and structures of reason and representation, and is in this way an affirmation of the ontological disorientation that occurs in the transgressive unrepresentability of the sublime. Indeed, "the sublime could be figured as the religious *par excellence*."[25]

---

[20] Ibid, 73.

[21] Clayton Crockett, *A Theology of the Sublime* (London: Routledge, 2001), 12-13.

[22] Tillich, *Theology of Culture*, 137. Compare with Immanuel Kant, *Critique of Pure Reason*, trans. Norman Kemp Smith (New York: St. Martin's, 1965), A33/B50.

[23] Crockett, *A Theology of the Sublime*, 16.

[24] Ibid, 16.

[25] Ibid, 19. Also see, "As the depth dimension of individual faculties or functions, religion appears as sublime, because one can identify a sphere of or phenomenon as religious only when its self-representation breaks down" (ibid, 103).

We are here clearly far from the theological sensibilities of Balthasar, for whom beauty is a transcendental concept that, by way of analogy, renders a transcendent God knowable to those open to revelation. It is thus, to some extent, unsurprising that Balthasar's intellectual descendents have bristled mightily at what they regard as the denigration of beauty in the wake of Kant. David Bentley Hart has perhaps been more vocal than most when he decries the postmodern:

> That the unrepresentable *is*; more to the point, that the unrepresentable... is somehow truer than the representable (which necessarily dissembles it), more original, and qualitatively *other*; that is, it does not differ from the representable by virtue of a greater fullness and unity of those transcendental moments that constitute the world of appearance, but by virtue of its absolute difference, its dialectical or negative indeterminancy, its no-thingness.[26]

All that results from this, for Hart, is the formlessness of a nihilism bereft of goodness and love, and for that violence and oppression.

This is all quite dramatic stuff, and indeed the Balthasarian defenders of beauty in the Radical Orthodoxy movement in particular have made use of it regularly to a much ballyhooed, bombastic effect. Interestingly, though, the most damning criticism that might be levelled at the champions of the sublime is perhaps also the one least palatable to a Balthasarian: namely, that the problem with inverting Kant, by way of "ontologizing" the sublime, misses the fact that such an inversion is, at once, unnecessary and counterproductive to the privileging of heterogeneity. As we will see in what follows, the rupturing of difference (or in Crockett's terminology, *disorientation*) between the sensible and thought, that is, between imagination and understanding, is not exclusive to the experience of the sublime. On the contrary, far too much is ultimately conceded by a theology of the sublime, with far too little a return. Our contention in what follows is that such a rupture is, rather, already at the heart of aesthetic experience, including that of beauty, and should be understood as a form of piety.

---

[26] David Bentley Hart, *Beauty and the Infinite: The Aesthetics of Christian Truth* (Grand Rapids: Eerdmans, 2003), 52. John Milbank, 'Sublimity: The Modern Transcendent," in *Religion, Modernity and Postmodernity*, ed. Paul Heelas (Oxford: Blackwell, 1998), 259.

II.

We follow Grace Jantzen in affirming that those who have transcendentalized beauty (though, as Jantzen illustrates in her survey of recent perspectives, not all are strictly Balthasarians[27]) and those who have ontologized the sublime have essentially fashioned the foundation and horizon for the contemporary thinking of aesthetics and theology. They have both, however, in blunt terms, "gotten Kant badly wrong". If we are more critical of those who emphasize the sublime, it is not because we feel that they should know better. On the contrary, their appeal to the sublime is based on an intentional and knowing inversion of Kant; that is, an inversion constructed not around blindness or ignorance but upon an overwhelmingly self-conscious late-modern/postmodern tradition of thought. We are critical because, though theirs is a strong intellectual genealogy (one often deeply invested in the future), it nevertheless fails the present.[28]

But make no mistake, by insisting on the specificity of an aesthetic rupturing of the sensible we are not providing succour to the ecclesial guardians of beauty. Although they misidentify Kant as a kind of proto-postmodernist, and in doing so parrot the position against which they rage—that is, concerning the ontologized sublime[29]—rejecting the ontological inversion of Kant that de-emphasizes beauty in no way diminishes the unsettling implications of his thought for theological orthodoxy. Indeed, if anything it may in fact result in a position even less appealing to it. Our aim, however, is not to resolve or referee the divide, but to resituate it completely. For as long as the lines of debate are situated between, on the one hand, the purity of beauty, and on the other, the absoluticization of the sublime, we feel that the debate establishes a false, debilitating foundation for the directing of attention (which we will call piety).

---

[27] And yet they are unified in "not allow[ing] beauty to challenge doctrine: beauty must be fit or it must be banished. Thus for all their commitment to the significance of beauty, they in practice keep beauty firmly subordinate to truth. Doctrine can and does question the place and understanding of beauty, not the other way around" (Grace Jantzen, "Beauty for Ashes: Notes on the Displacement of Beauty," *Literature and Theology* 16 (December 2002), 442).

[28] On this point, see especially Agata Bielek-Robson's piercing critique of Crockett, "The Traps of the Sublime," in *Journal of Cultural and Religious Theory* 9.2 (Summer 2008), 59-75.

[29] "Even when Kant's sublime is not directly invoked, its logic (at least, construed in a certain way) is always presumed" (Hart, *Beauty of the Infinite*, 44-45).

At this point, however, it is important first to step back and evaluate what exactly is going on in Kant's evaluation of the judgment of beauty and taste. As is well rehearsed, Kant bases this judgment on a fundamental antinomy:

> 1. *Thesis.* The judgment of taste is not based on concepts, for otherwise it would be possible to dispute about it (decide by means of proofs).
> 2. *Antithesis.* The judgment of taste is based on concepts, for otherwise, despite its variety, it would not even be possible to argue about it (to lay claim to the necessary assent of others to this judgment).[30]

This amounts to roughly the same thing as Kant's assertion earlier in the third *Critique* about the crucial peculiarity of this judgment, which "determines its object with regard to satisfaction (as beauty) with a claim to the assent of *everyone*, as if it were objective."[31] This peculiarity/antinomy emerges from an evolution in Kant's thinking about "the power of judgment" [*Urteilskraft*]. Having already in the first and second *Critiques* articulated the necessity of differentiating the subjective process of Reason [*Vernunft*] from the objective stability of Understanding [*Verstand*][32], Kant here reflects on how exactly we transition from any particular, empirical intuition to a general rule that actually allows for intelligible cognition. This transition, he argues, occurs in two ways. The first is by a "determining judgment," in which a conceptual category already exists and simply needs to be applied to a particular intuition. There is, though, he notes, a crucial deficiency with this judgment. Namely, that it is fundamentally unable to realise the absolute ("mechanical") systemization of knowledge to which it aspires. The laws of determining judgment can only provisionally suggest the appearance of a systematic relationship— anything more requires a higher metaphysical principle that it ultimately cannot provide. Kant contrasts this mechanical form of judgment with the *technē*, or artistry, of "reflective judgment." Here, instead of moving from pre-existent conceptual categories to intuitions, judgment begins with intuitions and proceeds to conceptual categories. Now, of course, to do this assumes a regulative higher principle as well, specifically that of purposiveness, and while Kant certainly makes much of our moral responsibility to think this higher principle, it is known as such only as a

---

[30] Immanuel Kant, *Critique of Power of Judgment,* trans. Paul Guyer and Eric Matthew (Cambridge, Cambridge University Press, 2000), 215.
[31] Ibid, 162.
[32] Kant, *Critique of Pure Reason*, A300/B357.

necessary fiction.[33] As such, the stuff of nature is, on the one hand, mechanical in terms of its adherence to empirical laws, while, on the other hand, "with regard to its products as systems, e.g. crystal formations, various shapes of flowers, or the inner structure of plants and animals, it proceeds *technically*, i.e. at the same time as an *art*."[34] With this assertion Kant becomes the harbinger for Continental philosophy's re-positioning of aesthetics away from its traditional confines of dealing principally "with those aspects of experience which are the least amenable to categorization" (e.g., beauty, emotion, sensory delight, etc.), to a privileged place in the rethinking of the relationship between mind and world, individual and reality.[35] (As we will see, in doing so aesthetics thus becomes a significant challenge to the maintenance of existing discursive hierarchies and boundaries imposed by our disciplinary and political forces.)

Kant's understanding of nature's "technical" relationship to art highlights a radical reformulation of our commonsense understanding of causation. Art and nature are alike, he contends, in that the pleasure we derive from either is the product of "mere judging" (which Kant also refers to as "mere reflection"), and is thus rooted neither in "mere sensation (something merely subjective)" nor through the application of an existing concept. By this, he means that while art (unlike nature) is identifiable as the product of an intentional, purposive act, it (like nature) seems "unintentional" [*unabsichtlich*].[36] As such, the beautiful object walks the tightrope of being *recognized* as a purposive production while at the same time *appearing* undesigned and unpurposive. Indeed, Kant explains, this is, the only way to preserve the freedom of our imagination from the determining grounding of concepts ("the free play of the faculties of cognition with a representation"), and results in our feeling of pleasure in the face of beauty.[37] The regulative importance of "representation" in this free play of the imagination in beauty should not be overlooked, however. Without it, Kant explains, we are left with the emptiness of merely "agreeable" art that reflects on nothing, which facilitates passive, momentary enjoyment at parties or over dinner ("an odd thing, which is supposed to sustain the mood of joyfulness merely as an agreeable noise,

---

[33] Kant, *Critique of the Power of Judgment*, 14. Otherwise, he continues, we would be lost "in a labyrinth of the multiplicity of possible empirical particular laws" (17).

[34] Ibid, 20.

[35] Clive Cazeaux, ed., *The Continental Aesthetics Reader* (London: Routledge, 2000), xiii.

[36] Kant, *Critique of the Power of Judgment*, 185-86.

[37] Ibid, 102-03.

and to encourage the free conversation of one neighbour with another without anyone paying the least attention to its composition.") In contrast, beautiful art invites active "sociable communication" by producing the material for aesthetic reflection that elicits the "universal communicability of pleasure."[38]

If we have established the significance of purposive representation we have yet to determine its actual status or how it avoids conceptual determinability in our aesthetic judgments. Establishing this point is crucial, as the theology of the sublime we are resisting rests on the position that Kantian Reason cannot countenance disorientation, and instead grips to the stable ground of the supersensible (that which informs the idea of a purposive representation) like a guardrail, lest it lose itself.[39] Crockett quotes John Sallis approvingly when the latter wonders, "What if now—today—such assurances [of stability] were no longer available," but concedes that the question is probably anachronistic, as Kant was an Enlightenment thinker and clearly possessed a faith in reason that our postmodern age may not. We have no interest in indicting or defending the Enlightenment here; nor will we dwell too closely on Kant's specific intentions. Rather, to reiterate what is at stake, much like Crockett and other proponents of theological sublimity, we too are concerned to explore the implications of Kant's aesthetic thinking for contemporary theology. We do so, however, without the assumption that this aesthetic thinking is inadequate to the cause and must therefore be fundamentally inverted. Like any lasting contribution of art ('art' broadly defined by intention), Kant's thinking is robust enough to incorporate conclusions alien to his cultural milieu or original intent. That the fecundity of Kant's thought invites both interpretive inversion and spirited defence speaks to its place *as an (aesthetic) object of reflection*. Which is to say it represents a specific site out of which the disorienting rupture of equality, which we identify as the possibility of "universal communicability," takes place. Strange as it may sound to so many of my postmodern peers, the specificity of *this* rupture takes primacy over the assertion of ontological rupture and disorientation.

The specificity of a work of art, whether it be hung on a wall, installed in a gallery space, performed on a stage, or published as a philosophical treatise, has such a potential insofar as it provokes what Kant calls "aesthetic ideas." By this he means "that representation of the imagination that occasions much thinking though without it being possible for any determinate thought, i.e., *concept*, to be adequate to it, which, consequently,

---

[38] Ibid, 184-85.
[39] Crockett, *A Theology of the Sublime*, 18, 77.

no language fully attains or can make intelligible."[40] Such ideas point directly to the powerful capacity of the imagination to create "another nature, out of the material which the real one gives it."[41] In other words, while imagination is reliant on nature to provide its materials (of thought and intuition), it uses these tools to fashion the aesthetic ideas that end up surpassing nature by providing indirect intimations of "something lying beyond the bounds of experience."[42] Kant's examples of such "invisible beings" include heaven and hell, eternity, death, envy, love, fame, etc., but as we have suggested above these are suggestive less of the stability that issues from dogmatic metaphysics than they are of what he regards as our necessary (moral) inclination toward the *idea* of a "supersensible substratum" of purposiveness.[43] Indeed, in contrast to ideas of reason, in which the supersensible stands outside the intuition as a safety-point or "guardrail," aesthetic ideas actively engage the supersensible limits of their constitutive (conceptual) material. In this way, an aesthetic idea thus "occasions much thinking" while also defying determinability.[44]

For Kant, aesthetic ideas are significant in that they embody the transition (but not disengagement) of our thinking "from the lawfulness of [the sensible world's] form" to our thinking "in accordance with the laws of freedom."[45] For Kant, this transition is most pronounced by the ability of genius, to "give the rule to art."[46] Apropos our present critique, while the primary characteristic of genius is its originality, in that it follows no prescribed or determinate rule, Kant insists that an originality concerned only with its own heterogeneity leads to the incoherence of "original nonsense." As such, genius must also be exemplary, in the sense of serving as a model or norm for others. Nevertheless, this exemplarity does not extend to describing "scientifically how it brings its products into being, but rather that it gives the rule as *nature*."[47] On the contrary, not even the author/artist knows from where or how the ideas emerged. In this way, the genius consists in the union of imagination (free play) and understanding, and thus in the capacity of genius to discover and express aesthetic ideas. Kant writes:

---

[40] Kant, *Critique of the Power of Judgment*, 192.
[41] Ibid, 192.
[42] Ibid, 192.
[43] Ibid, 220-21.
[44] Ibid, 192.
[45] Ibid, 63, 82.
[46] Ibid, 186.
[47] Ibid, 186-87.

Genius really consists in the happy relation... of finding ideas for a given concept on the one hand and on the other hitting upon the *expression* for these, through which the subjective disposition of the mind that is thereby produced, as an accompaniment of a concept, can be communicated to others... That requires a faculty for apprehending the rapidly passing play of the imagination and unifying it into a concept (which for that very reason is original and at the same time discloses a new rule, which could not have been deduced from any antecedent principles or examples), which can be communicated without the constraint of rules.[48]

The practice of the genius, then, is that of a strangely *unintentional intentional* practice. One might harness productively the harmonisation of imagination and understanding, but such a harmony cannot be produced by rules, "whether of science or of mechanical imitation"—they are ultimately unexplainable (or, at best, "explainable" only after the fact) and spontaneous.[49]

Provocatively,[50] Kant concludes that the genius is "the exemplary originality of the natural endowment of a subject for the *free* use of his [sic] cognitive faculties."[51] It is here especially, we suggest, that Kant's aesthetics resists the perceived necessity of so many representatives of postmodernism and postsecularity to ontologize the sublime in order to explain heterogeneity. In our estimation, few contemporary thinkers have articulated the implications of this resistance as coherently as Jacques Rancière. We will suggest that his recent reflections on politics and aesthetics help lead the way toward a conception of theology in which disorientation is not absolute, and for that even more radical than if it was.

III.

For Rancière, the ontological privilege given to heterogeneity and disorientation transforms 'art' (which he understands broadly to refer to

---

[48] Ibid, 194-95. Henry Allison is particularly good in teasing out the intricacies of Kant's presentation of genius in his *Kant's Theory of Taste: A Reading of the Critique of Aesthetic Judgment* (Cambridge: Cambridge University Press, 2002), 279-86.

[49] Kant, *Critique of the Power of Judgment*, 195.

[50] So provocative, in fact, that even within the pages of the third *Critique* Kant is unsure about what he has just articulated, and twists himself and his interpreters into knots constructing an ambivalently contradictory position that denies he ever privileged the freedom of genius at all. For a discussion, see Allison, *Kant's Theory of Taste*, 298-301.

[51] Kant, *Critique of the Power of Judgment*, 195.

anything made or done, in the spirit of the Greek term *poiēma*) into a "deliberation on mourning."

> The reinterpretation of the Kantian analysis of the sublime introduced into the field of art a concept that Kant had located beyond it. It did this in order to more effectively make art a witness to an encounter with the unpresentable that cripples all thought, and thereby a witness for the prosecution against the arrogance of the grand aesthetico-political endeavour to have 'thought' become 'world'. In this way, reflection on art became the site where a mise-en-scène of the original abyss of thought and the disaster of its misrecognition continued after the proclamation of the end of political utopias.[52]

While it should be noted that Rancière is not a card-carrying Kantian with respect to his understanding of aesthetics, his project helps tease out from the third *Critique* some of the important implications that Kant himself certainly did not readily identify.[53]

As hinted at already in the long quotation above, for Rancière politics plays a crucial role in both understanding and actualising the importance of aesthetics. Throughout much of his philosophy, Rancière's focus is on a class/status of people who have no proper place in the political community, and who thus lack (that is to say, are denied) the capacity to freely and coherently synthesize and articulate their perspectives of the sensual world. Theirs is, in short, the forced evacuation of the Kantian imagination—the denial of freedom. As a result, they play no role or part in the giving or taking from the shared world of experience (the *sensus communis*). Rancière regards politics as the event when this people nonetheless (in a kind of force) partake in that experience, and thus in that community. For Rancière, politics is inseparable from a truly democratic

---

[52] Jacques Rancière, *The Politics of Aesthetics: The Distribution of the Sensible*, trans. Gabriel Rockhill (London: Continuum, 2004), 9-10.

[53] A by-the-book Kantian aesthetics would more or less fall squarely in what Rancière calls "the poetic—or representative—regime of the arts," in that it focuses its energies on developing the norms "that define the conditions according to which imitations can be recognized as exclusively belonging to an art and assessed, within this framework, as good or bad, adequate or inadequate: partitions between the representable and the unrepresentable; the distinction between genres according to what is represented; principles for adapting forms of expression to genres and thus to the subject matter represented; the distribution of semblances according to principles of verisimilitude, appropriateness, of correspondence; criteria for distinguishing between and comparing the arts, etc." (*The Politics of Aesthetic*, 21-22). Rancière compares this to the ethical and aesthetic regimes of art, the latter being his clear preference and our object of analysis below.

justice, whereby a people create the sensibility they have been denied all along. This occurs, he explains, by the people's aesthetic/intentional practices that, in effect, lay claim to the "distribution of the sensible". Rancière writes:

> The distribution of the sensible reveals who can have a share in what is common to the community based on what they do and on the time and space in which this activity is performed. Having a particular 'occupation' thereby determines the ability or inability to take charge of what is common to the community; it defines what is visible or not in a common space, endowed with a common language, etc.[54]

Invoking Kant (though he adds, Kant "reexamined perhaps by Foucault"), inasmuch as it "revolves around what is seen and what can be said about it, around who has the ability to see and the talent to speak, around the properties of spaces and the possibilities of time," politics is inseparable from aesthetics. If this is so, Rancière continues, it is then possible to think and fashion aesthetic practices—which as we have seen above in Kant are ways of doing and making that involve the peculiarities of intentional practice—that are not divorced from their own materiality, but that rather intervene in the accepted "distribution of ways of doing and making," and in the process rupture the existing modes and horizons of being and visibility.[55]

In his treatise *Disagreement,* Rancière illustrates this dynamic of aesthetics and politics primarily by way of Aristotle's ideal political community.[56] Here, the demos are indistinguishable from slaves, in that both are necessarily different in kind from the master. The soul of the master is one of deliberation and discernment, which gives him the natural right of sovereignty, rule and law. The slave, however, has no such capacity, and indeed has no soul or essence at all. As such, while the slave can understand the reason and law of the master, this only affords the slave the ability to obey the master's orders. Reason and law, rather, are imposed upon the slave. Indeed, the slave only has a proper place in the political community at all inasmuch as s/he obeys the master. The slave's is a place of (natural/essential) subservience, "doomed to the anonymity of work and reproduction."[57]

---

[54] Rancière, *The Politics of Aesthetics*, 12-13.
[55] Ibid, 13.
[56] See especially Jacques Rancière, *Disagreement: Politics and Philosophy*, trans. Julie Rose (Minneapolis: University of Minnesota Press, 1999).
[57] Ibid, 7.

For Rancière, the proletariat are slaves who have rejected their "essential" place in the political community, that of the no-place. In other words, they are the slaves who have ceased to be subservient; they have, rather, denounced subservience and have staked a claim to the "distribution of the sensible," and thus a claim to freedom. A highly significant dynamic is at work in this claim. On one hand, they effectively position themselves outside of the existing political community's partitioning of the sensible. On the other hand, they lay claim to a freedom that belongs only to those with a part in this political community. Notice, though, that the slave's claim to freedom is fundamentally different than that of a claim to wealth or nobility. These claims assert particular qualities as proper and/or essential to those who lay the claim. In terms of the Aristotelian community, such claims are just only insofar as the wealthy and noble fulfil the roles they are naturally and essentially capable of fulfilling in the community. A slave's claim to freedom (that is, to sensibility), however, is an immediate claim, devoid of any justification by way of their proportional, contributing quality. In such a claim, the slave insists that the correlation between social position or role and natural capacity is purely theatrical, and thus artificial to the core.[58]

A political subject, then, should not simply be identified as "a group that 'becomes aware' of itself, finds its voice, imposes its weight on society," and in the process shuts out the voices of others.[59] Rather, it is also an aesthetic subject concerned with the configuration of what counts as a voice at all. In this way, political statements are informed by aesthetics in that they

> define models of speech or action but also regimes of sensible intensity. They draft maps of the visible, trajectories between the visible and the sayable, relationships between modes of being, modes of saying, and modes of doing and making. They define variations of sensible intensities, perceptions, and the abilities of bodies. They thereby take hold of unspecified groups of people, they widen gaps, open up space for deviations, modify the speeds, the trajectories, and the ways in which

---

[58] "There are moments when the community of equals appears as the ultimate underpinning of the distribution of the institutions and obligations that constitute a society; moments when equals declare themselves as such, though aware that they have no fundamental right to do so.... . They thus experience the *artificial* aspect of their power—in the sense that 'artifice' may mean both something that is not necessary and something that is to be created" (Jacques Rancière, *On the Shores of Politics*, trans. Liz Heron (London: Verso, 2007), p. 91). Also see Ranciere's discussion of history as a kind of fiction, in *The Politics of Aesthetics*, 37-38.

[59] Rancière, *Disagreement*, 40.

groups of people adhere to a condition, react to situations, recognize their images. They reconfigure the map of the sensible by interfering with the functionality of gestures and rhythms adapted to the natural cycles of production, reproduction, and submission.[60]

Importantly, the lines of fracture created by the uncounted's "intentional" aesthetic practices are rooted in "unintentionality." As we saw above with the Kantian genius, the freedom to assert one's cognitive faculties is not merely an assertion of one's rights or individuality, that is, of one's intentionality. The latter implies a predefined lawfulness to which one might appeal. It is precisely the status of this predefinition that aesthetics calls into question. For Rancière this means: *what and who gets to count as intentional*? He writes: "There is a politics when there is a part of those who have no part, a part or party of the poor. Politics does not happen just because the poor oppose the rich. It is the other way around: politics (that is the interruption of the simple effects of domination by the rich) causes the poor to exist as an entity."[61] This is to say, intentionality neither precedes nor is fractured (deconstructively) by unintentionality, but emerges from the unintentionality of aesthetic practice. Sensibility, as such, is not awaiting to be apprehended; it is, rather, forcibly and creatively asserted, without appeal to rule or precedent, the imagination made real.[62] We emphasize, then, with Rancière that the subjectification of the uncounted should not be understood to result in a newly stable collective body. Rather, the political result of "unintentional intentional practice" is the formation of *imaginary* collective bodies, which Rancière describes as "uncertain communities that contribute to the formation of enunciative collectives that call into question the distribution of roles, territories, and languages." [63] Such practice thus becomes exemplary for (might we say, even the moral responsibility of) a radically anarchic political subjectification/intentionality fundamentally disposed to challenging any given distribution of the sensible.

---

[60] Rancière, *The Politics of Aesthetics*, 39.

[61] Rancière, *Disagreement*, 11

[62] See Novalis: "When we speak of the external world, when we depict real objects, then we are acting as genius does. Thus genius is the ability to treat imaginary objects like real ones, and to deal with them as if they were real as well" (*Philosophical Writings*, trans. and ed. Margaret Mahony Stoljar (Albany: SUNY, 1997), 26).

[63] Rancière, *The Politics of Aesthetics*, 40.

IV.

For some, all this may seem far from the concerns of theology. And perhaps this is true. We submit, however, that this is more a failure of theology than it is a fault of aesthetics. As Philip Goodchild has noted, "We experience that to which we pay attention,"[64] and "that which presents no form may still affect the distribution of attention."[65] Consequently, piety, which Goodchild defines as "any determinate practice of directing attention," need not (and perhaps cannot) be directed fully to the existence or essence of God, but most potently to the unthinkable.[66] This description seems especially apt for the political subject that emerges from an aesthetic act. For if that which has no form or essence of which one might speak, or with which to speak or see, is the uncounted, the assertion of such via aesthetic practice—in which, the intentional emerges from the unintentional—may also be called an experience, borne from attention to the unconditional.

As we have seen, the theology of the sublime clearly aspires to a similar sphere of attention. We have argued, however, that this attention is fundamentally deficient. This is to say, our criticism is not simply that it is a misunderstanding of Kant (indeed, there is a strong intellectual tradition of privileging the Kantian sublime at the expense of genius, which we do not discount *tout court*), but primarily that it fails to live up to its emphasis on "ultimate concern." On the contrary, as Agata Bielik-Robson has noted, in its celebration of absolute disorientation, the theology of the sublime really only leaves us with "terror, apathy, paralysis, and resignation."[67] While it insists on the potential of the radically unbounded openness and possibility that absolutely disorientation offers, we contend it can only ever be empty, unmet potential—the circulation of "innovative" noise. This is because, like the traditional theology it attempts to challenge, the theology of the sublime begins and ends with the *naming* of its ultimate concern. In this way, it says both too much and too little. The theological vision borne from aesthetics, however, is concerned with why and how the naming of the unconditioned occurs at all. This does not mean that Kant and Rancière are theologians against their wills, but rather that their

---

[64] Philip Goodchild, *Capitalism and Religion: The Price of Piety* (London: Routledge, 2002), 210.

[65] Ibid, 223.

[66] "Life is no longer brought before the categories of thought; thought must be plunged into the categories of life" (Goodchild, *Capitalism and Religion*, 223).

[67] Bielek-Robson, "The Traps of the Sublime," 60.

concern for the unconditioned conditions of existence is exemplary for a new theological thinking.[68]

There is, of course, a crucial difference between a theologian, the one who names, and a philosopher, whose attention is the conditions of naming itself. Indeed, in tracing the implications of our argument here, perhaps only the latter, the non-theologian, can be truly attuned to the promise that crosses religious divides, that of a "new creation" (or "enlightenment")—the creation of a new existence, one incommensurate with the present order of reality and its existent horizon of expectations. If this is so, the world is made new not by the teleology or phenomenology of the promise or progress, nor by any kind of messianism. The world would be made new, rather, through the unintentional intentional practice of aesthetics; that is, through an active ethics of thinking embodied by the attention paid to that which is unthinkable *in the thinkable*—that which is/those who are constitutively silenced, the count of which there is no count.

Bibliography

Allison, Henry. *Kant's Theory of Taste: A Reading of the Critique of Aesthetic Judgment.* Cambridge: Cambridge University Press, 2002.

Balthasar, Hans Urs von. *Seeing the Form.* Vol. 1 of *The Glory of the Lord: A Theological Aesthetics.* Translated by Erasmo Leiva-Merikakis. San Francisco: Ignatius Press, 1982.

—. *Truth of the World.* Vol. 1 of *Theo-logic: Theological Logical Theory.* Translated by Adrian Walker. San Francisco: Ignatius Press, 2000.

Begbie, Jeremy. *Voicing Creation's Praise: Towards a Theology of the Arts.* Edinburgh: T&T Clark, 1991.

—. *Theology, Music and Time.* Cambridge: Cambridge University Press, 2000.

—. edited. *Beholding the Glory: Incarnation Through the Arts.* Grand Rapids: Baker, 2000.

—. edited. *Sounding the Depths: Theology Through the Arts.* London: SCM, 2002.

Bielek-Robson, Agata. "The Traps of the Sublime." *Journal of Cultural and Religious Theory.* 9.2 (Summer 2008): 59-75.

Cazeaux, Clive edited. *The Continental Aesthetics Reader.* London: Routledge, 2000.

---

[68] Anthony Paul Smith's appeal to François Laruelle's "non-philosophy" in this volume may give us more tools to further articulate the possibilities for this new theological thinking in the immanent praxis of non-theology.

Crockett, Clayton. *A Theology of the Sublime.* London: Routledge, 2001.

Goodchild, Philip. *Capitalism and Religion: The Price of Piety.* London: Routledge, 2002.

Hart, David Bentley. *Beauty and the Infinite: The Aesthetics of Christian Truth.* Grand Rapids: Eerdmans, 2003.

Jantzen, Grace. "Beauty for Ashes: Notes on the Displacement of Beauty." *Literature and Theology* 16.4 (December 2002): 427-49.

Kant, Immanuel. *Critique of the Power of Reason.* Translated by Paul Guyer and Eric Matthew. Cambridge, Cambridge, University Press, 2000.

—. *Critique of Pure Reason.* Translated by Norman Kemp Smith. New York: St. Martin's, 1965.

Kierkegaard, Søren. *Concluding Unscientific Postscript to* Philosophical Fragments. 2 Vols. Translated and edited by Howard V. Hong and Edna H. Hong. Princeton: Princeton University Press, 1992.

Milbank, John. 'Sublimity: The Modern Transcendent." In Paul Heelas edited, *Religion, Modernity and Postmodernity.* Oxford: Blackwell, 1998. 258-84.

Nichols, Aidan. *The Word Has Been Abroad: A Guide Through Balthasar's Aesthetics.* Edinburgh: T&T Clark, 1998.

Novalis. *Philosophical Writings.* Translated and edited by Margaret Mahony Stoljar. Albany: SUNY, 1997.

Rancière, Jacques. *Disagreement: Politics and Philosophy.* Translated by Julie Rose. Minneapolis: University of Minnesota Press, 1999.

—. *The Politics of Aesthetics: The Distribution of the Sensible.* Translated by Gabriel Rockhill. London: Continuum, 2004.

—. *On the Shores of Politics.* Translated by Liz Heron. London: Verso, 2007.

Tillich, Paul. *Systematic Theology.* 3 vols. Chicago: University of Chicago Press, 1951-63.

—. *Theology of Culture.* Edited by Robert C. Kimball. New York: Oxford University Press, 1964.

—. *On Art and Architecture.* Edited by Jane and John Dillenberger. New York: Crossroads, 1987.

Van Erp, Stephan. *The Art of Theology: Hans Urs von Balthasar's Theological Aesthetics and the Foundations of Faith.* Leuven: Peeters, 2004.

AFTERWORD

HYPOCRISY

PHILIP GOODCHILD AND N. OTHERS

Can philosophy of religion be pursued as a conversation? Perhaps only under conditions that are somewhat rare, involving both a careful attentiveness to the purport of the other's speech, and the opportunity to develop thought as far as it will lead. This paper is composed of just such a conversation: a highly provocative challenge (anonymous), followed by an extended yet indirect response from an author known pseudonymously as Eryximachus. My own reflections bring the conversation to a close.

The central concern here is analogous to an old chestnut of philosophy of religion: if God is ultimately mysterious and unknowable, in what sense is it possible to believe in, worship, or love such a God? What does one actually do when one takes oneself as doing so? A similar difficulty also arises when one attempts to address another from the heart, speaking to the heart. If one cannot designate the true referent of a proper name, how is it possible to intend or love anyone? Furthermore, how is it possible to manifest one's true meaning in one's speech, and therefore, how is it possible to escape hypocrisy? The problem explored here, however, is how it might be possible to articulate or express the meaning of what is meaningful in life, so as to make life more meaningful.

I. Prologue

Anonymous

Our world is full of thoughtless chatter. If rapid judgements always sting a little, one can at least bear in mind these consoling thoughts: the author of the judgement did not really mean it. The judgement just expressed a passing emotion. At another time, in a different context, a different judgement might be made. The reasons for the judgement did not run deep. There is no real authority behind such an opinion. If only the author had understood more, then such a facile judgement could never have been spoken. Unless, of course, the author of the judgement has seen and understood what one has not, making the judgement valid.

The predicament is the same for praise as it is for blame: thoughtless chatter may have no truth behind it. Of course, one hopes that the author has glimpsed some deep truth, but this is just a consoling thought. Judgements that praise may just express a passing emotion. At another time, in a different context, a different judgement might be made. One fears friends when one suspects that the bonds of affinity do not run deep. There is no real steadfastness underlying such friendship. If only the author had understood more, then such a deceptive judgement could never have been spoken. Unless, of course, the author of the judgement has seen and understood what one has not, and deliberately strives to protect one from that insight into one's own failings.

Perhaps the purpose of philosophy is to train and enable us to mean what we say. Perhaps the purpose of philosophy is to discover grounds for judgements, or reasons. Perhaps the purpose of philosophy is to lend authority to our judgements. Perhaps the primary fault that philosophy seeks to correct in idle chatter is not error, but hypocrisy. Hypocrisy would be the expression of thoughtless judgements for the sake of approval by others. For perhaps the purpose of making judgements often has more to do with eliciting approval from a sympathetic constituency than it does with expressing reasons.

The same judgement may therefore signify a quite different purport depending on why it was issued, how deeply it was meant, how much the author has understood, and the quality of the reasons that support it. Before one comes to a judgement on such a judgement, then, it is necessary to interpret the sense in which it was meant. One seeks out informed guesses on matters of motivation, intention, comprehension, and reasoning. One places the judgement back within a context. One weighs its authority and authenticity. One tests whether it might be expressed otherwise in a different context. One assesses its resilience before determining its meaning. Finally, the philosopher expresses a conclusion, along with the reasoning that led to it. The reasoning endeavours to make the purport, resilience, and authority of a judgement transparent.

But isn't understanding lost as soon as the reason is given? For reasons are themselves judgements that depend upon the authority of the thinker: they have their own purport. Yet reasons are offered as judgements that may be adopted by anyone. They appeal to all who share in common sense. The philosopher attempts to establish an affinity with all right-thinking people who will recognise their own sentiments and perceptions reflected in the given grounds. In short, the philosopher attempts to conceal individual subjectivity beneath a public display of reasoning. There is no longer a distinction between a judgement and its purport. There is no longer scope for interpretation. There is only persuasion, eliciting approval. Philosophy becomes a form of rhetoric.

The predicament is the same whether the subjective sentiments of the philosopher are in tune with the expressed reasoning or at variance with it. The matters of why the reasoning was issued, how deeply it was meant, how much the philosopher has understood, and the quality of the sentiments and perceptions that support it, are put aside in favour of the intrinsic merits and force of the argument, given the premises. One sets aside the sense in which the reasoning is meant for the sake of attracting agreement. Philosophy is hypocrisy. The method of this putting aside is abstraction: the subjective variables are put aside by taking reasoning out of any context. Philosophy is hypocritical not because its judgements are wrong, but because they are abstract. They have no purport. They are like empty, whitewashed tombs. None of the results of rational argument are deeply meant, for they await an overturning by the next reason. Shallowness is inevitable as soon as one tries to make reasons explicit. For explicit reasoning requires that we all mean the same by our judgements. There is no more scope for a difference in meaning or level. Interpretation of the purport is laid aside in favour of an attention to the weight of the argument. In weighing reasons, philosophy abandons the imperative to know itself, to read the purport of its own judgements. Thus philosophy inevitably falls into hypocrisy.

Consider the purport of the following scenario. There is a certain philosopher who has a gift of touching and moving the souls of others. When he speaks, or when he is read attentively, some of the most profound and significant insights parade before thought. This virtue he has cultivated largely at the expense of others. Indeed, perhaps his greatest service to humanity lies in his withdrawal for the sake of thinking, so saving others from being afflicted by his presence for much of the time. There is no end to his vanity. He displays his thinking not to inspire but to seduce. Yet the secrets of his character are often carefully concealed beneath the cloak of a modest exterior, all the better to propagate an image of sagacity. Few see through him directly. He no longer measures his worth by the numbers of personal expressions of praise or gratitude, nor by the numbers of strangers who write to him about his work, nor by the range of speaking invitations he receives, nor even by the vitriol of harsh reviews. Instead, he is moved by those who send him their poems or fairy stories, by strangers who offer him money, and especially by the women who, being touched by his mind, desire also that he touch their bodies. So, one day our hypocritical philosopher meets a tall and beautiful woman who will not be separated from his company, who pursues intense conversations about the possibility of living life as a work of art, whose demonstrative hand gestures during speech strike him on the chest so hard that it is as if she is trying to reach directly into his heart. Once his feigning of nonchalant unconcern has the desired seductive effect, a few well-timed compliments and well-placed caresses raises the intensity of her desire to a plateau where it overwhelms any more subtle sensitivities of her soul, whence she declares, "I can't feel the spiritual connection, but right now that no longer seems to matter. I can't understand why you excite me so much more than other lovers. It must be because you are *N*. [she speaks his name]." Immediately he is dumbfounded. Does she delight in his projected image alone, one that, even if it blends seamlessly into his inflated ego, is not the person and body beside her? Is there any relation here? Or does she use his name to designate some kernel of virtue that she has divined, whether in his work, or concealed beneath his vanity in the soul of the person she encounters? Does the name that awakens her desire refer in any way to him?

And here is the question for the philosopher: how do you ascertain the true reference of a spoken name?

(Note by Philip Goodchild: I must say that I am very reluctant to condone the purport of this provocation. Insofar as it neither bears a name, nor names the philosopher in question, it can itself be suspected of being gossip or idle chatter. Philosophical work is entirely about constructing arguments and showing reasons, an activity that I and many others find powerful and meaningful. The challenge at the end is, of course, impossible to fulfil. For while a name is a public designation, the true identity and character of a person remains secret. Even if one becomes capable of knowing a person, that knowledge cannot be made public without rendering the description impersonal.

One suspects that the provocation of charging philosophy with hypocrisy is a false problem, born of abstraction, which only arises for one who struggles to give his reasoning any purport. One may even suspect that it is motivated by jealousy of the vain philosopher who touches bodies as well as souls, even though this character is no doubt fictitious, since vanity is incompatible with moving insight. Indeed, the use of such an imaginary scenario itself is hypocritical, since it does not arise directly from experienced problems.

Yet I think that there are real philosophical problems at stake here, such as questions about the nature and possibility of meaning, and the nature and possibility of love. The response that follows wisely avoids direct discussion of the challenge, but addresses these underlying problems.)

II. Response: On Meaning and Conversation

Eryximachus

Supposing you were offered living immortality in a virtual reality machine—would you accept it?

Here's the deal: your brain is to be placed in a protective environment, where the nerve cells are directly connected to a computer. An imaginative application of stem cell technology enables any failing brain cells to be replaced. The computer generates your chosen experiences in a manner that can no longer be distinguished from real life. It is not merely touch, taste, sound and sight that are identical. Your entire life becomes a waking fantasy. Your looks, voice and abilities are perfected. You may become the star that delights thousands of admiring fans, or the hero who saves the world from destruction. You may become a great artist or musician or inventor. You may acquire the greatest of riches, and possess whatever you wish. You may travel to all the most wondrous and exotic locations, on this planet and beyond, real or possible. You may become a great lover, commanding complete devotion from the most beautiful of people. You may pass through all the available states of consciousness, from the highest to the lowest. All this is to be your experience, exactly as you choose. All this will feel real; indeed, it will be real, for your brain and the computer. But it will not be experienced by any other.

Would you accept such a deal?

This thought experiment brings to light certain deep questions about what it is to live a meaningful existence. Is the quality of life to be measured by experience? Can meaning be recorded in a computer? Are you tempted by the freedom offered by this detachment from the constraints of our fallible reality? Could you educate yourself through experience in the machine to desire only the most fulfilling of experiences? Could you create your own heaven? Could you even spend the time making yourself into a great philosopher by carrying out all kinds of conceivable thought experiments? Or might you feel compelled, once there, to seek satisfaction of the same old base urges in a continual repetition compulsion? Would you develop hungers that can never be assuaged? Would your desires, meeting no resistance, descend to the level of lust and aggression? Would your immortality turn into hell, so that you long to escape the computer, escape yourself, longing only for your own abolition? Would you endlessly fantasise your own demise, and experience a thousand times your own death?

The temptation to find meaning solely in experience and feeling is mirrored by an opposing temptation: to find meaning solely in activity.[1] Only what you do is actual and real; all sensation is insignificant or illusory. Action must be performed without regard to the fruit. The highest

---

[1] Herbert McCabe OP draws on a similar thought experiment, Robert Nozick's "Experience Machine", to argue the Thomist case of the priority of activity over experience. Herbert McCabe, *The Good Life* (London: Continuum, 2005), 50.

experiences in life are those of rapt attention where one is so engaged in an activity that one loses all sense of self or time.[2] Even here, experience no longer counts, but only the activity which can be measured as actual effort or achievement. It is better to play a sport than to watch. It is better to make music than to listen. It is better to give than to receive. It is better to make the news than to hear it. It is better to love than to be loved. For, perhaps in the secret part of one's soul, there is one who watches the activity of one's virtue and knows. Only such a one perceives meaning. If one holds this view, then one would surely renounce the temptations of the virtual reality machine for the sake of acting in the world, in however minor or temporary a manner. Even a short life is a real one. A *fortiori*, then, one should also renounce all the temporary and inadequate pleasures provided as entertainment in a consumer society, which similarly occupy one's time for far less satisfaction than that afforded by the virtual reality machine. According to this view, one may rest and consume only in order to work: for serious, purposeful activity is the true end of life.

One can test whether this alternative is any better by proposing another thought experiment: suppose a demon were to offer you a drug that transformed your soul, filling it with excellence in every skill and virtue, for a small price: your consciousness. The rest of your life could be an exercise in spontaneous magnanimity, but you would live as though dead drunk or a sleepwalker: your own character would be expressed to others, but you would have no knowledge or memory of what you had done. Would you make that sacrifice for the sake of virtue, or for the sake of what you could then do for others? Is the sacrifice of one's entire life easier than such a sacrifice of consciousness alone?

These hypothetical reflections may seem somewhat abstract, at a great distance from reality. No judgements about them could sincerely be meant. Nevertheless, the decision between these alternatives is at bottom very real insofar as it may guide the practical conduct of life. It raises a profound philosophical question: where do we find meaning in life? Is meaning to be found in experience or activity? Moreover, even if we do not yet possess a virtual reality machine that generates a realistic experience, we do possess machines for recording and generating meaning—not only computers, but also film, art, architecture, music, and language, for example. The alternative can be posed as follows: is it better to listen or to speak? Is it better to read or to write? Moreover, is our language capable of recording the meaning that we find, or is our language the machine that

---

[2] Winifred Gallagher, *Rapt: Attention and the Focused Life* (New York: Penguin, 2009).

generates meaning? Do we speak or are we spoken? Does meaning reside in the saying or the said?[3]

It may be possible to take the view that meaning belongs entirely to the sphere of language. Where nothing is spoken or written, all interactions would then be without sense. Even the signs of physical passion would have to be read as the language of love. Yet a purely linguistic meaning may seem to hold signification without significance. It does not matter to the bookworm what is written on the page. The non-human world has no concern over what is written in human libraries. The world still matters even when it does not signify. The alternative view would be to hold that signification only takes on a meaning when it is related to a subject as a focus of experience or activity. On this account, meaning comes to light only in relation to something kept secret. Experience is meaningful when it engages or resists some hidden desire; otherwise, it is merely noise. Activity is meaningful when it expresses some personal virtue; otherwise, it is merely mechanical. While the subject of experience or action is not directly perceived, we can at least pay attention to the meaning found in experience and activity. It would then be this source of meaning that is designated by a proper name.

The more fundamental question, however, is this: how does one lead a meaningful life? The quest, here, is not merely to find a life that is happy, or busy, or sophisticated, but to lead a life that matters. Can one find what matters in sensation, or activity, or linguistic sense? To be sceptical about one or the other of these is to suggest that what matters is something that either cannot be felt, or cannot be done, or cannot be spoken. So, for example, to be sceptical about whether the meaning that is said is the meaning that matters is also to be sceptical about whether philosophy can ever articulate what matters in a proposition. It is to regard language as an imperfect virtual reality machine for recording and generating meaning. It is to suggest that what really matters is never to be found in books of philosophy. So if, for example, we use the word "soul" to designate what matters in a human life, what gives it meaning, then we could never say what that soul is. Even to call it a "subject", a focus of experience or activity, may say too much or not enough. Similarly, if we use a proper name to designate what matters in an individual person's life, then we can never explain what is the referent of such a name. By contrast, to engage in philosophy as an attempt to articulate what matters may be an attempt to create a virtual reality machine. This very enterprise may prevent a philosopher from manifesting a soul.

---

[3] Emmanuel Levinas, *Otherwise than Being, or, Beyond Essence* trans. Alphonso Lingis (Pittsburgh: Duquesne University Press, 1998).

Of course, it is perfectly possible to live without posing such dilemmas. Nevertheless, there is a practical correlate for such problems. When one cares about someone, does one care primarily about what they feel, or what they do, or what they say? What is it about them that matters, or is meaningful? If one cares about each of these, does one care about these in themselves, or for the sake of something else, such as the person, or the good? Indeed, instead of wrestling with the dilemmas of self-knowledge, it may be more fruitful if we wrestle with the dilemmas of benevolence or love.

There is a conception of human love that makes it independent of conditions or qualifying reasons. As Gene Outka explains, "A person is valued as, or in such that he is, a person qua human existent and not because he is such-and-such a kind of person distinguishing him from others."[4] Or in the famous phrase of Karl Barth, one "identifies with his interests in utter independence of the question of his attractiveness."[5] In comparison with such disinterested love, the preferential relations found in friendship or erotic love seem to be self-interested: the other may be a means, and not simply an end.

On the other hand, a sexual impulse directed to the human qua human existent would be the most base and ignoble, because it shows no discrimination in the object of desire, and threatens to initiate entirely inappropriate liaisons. As Arthur Schopenhauer explained, if sexual impulse in general without direction manifests a will to live, one directed to a definite individual is a will to live as a precisely determined individual.[6] So do we make ourselves by what and whom we love? Could the meaning of our lives be given by the object of our devotion? Does speech hold significance only when it addresses the heart? Do words only gain meaning when spoken out of love?

This would have considerable implications for how we think about unconditional love. Why should this love that always treats the other as an end, never a means, require an entirely different nature from erotic love? Why should universal benevolence be so different from singular devotion? Is love to be considered as the negation of the self or the realisation of the self? Does the lover lose or gain meaning? Should one love the person who is already beautiful and good, or does one's love create the possibility

---

[4] Gene Outka, *Agape: An Ethical Analysis* (New Haven: Yale University Press, 1972), 12.

[5] Cited in Outka, *Agape*, 4.

[6] Arthur Schopenhauer, *The World as Will and Representation* Vol. II, trans. E. F. J. Payne (New York: Dover, 1966), 535.

for the other's being beautiful and good?[7] If the latter, then our moral virtue may be entirely at the mercy of the capacities of our neighbours to love us without regard to our virtues and vices. Indeed, what they really love might not be ourselves as we are, but the possibility of our acquiring virtue. When we love someone, do we really love the virtuous person that they might be? In other words, do we love the possibility of their learning to love, which is to say, learning to disregard themselves for the sake of another? Do we love their self-sacrifice, their self-emptying of meaning? If we disregard ourselves for the sake of another, do we secretly wish them to disregard themselves for our sake? Or is such unconditional love only pure when it is passed on unrequited?

What these dilemmas illustrate is the difficulty of engaging with what is meaningful in a human life. For we love only what matters or is meaningful. Then one wonders whether there is some meaning in a human person capable of being loved that is not to be encountered in a virtual reality machine, nor in sense experience, nor in activity, nor in language. Moreover, insofar as actual love is always for a definite individual—unlike benevolence which is potentially distributed universally to all human beings—does this meaning always have a definite character?

Nevertheless, the meaning of love is perhaps poorly understood as a dyad, whether it is considered as the sacrifice of self for the sake of the other or affirmation of self through the other. For neither self nor other can become the object of intention or attention. At best, one can pay attention to how meaning is inhabited or cohabited. In this respect, love is inseparable from a mutual third term. Schopenhauer proposed an interesting suggestion on this issue:

> The quite special and individual passion of two lovers is just as inexplicable as is the quite special individuality of any person, which is exclusively peculiar to him; indeed at bottom the two are one and the same; the latter is *explicite* what the former was *implicite*... The moment when the parents begin to love each other—*to fancy each other*, as a very apposite English expression has it—is actually to be regarded as the very first formation of a new individual, and the true *punctum saliens* of its life.[8]

Schopenhauer does seem to hesitate here between whether the new germ of individuality belongs to the lovers themselves, or whether it belongs to a child who has yet to come into existence. It is, of course, tempting to

---

[7] Anders Nygren, *Agape and Eros*, trans. Philip S. Watson (London: SPCK, 1954), 78.

[8] Schopenhauer, *The World as Will and Representation*, 536.

objectify meaning in the person of the child, for then one can at least designate what one is talking about. But this is simply to postpone the problem of meaning. It leads Schopenhauer to the pessimistic view that erotic love is not in the lover's interests, but only in the interests of the child.[9] After the "consummation of the great work", the lovers find themselves duped, since a sexual impulse operates in the interests of the species to select the next generation. Sexual impulse is an instinct, "an action as if in accordance with the conception of an end or purpose, and yet entirely without such a conception".[10] In other words, Schopenhauer views sexual behaviour in terms similar to the somnambulism we described in the earlier thought experiment, except that the lovers do have a consciousness as an afterthought that finds itself to be deceived. All lovers are seducers, deceivers and hypocrites, just as they are all deceived. While Schopenhauer celebrates the precise determination of the individualities of the next generation as a much higher aim than "the exuberant feelings and immaterial soap-bubbles" of those who pursue romantic love,[11] such a purpose is enacted outside of the consciousness of lovers, within which love comes to nothing. On this account, which seems to prioritise activity over experience, the end result is also prioritised over the activity, leaving meaning to be perpetually postponed. Thus all lovers are deceived. All impulses are hypocritical.

What if, by contrast, love is a matter of determining the individualities of the current generation? What if the human person remains in respect of meaning a kind of unformed matter until they cohabit in love? What if the sexual impulse is not the ultimate motive and goal of almost all human effort, but a paradigm of the transformation of meaning effected by love? What if reproduction is not the primary goal of sexual behaviour, but instead it is the production of meaning? What if all the shades and varieties of love between persons, beginning with that between parent and child, are the progressive determination of individuality? What if satisfaction and fulfilment is to be found in human relationships rather than in entertainment and activity? What if the meaning of entertainment, activity and discourse is only to be found in the fact that it is undertaken together?

The inhabited relation is itself the germ of meaning, the third term that may become the collective object of attention. One does not desire an inaccessible other, but the relation itself. The mutual relation fails if one party attempts to dominate the terms of shared life, or if one party restricts

---

[9] Ibid, 555.
[10] Ibid, 540.
[11] Ibid, 535.

activity in favour of pure attention. Instead, a relation operates most effectively like those turning tables in nineteenth century séances. The table, whose legs have well-lubricated castors, begins at rest, with several people placing their hands upon it. A slight disturbance from the muscles of one participant causes a small movement, which is compensated for by a response from the others. Instead of returning to equilibrium, however, the response imparts a new motion, leading to further compensations, until the table moves around the room in a chaotic manner, like a stock market, leading the participants with it, while none of them have any control over its motions. The motion of the table appears autonomous, in spite of the fact that it is reflexively determined by resistance to the stimulus of others. A relation will grow and change until one party lets go, or until it finds a regular pattern of equilibrium behaviour. Its meaning is its apparently autonomous movement. Such séances may be performed each night in the bedroom. Love carries its inhabitants away with it, so long as mutual attention and response to the motion continue. In this respect, its course is not determined in advance by the prior individuals; on the contrary, the individuals learn to express their individuality through the attention and response enabled by cohabited relation. The human person is a being capable of tuning in to the rhythms of love, not an author of love. Meaning cannot be reified and made explicit since it is the environment and dynamism in which we dwell.

Then how might such a conception of inhabited meaning relate to philosophy? Is philosophy to be reduced to playful conversation or idle chatter? Does philosophy betray inhabited meaning when it seeks to articulate reasons? Or does philosophy educate by catching us out in the hypocrisy of our explicit utterances by demonstrating that what we say is not what we mean? Two relevant insights may be helpful here. Martin Buber proposed that only encounter is actual.[12] This is as much as to say that only actual relations matter or are meaningful. The virtual reality machine, then, would lack meaning because it involves no encounter. The same would also hold for certain uses of language, and even certain uses of proper names: language can participate in and bear witness to meaning, but it does not disclose or contain it. At best one can bear witness to truth, but all that we say has no actual being. One can never articulate the end, or purpose, or final cause, or that for the sake of which one acts, because such reasons are not intelligible within language.

Another relevant insight may be drawn from Schopenhauer's discussion of music. Schopenhauer drew a distinction between music,

---

[12] Martin Buber, *I and Thou*, trans. Walter Kaufmann (New York: Charles Scribners Sons, 1970), 62.

which expresses the stirrings of the will itself, and concepts denoted by words that are the most indirect method of representation.[13] Even if he is somewhat optimistic about the powers of music, the sheer fact of its existence as a bearer of meaning alongside language, where the meanings of one cannot be translated into the meanings of the other without near complete loss, means that neither music nor language alone is capable of containing meaning by itself. Nevertheless, Schopenhauer is surely correct in noticing a greater affinity between music and the will: "For only the passions, the movements of the will, exist for it, and, like God, it sees only the heart."[14]

This suggests an alternative approach to philosophy, one partially noticed by Ludwig Wittgenstein: "What has to be overcome is a difficulty having to do with the will, rather than the intellect."[15] This is perhaps why he regards the attempt to make the spirit explicit as a "great temptation",[16] and compares those who seek reasons, who perpetually ask, "why?" to tourists who are so busy reading the guide book that they cannot see the building in front of them.[17] Working in philosophy is then a working on oneself, on one's own interpretation, on one's way of seeing things.[18] Even Jacques Derrida saw the primary purpose of a book as forming a reader.[19] Meaning is only lacking for those who expect to find it in the wrong place. Drawing upon Buber and Schopenhauer, we may suggest that meaning consists in encounter and performance. Drawing upon Wittgenstein and Derrida, we may suggest that philosophy is a way of working on and through meaning and language so as to enable one to see meanings. So if experience, or activity, or language are not bearers of meaning in and of themselves, then this would imply that the decisive factor is that they should be formed, worked on, animated and inhabited. Of course, little can be achieved by trying to make this animating spirit explicit, for what is essential would be lost in the translation into language. On the other hand,

---

[13] Schopenhauer, *The World as Will and Representation*, 449.

[14] Ibid, 449.

[15] Ludwig Wittgenstein, *Culture and Value*, trans. Peter Winch (Oxford: Basil Blackwell, 1980), 17.

[16] Ibid, 8.

[17] Ibid, 40.

[18] Ibid, 16.

[19] Derrida continues: "The mass productions that today inundate the press and publishing houses do not form their readers; they presuppose in a phantasmatic and rudimentary fashion a reader who has already been programmed. They thus end up preformatting this very mediocre addressee whom they had postulated in advance." Jacques Derrida, *Learning to Live Finally: The Last Interview,* trans. Pascale-Anne Brault and Michael Naas (Basingstoke: Palgrave Macmillan, 2007), 31.

it is possible for philosophy to inhabit and animate language, whether one is speaking or reading. The spoken word has the advantages of expression, tonality, rhythm and cadence, capable of displaying emotion and the heart. Similarly, the word that is attentively read can recreate all these features through imagination. In either case, inhabited meaning has to be embodied, whether in imagination and speech, or in habits and institutions. It has to become extended and differentiated. Of course, this is precisely what happens in the virtual reality machine which merely extends the powers of imagination. If there is no resistance to the force of thought, then its power of action is without meaning. For expressed imagination to take on coherence, solidity, and objectivity, then it is not sufficient that it is inhabited by a monad, a ghost in the machine—it is necessary that it should be cohabited. Thought is both performance and encounter. This implies more than the need for a spectator or audience. One does not speak or write simply in order to be heard or read. One invites a response, the co-creation of the meaningful world. Philosophy becomes meaningful in conversation.

This is, of course, the blandest of observations. Most conversation is idle chatter, not philosophy. To have a meaningful conversation is a difficult skill. It demands courage and sensitivity. One has to be bold enough to shape and disrupt the world with what one says. One has to be sensitive enough to attend to what is meaningful in what is said. A philosophical problem is bold and disruptive because it interrupts a train of thought or a habitual pattern of behaviour. It poses the question of what is meaningful and decisive here. Idle chatter is idle because it determines nothing. A philosophical problem, by contrast, is always a quest for meaning.

Of course, in philosophy, as in relationships, the life of continual mutual attention and response is an impossible ideal. It is also radically unstable. It threatens to displace mutually beneficial arrangements with continual change and forgetting. A meaningful relation can only grow in complexity and depth when its habits and practices become institutionalised. An institution is the memory or writing that belongs to collective life. It provides the structure and stability through which complexities of meaning and relation can be fostered and negotiated without risking the dangers of destructive behaviour.

There are institutions that impose obligations upon collective behaviour. There are also institutions that are ways of seeing and paying attention. These are the institutions of the soul. They are habits and practices that enable one to notice things, to count certain things as significant. And philosophy as a pedagogical exercise is an attempt to develop the institutions of the soul, to notice what is significant, what counts, and what matters. Indeed, the situation is the same in conflict as it is in pedagogy. Disagreement arises over perceptions of what is decisive and significant. Rational argument will not be persuasive when there is no agreement over underlying premises. Yet there can be inequality when one party understands the other's point of view, while the other sees the first as perverse, irrational, or stupid. Since one is always convinced of the merits of one's own point of view, it is often hard to grasp why another will refuse to adopt it. A child will fail to notice how much a parent see and understands. One is usually blinded by the light of one's own understanding, and by the significance of what one takes as being decisive. The wise person sees what the foolish sees and understands, but discounts it for reasons the fool does not see and understand. The wise understands the fool, but the fool does not understand the wise. Inequality of point of view occurs when one party learns to see the viewpoint of the other in secret. Moreover, growth in understanding occurs when one learns to encompass the other's point of view, and to see what is taken as decisive and significant.

While there is a place for disclosing reasons in any attempt to bring another to one's own understanding, this strategy will often meet with opposition and blindness. It is often more effective not to respond directly to the concerns and questions raised by a given perspective, and to refuse engagement. For such direct engagement has to operate in the terms given by the opposing perspective. If, by contrast, one dramatises and lives out of one's own differing perspective, the opponent may have the opportunity to observe what counts and is decisive for oneself.

So philosophy is a matter of learning ways of seeing. One rarely makes progress in philosophy by constructing the most effective arguments, but more often by attending to and understanding different points of view. At the level of the will, what is required is humility, not vanity. It is essential to learn to see in secret. "In the domain of the intelligence, the virtue of humility is nothing other than attention."[20] Simone Weil went so far as to think that the development of attention ought to be the sole aim of education.[21] Nevertheless, attention is one-sided since it does not manifest to others a way of seeing, a way of counting things as significant. Philosophy will have little meaning until it manifests encounter, conflict, and resistance. Of course, it serves little purpose to simply state opposing judgements and countervaluations. Instead, it is necessary to think and act

---

[20] Simone Weil, *Notebooks* Vol. I, trans. Arthur Wills (London: Routledge, 1956), 245.
[21] Ibid, 251.

in such a way that what one's companion or opponent takes as decisive no longer seems significant, and what matters most to one's opponent is barely counted at all. One best pursues philosophy by playing the fool. For the fool may have a capacity to reach behind defences thrown up against the wise. In seeking to educate the fool, one tries to show what matters. One attempts to display one's reasons. And in searching to make one's reasons so clear that even a fool could understand them, one may run across circumstances in which such reasons no longer evidently apply. The clever fool lays traps wherein one encounters problems. And problems are the meat and drink of the performance of philosophy.

III. Epilogue: Response to Eryximachus

Philip Goodchild

I know someone who spends his time seeking to acquire money. He wants to be rich. What does he want to spend the money on? Nothing. He just wants the money. I know someone else who longs to be famous and admired. She wants to be a celebrity. What does she want to be admired for? Nothing more than herself. She just wants to be admired by strangers. I know someone else who is driven by the desire for sex. On every occasion, he is on the lookout for opportunities. What kind of sex, with what kind of people? It doesn't matter, he just wants sex with as many people as possible. I know someone else who wants to be reasonable. In everything that is said and done, she wants to find the reason. What kind of reason does she seek? It doesn't matter, just so long as it is a reason. I know of yet another person who longs for virtue. He wants to be thoroughly good and excellent, whether others notice or not. What kind of virtue does he seek? It doesn't matter, just so long as it is virtuous. Finally, I know someone who seeks God. She wants to be close to God. What is it like to be there? It doesn't matter, just so long as it feels spiritual.

Many of us live our lives by abstractions that nevertheless seem to name the most important matter of all. What, then, are we to make of a person who longs for meaning? What are we to make of a person who seeks to respond to others from the heart? What are we to make of a person who seeks to evade hypocrisy, who makes a virtue of sincerity? Are they, too, driven by bloodless abstractions? Is the end that each projects and seeks anything more than an illusion, even if that end attained would be very real? Do the words that we propose and the promises that we make become capable of bearing meaning before that meaning is instantiated in the rich experience of the past? Is all self-determination a wager, a gamble, a speculation, for we do not know what our experience will prove to have been?

The anxiety that is provoked in me by both yourself and your interlocutor results from the fact that I cannot hear expressed in your discourse the inhabited experience that would lead you both to pose your problems as the result of passionately-felt dilemmas. Who loses sleep at night over virtual reality machines? Who constructs a fantasy scenario out of gossip and idle chatter? Who sees a contrast between expressed reasons and the purport of discourse apart from one who struggles to find any purport for what they say? Who finds it necessary to articulate the nature of love apart from one who seeks to name what they lack? My anxiety is that your lives are not rich enough for your hopes. Do you pay attention to thought and questioning at the expense of listening to your hearts?

Both you and your interlocutor have given numerous suggestions as to what we might understand by the "heart". Your interlocutor suggests that it is not a public face but a site of grounds, reasons, or deeply felt judgements arising from extensive understanding. It is that which makes sense or gives sense, rather than appealing to an existing common sense. It holds a purport, an application, an address, and a relevance, so that its insights are capable of touching and moving hearts and souls. It is the site of personhood, character, virtue and identity. You suggest that the heart is the possibility of living a meaningful existence, one that is distinguished from experience, activity and language. It holds the secret desire or secret virtue that gives meaning and significance to experience and activity. Its individuality is constructed from its objects of devotion and its manner of devotion. It is the transformation of meaning effected by the cohabiting of relation, whether this occurs through desire or resistance. It has a beat, a rhythm, an expression, tonality and cadence; it is the contribution to meaning made by music. It knows only performance and encounter. The heart may even be a memory of the institutions of the soul, of ways of seeing and understanding, and of the grounds for these ways of seeing and understanding. These suggestions are multiple and irreconcilable because meaning cannot be reified and made explicit since it is the environment and dynamism in which we dwell. In any case, the task of philosophy is changed: to find grounds or reasons is now to find the meaning produced by the heart. Instead of seeking the universal idea, one seeks a singular point of view.

Perhaps all philosophers of religion should be equipped with stethoscopes. Perhaps it is necessary to redefine the Christian concept of God as on the one who sees in secret into all hearts. More significant than the sense of responsibility that devolves from a faith in the observed nature of all moral action is the faith that life itself has a meaning, a meaning that can be observed from the perspective of one who sees the heart. Then the philosopher of religion would have less need to construct precise concepts of God or love than to learn to listen to the heart. The one who discerns the rhythms of the music of experience is the one who understands God because that one hears the heart as God hears it: one knows God through understanding meaning; one does not understand meaning by knowing God.

Moreover, there is no need for meaning to be created afresh by inhabited encounters. Meaning is already available for those who are willing to listen. What such encounters offer is the resolution of perspectives, the emergence of ways of seeing, of ways of hearing, and of ways of expressing. There is nothing significant about the random fluctuations of idle chatter, of turning tables, of stock market indices, or of bedroom antics. Yet when they develop a rhythm, a structure, a predictability and a malleability, in short, when they become habitual or institutionalised, then they form in themselves an eardrum that is sensitive to modifications. We all need such organs and prostheses to discern the flows of energy that emerge from the heart, both our own heart and that of others. We need concepts that are taut, flexible, responsive, selective and sensitive to discern the meaning that flows from the problems we encounter in real life. Human nature has still to be created.

What you have suggested is that a meaningful life is to be found in encounter, performance, and relation. Philosophy changes from an exercise of writing, storing up meaning in the virtual reality machine of language, to an enactment of encounter, performance, and relation. The philosopher touches souls and perhaps, on rare occasions, even bodies. One can imagine the continuation of the imaginary scenario: perhaps once the lady in question starts to respond in kind to the dumbfounded philosopher, his philosophical quandary will recede so that he declares: "I don't know who *N.* is, but right now that no longer seems to matter." For physical intimacy is the performance of meaning, the event which, lacking an intelligible meaning in itself, gives shape, meaning and desire to both prior and subsequent experience. The spiritual connection or meaning is then a repetition of this pure event, in anticipation or recollection, an event belonging to these two and no other.

So what matters in the initial scenario is not primarily whether the fictional philosopher is vain or whether his lover deceives herself. The question of whether their relation is real, or involves any spiritual connection, is a matter of whether it opens up new possibilities of seeing and hearing. It is whether it casts a new light on an experience that has not been understood, or whether it makes audible a meaning that has not been heard. A spiritual connection comes with habitualisation or repetition. A philosophical body of thought is a mechanism for hearing, for counting and for feeling. And through our conversations we must seek to gather, form, assemble and empower a body of understanding that will make audible the most significant problems of our era.

Nevertheless, I do suspect that both you and your interlocutor have been somewhat harsh on abstraction. An abstraction may not be simply an attempt to represent, contain, or possess meaning. An abstraction may also be a proposition, understood as an invitation, a proposal. It may be an offering of relation, a common activity or experience, and the intimacy of the shared meaning and perspective that arises as a result. It may even be a promise. Of course, the experience of a proposal accepted or a promise fulfilled may be much richer than the initial meaning signified by the proposal or promise. Yet the purpose of the proposal or promise is to make this experience and meaning possible, not to anticipate it. Philosophical abstractions may be regarded as attempts to introduce encounter, performance, and shared meaning. Then the aim of philosophy is not to eliminate hypocrisy from idle chatter, but to open up the possibility of a depth of shared meaning. The aim of philosophy is not merely to inspire but to seduce. Philosophy is an invitation to enable a certain depth of encounter to happen.

Bibliography

Buber, Martin. *I and Thou*. Translated by Walter Kaufmann. New York: Charles Scribners Sons, 1970.

Derrida, Jacques. *Learning to Live Finally: The Last Interview*. Translated by Pascale-Anne Brault and Michael Naas. Basingstoke: Palgrave Macmillan, 2007.

Gallagher, Winifred. *Rapt: Attention and the Focused Life*. New York: Penguin, 2009.

Levinas, Emmanuel. *Otherwise than Being, or, Beyond Essence*. Translated by Alphonso Lingis. Pittsburgh: Duquesne University Press, 1998.

McCabe, Herbert. *The Good Life*. London: Continuum, 2005.

Nygren, Anders. *Agape and Eros*. Translated by Philip S. Watson. London: SPCK, 1954.

Outka, Gene. *Agape: An Ethical Analysis*. New Haven: Yale University Press, 1972.

Schopenhauer, Arthur. *The World as Will and Representation.* 2 volumes.
    Translated by E. F. J. Payne. New York: Dover, 1966.
Weil, Simone. *Notebooks.* Volume I. Translated by Arthur Wills. London:
    Routledge, 1956.
Wittgenstein, Ludwig. *Culture and Value.* Translated by Peter Winch.
    Oxford: Basil Blackwell, 1980.

CONTRIBUTORS

Pamela Sue Anderson is Reader in Philosophy of Religion at the University of Oxford. Her works in this field include *A Feminist Philosophy of Religion* (Blackwell, 1998) and the edited collections, *Feminist Philosophy of Religion: Critical Readings* (co-edited with Beverley Clack; Routledge, 2004) and *New Topics in Feminist Philosophy of Religion* (Springer, 2009).

Alex Andrews is a Ph.D. Candidate at the University of Nottingham's Department of Theology and Religious Studies. His main interests are neoliberalism, the power of economic discourse and the relations of these to religion.

Daniel Colucciello Barber teaches in the Department of Philosophy and Religious Studies at Marymount Manhattan College. His articles have appeared in *Southern Journal of Philosophy*, *Political Theology*, and *Modern Theology*. He received his Ph.D. in Religion from Duke University with a dissertation entitled, *The Production of Immanence: Deleuze, Yoder, and Adorno* (2008). His current research addresses the relationship between immanence, secularism, and biopolitics.

James C. Brown is a Visiting Fellow at the Institute of Philosophy (London) and also works at the École Centrale (Paris). He received his doctorate in 2007 from the Université de Paris X—Nanterre. His research focuses primarily on seventeenth and eighteenth century philosophy.

Michael O'Neill Burns is a Ph.D. student in Philosophy at the University of Dundee where he is writing a thesis on Kierkegaard, contemporary French philosophy, and political subjectivity. He has published articles in *The Heythrop Journal* and *Political Theology*.

Clayton Crockett is Associate Professor and Director of Religious Studies at the University of Central Arkansas. He is the author of *A Theology of the Sublime* (Routledge, 2001), *Interstices of the Sublime: Theology and Psychoanalytic Theory* (Fordham University Press, 2007), and a forthcoming book on radical political theology.

Rocco Gangle is Assistant Professor of Philosophy at Endicott College. His work has appeared in multiple journals and edited collections. Most recently he is the translator of François Laruelle's *Philosophies of Difference* (Continuum, 2010).

Philip Goodchild is Professor of Religion and Philosophy in the Department of Theology and Religious Studies, University of Nottingham. He is the author of *Gilles Deleuze and the Question of Philosophy* (Fairleigh Dickinson University Press, 1996), *Deleuze and Guattari: An Introduction to the Politics of Desire* (Sage, 1996), *Capitalism and Religion: The Price of Piety* (Routledge, 2002), and *Theology of Money* (SCM, 2007 and Duke University Press, 2009). He is also co-editor of the New Slant Book Series on Religion, Politics and Ontology with Duke University Press.

Clare Greer is a Ph.D. candidate in the University of Manchester, writing a thesis with the title: "The critical conversation between John Milbank and Gillian Rose, and its consequences for an aporetic political theology". Her research interests include the intersection of religion and politics, ethics and law, particularly in the work of Gillian Rose. Other publications include "On Jantzen and Theology: A Conversation with William Desmond" in Elaine Graham edited, *Redeeming the Present* (Ashgate, 2009); and "Review of *Law and Transcendence: On the Unfinished Work of Gillian Rose* by Vincent Lloyd and *After Innocence: Gillian Rose's Reception and Gift of Faith* by Andrew Shanks." in *The Heythrop Journal* (forthcoming, 2010). She would like to acknowledge the support of the Arts and Humanities Research Council.

Bradley A. Johnson is an independent researcher whose articles on philosophical aesthetics, theology and politics have appeared in the *Journal of Religion*, *Political Theology*, and *Postscripts*. His forthcoming book is entitled *The Characteristic Theology of Herman Melville: Aesthetics, Politics and Duplicity*.

Michael Kolkman will have completed his Ph.D. (*Towards a Philosophy of Freedom, Fichte and Bergson*, 2009) in Philosophy at the University of Warwick at the publication of this chapter. His research interests concern the modification of transcendental philosophy towards the thought of spontaneous organisation, as found primarily in the works of Kant, Fichte and Bergson. In a wider sense this project is also informed by Spinoza,

Kierkegaard, Stirner, Deleuze and Nancy, the theory and practice of anarchist organisation and theory and practice of Buddhism.

Adam Kotsko holds a Ph.D. from the Chicago Theological Seminary and is currently Visiting Assistant Professor of Religion at Kalamazoo College (USA). His research interests include historical theology and continental philosophy. He is the author of *Žižek and Theology* (T&T Clark, 2008) and *Awkwardness* (Zer0 Books, forthcoming) and is currently working on a translation of Agamben's *The Sacrament of Language: Archeology of the Oath* (under contract with Stanford University Press).

John Mullarkey is Professor of Film and Television Studies at Kingston University, London. He has also taught philosophy and film theory at the University of Sunderland, England (1994-2004) and the University of Dundee, Scotland (2004 to 2010). He has published *Bergson and Philosophy* (Edinburgh University Press, 1999), *Post-Continental Philosophy: An Outline* (Continuum, 2006), *Philosophy and the Moving Image: Refractions of Reality* (Palgrave, 2010), and edited, with Beth Lord, *The Continuum Companion to Continental Philosophy* (Continuum, 2009). He is an editor of the journal *Film-Philosophy*, and chair of the *Society for European Philosophy*. His work explores variations of 'non-standard-philosophy', arguing that philosophy is a subject that continually shifts its identity through engaging with supposedly non-philosophical fields such as film theory (the realm of 'outsider thought' with which he is most acquainted).

Karin Nisenbaum is a Doctoral Candidate at the University of Toronto. Her research focuses on the trajectory of metaphysics from Kant through German Idealism to modern Jewish thought. She is interested in contemporary debates over secularisation informed by phenomenology or critical theory, and she is interested in the interrelation between philosophy, religion, and literature. Her work has been published in *Perspectives, The International Journal of Philosophical Studies,* and *Letras Libres.* She is the Executive Editor of *The University of Toronto Journal of Jewish Thought.*

George Pattison is Lady Margaret Professor of Divinity at the University of Oxford. He has written extensively on Kierkegaard and Heidegger and is currently working on a book on God and Being.

Nina Power is Senior Lecturer in Philosophy at Roehampton University and the author of *One-Dimensional Woman* (Zer0, 2009). She is currently working on a book about Feuerbach.

Anthony Paul Smith is a research fellow at the Institute for Nature and Culture (DePaul University) and received his Ph.D. in Philosophical Theology from the University of Nottingham. He is the translator of François Laruelle's *Future Christ: A Lesson in Heresy* (Continuum, 2010) and has published in *Polygraph, Political Theology, SubStance, Journal of Cultural and Religious Theory*, and *Analecta Hermeneutica* on religion, nature, politics, and non-philosophy.

Alberto Toscano is Senior Lecturer in Sociology at Goldsmiths, University of London. He is the author of *The Theatre of Production: Philosophy and Individuation Between Kant and Deleuze* (Palgrave, 2006) and *Fanaticism: On the Uses of an Idea* (Verso, 2010) as well as the translator, most recently, of Alain Badiou's *Logics of Worlds* (Continuum, 2009) and *The Century* (Polity, 2007). His current research is focussed on the aesthetic problems posed by representing or mapping capitalism and on theories of 'real abstraction' in philosophy and political economy.

Ashley U. Vaught is a Post-Doctoral Fellow in the Department of Philosophy of Fordham University. His work examines how German idealism rehabilitates Spinoza's "dogmatic" metaphysics and ethics despite the acknowledgment of the speculative limitations established by Kant's critical philosophy. He has essays forthcoming on immanence and on eternity and temporality in the *Freiheitsschrift*.

Daniel Whistler is Lecturer in Philosophy at the University of Liverpool. He is co-author of *Spinoza and Theology* (T&T Clark, 2012) and co-edited the volume, *Moral Powers, Fragile Beliefs: Essays in Moral and Religious Philosophy* (Continuum, 2011).

INDEX